MW01199656

Ecumenism in Praxis

STUDIEN ZUR INTERKULTURELLEN GESCHICHTE DES CHRISTENTUMS
ETUDES D´HISTOIRE INTERCULTURELLE DU CHRISTIANISME
STUDIES IN THE INTERCULTURAL HISTORY OF CHRISTIANITY

begründet von / fondé par / founded by
Richard Friedli, Walter J. Hollenweger und /et/and Hans J. Margull †
herausgegeben von / édité par / edited by
Mariano Delgado, Université de Fribourg
Jan A. B. Jongeneel, Universiteit Utrecht
Klaus Koschorke, Universität München
Frieder Ludwig, Hermannsburg
Werner Ustorf, University of Birmingham

VOL. 159

PETER LANG
EDITION

Joseph Daniel

Ecumenism in Praxis

A Historical Critique of
the Malankara Mar Thoma Syrian Church

PETER LANG
EDITION

Bibliographic Information published by the Deutsche Nationalbibliothek
The Deutsche Nationalbibliothek lists this publication in the Deutsche Nationalbibliografie; detailed bibliographic data is available in the internet at http://dnb.d-nb.de.

The publication of this volume has been supervised by
Professor Dr. Klaus Koschorke.

Library of Congress Cataloging-in-Publication Data
Daniel, Joseph, Rev.
Ecumenism in praxis : a historical critique of the Malankara Mar Thoma Syrian Church / Joseph Daniel. -- 1 [edition].
    pages cm. -- (Studies in the intercultural history of Christianity, ISSN 0170-9240 ; VOL. 159)
Includes bibliographical references.
ISBN 978-3-631-65480-4
1. Mar Thoma Syrian Church--Relations. 2. Mar Thoma Syrian Church--History. 3. Christian union. I. Title.
    BX166.3.D365 2014
    281'.54--dc23
                        2014027192

ISSN 0170-9240
ISBN 978-3-631-65480-4 (Print)
E-ISBN 978-3-653-04717-2 (E-Book)
DOI 10.3726/978-3-653-04717-2

© Peter Lang GmbH
Internationaler Verlag der Wissenschaften
Frankfurt am Main 2014
All rights reserved.
Peter Lang Edition is an Imprint of Peter Lang GmbH.

Peter Lang – Frankfurt am Main · Bern · Bruxelles · New York · Oxford · Warszawa · Wien

This publication has been peer reviewed.

www.peterlang.com

Message from His Beatitude Dr Joseph Mar Thoma, Metropolitan of the Malankara Mar Thoma Syrian Church

If we believe God has engaged and continues to engage in history, we can never stay static and be happy with the status quo.

The history of the *Malankara* Mar Thoma Syrain Church cannot be told without looking deeply at its relationship with the global ecumenical movement and at how the church shaped, and was shaped by, the evolution of ecumenical thinking. At the same time, the church has also been influenced by India's social ethos, cultural structures and political movements – imbibing from and contributing to these realms in a profound manner.

The Mar Thoma Church has incorporated the values of the Kingdom of God and the manifestation of these values can be seen in its activities encompassing economic development, social engineering and women's empowerment programmes.

The involvement of the church in these post-independent moves has also meant that it has kept its position as an autonomous and independent Indian church. These moves have been extended further in the practical expressions of the church's stand on safeguarding justice, peace and freedom in India at critical periods when these values came under threat in the country. This further enhanced the autonomous and independent nature.

The autonomous and independent nature of the church can be traced back to the late 15th Century, which saw the discovery by Vasco Da Gama of the trade route from Europe to India. The then Roman Catholic campaign to gain a controlling hold of the Indian church, the Malankara church's round opposition to the move, the subsequent Synod of Diamper and the Coonen Cross oath possibly marked the early manifestations of that nature.

But we should also go back to the historical context of the origin of Christianity in India during the first century CE to understand the genesis of the *Malankara* Church's ecumenical outlook. There is reason to believe that the first converts of Christianity in India were from different Hindu religious traditions – people of the land, the *Dravidians* and the *Brahmins* – although a section of the Mar Thoma Christians claim an exclusive *Brahmin* descendance. Thus the very constitution of the Malankara church was ecumenical, with Christ the cornerstone showing the path towards a greater unity.

The Malankara church has continued to affirm its oriental heritage and traditions, although it took on a distinct reform focus at a defining moment in its history. It continues to be open to fresh insights from the global ecumenical movement. In fact, imbibing these insights and implementing them into the Indian space has become the church's forte. At the same time, the church also helped inspire and guide the global ecumenical movement through original insights from its own leaders and learned sons.

The historian and theologian in Rev. Dr Joseph Daniel, a priest of the Mar Thoma Church, has come out yet again with another book on the history of ecumenism, which profoundly captures the scope and thrusts of the ecumenical movement as it evolved over the years.

It takes us on a trip down the historical path that the Mar Thoma Church traversed in its dynamic relationship with the ecumenical movement and the Indian society. Indeed, the church's history is one of *Ecumenism in Praxis*, as this book is aptly titled. This is not just a chronological account, but offers a careful evaluation of and value judgements on the church's evolution.

The author's scholarly knowledge has already been brought to the limelight by his first book, *One Family Under Heaven,* that goes deep into the history of the emergence of the Ecumenical Christian Centre (ECC) in Bangalore, India. That was originally done as a thesis for Rev. Dr Daniel's Master of Theology course of the Federated Faculty of Research in Religion and Culture, Kottayaum, affiliated to the Serampore University.

The book, *Ecumenism in Praxis – A Historical Critique of the Malankara Mar Thoma Syrian Church,* is modified from Rev. Dr Daniel's PhD thesis, *Historic Praxis of Ecumenism in the Malankara Marthoma Syrian Church.* I need to mention here that his efforts earned for the author a PhD from the University of Berne, Switzerland, with the honour, *Insigni cum Laude* (thesis defence) and with *Magna cum Laude.*

We commend him for his efforts and wish him all the best in all his endeavours. Our prayers are always with him.

Joseph Mar Thoma, Metropolitan
Metropolitan of the Malankara Mar Thoma Syrian Church
Poolatheen
Tiruvalla

Zum Geleit (Forward)

In the summer of 2009, the bishops of the Malankara Mar Thoma Syrian Church sent Rev. Joseph Daniel to the *Departement für Christkatholische Theologie* at the University of Bern, in Switzerland, to undertake his doctoral studies. In the long history of this department, which was founded in 1874 as the Faculty for [Old] Catholic Theology in the canton of Bern and capital of Switzerland, there have been more than 250 PhD students, about half of whom have been of Eastern European Orthodox background. They were provided a generous grant by the *Christkatholische Kirche der Schweiz* (Old Catholic Church of Switzerland).

Of this long series of doctoral students Dr Daniel was the first doctoral student to come from the Malankara Mar Thoma Syrian Church to study at this renowned institution for theological research and the education of Old Catholic theologians. A primary reason for his arrival in Europe was the establishment of closer contacts between the Old Catholic Churches of the Union of Utrecht and the Malankara Mar Thoma Syrian Church.

In his doctoral thesis, "The Historical Praxis of Ecumenism in the Malankara Mar Thoma Syrian Church" Dr Daniel offers a historical reconstruction of the evolution of this Church's deep-rooted focus on ecumenism and its ecumenical attitudes that have shaped its history as an Indian church. The main period under consideration is the twentieth century. In this thesis, Dr Daniel offers a significant contribution to the history of the ecumenical movement from a non-European perspective and presents an important study of the history of this indigenous, ecumenically-oriented church and of the complexities of its relationships to Europe. The book is an adaptation of the author's PhD thesis, *Historic Praxis of Ecumenism in the Malankara Marthoma Syrian Church.* The publication of this volume in the prestigious series, **Studies in the Intercultural History of Christianity**, would not only help to disseminate these results, but would make possible a deeper understanding of this church's history and identity amongst theologians and church historians not only in India, but in Switzerland, across Europe and indeed globally. Moreover, the publication of his doctoral dissertation coincides with the rapprochement between the Old Catholic Churches of the Union of Utrecht and the Indian Church growing deeper, as visible in a report of the recent dialogue (the report awaits ratification by the two churches).

During his time in Switzerland, Joseph Daniel contributed to the establishment of closer contacts between the Old Catholic church and the Mar Thoma church. He spent four and a half years in Bern. During this time, he made possible a living encounter with the Mar Thoma church and its spiritual riches for those with whom he studied at the *Departement für Christkatholische Theologie* and at the Faculty of Theology. He participated actively in the life of the Old Catholic student house at Bern, the *Christkatholisches Studentenheim*, contributed to several international conferences and took part in services both in his local parish and at ecumenical events. His thesis defence, which took place on 28 February 2014, demonstrated the high regard in which Joseph Daniel and his work are held: not only staff and students of the Faculty were present, but also many members of both the Swiss Old Catholic and the Mar Thoma Church. It was a privilege and an enriching experience to serve as Joseph Daniel's doctoral supervisor. The department and the faculty wish him well for the future, and hope that he will find a position in which he can use his talents in order to bring about deeper reconciliation of cultures and church traditions.

I wish the readers of this book a living encounter with recent ecumenical church history!

Professor Dr Angela Berlis
Head of the *Departement für Christkatholische Theologie*
Vice Dean Faculty of Theology

Preface

It is an honor to write a foreword to this illuminating study on the Malankara Mar Thoma Syrian Church (Mar Thoma Church). I have been privileged to advise the author, Joseph Daniel, during his stay at Berne until the completion of his competent and most impressive doctoral disputation in February 2014. As a doctoral student at the Theological Faculty of the University of Berne, he was exceptional in various respects. Far from limiting himself to academic study, he embodied the topic of his research in a holistic manner and practiced in a convincing way what he was writing about. As a *missionary* minded person, Joseph Daniel established and pastored a congregation of the Mar Thoma Church in Switzerland. At the same time, he also participated regularly at the worships of the Old Catholic Church in Berne. As an Indian abroad, he became a friend and partner in dialogue to foreigners from India representing diverse religious backgrounds. As a fellow student he shared his expertise of Indian Christianity and was appreciated as a spiritual friend accompanying students with his prayers. As an ecumenist he joined ecumenical conferences in Switzerland and abroad. All in all Joseph Daniel has left his mark in Berne as a living witness and transmitter of the Christian faith academically and practically, locally and internationally.

The book highlights the almost two millennia of Christian presence in India from an ecumenical and missional angle. That double perspective is exceptional compared with the current state of research on Thomas Christianity. This is indeed a reason why the study presented here deserves the attention not only of members of the Mar Thoma Church and experts of Thomas Christianity in India, but also the interest of the wider ecumenical community and people interested in the history of World Christianity altogether. Ecumenicity is not a purpose for its own sake. It always implies a new challenge irrespective of what the actual self-understanding and inter-church relationships of a given church may be. Ecumenicity demands to revise one's opinion and way of life when it is exposed to the encounter with other churches, different cultures and new social situations. Ecumenicity always implies a risk, requires *metanoia*, leads to the insight that being true and truly church is possible only together with other churches, neither separated from them nor against them. Ecumenicity is the expression of what the biblical metaphor, Body of Christ, means:

the Church, while embracing many members – or churches – with diverse functions, gifts and historical journeys, is nevertheless one and whole (1Cor 12).

Joseph Daniel's analysis sheds light on the ecumenical spirit in the tradition of Thomas Christianity in India from antiquity throughout medieval and colonial times until the 20th century. As the study shows, an ecumenical spirit was alive on the Indian continent already long before *ecumenism* has been coined as a term. According to the author, openness and autonomy have served as guidelines for the Mar Thoma Church's attitude to other branches of World Christianity throughout its history. Faithfulness to the apostolic tradition is intertwined with openness "to fresh insights and ideas from other denominations and other faiths" (p. 2). Joseph Daniel discloses a constant quest for creative tension and equilibrium between plurality and unity throughout the long history of the Indian Thomas tradition.

The Mar Thoma Church, established in 1889, shares the long liturgical, spiritual and doctrinal tradition of Thomas Christianity and is deeply rooted in it. What is exceptional about the Mar Thoma Church is that it functions, at the same time, as a bridge church connecting Asian and Western as well as oriental-orthodox, Latin and protestant – especially Anglican – legacies. Without losing its oriental-orthodox character in liturgy and doctrine, it also embodies core elements of churches that emerged from the Reformation, visible most of all in its far-reaching diaconial agency and missionary outreach among Indians of scheduled castes. According to a wide spread opinion, *missional* outreach is not a salient feature of the Thomas Christianity. It rather consolidated itself within the boundaries of high caste Indian communities and identified closely with specific high caste traditions. *Missional* outreach is not only in India, but all over the globe a risk for introverted churches that fear to lose their ecclesial identities. *Missional* outreach challenges closed identities by transgressing boundaries of culture, caste, class and language. The Mar Thoma Church has taken that risk by exposing itself to all kinds of unpleasant social realities in India. The outreach move has driven the church to take responsibility for social injustice and reflect its new engagement in public theology. Crucial impacts and hotly debated questions on church life followed immediately: How can new church members from a scheduled caste background participate fully and equally in the life and leadership of a church that has a century long tradition of high caste culture? Joseph Daniel does not hesitate to name the failures and ambivalences of how the Mar Thoma Church is struggling with that question even today.

Ecumenicity is at stake when one church claims juridical supremacy over another church or when a church is even forced to incorporate into the former.

Thomas Christianity in general and the Mar Thoma Church in particular have several times experienced such threats from its ecumenical partners. Under the auspices of Portuguese colonialism, the Roman-Catholic church put an end to the independence of Thomas Christianity at the turn of the 17th century (1599) and unleashed among Thomas Christians a never-ending process of splitting. A lesson can be learned from the Mar Thoma Church in how it dealt with precarious inter-church relationships when they entered a struggle for spiritual and juridical (canonical) supremacy. A crucial time of a different kind occurred when the Mar Thoma Church was invited to join the Church of South India (CSI). This time it was not a question of an alien authority being imposed on the Mar Thoma Church, but an offer to join the emerging church union out of free will. It launched an intensive discourse among Mar Thoma Church leaders on how its own principle of openness and autonomy should be applied. The model of *organic union* preferred by CSI was carefully measured against another model: *conciliar union* respectively *organic oneness*. Priority was given to the latter as it gives the Mar Thoma Church space to preserve its autonomy and identity while committing at the same time to many different forms of close ecumenical cooperation with the CSI.

Organic union – conciliar union – conciliar oneness: these are but some of many guidelines to practice ecumenicity and celebrate at the same time ecclesial plurality in contemporary World Christianity. One of the features of World Christianity in the 21st century is that creative and viable ecumenicity derives increasingly from outside the Western world, particularly in Asian settings where churches are accustomed to existing as minorities in the midst of many other faith communities. Asian ecumenism has not only since long come of age but has taken a leading role on the regional and global levels alike.

In Asia, ecumenists of Indian churches including the Mar Thoma Church (M.M. Thomas!) have taken up a special role in ecumenism both past and present. Asians have appropriated ecumenism as a genuinely Asian cause. Among their priorities are the aims to overcome denominational conflicts originating from Western mission to Eastern lands, to bridge the ecumenical-evangelical divide, and to build up confidence between separate branches in the modern ecumenical movement. 'Wider' ecumenism with other religious communities is given special priority with regard to ethical concerns so that contours of an inter-religious public theology are visible. Joseph Daniel's study blends seamlessly in this broad Asian ecumenical horizon. He introduces the Malankara Mar Thoma Syrian Church as a bridge and ecumenical link with churches of many different denominational traditions all over the globe. At the same time, he also appreciates distinctiveness as a precious treasurer and feature of the Body of Christ. May his marvellous book find an

11

audience across the ecumenical world and open as well the eyes of members of his church for intra-Christian and wider ecumenism.

Christine Lienemann-Perrin, Berne
Prof.em.für Ökumene- und Missionswissenschaft
Theologische Fakultät
Universität Bern

Acknowledgements

It has been my privilege to pursue my doctoral study at the *Departement für Christkatholische Theologie*, the Department of the Old Catholic Theology in the University of Bern. This book is the revised version of the doctoral dissertation that I submitted as part of the doctoral requirement to the *Departement für Theologie* in the University of Bern. When I look back over the four years of my studies at the *Departement für Christkatholische Theologie*, I have so many things to be grateful for, especially for all the love and support that was shown to me by many devoted people. I thank them all.

This study is a result of the constant guidance, encouragement, inspiration and wholehearted support of **Prof. Dr Angela Berlis**, my professor and thesis supervisor. She was always available for discussions and it was her timely guidance and valuable corrections that made this project bear fruit. I am indebted to her for her right and thought-provoking suggestions and criticisms. I place on record my gratitude to her for granting me avenues to present papers at various international conferences.

Prof. Dr Christine Lienemann, my second dissertation supervisor and professor, was always forthcoming with inspiring suggestions, constant guidance, encouragements and insightful comments. I extend my gratitude to her for having taken the pain to read and correct the manuscript and for her rigorous and insightful motivation and comments. She opened doors for me to be guest lecturer in theology classes at the University of Basal and University of Bern.

I am thankful to both my professors for writing appropriate forward and preface to the book.

I am thankful, to **Prof. Dr. Klaus Koschorke** for including this book into the series – **Studies in the Intercultural History of Christianity**. The book was accepted for publishing by *Peter Lang GmbH, Internationaler Verlag der Wissenschaften*. In this regard, I am grateful to **Prof. Dr Klus Koschorke** and **Dr Ute Winkelkötter** for their guidance and help in the publication process.

Thanks are due to the *Eugène-et-Louis-Michaud-Fonds* of the *Departement für Christkatholische Theologie* in the University of Bern, for giving permission and grant to publish the dissertation with revisions.

13

My heartfelt thanks to His Beatitude **Dr Joseph Mar Thoma**, Metropolitan, for granting me permission for higher studies and for his fraternal care, support and prayers throughout my ministry and study. Thank you, dear *Thirumeni*, for writing an appropriate message to the book.

I am indebted to **Bishop Dr Harald Rein**, *Bischof der Christkatholischen Kirche der Schweiz*, who granted me scholarship, prayer support and fraternal care during my study.

The proof reading of this book was done by **Mr Shibu Itty Kuttickal**, a resident in Dubai, UAE. I am thankful to him for the long hours he spent with me and his readiness to discuss any question with regard to the editing of this book. I place on record his selfless and sincere effort and goodwill in meticulously correcting the language and technicalities of the manuscript.

I extent my gratitude to the office staff of the Mar Thoma Syrian Church Office, India, the library staff at the Mar Thoma Theological Seminary, Kottayam, India, the University of Bern, University of Cambridge, U.K, University of Basel, Basel Mission archives and the University of Oxford, UK for their guidance in collecting the sources for my study.

I am thankful to **Dr Urs von Arx**, professor emeritus, for his guidance and support in my admission for study to the University of Bern. His unassuming fraternal care, prayers and support during my study deserves a special mention. With the deepest sense of gratitude, I acknowledge the brotherly encouragement and support of **Dr Mathews George Chunakara** for writing an appropriate review of this book.

For their encouragement and help, I am thankful to **Prof. Dr Zac Varghese, Prof. Dr Anitha Daniel, Prof. Dr Martin George, Prof. Dr Martin Sallmann, Fr Christoph Schuler, Fr Peter Potter, Fr Peter Feenstra, Prof. Dr Peter-Ben Smith, Jurist Samuel Chacko, Mr Sam Panthradiyil, Mr Mathew Joseph (Ronnie), Mrs Annie Elizabeth Thomas, Mr Thomas Vergis, Prof. Dr Roy Joseph, Dr Martin Robra, Dr Max Beat Fleukiger,** and all others who helped me in this study. I must also thank **Rev. Prof. Dr M.V. Abraham, Rev. Prof. Dr T.P. Abraham, Rev. Prof. Dr M.J. Joseph, Rev. Prof. Dr K.G. Pothen, Rev. Prof. Dr Cherian Thomas, Very Rev. George Zachariah** and **Very Rev. Skariah Abraham** for their continued encouragement, prayers and fraternal care in my academic pursuits.

My sincere "thank you" goes out to **Most Rev. Dr Philipose Mar Chrysostom**, Metropolitan emeritus, **Most Rev. Dr Zacharias Mar Theophilus**, my previous diocesan bishop, **Rt Rev. Dr Geevarghese Mar Theodosius**, my diocesan Bishop, and **Rt Rev. Dr Issac Mar Philoxinos**, chairman of the higher studies commission, and the holy Episcopal synod for their fraternal care, prayers, encouragement and support during my studies.

I shall gratefully remember the brothers and sisters of the *Christkatholische Studentenheim* community, especially **Fr Peter Feenstra**, our *Seelsorger*, **Nick Rüthy, Bruno Worni, Norbert Naggy, Peter Vins, Jiri Dvoracek, Elena Primushko, Mariam Kartasyan, Kyriaki Meletzi, Julia Detelaff, Ravasz Hajinalka, Anna Dimura, Nancy Rahn, Milan, Eleni Kalogera, Markus Hupp** and **Christa Schwendener**, with all of whom I shared my fraternity. They have all partaken in this work in some way. I thank all my church members at the Mar Thoma Congregations in Switzerland and Germany, St. Paul and St. Peter *Christkatholische Kirche,* Bern, St. Ursula Anglican Church, Bern, and friends, especially my brother **Mr Oommen Varghese**, without whose prayers, encouragement and assistance, this study would not have reached its present form.

I bow in gratitude before my loving parents, **Thomas Daniel and Saramma Thomas**, my brother, **Daniel Thomas**, and sisters – **Rachel Thomas, Mariamma Thomas** and their families for their unbound love and prayers.

My deep gratitude to the Triune God for His providence, blessings and enlightenment all through my life and especially during my studies at the Department of Theology in the University of Bern. Divine guidance is what sustained me all these years.

I dedicate this book to the fond memory of the late Mar Thoma Metropolitan, **Dr Alexander Mar Thoma.**

Joseph Daniel
Bern, 29 April 2014.

Table of Contents

Introduction

This book attempts primarily to reconstruct the evolution of the Malankara Mar Thoma Syrian Church's pragmatic principle of ecumenism as it appears in history since its beginning in 52 CE and particularly during the period between the significant changes of 1889 and the present times. The study also looks at investigating instances when it skewed its pragmatic principle of ecumenism in its praxis.

The ecumenical outlook – marked by twin facets of openness and autonomy – has been the underlying ethos guiding the ecumenical history of the Malankara Mar Thoma Syrian Church.[1] The subject matter of this study, the Mar Thoma Church, as it is commonly called, is believed to have been founded by St. Thomas, one of the 12 apostles of Jesus Christ, in India. The church adopted the Persian East Syrian liturgy in the 4th century. In the 17th century, the church started fresh ecumenical engagements with the Antiochian Church and it eventually adopted the west Syrian liturgy, or St James Liturgy in 1836.

The church has seen significant reforms since 1889, a year when it took on a new existence. The faith of the church is anchored in the Holy Scripture and the three ecumenical councils of Nicaea in 325, Constantinople in 381 and Ephesus in 431. Currently the church consists of 12 dioceses, of which two are overseas dioceses with a membership of about 1 million.[2] The other denominations that claim the St. Thomas tradition in India are: Malankara Orthodox Syrian Church, Malankara Syrian Orthodox Church (Jacobite Church), Syro-Malabar Rite of the

---

1   Malankara Mar Thoma Syrian Church is hereafter reffered to as "Mar Thoma Church".
2   There are differences in the stastistics provided by different writers on the number of members of the Mar Thoma Church and other churches in India. For instance, the number of the Mar Thoma Church members as per the stastics provided by *Malankara Mar Thoma Syrian Church Diary* 2014 is 1.5 millon. Acording to Karl Pinggera the number of the Mar Thoma Church members is 600,000. In the Cambridge Dictionary of Christianity, the number of members in the Mar Thoma Church is 1,061,940.
See, *Malankara Mar Thoma Syrian Church Diary* 2014, 14; Karl Pinggera, "Die Kirche der Syrisch-Orthodoxen Tradition" In: Christian Lange, Karl Pinggera, (eds.) *Die altorientalischen kirche-glaube und geschichte,* (New York: Cambridge University Press (WBG), 2002), 87–89; Daniel Patte, (eds.) *The Cambridge Dictionary of Christianity,* (New York: Cambridge University Press, 2010), 253–254.

Roman Catholic Church, Malankara Rite of the Roman Catholic Church, Malabar Indepedent Syrian Church and Chaldean Syrian Church of the East.[3]

The ecumenical disposition of the Mar Thoma Church can be traced back in history to the time when it applied ecumenical outlook in practice by bringing together converts from three ethnic Indian groups – the *Brahmin*, the *Dravidian*[4] and the people of the land[5] – under the ambit of the church. This ecumenical ethos led to the church establishing its own unique self-identity. The self-consciousness of the church of being a participant in the common cultural heritage of India has helped it to share in India's socio-cultural disposition towards unity in diversity and the spirit of tolerance with other faiths and church denominations. The church had no qualms about receiving episcopal supervision from the Persian church and in effecting inter-communion agreements with other church denominations even before the idea of inter-communion between churches surfaced in the history of the ecumenical movement.

The underlying hypothesis of the study is the church's ecumenical outlook that underpins its inherent quality of openness and autonomy. This conforms to the meaning-content of the word, "ecumenism", as referred to by the modern ecumenical movement in its relation to other religious faiths (wider ecumenism) and other Christian denominations. This underlying premise, which guided the selection of source materials and its interpretation, underscores the fact that the history of the Mar Thoma Church evolved over the years through its ecumenical engagements with other churches. The church has also been a source of enrichment to India's socio-religious history.

---

3   Acording to Karl Pinggera the number of members of the churches that claim St. Thomas traditions in India are as follows: Malankara Orthodox Syrian Church (1 million), Malankara Syrian Orthodox Church (Jacobite Church) (1million), Malabar Independent Syrian Church (10,000), Syro- Malabar Rite of the Roman Catholic Church (3700,000) and Malankara Rite of the Roman Catholic Church (400,000). See, Karl Pinggera, "Die kirche der Syrisch-Orthodoxen tradition" In: Christian Lange, Karl Pinggera, (eds.) *Die altorientalischen kirche-glaube und geschichte, op.cit.*, 253–254.

4   The *Dravidians* belong to the Mediterranean race. They are believed to be the main racial element in the *Dravidian* population in South India. They are considered as the relatives of the people of the Indus Valley civilization. Nairs, Vellalas, Ezhavas may belongs to this group. This race also consists of the scheduled castes – *Pulayas, Parayas, Kuravas* and others.
     See, A. Sreedhara Menon, *A Survy of Kerala History*, (Madras: S. Visvanathan Publishers, 1988), 44.

5   The "people of the land" are the hill tribes of Kerala. They belong to the *dalit* community such as "adivasis" in India.

Rooted in tradition, open to fresh ideas

The Mar Thoma Church has shown this ecumenical outlook throughout its entire historical development and progress and particularly when it encountered challenges in its engagements with the Persian Church, the Roman Catholic Church, the Antiochian Church, the Malabar Independent Syrian Church (MISC), the Anglican Church, the Church of South India (CSI), the Church of North India (CNI) and the world-wide ecumenical movement. The history of the Mar Thoma Church should thus be viewed in the light of its continuous engagement to bring into fruition the centuries-old tradition of openness and autonomy in its life and witness. This book attempts to give an explanation of its unique identity and highlight instances of this reality by investigating into the church's historical and theological aspects.

The Mar Thoma Church has cherished its apostolic tradition and at the same time remained open to fresh insights and ideas from other faiths and Christian denominations. Based on this, the reforms within the church during the 19th century can be understood as being partly a result of its wish to keep age-old church traditions and partly a result of its ability to receive fresh ideas from the reformation and CMS missionaries to contemporize it. Consequently, when the Mar Thoma Church started engaging other churches and faiths, it listened, respected differences and adopted new insights and resources including the liturgy for enriching its life and witness. In this process, the Mar Thoma Church upheld its special vocation as part of the "one, holy, catholic and apostolic church" and its richness as a separate indigenous church.

In the light of these facts, this study attempts to deal with questions such as: How did the church start practising an ecumenical outlook, even prior to the word, ecumenism, being coined in the ecumenical movement? Could it be the result of the church's interaction with Indian culture, which upholds unity in diversity? Or, could the church have considered openness and autonomy as a requirement for its existence in India's multi-religious and pluralistic context? I would think it more appropriate to equate the life principles of openness and autonomy of the Mar Thoma Church with the term: "ecumenism", in order to emphasise that the church remained part of the "one, holy, catholic and apostolic church". Again, the church's ability to project mutual respect and church unity engagements, while preserving its autonomy, brings to mind such a reasoning.

25

Historical-critical analysis

This book follows the historical method of the Church History Association of India that is the commonly accepted historical method in reconstructing the history of Christianity in India.[6] The Church History Association of India (CHAI) highlighted the role of Indian churches and Indian Christians in the development of Christianity, by the process of historical-critical analysis of the data available for the reconstruction of Indian Christian history. It deals with different aspects of Christianity – social, cultural and ecumenical – in relation to other religious and cultural movements. A particularly focussed analysis of Indian Christian participation and ideas is pertinent in this method. Its main emphasis is on the contribution of Indian Christians to the development of Christianity in India.

One of the perennial questions challenging and disturbing the Mar Thoma Church has been the "unity in diversity" concept. The church has attempted to find answers to this in different historical contexts, and a permanent solution to the issue could have been found in its ecumenical outlook. This work thus inquired into the evolution of the Mar Thoma Church's pragmatic ecumenical life principle and its historic praxis in India's multi-religious and multi-cultural context. The church's pragmatic ecumenical outlook took shape through its

---

6   Church History Association of India has published six volumes on comprehensive history of Christianity in India, using this method. See, John C.B. Webster, "History of Christianity in India: Aims and Methods", In: *Indian Church History Review*, Vol. XIII, No. 2 (December/1979), 87–122, "A Scheme for the Comprehensive History of Christianity in India", In: *Indian Church History Review*, Vol. VIII, No. 2 (1974), 89ff; Kaj Baago, "Indigenization and Church History", In: *Bulletin of the Church History Association of India*, Special Number (February/1976), 24–28; T.V. Philip, "Conclusion", In: H.C. Perumalil, E.R. Hambye, (eds.) *Christianity in India: A History in Ecumenical Perspective*, (Alleppey: Prakashan Publications, 1972), 300ff; A. Mathias Mundadan, "The Changing Tasks of Christian History: A View at the Onset of the Third Millenium", In: Wilbert R. Shenk, ed. *Enlarging the Story: Perspective on Writing World Christian History* (New York: Orbis Books, 2002), 44; George Thomas, *Chrisitian Indians and Indian Nationalism 1885–1950* (Frankfurt: Verlag Peter D.Lang, 1979); Mathias Mundadan, "Changing Approaches to Historiography", In: *Indian Church History Review* (June/2001), 51ff; A. Mathias Mundadan, "Rewriting History: Orientations" In: *Journal of Dharama*, Vol. XXVIII, No. 2 (April/June/2003), 168; K.N. Panicker, "Alternative Historigraphies: Changing Paradigms of Power", In: *Jeevadhara*, Vol. XXXII, No. 187 (January/2002), 11; George Oommen, Historiography of Indian Christianity and Challenges of Subaltern Methodology", In: *Journal of Dharama*, No. 28, 2 (April–June/2003), 21–231.

active engagement in the struggles against the "caste system", its association with other churches, and its impact of the church's leadership on socio-political movements as well as on the institutional expressions of modern ecumenism such as the International Missionary Council (IMC) and later, the World Council of Churches (WCC).

This book follows a chronological sequence of the Mar Thoma Church's life and witness since its inception and particularly after 1889. However, due to the interplay of historical reasons and the simultaneous historical functioning of ecumenism in the church's multi-faceted realms, a chronological sequence of the historical analysis is discarded for consistency and clarity in some respects. Therefore, there appears to be an overlapping of historical periods in the presentation of facts and their interpretations in this book.

History versus agenda

Methodologically, the writing of history is supposed to be objective and free from prejudice. However, the historical interpretation of the source materials often reveals the writer's attitude and bias towards the materials and their interpretation. The Indian church historiography contains the writings of the history of various church traditions; they often claim to be the direct custodians of the history of the *Malankara* Church, founded by St. Thomas in India. Therefore this study has taken precautionary steps to avoid such clandestine writing of history.

At the same time, as an ordained priest of the church that is being studied, I have had to guard against the possibility and tendency to unintentionally collect available data for the reconstruction of history in an apologetic mode. While searching for the church's own identity, the Metropolitans, bishops, the episcopal synod and the general body of the church have received more attention in this analysis than the laity – the worker bees in the making of the history of the church at the grassroots or parish level. The church's administrative structure has a well-defined hierarchical structure, but also democratic agencies to formulate and implement the church's ecumenical life principle at the level of the local parishes. Therefore, while the role of the church leaders could be overstated, the study has taken precautionary measures to investigate the available sources using historical-critical method, in order to avoid the skewing of metanarratives.

Praxis, openness, autonomy ...

The conceptual clarity of the terminology is essential in understanding this study. The term "**historic praxis**" is used by several writers attributing different connotations, based on different perspectives. However, the term, as used in this study, to signifies the church's conceptualisation of the internalised meaning of ecumenism – from its multi-religious and ecumenical experiences – and indicates how those meanings could be practised in its life and witness. In plain term, it refers to the church's process of using its internalised and digested knowledge of ecumenism into its life and witness.

The term, "**ecumenism**" used in this study signifies a particular rational view and pragmatic functioning principle that emerged within the Mar Thoma Church and the manifestation of that principle in its historic praxis, which led to the church becoming open to other churches and movements by imbibing their insights and resources to forge unity, while remaining an autonomous and indigenous church. The central thesis is that ecumenism is the principal underlying ethos moulding the church's core, around which the church evolved through centuries. This is not to say that the church has perfectly adapted to its pluralist, multi-religious and multi-cultural environments. This study is both an exposition of ways in which the Mar Thoma Church views the world, the other denominations and other religions as well as an account of what the church has learned about its evolution from its historical engagements with other churches, ecumenical movements and other religions.

"Ecumenism", in this sense, is in conformity with the meaning of the Greek word *oikoumene*, which has been referred to as the "whole inhabited world"[7], the "whole of the Roman Empire"[8], "the whole of the Church"[9], "universal ecclesiastical validity"[10], "world-wide missionary outreach"[11], and "unity of churches"[12]. This refers to the plurality of the world including the plurality of religious and denominational existence. This is also a way of relating the church to other denominations and religions to enhance mutual respect, promotion of an informed understanding of each other and building of mutual relationship. However, it

---

7   Willem Adolf Visser't Hooft, "The Word Ecumenical – Its History and Use", In: "Appendix I", Ruth Rouse and Stephen Charles Neill, ed., *A History of the Ecumenical Movement*, Vol. 1, Third Edition, (Geneva: World Council of Churches, 1986), 735–740.
8   *Ibid.*
9   *Ibid.*
10   *Ibid.*
11   *Ibid.*
12   *Ibid.*

neither advocates uncritical adaptations nor syncretism by damaging the core fundamental values of the church for the sake of unity. Rather it is an attempt to practise unity in diversity, with mutual respect helping to form a community of communities.

The term, "**openness**", as used in this study, is the pragmatic functioning characteristic of the Mar Thoma Church to the fact of the existence of different church traditions and religions. This characteristic feature of the church equips it to listen and entertain new ideas, when it encounters other church traditions and religions. This quality helps the church to adopt new ideas, symbols and customs from those church traditions and religions that it encounters.

The term, "**autonomy**", has different connotations in the Roman Catholic, Oriental and Eastern Orthodox traditions, based on the different perspectives in which they see the term in the context of the local church's relation to its mother church.[13] However, the term used in this study signifies the Mar Thoma Church's self-understanding of its internalised meaning of independence, from other churches of the St. Thomas tradition in India and how that independence can be maintained in its life and witness, while keeping ecumenical engagements with other churches and religions. In other words, it refers to the Mar Thoma Church's status as a self-governing, independent church that is subject to its canons and Constitution. "Autonomy" is not used in the sense of the Mar Thoma Church's status as an autocephalous Oriental church, but in the sense of it being an independent church governed by its own Metropolitan, episcopal synod, general assembly and appointing its own Metropolitan.

This book has 15 chapters that wraps the evolution of Mar Thoma Church's ecumenical journey starting from its earliest history and moving through posers on its assimilation of external influences, while keeping its autonomy. The study has sought to analyse critically the church's relation to Indian culture and its caste affiliations, from an Indian cultural perspective.

The part played by the Mar Thoma Church's Archdeacon, the reaction of its members to subjugation moves by other churches and its response when faced with a leadership vacuum, are among the various landmarks in that ecumenical journey that the book looks at.

The first few chapters cover a brief historical survey of the church after its inception to a newfound existence in 1889. The study then deals with how it preserved

---

13   John H. Erickson, "Autocephalous Church", In: John H Erickson, *The Challenge of Our Past, Studies in Orthodox Canon Law and Church History,* (New York: St. Vladimir's Seminary Press, 1991), 91–113.

its indigenous church identity, while participating in the larger ecumenical movement. The book analyses the church's underlying ecumenical life principle and its application to India's social, religious and political context. The church's oriental liturgical base and reforms are analysed against this background. I found the church's auxiliary organisations having a powerful influence in keeping the centuries-old ecumenical vision in its core. From an administrative and structural perspective, the part played by the Metropolitans, the head of the church, the episcopal synod, the church council and the general assembly are examined critically.

This book also seeks to dive deep into the church's ecumenical engagements with the MISC and the Church of India, Burma and Ceylon (CIBC), the Church of India, Pakistan, Burma and Ceylon (CIPBC) as well as its participation in the national, regional and global ecumenical movements. The study seeks to unravel the ecumenical ethos that drives the church to define its relation with other churches and to the national, regional and global ecumenical movements. The church's conciliar model of ecumenical relations with the Church of South India (CSI), the Church of North India (CNI) and the Communion of Churches in India (CCI) are also dealt with in this book. The book assesses the progress of the church's ecumenical process by employing a detailed study on the ecumenical engagements with the churches of the world-wide Anglican Communion, the CSI, the CNI and the Nilackal Ecumenical Trust.

The final part of this book looks at the response of the church to the programmes of the WCC by outlining how the Mar Thoma Church has responded to those programmes in its life and witness. The church's life and work through auxiliary organisations – Development Department, and Christian Agency for Rural Development (CARD), Mar Thoma Gospel Women's Association (MTSSS) – are analysed at length in this chapter. It also covers the church's response to the political crisis following the declaration of emergency rule in India in 1975. Chapter 15 wraps the general conclusions of this study.

Joseph Daniel
Bern

Chapter I
An Indian Church

Call it colonialism of the religious kind – Vasco Da Gama's discovery of the trade route from Europe to India in 1498 saw the beginning of a Roman Catholic campaign to gain a controlling hold on the Indian church. The *Malankara* Church (Church of St. Thomas or Mar Thoma) roundly opposed it.

The Roman Catholic-Portuguese project was to bring Roman Catholicism to the East and to bring the Mar Thoma community wholly under its fold. Towards this end, the Pope sent Archbishop Alexis De Menezis (1559–1617) to India with the express order "to take control of the Bishopric".

The Archbishop set up shop in Goa in 1592 and set out to bring the Mar Thoma Church in conformity with the doctrines and customs of the Roman Catholic Church. *Extra ecclesiam nulla salus* – there is no salvation outside the (Roman Catholic) Church – became the watchwords of the Menezis regime. This put him in direct confrontation with Archdeacon Thomas, the spiritual head of the Mar Thoma church and representative of the Persian bishop. The Archdeacon used to be then considered the "prince of all Christians" (*jathikkukarthavyam*) in Malabar.

Overriding the strong opposition of Archdeacon Thomas, the Pope's agent convened a synod to separate the *Malankara* Church from the influence of the Persian Church and to subject it under the Roman Catholic diocese of Goa. The Synod was convened for six days in Udayamperoor (Diamper) in 1599. In the book, *The History of Christianity in India: From the Commencement of the Christian Era*, James Hough writes about the actions of Menezis:

> By thus winning over the civil powers, by threatening to excommunicate the Archdeacon, by ordaining a majority of clergy who would zealously lend their valuable aid to the reform in the Chaldean liturgy, and cajoling those already in Holy Orders and conciliating the chief of laity, he prepared them all to listen obsequiously to the decrees which he had already composed for their acceptance.[14]

---

14   James Hough, The *History of Christianity in India; From the Commencement of the Christian Era,* (London: R.B. Seeley and W. Burnside, 1839) 462.
      James Hough was a chaplain to the English East Indian Company. He travelled widely in India and wrote a monumental work on the "History of Christianity in India"

It was a one-point programme – to obliterate an Indian church that had dared to start taking on an increasingly autonomous nature of functioning. Menezis' personal mission strategy was to bring the *Malankara* Church under the Pope by whatever means necessary, fair or foul. For instance he anathematized the *Malankara* Church's customs and practice and condemned its Syriac documents. Ahead of the Synod, Menezis, without authorization from Archdeacon Thomas, ordained a large number of clergy, 90 in all, to exercise episcopal duties in the *Malankara* Church, but mainly with a view to ensure a majority of votes of clergy at the synod.[15]

Diamper decisions

Four radical decisions that were passed during the Synod against the *Malankara* Church's ecumenical outlook can be identified – anathematization of the *Malankara* Church's practices and customs on the guise of being heathen, the suspension of the church's theological vision of mission[16], the condemnation of its Syriac liturgy and manuscripts and the establishment of the Pope's supremacy.

First, the Synod forbid the church to continue its centuries-old practices and customs, which had been designed in conformity with India's social and religious culture.[17] It condemned the *Malankara* Church's theological vision on mission as

---

in 1824 and in which, he made a special study on the history of the Mar Thoma Christians. His book is one of the earliest available written books about the history of Christianity in Kerala.

15 C.P. Mathew and M.M. Thomas, *The Indian Churches of St.Thomas,* Second Edition (New Delhi: ISPCK, 2005), 34. According to George Milne Ray, the synod was convened "for the increase and exaltation of the Catholic faith among the Syrians in Malabar; for the destruction of the errors and heresies, which had been sown in the diocese by several heretics and schematics; for the purging of books from the false doctrines contained in them; for the perfect union of this Church with the whole Church Catholic and Universal; for the yielding of obedience to the Supreme Bishop of Rome, for the extirpation of simony, which had been much practised in the diocese; for the regulation of the administration of the holy sacraments of the Church, and the necessary use of them; and for the reformation of the affairs of the Church and the clergy and the custom of all the Christian people of the diocese". See, George Milne Rae, *The Syrian Church in India* (Edinburgh: William Blackwood and Sons, 1896), 226–227.

16 "Act III, Decree IV of the Synod of Diamper", In: Michael Geddes, *A Short history of the Church of Malabar Together with the Synod of Diamper*, In: George Menacherry ed., *Indian Church History Classics, The Nazranis* (Trissur: SARAS, 1998), 62.

17 *Ibid.*, 62, 84.

a "manifest heresy".[18] These acts were also visible expressions of the inability of Menezis and his Jesuit advisors to see that "the positive elements in non-Christian religions and their providential salvific role for millions of people were not taken seriously in the synod".[19] It declared that

> "Schism and heresy, there being but one Law to all Christians, which is that which was given and declared by Jesus Christ the son of God, and preached by the Holy Apostles all over the world, as one faith, one Baptism, there being but one Lord of all, and one catholic and apostolic church, of which our Lord Jesus Christ, God and man, who founded it, it is the only Spouse; the only universal Pastor, to whom all other Prelates owe obedience, the Pope and the Bishop of Rome, successor in the Chair of St. Peter, the prince of the apostles ; to whom our Lord Jesus Christ bequeathed that supreme authority, and by him to his successors; which Catholic doctrine is necessary to eternal life…"[20]

The Synod condemned *Malankara* Church's Syriac liturgy and manuscripts to be either corrected or to be burned. "Wherefore this Synod knowing that this Bishopric is full of books written in Surian (sic) tongue, by Nestorian heretics …",[21] it commanded that "no person, or of what quality and condition so ever, shall from henceforward presume to keep, translate, read, or hear read to others …"[22] these volumes. After the Synod, they collected all the Syriac documents and liturgies and burnt them, introducing instead Latin liturgy.

---

18 *Ibid.*
19 *Ibid.*
20 *Ibid.*, 63. This reflects "the unawareness of the Latin missionaries about the non-Christian religions. This unawareness instigated them to narrowly interpret the dictum, "outside the Church there is no salvation". See, A.M. *Mundadan, History of Christianity in India, From the Beginning up to the Middle of the Sixteenth Century, vol. I,* (Bangalore: Church History Association of India, 1989) 493; Joseph Kuzhinjalil explores that that most of the disciplinary norms of the synod were fruits of ignorance concerning the Eastern Liturgico-sacramental discipline and the indigenous customs and traditions of *Malankara* Church. Joseph Kuzhinjalil, *The Disciplinary Legislation of Synod of Diamper,* (Ph. D Dissertation, Faculty of Canon Law, Oriental Institute, Rome: 1975), 102; The Syro – Malabar Church (Roman Catholic) has made modifications in the liturgy of "Adai and Mari" of the Persian Church and it was restored in their liturgy in vernacular *Malayalam* language five centuries after the Synod of Diamper, in 1962.
21 "Act III, Decree IVX, of the Synod of Diamper", In: Michael Geddes, *A Short history of the Church of Malabar Together with the Synod of Diamper, op.cit.,* 64.
22 *Ibid.*

The most shocking act of the Synod of Diamper was its move to suspend the *Malankara* Church's centuries-old autonomy. By a decree, the Synod brought the church under the see of Pope in 1599. Here's what the decree states:

> That there is one Law of St. Thomas, and another for St. Peter; which made two different and distinct Churches; and both immediately from Christ; and that the one had nothing to do with the other, neither did the prelate of the one owe any obedience to the Prelate of the other; and that they who have followed the Law of St. Peter, had endeavoured to destroy the Law of St. Thomas, for which they had been punished by him; all which is manifest, Error, schism and Heresy, there being but one Law to all Christians.[23]

The decree unified laws of both churches. By one stroke, it took away the autonomy and independence that the *Malankara* Church enjoyed historically as a church founded by St. Thomas. The decrees in fact articulated the innermost feeling of the Roman Catholic exclusivist claim of being the sole custodian of salvation. What was being brought to the fore was the Roman Catholic Church's self-understanding of being the one and only Church on earth. To cement the Pope's authority over the *Malankara* Church, the Synod also accepted the Council of Trent (1545–1563), which addressed doctrinal, sacramental and ecclesiastical corruption, and the Roman Catholic Court of Inquisition.[24]

Moreover, celibacy of clergy was made compulsory, against the *Malankara* Church's tradition. Horror of horrors, married clergy were called upon to put away their wives as well!

Even though Menezis and the Roman Catholic Church were able to suppress the *Malankara* Church for a short while and managed to burn valuable Syriac manuscripts, the Synod of Diamper triggered a wave of unrest among the Mar Thoma Christians against the Roman Catholic Church. For the first time in its history, the *Malankara* Church was confronted by authoritarianism, but responded robustly. The aftermath of Diamper saw the seeds of unrest being sowed among the Mar Thoma community which took on the shape of a revolt eventually.

The Coonen Cross revolt

The struggle between the Roman Catholic Church and the *Malankara* Church in the aftermath of the Synod of Diamper culminated in the "Coonan Cross Oath"[25]

---

23   *Ibid.*, 62–63.
24   *Ibid.*
25   The *Coonan Cross Oath* was a public avowal by members of the Mar Thoma community on January 3, 1653 that they would not submit to the Roman Catholic domination.

of 3 January, 1653, an epoch-defining episode in Indian church history. The oath cut off all links of Mar Thoma Christians to the Roman Catholic Church. Here's how the events unfolded.

A group of people under Archdeacon Thomas, which had been searching for an opportunity to re-establish and re-affirm the identity of the centuries-old *Malankara* Church, realized the importance of scrapping its union with the Roman Catholic Church. The church, in this instance, had to depart, albeit temporarily, from its centuries-old policy of tolerance to other churches. But it was a pragmatic move for a greater cause to safeguard its autonomy and independence.

It was just a matter of time before the struggle found the trigger that brought things to a head. In 1653, a sporadic event was to ignite the embers of resentment to a fire of revolt. The resentment that brewed over the years fermented into a violent reaction on the part of the Mar Thoma Christians, when Mar Ahatalla, who was a bishop sent by the Patriarch of Antioch on the request of Archdeacon Thomas, was prevented from entering India at Cochin. He was kept as a prisoner by the Portuguese.[26]

This oppressive action of the Portuguese provoked those who rallied under the Archdeacon to receive the bishop at Cochin. The infuriated people, who assembled at Cochin to receive bishop Ahatalla, moved towards a cross installed in Mattancherry, Cochin, on 3 January, 1653, and took a solemn oath, renouncing all allegiance the Pope. This event came to be known as the *Coonan Cross Oath*. Says A.M. Mundadan, a Roman Catholic priest and church historian:

> "It was a painful outward manifestation of the deep trauma the community had been experiencing at the distortion of their identity and loss of autonomy".[27]

Roman Catholic historians called this event as "Coonan Cross Revolt" whereas, other historians called this event as *Coonan Cross Oath*.

26 Itty Daniel, "The Syrian Church of Malabar", In: George Menachery., ed., *Indian Church History Classics, The Nazranis, op.cit.*, 405–406. A. Sreedhara Menon, *A survey of Kerala History*, (Madras: S. Viswanathan Printers and Publishers, 1988) 195; Joseph Thekkedathu, *History of Christianity in India, Vol. II*, (Bangalore: Theological Publication of India for Church History Association of India, 1982), 94–96. Itty Daniel (1905–1988) was an ordained priest of the Malankara Orthodox Syrian Church. He was a scholar and a writer. This work is the published copy of his doctoral dissertation at the Erasmus Theological College, California in United States of America.

27 A.M. Mundadan, *Indian Christians Search for Identity and Struggle for Autonomy*, (Bangalore: Dharamaram, 1982) 51; Joseph Thekkedathu, *History of Christianity in India, Vol. II, op.cit.*, 95.

Their trauma was aggravated by "the attempt of the Jesuit Archbishop[28] to eliminate the age-old authority and special position of the Archdeacon", adds Joseph Thekkedathu, another Roman Catholic priest and historian.[29] A.T. Philip, a Mar Thoma Church historian, suggests the revolt was "a reaction of the Mar Thoma Christians against the liturgical circumvention by the Roman church".[30]

The majority of historians, including those in the Roman Catholic Church, considered *Coonen* Cross as the epicentre of a chain of reactions of the Mar Thoma Christians against the unilateral decisions of the Synod of Diamper[31].

It resulted in the first split in the Mar Thoma community.[32] The major faction recognized the Archdeacon as the supreme head of the Church, who after a valid act of consecration, came to be known as Mar Thoma I (1653–1670).[33]

The classical thesis, *Christianity in Travancore*, by G.T. Mackenzie, a former British Resident in Travancore and Cochin states is considered the first monumental work on the history of Christianity in Kerala. He says: "Of the whole number of Syrian Christians, computed to amount two hundred thousand persons, only four hundred remained under archbishop Gracia"[34] of the Roman Catholic Church.

---

28 Francis Ros (1600–1624), Stephen Britto (1624–1641) and Francis Gracia (1641–1659) were three Jesuit archbishops of the Roman Catholic Church, who ruled the Roman Catholic Church since the synod of Diamper in 1599.

29 Joseph Thekkedathu, *History of Christianity in India, Vol. II, op.cit.*, 95.

30 A.T. Philip is an ordained priest of the Mar Thoma Church and a Church Historian. He was a Professor at the Mar Thoma theological seminary, Kottayam. See, A.T. Philip, "Liturgical Imperatives of the Mar Thoma Church", In: M.V. Abraham, Abraham Philip and et al, (eds.), *A Study on the Malankara Mar Thoma Church Liturgy*, (Manganam: TMAM Orientation Centre, 1993), 22–42. When the Synod of Diamper forbade the use of this liturgy and instead introduced the Latin Liturgy, the church members have not welcomed the new liturgy.

31 Roman Catholic historians like A.M. Mundadan, Joseph Thekkedathu and Jonas Thaliath are in favour of this view.

32 Those who remained in the Roman Catholic Church were called *Pazhayakoor* and those who wanted to keep their independent status were called *Puthenkoor*.

33 Those who took the "Coonan Cross Oath", later in the month of May in 1653 held a council at *Alangad* in Kerala and have chosen Archdeacon Thomas as their bishop by the laying-on-of-hands by 12 priests. Later, when Mar Gregorios, the Bishop of Jerusalem arrived in Kerala in 1663, the Archdeacon was consecrated as the bishop – Mar Thoma I (1663–1660). This was the first occasion, when the *Malankara* Church came into the direct relation with the Antiochian Church. See, I. Daniel, *The Syrian Church of Malabar, op.cit.*, 406.

34 G.T. Mackenzie, *Christianity in Travancore, op.cit.*, 120.

This fact supports the intensity of the Coonen Cross action as one that manifested not merely the opposition of the Mar Thoma Christians against the Roman Catholics, but underlines the long history of a cherished autonomous identity of the *Malankara* Church. The oath reestablished the validity of that identity, which could be traced back to the time of the founding of the *Malankara* Church.

At the same time, it created a situation that forced the church to seek help from the Patriarch of Antioch for the consecration of the first Metropolitan of the *Malankara*. That event marked the beginning of an apostolic succession from the Antiochian patriarchate that continues till date.

The importance of "Coonan Cross Oath" in the history of the *Malankara* Church cannot be overemphasized. The intense resentment against the Portuguese in the 17th century for imprisoning Mar Ahatalla and the resultant "Coonan Cross Oath" were forerunners of the Indian liberation movement. The "Coonan Cross" fervour seemed to endure in the following decades as it enabled Mar Thoma Christians to stand up for reforms and to revolt against the jurisdictional claims of the Antiochian Patriarch during the 19th century. The following analysis would shed light on this fact.

The Antiochian connection

The antagonism of the Roman Catholic Church resulted in the *Malankara* Church being prevented from consecrating its bishop canonically till 1663. It was Antiochian Bishop Mar Gregorios of Jerusalem, with the help of the Dutch political power, who consecrated Mar Thoma I (1653–1660) in 1663. This marked the beginning of the *Malankara* Church's relation with the "Monophysite"[35] Jacobite Patriarch of Antioch.[36]

---

35   The *Monophysitism* was a theological position to counter the Nestorianism and it held that "there is only one nature in the incarnated Christ" after the union. It was since 6th century; the Monophysites separated themselves and called themselves Jacobites. The Patriarch of Antioch was its head. See, Placid J. Podipara, *The Thomas Christians,* (Bombay: St. Paul Publication, 1970) 66–67.

36   The non- chalcedonian churches are the Persian, the Assyrian, the Egyptian, the Armenian and the Indian. Generally the Monophysites are the name associated with these churches. These churches did not accept the chalcedonian formula in 451 CE. *Malankara* Church had no engagements with the *Monophysite* Jacobite church until 1665. It was Mar Gregorios, who belonged to the "Monophysite" Jacobite church

Two major effects of the church's relation with the Antiochian Church can be identified. These are: the adoption of the west Syrian liturgical tradition unofficially, and the church's approval of the Antochian Patriarch's spiritual supremacy. These eventually resulted in another fresh schism within the church, which will be dealt with later.[37]

Before moving to the reforms that ensued in the *Malankara* Church, it will be educative to take a look at the historic background of the evolution of a wider ecumenical outlook that the church practised well before the concept became accepted and followed in the world at large.

---

brought the Mar Thoma Church in relation with Antiochian (Jacobite) Church. See, Placid J. Podipara, *The Thomas Christians, op.cit.*, 66–67.

M.M. Thomas commented on the nature of Mar Gregorios "as a good Jacobite Syrian, he sought to reintroduce oriental customs such as eastern liturgical vestments, leavened bread in the Eucharist and clerical marriage". See, C.P. Mathew and M.M. Thomas, *The Indian Churches of Saint Thomas, op.cit.*, 43.

37 Ever since that time the Jacobite bishops were sent to India by the Patriarch of Antioch, and this relation later went into extreme hatred and spilt within the church in 1889 and in 1912. The details of which will be dealt with in detail in the following section of this study. See, A.M. Mundadam, *Indian Christians Search for Identity and Struggle for Autonomy, op.cit.*, 118–120.

Chapter II
A Wider Ecumenical Outlook

In order to find out the reason for the genesis of the *Malankara* Church's ecumenical outlook, we must go back to the historical context of the origin of Christianity in India during the first century CE. There is reason to believe that the first converts of Christianity in India were from different Hindu religious traditions – people of the land, the *Dravidians* and the *Brahmins*[38] – against the exclusive *Brahmin* descendant claim of the Mar Thoma Christians. It is therefore methodologically right to explore the ethnic background of the first Christian converts in India and their attitude towards the Hindu religious traditions, as we seek the reason for the genesis of the wider ecumenical outlook of the *Malankara* Church.

This outlook can be traced back to the Third Century CE, when the *Malankara* Church started conversions and in the process, brought together the three different Hindu religious traditions mentioned above. But the Church's openness was visible even from the First Century CE, when St. Thomas is believed to have founded seven churches in the Malabar Coast.

There is ground to believe that the *Malankara* Church[39] has been in existence in the south-western coast of India, or Malabar, since 52 CE. This becomes clear as

---

38 *Brahmins* are the highest class of religious community in the caste system in India. The "caste system" in India has been dealt with in detail in the following chapters of this study.

39 The *Malankara* Church entered into a relationship with the Persian East Syrian Church and inherited its language and liturgy. (Since the 4th century) The East Syrian Christian heritage was transmitted to the *Malankara* Church through the Syriac language, which is a dialect of Aramaic. Until the Roman Catholic domination in India, the Christians of India were called the "Mar Thoma Christians" or "Nazrani Christians". In the 16th century the Roman Catholic Church tried to unite the Mar Thoma Christians to the Roman Catholic Church and it eventually led to a spilt in the church. Those who did not follow the Roman Catholic fold were known as "Syrian Christians of Malabar" or "*Malankara* Christians" and they continued the *Malankara* Christian tradition in India. The spilt within the "*Malankara* Christians" in 1889 led to parting of the *Malankara* Church into two pathways namely; "Malankara Mar Thoma Syrian Church" and the "Malankara Jacobite Syrian Church."

we look at the history of the *Malankara* Church in the backdrop of the St. Thomas tradition.

But some basic questions need to be pondered here. How did Christianity reach Kerala? How did the *Malankara* Church practice an ecumenical outlook, even prior to the rudimentary understanding of *oikumene* being transformed into a well-developed concept of "ecumenism", as we understand it, in the world ecumenical movement? Could it be the result of the church's interactions with Indian culture, which upholds the idea of "unity in diversity", while maintaining its relationship with other churches?

Origin of the *Malankara* Church in India

The history of the *Malankara* Church during the first four centuries of the Common Era can be traced only with the help of a study of traditions, legends and apocryphal texts as authentic historical data was not available to reconstruct its history during this period. Hence, any account of this period can only be called a historical probability.

The relation between *Malankara* Church's self-awareness as an oriental, indigenous Indian church and its reverential consciousness of the St. Thomas apostolic tradition is a crucial point to be considered while studying the church's history. Autonomy and openness are crucial elements of its ecumenical outlook, which is an integral part of its identity, along with its apostolic consciousness. Historians base the church's apostolic consciousness on two theories – the South Indian Tradition Theory and the North Indian Tradition Theory.

The South Indian Tradition Theory refers to the missionary work of St. Thomas that resulted in the origin of a Christian community in the extreme south-west of India (Kerala) during the First Century CE. The tradition suggests that Apostle Thomas came to the south-west coast from the island of Socotra in 52 CE, and by the time that he finished his work as an apostle in Kerala, he had founded seven churches[40] on the Malabar coast. Thomas later went over to the Madras coast, where he converted some to the Christian faith, but was finally martyred at

---

40   The churches that founded by St. Thomas in India are *Crangannore, Kottkkayal, Palur, Kokkamangalam, Niranam, Quilon,* and *Nilackal.* See, Alexander Mar Thoma, *The Mar Thoma Church Heritage and Mission* (Tiruvalla: National Offset Printers, 1985), 2.

Mylapore near Madras in Tamil Nadu in 72 CE.[41] There seems to be a lot of local traditions, stories and songs that still support this tradition in Kerala.[42]

So, does the voyage of St. Thomas to South India have historical basis, or is it just based on traditions and folklore? While the following explanation on the historical methodology may seem a diversion from our topic of discussion, it is important to appreciate the basis of the St. Thomas Apostolic tradition that the church has been founded.

Historians like A.E. Medlycott, the author of a Third Century work, *India and the Apostle Thomas: An Enquiry with a Critical Analysis of the Acta Thomae*,[43]

---

41 G. Milne Ray, *The Syrian Church in India* (Edinburgh: William Blackwood and Sons, 1892), 22–23; J.N. Farquhar, *The Apostle Thomas in North India* (Manchester: The Bulletin of the John Ryland's Library, Vol. 10, No. 1, January 1926; J.N. Farquhar, *The Apostle Thomas in North India* (Manchester: University Press, 1926); Alexander Mar Thoma, *The Mar Thoma Church Heritage and Mission* (Tiruvalla: National Offset Printers, 1885), 2; A.E. Medlycott, *India and the Apostle Thomas: An Enquiry with a Critical Analysis of the Acta Thomae* (London: Ballantyne Press) 1905 in George Menacherry ed., *Indian Church History Classics, The Nazranis* (Trissur: SARAS, 1998), 188–200.

J.N. Farquhar (1861–1929) was a Professor of Comparative Religions at the University of Manchester. He was a scholar and a theologian. His analyses on the apostolate of St. Thomas have provided valuable insights on the text of the *Acta Thomae*. His monumental work "Crown of Hinduism" reflects his knowledge of Hinduism and Christianity.

A.E. Medlycott (1838–1896) was the vicar apostolate of Trichur in the Cochin State and a Bishop of Tricomia, the first Bishop of the Syro-Malabar Church, a wing of the Roman Catholic Church in India during 1887–1896. His work – "Indian and the Apostle Thomas: An Enquiry with a Critical Analysis of the *Acta Thomae*" –, which has been published in 1905, is an exhaustive pioneering work for the study on the history of Christianity in India. He has produced several ancient documents to prove the validity of the tradition. It remains a standard reference book about the Mar Thoma Christians in India.

Alexander Mar Thoma (1813–2000) was the Metropolitan of the Mar Thoma Church during 1976–1999. He was a scholar in Hinduism and Church History.

42 *Margam Kali* songs, local church traditions and family histories of the Christian families in Kerala provide evidences in support of this theory.

43 *Acta Thomae* is a third century document, which contains the story of the arrival of St. Thomas in India. It has a Gnostic affiliation. There are several ancient texts of the *Acta Thomae* in existence in various languages such as Syriac, Greek, Latin, Armenian and Ethiopic of this book. The original manuscript of this book is found in the British Museum. This book gives a detailed account of Apostle Thomas' missionary work in Persia and India. A gist of it is summarised here: At the disciples' meeting in Jerusalem, after the ascension of Jesus Christ, all the countries of the world were

maintained that there is ample evidence for the acceptance of the South Indian Tradition. He writes: "After the demise of the Blessed Virgin Mary ... Thomas commenced his second apostolic tour ... he passed on to Socotra ... going thence he would have landed on the west coast of India".[44] Besides, Medlycott translated the writings of the Persian church's St. Ephraem,[45] titled *Carmina Nisibena.*[46] We surmise from St. Ephraim's hymns that the apostle was martyred in India and that his relics were taken to Edessa.

By quoting the *Nisibine* hymn 42, Medlycott argued the following points to support the South Indian Tradition Theory: 1. the apostle suffered martyrdom in India; 2. his body was buried in India; 3. his bones were later taken to Eddessa, and

---

divided among themselves for evangelisation and India was assigned to St. Thomas. India, which at that time included all Middle East to the present India. The story tells that a merchant by name Habban of Indian King Gundnaphor came to Jerusalem, looking for a carpenter to take home to the King. Christ appeared to him and sold his slave Thomas to Habban for 20 pieces of silver. They took the sea route to India and landed in a port – *Sandruk Mahosa* – where Habban was received by the local King. They attended the wedding of the King's daughter and St.Thomas demonstrated his ability of performing miracle to the King's daughter and it attracted the King. With his help, they reached the Kingdom of Gundaphorus and Thomas was commissioned to build a palace for the King on the bank of the river. However St. Thomas distributed the money that he received from the king for the building, to the poor and therefore he could not build the palace. So the king put him in prison. However that night the King's brother Gad died and he was told the beautiful palace beside the river in the heaven was his brother's. He came back from the dead and told the story to the King. They were later converted to the Christianity. See, For a concise account of the text See, C.B. Firth, *An Introduction to Indian Church History, revised edition* (Serampore: Indian Theological Library, 1992), 9–11.
C.B. Firth (1894–1931) was a missionary of the London Mission Society (LMS) in India and a graduate from the Cambridge University in England. He was the secretary of the "Conference of the British Missionary Societies in London". His contribution to Indian church history and literature was immense.

44   A.E. Medlycott, *India and the Apostle Thomas: An Enquiry with a Critical Analysis of the Acta Thomae, op.cit.*, 161–162.

45   St. Ephraem was a hymn writer of the Edessan Church, who lived around 300–370 CE. In his hymns he states that Apostle Thomas was martyred in India and that his relics were taken to Edessa by a merchant.

46   This is a collection of hymns edited by Bickell from British Museum, *Add.MSS14572.* The MS consists of 117 folios and is assigned by Bickell to the sixth century. Some folios of the text have been lost. Medlycott has translated the first three strophes of Hymn 42. The remaining strophes have no direct bearing on the subject.

4. his power and influence were felt in both places of India and Persia.[47] He used another Syriac document titled, *"The Doctrine of the Apostles"*[48] to prove the Apostolic mission of St. Thomas to India.[49] He quotes a statement from the translation of Curaton on the ancient Syriac manuscript: "India and all its own countries, and those bordering on it, even to the farther sea, received the Apostle's hand of priesthood from Judas Thomas, who was a guide and ruler of the Church that he built and ministered".[50] He emphasizes the South Indian tradition in support of the claim of Mylapore that it holds the tomb of the apostle.[51] Most of the Christians, who claim the Apostolic origin in India, are holding on to this tradition.

North Indian tradition

The North Indian Tradition Theory refers to the origin of Christianity in India by the Apostle Thomas' mission to North India. The theory is developed on the basis of the *Acta Thomae*[52], which is the earliest available record about St. Thomas' travel and missionary work in India. The theory suggests that St. Thomas went by sea to the kingdom of Indian King Gondaphorus'[53] and preached the gospel there, and also met the king and his brother.[54] Then he was sent to another king called

---

47   A.E. Medlycott, *India and the Apostle Thomas: An Enquiry with a Critical Analysis of the Acta Thomae*, 1905, In: George Menacherry ed., *Indian Church History Classics, The Nazranis, op.cit.*, 194–197.

48   "The Doctrine of the Apostles" is an ancient Syriac document, edited by Curaton, *Ancient Syriac Documents*, London, and previously by Cardinal Mai, *Scriptorum Veterum Nova Collectio*, Rome: 1838.

49   A.E. Medlycott, *India and the Apostle Thomas: An Enquiry with a Critical Analysis of the Acta Thomae, op.cit.*, 197.

50   *Ibid*, 198. Also Cited In: William G. Young ed, *Handbook for Source Materials for Students of Church History,* (Madras: CLS, 1969), 26.

51   A.E. Medlycott, "St. Thomas Christians", In: *Catholic Encyclopedia*, Vol. XIV, (New York: The Gilmary Society, 1914), 678–88.

52   *Acta Thomae* is sometimes called by its full name *Acts of Judas Thomas*. The book ends with a statement, which says: "the *Acts of Judas Thomas* is completed, which he wrote in the land of the Indians, fulfilling the command of him, to whom be glory forever and ever". See, T.V Philip, *East of the Euphrates* (New Delhi: ISPCK, 1998), 96.

53   Various spellings of the name Gundaphar are seen in different versions of this story such as Gundaphar, Gondophores etc.

54   J.N. Farquhar, "The Apostle Thomas in North India", In: the *Bulletin of the John Rylands Library*, Vol. 11, 1926 in George Menacherry ed., *Indian Church History Classics, The Nazranis, op.cit.*, 313–322.

Mazdai in another part of India to heal his wife and daughter who were possessed of evil spirits. The women were restored to sanity and they decided to abandon marriage.[55] Many members of the royal family were converted. The king killed Thomas for some explained reasons.

We have to confront a question at this point: is King Gondaphorus a historical figure? The historical analysis of the *Acta Thomae,* the numismatic evidences of the first three centuries, and the local Christian traditions, as they exist in folklore, provide insights that are positively related to the St. Thomas apostolate theories. J.N. Farquhar, professor of comparative religious studies at the University of Manchester,[56] made a detailed study on the St. Thomas Apostolate to both North India and South India. Both studies are based on analyses of the text, *Acta Thomae.* He suggests that the voyage of St. Thomas to India, its kingdom and the king, which are referred in the *Acta Thomae,* are historical.[57]

Moreover, about 30,000 *Pali* language inscriptions[58] in coins that were discovered from Afghanistan and Punjab by the middle of the 19th century have thrown light on the history of the church that extends over first three centuries.[59] Among

---

55 *Acta Thomae* supports celibacy and asceticism and it considers such kind of life as a highest form of life.

56 J.N. Farquhar had made two monumental studies on the St. Thomas Apostolate to South India and North India. "The Apostle Thomas in North India" is an amplification of the lecture that he delivered in the John Rylands Library in October 1925 and it published in the Bulletin of the Library in 1926. "The Apostle Thomas in South India" is his work that appeared in the same Bulletin in 1927.

57 J.N. Farquhar, "The Apostle Thomas in North India", *op.cit.*, 313–322.

58 *Pali* is a literary language of the *Prakrit* language family in India. Most of the early Buddhist writings were written in the *Pali* language. The early Buddhist *Pali* was considered linguistically similar to, or even a direct continuation of the old *Magadhi* language, which was an ancient Indian language.

59 Sir. Alexander Cunningham, (1814–1893) was an English archaeologist and an army engineer. He retired (1861) as a major general after 30 years of his service with the Bengal engineers and then he served as the head of the Archaeological Survey of India during 1861–1865, 1870–1885. Among his books are *Bhilsa Topes* (1854), "A History of Buddhism Based on Architectural Remains", "The Ancient Geography of India" (1871, 2d ed. 1924), "The Book of Indian Era" (1883) and "Coins of Ancient India" (1891). His collection of rare coins is kept in the British Museum. In 1854, General Alexander Cunningham in his writings in the Journal of the Asiatic Society in Bengal says about the discovery of not less than 30,000 coins, bearing Greek and Indian legends and extending over a period of more than three centuries in Afghanistan and Punjab. There is a clear mention of the dynasty of the King Gondaphorus in

44

these coins, the coins of Gondaphorus were common in Kabul, Kandahar and Seistan and in the western and southern Punjab. Besides, some documents in the ancient Edesan church reported the arrival of St. Thomas in India. Farquhar also listed a few such writings along with numismatic evidences to prove that the visit of St. Thomas to North India was historical.[60]

Farquhar thus arrived at the assumption that the Kushan war drove the apostle out of Punjab and the dates tallied with this inference.[61] Habban, a merchant who accompanied Thomas, probably expressed the opinion that the best thing that the Apostle could do was to move to the South Indian port of *Muziris*,[62] where the Europeans, Egyptians and Romans had trade routes even prior to the Common Era. When St. Thomas left Gondaphorus' kingdom, he went to another part of India, where he won converts but was finally put to death by order of the king.[63]

It is important to note from the numismatic inscriptions that by about 50 CE, the Kushans[64] had defeated the Scytho-Parthian Empire.[65] The inscriptions on the coins deciphered by archeologists as those from the time of King Gondaphorus prove that he was still reigning in 45 CE. Another inscription on the coin, which was dated 64 CE, proves that the Kushan king was then supreme. Therefore, we

---

it. The specimens of these coins are available at Berlin Museum, British Museum and the Bibliotheeque Nationale, Paris. See, "Alexander Cunningham", In: *Journal of the Asiatic Society in Bengal,* Vol. xiii, (1837), 679–712.

60 The list of evidences that Farquahr presents in support of his argument are: the *Acta Thomae* (180–230), Ephraim of Nisibis and Edessa in his hymns (373), Gregory of Nazianzus, *Hom.XXXIII*, Ambrose, Ballerini, II, 389, Jerome, Mingne, P.L., XXII., 558; Origen, *Commentary on Genesis, III*, Eusebius *Ecclesiastical History, II, I.* and other writings. See, J.N. Farquhar, "The Apostle Thomas in North India", In: *op.cit*, 319–320. It was by the middle of the first century BCE that the Parthian empire became powerful in Persia and Greater India.

61 *Ibid.*

62 A. Sreedhara Menon, *A Survey of Kerala history, op.cit.*, 5.

63 J.N. Farquhar, "The Apostle Thomas in South India", In: the *Bulletin of the John Rylands Library*, Vol. 11, 1927 In: George Menacherry ed., *Indian Church History Classics, The Nazranis, op.cit.*, 324–331. The writer of the *Act of Thomae* has not mentioned the name of the kingdom of Gondaphorus in the original text.

64 *Kushans* belonged to the steppes of Central Asia. They invaded India in the first century CE. The Kushans first occupied Bactria (North Afghanistan) and moved to Kabul, after defeating the Indo-Parthian rulers. They invaded India by the middle of the first century CE.

65 Edward James Rapson, The Cambridge History of India, cited In: *ibid.*, 321. S.L. Kaeley, V.K. Bhandari, et al., *Indian History and Culture* (New Delhi, Inter University Press, 1986), 92–95.

45

can infer that the King Gondaphorus was an Indian king before the Kushan rule was established in India. The Kushan war might be the reason why St. Thomas abandoned his chosen field of evangelization and sought the advice of merchant Habban[66] before sailing towards South India, where he reached in 52 CE and was martyred in 72 CE.

In the light of additional references in early church historian Eusebius' works, *Ecclesiastical History*[67] and *Edessan literature*, Farquhar held the view that both the South Indian and North Indian Apostolate of St. Thomas were valid traditions. He stated that St. Thomas first went to North Western India travelling by sea and up to river Indus, but had to leave due to the Kushan invasion, which eventually wiped out Christians of that region, so that no trace remained. Then he left India by sea, landed in Socotra and afterwards sailed for South India and came to Malabar. He then moved to Burma, only to return to India before being martyred at Mylapore.[68]

An Indian historian, T.V. Philip,[69] also held the view that "it is reasonable to believe that Thomas was apostle to all India".[70] Although South Indian tradition gained more importance because of the existence of Christian and Jewish communities there in the First Century CE, "both theories are reasonable and far from being exclusive, strengthen each other",[71] says Philip. An American historian S.H. Moffett also held the view that St. Thomas visited both places. Moffett states:

> The consensus of the majority is that both theories are reasonable and far from being mutually exclusive, can be interpreted as strengthening each other. It is not implausible to believe that after preaching in Gundaphar's kingdom in the North, Thomas moved on as all traditions affirm to preach the gospel to other kingdoms as well, the kingdoms of south western and south eastern India until he was put to death, perhaps in Madras. If, as seems quite possible, he was the apostle to India at all, it is satisfying to believe with considerable reason that he was the apostle to the whole of India.[72]

---

66 J.N. Farquhar, *The Apostle Thomas in South India, op.cit*, 323.
67 Origen remarks in his *Commentary on Genesis* that "according to tradition, Thomas allotted the field of labour was Parthia". Cited In: *Ibid.*, 328. Eusebius quotes this passage in his "Ecclesiastical History", Eusebius, Ecclesiastical History, Vol. III, Cited In: *Ibid.*
68 J.N. Farquhar, The Apostle Thomas in South India, *op.cit.*, 323–331.
69 T.V. Philip was a Church historian and an ecumenist. He was a fellow of the Brisbane College of Theology, Australia.
70 T.V. Philip, *East of the Euphrates: Early Christianity in Asia*, (New Delhi: ISPCK, 1998), 102.
71 *Ibid.*
72 S.H. Moffett, *A History of Christianity in Asia, Vol. I*, (San Francisco: Harper and Row, 1992), 161.

This tradition is still maintained at the heart of Indian Christianity.[73] However, the traditions of both North Indian and South Indian St. Thomas apostolates are matters of controversy even today.[74] The possibility also exists that some foreign missionaries discouraged the notion of Apostle Thomas being in India for claiming the Indian mission field for themselves and writing their own history.

There are other random evidences to support the St. Thomas Apostolic traditions of the *Malankara* Church. Some of such evidences are as follows: One of the bishops present at the Council of Nicea in 325 CE signed the decrees of the

---

73   Indian ports were being referred in the accounts of the foreign travelers and the writers from Greece and Rome. The Greek ambassador Megastanese refers the "Chera Kingdom" an ancient Kerala kingdom in his account on ancient India. Pliny and Ptolemy also have written about the Kerala coast and its trade relation with Roman Empire through the ports of *Muziris, Tyndis, Barace* etc, See, A. Sreedhara Menon, *A Survey of Kerala History, op.cit.*, 10–11. In the coin collection of the *Maharaja's* palace at Trivandrum in Kerala, there are 9 Aurei of Augustus Ceaser's coinage, 28 of Tiberias, 2 of Caligula, 16 of Claudius and 16 of Nero... See, Nagam Aiya, *The Travancore State Manual*, (Trivandrum: Travancore Government Press, 1906), 231.
Nagam Ayya, (1850–1917) was a renowned government official in the state of Travancore, who compiled the history of Kerala, – "Travancore state Manuel" – in three volumes, by the support of the king. This work sheds light on the Kerala history and culture.

74   L.W. Brown states that "We cannot prove that the apostle worked in south India any more than we can disapprove that fact but the presence of Christians of undoubtedly ancient origin holding firmly to the tradition is the proof of very considerable commercial contact between the western world and the Malabar Coast". See, L.W. Brown, *The Indian Christians of St. Thomas*, (Cambridge: The University Press, 1956), 59. Brown rejects the St. Thomas tradition on the ground that it has developed on the basis of the apocryphal work *Acta Thomae*, which is dependent on the Edessa Church. The purpose of this text is to magnify the works of St. Thomas, not to establish Indian apostolate. But Brown misses some points. Firstly, although the Edessa Church had a special relation with St. Thomas, they never claimed him as the founder of their Church. Second, the Edessan Church started celebrating the feast of St. Thomas on July 3 in memory of the transfer of St. Thomas' bones from India to Edessa. Third, Medylcott's research on St. Ephrerm's hymns, suggest that the relics of St. Thomas were very much venerated in Edessa. Therefore it is a general opinion of the Edesan Church that St. Thomas died in India. See, L.W. Brown, *The Indian Christians of St. Thomas, op.cit.*, 45–65.
L.W. Brown (1912–1999) was an Anglican Bishop of Uganda, former principal of the United Theological College at Bangalore in India and a chaplain to the Jesus and Downing Colleges, Cambridge. He was a scholar in Church History. His work "The Indian Christians of St. Thomas" is an authoritative source on Indian church history.

council as John, bishop of Persia and Greater India.[75] St. John Chrysostom writes, "How could the apostle who spoke only Hebrew draw all these people to the faith. How were they able to preach, to the Scythians, the Indians and the Samaritans?"[76] On the analysis of the available evidences mentioned above, the St. Thomas Apostolate was the most probable hypothesis that could be reached. Having accepted that as historical, it is reasonable to surmise that the first ethnic converts from the three different Hindu religious traditions mentioned earlier on in this chapter were drawn to this Christian tradition. Adding to these evidences is the presence of the Syrian Christian diaspora community, which reached Kerala in the 4th Century CE from Persia, again drawn by the St. Thomas and Jewish traditions, along with the openness of the St. Thomas Christian community.

The blending of the three different traditions mentioned above has a definite historical basis. Indian historians generally believe that the vast majority of people in the *Sangham*[77] age had no special religion till 500 CE.[78] They were the *Dravidians* and the People of the land. The historians held that Buddhism and Jainism had its influence in Kerala during the early centuries.[79] An earliest account dating 630–640 CE speaks of Buddhism as the state religion in Kerala, but it also found a considerable presence of the Brahmin community.[80] The real

---

75   There is an evidence, which shows that one of the bishops, who present in the council of Nicea in 325 CE signed the decrees of the council, was John. He was a bishop of Persia and Greater India. See, G.T. Mackenzie, *Christianity in Travancore*, in *Ibid.*, 113–148; Claudius Buchanan, *Christian Researches in Asia; With Notes of the Translation of the Scripture* (London/Liverpool: Ward & Co, Paterson Row, Edward Howell Co, 1849), 71.
      Claudius Buchanan was the first chaplain of the English East India Company in India. He visited several churches in Malabar and met the King of Travancore. His book is a treasure house of his understanding about the Mar Thoma Church in India.

76   C.P. Mathew and M.M. Thomas, *Indian Churches of St. Thomas* (second Edition) (New Delhi: ISPCK, 2005), 12; Zaleski, *The Apostle St. Thomas in South India* (Mangalore, 1912), 44.

77   First five centuries of CE in south India was the period of the *Sanghom* age.

78   A. Sreedhara Menon, *A survey of Kerala History, op.cit.*, 80.

79   *Ibid.*, 74–87; K.P. Padmanabha Menon, *History of Kerala* (Cochin: Cochin Government Press, 1924), 47.
      K.P. Padmanabha Menon was a renowned secular historian in Kerala.

80   E. Kunjanpillai, *Chila Kerala Charithra Prasanagal* (Malayalam) (Kottayam: NBS Press, 1963), 221.
      E. Kunjanpillai was a secular historian in Kerala.

Brahmin migration to Kerala started only after the Sixth Century and they became powerful by the Eighth Century.[81] However, the earliest available source for the Brahmin presence in Kerala is the *Patittupattu*.[82] It speaks of the *Vedic* knowledge of the Brahmins in Kerala. The *Sangham* works also provide evidences for the presence of Aryan ideas and practices in Kerala in the early centuries of the Common Era.[83]

However, the Brahmins were very few in number and they were not a powerful community in Kerala during the First Century CE. As evidenced from these documents, we can infer a Brahmin presence during the first few centuries of the Common Era supporting the St. Thomas tradition theory of Brahmin conversion.[84] This theory has it that St. Thomas converted four Brahmin families to Christianity after reaching Muziris and the Mar Thoma Christians are descendants of these four families. It is equally logical to believe that St. Thomas converted the Dravidians and the people of the land, who were the majority population, during his mission in Malabar.

By these acts, he succeeded in blending the three different racial elements in Kerala, bringing them together under one umbrella of the Gospel in a tradition rooted in Indian culture.

India's social, political and religious spheres have definitely had a bearing on the *Malankara* Church's life and work. It has followed a policy of openness to other Indian religious communities,[85] accepting India's plurality and diversity as a gift. It is "Indian in culture, Christian in religion and oriental in worship", said Placid J. Podipara (1899–1985), a CMI priest in Kerala, who was an eminent

---

81 *Ibid.*
82 *Patittupattu* is a poetic work of the *sangham* period.
83 A. Sreedhara Menon, *A Survey of Kerala Histroy, op.cit.,* 80.
84 V. Naggam Aiya, *The Travancore State Manual,* Vol. II, *op.cit.,* 22–123.
85 The major religious communities in Kerala are Hindu, Muslim, and Christians. Within the Hindu community there are several sub-sections such as *Namboothiris, Nairs, Ezhavas, Parayas, Pulayas,* and *veluthedans.* The Mar Thoma Christians have maintained a close relationship with these religious communities. See, Xavier Koodapuzha, *Christianity in India* (Vadavathoor: OIRS, 1998), 32–33; Placid J Podipara, *The Thomas Christians,* (Bombay: St. Paul Publication, 1970), 76–77.

theologian and a prolific writer.[86] It has also been reported that the *Malankara* Church architecture of church buildings closely resembles that of the pagodas.[87]

There is no evidence of a centralized administration, or an overseer (bishop), to look after these early converts to Christianity in the First Century CE. On the other hand, the Indian concept of unity of living with differences, or unity in diversity, could have created a degree of harmony and unity.

The early Christian converts from these different communities attempted to give a justification for their conversion to Christianity by living together as a religious community. At the same time, they kept existing social and religious values that are embedded in Indian culture, even while embracing Christian values. They also accepted their brethren, who belonged to the Buddha, Jain and Hindu religious traditions, which themselves were well known for their religious tolerance and openness.[88] On Indian Christians, Upadyay says: "In matters other than

---

86   *Ibid.*, 79.

Mar Thoma Christians share the common destiny in their placing in the multi-religious and multi-cultural context of India. "Mar Thoma", is the Syriac translation of the name "St. Thomas". Mar Thoma Church shares the east Syrian liturgy until 1836. Since then, the church adopted the west Syrian liturgy as it had started a fresh relation with the Antiochian church. The new liturgical tradition was implemented by the decisions of the Synod at Mavelikara in 1836 in the church. The churches that claim St. Thomas Apostolate in India still use either translation of the Syriac liturgy or Syriac liturgy as such in their worship services. See, G.T. Mackenzie, *Christianity in Travancore*, (Trivandrum: Travancore Government Press, 1901), 1–10.

G.T. Mackenzie was a British Resident in Travancore and Cochin. His work "Christianity in Travancore" is a monumental work on the history of Christianity in Kerala. Even today, this book is considered as a classical one, which throw light on the history of Indian Christianity. He published it with the permission of the then King of Travancore in 1901.

87   *Pagoda* is a Buddhist religious building with several levels, each of which has a roof that sticks out. James Hough reported that Vincent De Lagos "was displeased at the sight of the Christian churches so closely resembling the heathen (Hindu) pagodas", when he visited Kerala. See, James Hough, *The History of Christianity in India From Commencement of the Christian Era Vol. 1*, (London/Madras: R.B Seeley and W. Burnside, 1839), 246; Also Quoted In: J.C. Panjikkaran, *The Syrian Church in Malabar* (Trichnopoly: St. Joseph's Industrial School Press, 1914), 277–290. J.C. Panjikkaran was a historian, who did a major historical work on the Mar Thoma Christians in 1914. His work "The Syrian Church of Malabar" is the revised and published dissertation, which he submitted to the University of Madras.

88   A. Sreedhara Menon, *A survey of Kerala History, op.cit.*, 80.

faith, we are essentially Hindu."[89] Therefore, the sense of openness and tolerance of other religious communities had a bearing on the social and religious outlook of the first Christian converts. This open and tolerant cultural milieu eventually developed into a sense of wider ecumenism within the *Malankara* Church. It also helped them to formulate a separate law for Christians in India.

Law of St. Thomas

The Law of St. Thomas stands for the vision of openness and autonomy, customs and disciplinary norms of the Mar Thoma Christians that they nurtured in the Indian socio-cultural milieu since the time of the Apostle Thomas. Says Roman Catholic Church historian Francis Thonipara: "The Law of Thomas stands for the whole life-style of the St. Thomas Christians. It includes the ecclesiastical, liturgical, spiritual, and socio-cultural lifestyle of St. Thomas Christians. This Law of St. Thomas was well-adapted to the cultural-religious milieu of Malabar."[90] The Decree of the Synod of Diamper (1599) also agrees with the separate religious and cultural existence of the *Malankara* Church against the church in Rome.[91]

The law of the *Malankara* Church mentioned in the Synod of Diamper is that "each one can be saved in one's own law and all which are right and lead men to heaven".[92] It accepts the self-sufficiency of other religious laws to lead men to salvation. It affirms the universal law of love. Christianity has a universal law of love that binds the Holy Trinity and the love that binds humanity and nature. This law opens another level of unconditional love of God, for God is love.

The Law of St. Thomas is not like Mosaic Law, which is rigid and not open to change, or any such laws. It is very vague, elastic and stretchable as it appeared in the Decree of the Synod of Diamper. In fact, the Law of St. Thomas describes the way in which the fact of India's religious plurality and religious teachings leading to salvation have been conceptualized and accommodated by the *Malankara* Church; even centuries before a theology of mission in relation to religious plurality emerged. Although Diamper branded it as heresy, the Synod document did

---

89 R.H.S. Boyd, *An Introduction to Indian Christian Theology* (Madras: CLS, 1969), 97.
90 Francis Thonipara, "St. Thomas Christians: the First Indigenous Church of India", In: *Christianity is Indian,* Edited by Roger E. Hedlund (New Delhi: ISPCK, 2004), 65.
91 "Act III, Decree VII, Acts and Decrees of the Synod of Diamper, 1599", In: Geddes, *A Short History of the Church of Malabar Together with the Synod of Diamper*, George Menacherry, ed., *The Nazranis, Vol. 1, op.cit.*, 62–63.
92 "Act III, Decree, IV, Acts and Decrees of the Synod of Diamper, 1599", In: *Ibid.*, 62.

imply the ecumenical outlook of the *Malankara* Church and its participatory social and religious Indian culture.[93]

Church soaks in Indian culture

Among the reasons for *Malankara* Church to identify with the social, religious and cultural traditions of India and to assume an independent position by formulating the Law of St. Thomas was its debt to the Indian culture. Indian historian A. Sreedhara Menon writes: "Nevertheless, the Christians have completely assimilated themselves in a community in which they live by adopting the language, dress, and habits of the Hindu brethren. Though Christian in faith, they are Keralites in all other aspects."[94]

They have imbibed the social and cultural practices and traditions of Hinduism, which represents the crux of Indian culture. This allowed the *Malankara* Church flexiblity to legitimatize the adaptation of Christians to the social, religious and cultural traditions of India. In India, the cultural trend has been the affirmation of pluralism – that different religious expressions are equally valid for a universal religious reality.[95] Consequently, India's social and religious openness and tolerance provided a standard for the development of the *Malankara* Church's social, religious and cultural milieu. While St. Thomas desired the propagation of the message of the love of God in India, the church could not ignore the fact that it was the religious tolerance and openness of Indian culture that helped it to develop an ecumenical outlook and to be a part of India's social, religious and cultural life.

The *Malankara* Church became an integral part of the socio-cultural history of Kerala by following the Law of St. Thomas. The Mar Thoma Christians opted

---

93   The Law of St. Thomas was against the Roman Catholic Church's teaching of "no salvation outside the church". Therefore, the Synod of Diamper branded the Law of St. Thomas a heresy. See, *Ibid.*, 62–62.

94   A. Sreedhara Menon, *A survey of Kerala History, op.cit.*, 86.

95   There was an undercurrent of religious unity and inter-religious engagements among diverse religious faiths in India by the influence of the Hindu culture. The Hindu Indian culture affirms that the "Truth is one and sages speak of it differently". (*Rig Veda* 1: 164.46). This means that different religions are equally valid expressions of the universal truth. Thus both facts of unity of religions and differences of religious experiences are affirmed by the Hindu culture in India.

deliberately to assimilate the culture and practices of Kerala Hindus.[96] For instance, they adopted the customs associated with the Hindu way of life in dressing, eating habits, and death and marriage rituals.[97]

Some of such customs could be cited here: "A new-born baby is fed with powdered gold mixed with honey"[98], immediately after the birth. A child beginning to learn the alphabet is made to write the first letter with their finger in rice.[99] The Christians also used to sing a special song called *Veerandiyanpattu*, which is a traditional Hindu "caste" song, at the time of the feast of the St. Thomas Christians.[100] At the same time, they have been deeply attached to their autonomous apostolic heritage, which they used to call *Thomayude Margam*.[101]

---

96   For instances, the Buddhist *pagoda* and the Christian church were called in vernacular as the *Palli*. Like the Buddhist *Sangha*, the executive committee of the Church is called the *Edavaka Sanghom*. Even in matters of dress, the Mar Thoma Christians maintained a style of their own with little difference with the dress pattern of the Hindus. See, Placid J. Podipara, *The Thomas Christians, op. cit.*, 79–98.

97   A.M. Mundadan, *Indian Christians Search for Identity and Struggle for Autonomy* (Bangalore: Dharamaram, 1982), 24.
There are several customs associated with the whole life of a person is practiced by both the Hindus and the Christians in India. Some of such practices are: First rice feeding custom, marriage customs, puberty customs, and so on. Both the Hindus and Christians practice arrange marriages. During the marriage solemnization, as in Hindu customs, at the end, after blessing the *tali* or *minnu*, in the Christian marriages also, the *minnu* is handed over to the bridegroom, who ties it round the brides neck with threads taken from her veil (*sari*), making a special kind of knot, while the priest holds it in front. Both communities respect and honour their parents, priests, teachers and elders.
See, L.K. Anantha Krisna Ayyar, *Anthropology of the Syrian Christians* (Eranakulam: Cochin Government Press, 1926) In: George Menacherry ed., *Indian Church History Classics, The Nazranis, op.cit.*, 485–507.
L.K. Anantha Krisna Ayyar was a Curator of the State Museum and the Superintendant of Ethnography in Kerala and his work is an earliest scientific study on the Anthropology of the Mar Thoma Christians in India.

98   Placid J. Podipara, *The Thomas Christians, op.cit.*, 80.

99   *Ibid*. This custom is still prevalent among both Hindu and Mar Thoma Christians communities. The *mantra, Om hari sree gana pathaye namaha* would be written on sand or in a tray of rice. The Sanskrit words, *Hari* refers to God and *Sree* refers to prosperity. It is a prayer for the God of Knowledge and alphabets. Writing on grains denotes the acquisition of knowledge, a source of prosperity.

100 Xavier Koodapuzha, *Christianity in India*, (Vadavathoor: OIRS, 1998), 32.

101 *Ibid. Thomayude margam* is a Malayalam word, which means the way of St. Thomas.

Second, the *Malankara* Church has adopted a policy to live in religious harmony, influenced as it is by the spirit of tolerance and interaction in India's social and cultural realms, as has been highlighted above. L.W. Brown notes that the Mar Thoma Christians "appear to have lived in two worlds at the same time, but with no consciousness of tension between them or disharmony within themselves".[102] They were Christians of faith and Syrians in worship and ethic; "they were Indians in all else".[103]

Therefore, "the communal harmony, spirit of tolerance and openness should be considered as a typical Indian Church's contribution to the world Christian vision".[104] This is the *Malankara* Church's ecumenical understanding on which the *Malankara* Church's mission strategies are based. This will be dealt with in detail in the next section of this study.

Third, the *Malankara* Church remained uncritical on the Brahmanical Hinduism's agenda of implementing "casteism"[105] during the eighth and ninth centuries in Kerala. When the Brahmanical Hinduism assumed a radical stand of ostracizing the "lower caste" communities, the *Malankara* Church was found to be more

---

102 L.W. Brown, *The Indian Christians of St. Thomas An account of the Ancient Syrian Church of Malabar, op.cit.*, 3–4.

103 *Ibid.*

104 A.M. Mundadan, *History of Christianity in India, From the Beginning up to the Middle of the Sixteenth Century*, vol. I, (Bangalore: Church History Association of India, 1989), 493.
The priests of the Malankara Church have high social position down through the centuries. Even the civil court cases were settled by the mediation of a priest, or bishop, only criminal cases used to be taken to courts. See, Placid J. Podipara, *The Thomas Christians, op.cit.*, 84.

105 The "caste system" in India has its debt to the Brahmanical Hinduism and its sacred texts – four *Vedas*. In the *Vedic* system, there were four basic social classifications in the society – *the Brahmans*, the *Kshatriyas*, the *Vaishyas*, and the *Shudras*. The *Brahmans* were priests and intellectuals. They practiced and preserved the *Vedic* rituals and processes of spiritual realization. The *Kshatriyas* were warriors, military and government administrators. The *Vaishyas*, were the merchants, bankers, farmers and the *Shudras* were common labourers, musicians, dancers. *Casteism* says that if anyone who born of a *Brahmana* family, then he/she be a *Brahmana,* no matter whether he/she truly exhibit the genuine characteristics of a *Brahmana* or not. Those who were not within this division were called "outcastes". They were deprived of all rights and privileges of four divisions within the community. See, *Report of the Commissioner for scheduled castes and scheduled Tribes for the second period ending 31st December, 1951*, 1ff; James Massey, *Roots – A Concise History of the Dalits*, (New Delhi: CISRS, 1991), 10–25.

vulnerable to the "caste system".[106] Eventually it led to the church assuming solidarity with the "caste system".

It might have been a quirk in the ancient history of the church, as the Mar Thoma Christians struggled for survival in the early stages as a very vulnerable and small community among the vast majority of Hindus. As a negative consequence, the *Malankara* Church was also influenced by the superstitious and caste-religious tendencies current in the medieval and modern Hindu culture. Purification rites related to death and puberty,[107] and negative social practices such as consulting fortune-tellers, keeping slaves, the practice of dowry,[108] "castiesm" and untouchability[109] were among the other Hindu ritualistic influenced that seeped through the church community. The Mar Thoma Christians wrongly preferred a social position within the "caste system", equivalent to the "high-caste" Hindus.[110] Consequently, the champions of "Hindu-castiesm" looked upon the *Malankara* Church as serving the cause of "castiesm" and looked for its promotion together with the Christian piety. Therefore, they accepted them as a "caste" within the "caste system" in Malabar. For instance, "for a High Caste Hindu, the touch of a Mar Thoma

---

106 The Mar Thoma Christians got the equal position of the *Kshatriya* community (*Nair*) in Kerala.

107 The women in their periods were considered unclean. Like Hindu girls and women, the Christian girls and women were under seclusion for three days during which they could not enter into the kitchen. See, L.K. Ananthakrishna Ayyar, *Anthropology of the Syrian Christians, op.cit.*, 491–492.

108 Dowry was an age-old practice going back to the Vedic period in the Indian society. Before a marriage is being fixed between a boy and a girl, the boy's parents fix a certain amount of gold and cash to be paid to them by the parents of the girl. Later, it became a custom to demand money from girl's parents. This became an evil practice and a matter of gender discrimination. The Government of India prohibited the practice of the dowry by the Indian Parliament in 1961 by passing Dowry Prohibition Act. See, L.K. Ananthakrishna Ayyar, *Anthropology of the Syrian Christians, op.cit.*, 490–491.

109 "Untouchablity" was a custom within the "casteism" in India. The "lower caste" people were considered as untouchables. In public roads the "lower caste" had to give way to the "high caste" including Christians. In case they happened to meet a "lower caste" either by seeing or touching, the "high caste" people would purify themselves by a bath. "Untouchability" is abolished and its practice in any form is forbidden in India by Law. The Constitution of India safeguards the equal rights and privileges of its citizens irrespective of race, "caste", religion, sex. See, Gangadhar Pantawane, "Evolving a New Identity:The Developement of a Dalit Culture" In: Barbara R. Joshy ed., *Untouchable!Voice of the Dalit Liberation Movement*, (New Delhi, 1986), 79ff.

110 L.K. Anantha Krisna Ayyar, *Anthropology of the Syrian Christians, op.cit.*, 498.

Christian was sufficient to purify articles defiled by the touch or near approach of the "low caste" people".[111]

This caste identity of the *Malankara* Church resulted in the exclusion of the "low-caste" people from the church, and the sidelining of the missionary goal, as ethnic and caste solidarity[112] issues gained more prominence. This was despite the fact that the church had developed a theological vision for mission, considering the pluralistic context of India. Both these attitudes have been changed by the church after its reform during the 19th century, which will be discussed later.

Ecumenical theological vision on mission

The implementation of the *Malankara* Church's social and ethnic solidarity with the socio-religious and socio-cultural milieu of India helped it to formulate a mission outlook in relation to other Indian religions. This outlook was based on the Law of St. Thomas[113] and in opposition to the imperialistic missionary agenda of saving the souls from heathens of the modern missionary movements.[114] The church's theological vision on mission affirms the mutual respect for all religious faiths, including the Christian faith, in relation to the universal. A.M. Mundadan says:

> It would be centuries before the Europeans would acquire a life experience of non-Christian religions, before a theology of the religions of the world would emerge,

---

111 Placid J. Podipara, *The Thomas Christians, op.cit.*, 82.
112 L.W. Brown and other historians' allegation against the Mar Thoma Christians was that they never possessed the spirit of Christian mission to their neighbours in India. However, historians like Medlycott, Cardinal Tisserant and other do not agree with this view. Yet, it is a fact that the Mar Thoma Christian's missionary spirit was not in the same way as that of the west. This has been dealt with length in the following chapters of this study. S.E. Tisserant, *Eastern Christianity in India* (London: Longman and Green Co, 1957), 11–26; L.W. Brown, *The Indian Christians of St. Thomas An account of the Ancient Syrian Church of Malabar, op.cit.*, 167–209.
113 "Act III, Decree, IV, Acts and Decrees of the Synod of Diamper, 1599", In: George Menacherry ed., *Indian Church History Classics, The Nazranis, op.cit.*, 62–64.
114 Modern missionary movements during the 18th and the 19th centuries considered mission as sending missionaries from the west to the east and making them similar to the west in religion and culture. It was associated with western imperialism. Therefore, most of the missionaries who came to India were not able to find the rich religious and cultural heritage of India. It was on the basis of their missionary consciousness; the modern missionaries have not found the same western missionary consciousness in the Mar Thoma Church.

which would give due respect to the positive elements in those religions and their providential salvific role for millions of people. But the Indian Christians had already been living for centuries in a positive encounter with the High caste Hindus and had developed a theological vision of Hindu religion which was more positive and liberal.[115]

This statement of Mundadan contains a basic disposition of the *Malankara* Church, in its liberal and pluralistic mission outlook, which is independent of the western mission theology in relation to other religions. The significance of the *Malankara* Church's attempt is that it sought to apprehend the challenges of Christian mission within the Indian pluralistic context. The *Malankara* Church thus tried to respond to the fact of Indian religious plurality by way of two major paradigms of the modern world, viz., inclusivism and pluralism, at a period when the world never thought of those paradigms in dealing with religious fundamentalism.[116]

The consequence of this outlook was the development of a conscious stand of the *Malankara* Church on mission strategy, with an emphasis on peaceful co-existence with other religious communities, and attracting others by their good deeds in the same way as the bees were attracted by the flower. Thus, long before the wider ecumenical outlook became a guiding principle in the global inter-religious dialogues respecting all faith and teachings leading to salvation, it had been a much desired quest within the *Malankara* Church.

Let us now analyze whether the same outlook serves as the basis for the *Malankara* Church's relation with other churches that came into contact with it.

---

115   A.M. Mundadan, *History of Christianity in India, Vol. I* (Bangalore: Theological Publication in India, 1984), 493–494.

116   The policy of religious tolerance and the respect for all religions in India was adopted by the Kushan emperor Ashoka (273–232 BCE). He says that "there should not be honour to one's own sect condemnation to another sect… On the contrary, the other's sect should be honoured on this and that occasion. By doing so, one promotes his own sect and benefits another's sect". See, S.L. Kaeley, V.K. Bhandari, and *et al.*, (eds.), *Indian History and Culture, op.cit.*, 86. The second major attempt was done by the Mughal Emperor Akbar (1556–1605), who introduced a new religion – *Din- i-llahi* – which was the fusion of different religious ideals and principles. See, *Ibid.*, 231–232.

Chapter III
In Communion

The Coonen Cross Oath of 1653 marked the culmination of a long-standing struggle against the imperialistic designs of the foreign Roman Catholic Church. That event reflected the fierce determination of the *Malankara* Church to remain an indigenous church. But this cannot eclipse the fact that tolerance and openness remained the church's watchwords in its relations with other communities, including other church denominations.

The *Malankara* Church has maintained positive ecumenical relations with churches that have came into contact with it since the Fourth Century CE.[117] It maintained links at different levels with the Persian Church, the Roman Catholic Church and the Antiochian Church, and adapted its Christian views and liturgical elements opportunistically from these streams.

The contact of the *Malankara* Church with other churches can be traced back to the middle of the Second Century CE, when it possibly developed contacts with the Alexandrian Church. Although there is no primary historical data available to corroborate this hypothesis, the visit of Pantaneus, the first known head of the catechetical school in Alexandria, to India in 180 CE is taken as an earliest reference of the relations of the *Malankara* Church with a church outside India.[118] However, the church was not able to develop a long-lasting ecumenical relation with the Alexandrian Church for unknown reasons. The burning of church documents and

---

117 Francis Thonipara, "St. Thomas Christians: the First Indigenous Church of India", In: *Christianity is Indian, op.cit.*, 65–66.

118 Eusebius states that when Panteneus arrived in India, he found persons, who knew Christ and the Gospel of St. Mathew in Hebrew language from India. It was believed that St. Bartholomew, who brought the Gospel of St. Mathew to India. See, Eusebius, *Ecclesiastical History*, 5: 10; Also cited in T.V. Philip, *East of the Euphrates: Early Christianity in Asia, op.cit.*, 105; Alexander Mar Thoma, *The Mar Thoma Church Heritage and Mission, op.cit.*, 3. Jerome and Clement of Alexandria speak of Pantaneus visit to India; I. Daniel, *The Syrian Church of Malabar* (Madras: The Diocesan Press, 1945) in George Menacherry ed., *Indian Church History Classics, The Nazranis, op.cit.*, 402. These references show the existence of a Christian Church in India during the second century. Origen also states that St. Thomas evangelized Parthians. Cited In: *Ibid.*

Syriac manuscripts by the Roman Catholic Church in the wake of the Synod of Diamper had destroyed historic data that could have supported such hypotheses.

Persian connections

The *Malankara* Church's relation to the Persian Church is linked to two migrant waves of Persian Christians to India. The first Persian Christian migration to India was associated with the arrival of Thomas of Cana and other Persian and Syrian Christians' to India in 345 CE.[119] The second started when the Persian *Caliphs* began persecuting Christians in 632 CE. The second wave resulted in a group of

---

119 A band of Christians that consists a bishop, priests, deacons and laymen from Bagdad, Nineveh, and Jerusalem migrated to the Malabar Coast of India under the leadership of Thomas of Cana and settled down at Cranganore in 345 CE. He obtained from the then King of Malabar Cheraman Perumal, certain rights and privileges for Christians. This migration was in the political context of the Persian persecution of Christians, which started during the reign of the Persian emperor Shapur II (309–379) in 343 CE. It was therefore quite likely that in order to escape from punishment, some Persian Christians migrated to India. See, A. Sreedhara Menon, *A Survey of Kerala History, op.cit.*, 84; G.T. Mackenzie, *Christianity in Travancore*, In: *Ibid.*, 113–148; V. Naggam Aiya, *The Travancore State Manual, op.cit.*, 233.; I. Daniel, *The Syrian Church of Malabar, op. cit.*, 402; P. Cherian, *Malabar Syrians and Church Mission Society 1816–1840*, (Kottayam: Church Missionary Press, 1935), 1–15.
The book "Universal Christian Topography" was written by Cosmos Indicopleustes. He was an Indian voyager set out his journey to India in 522 CE. He found the Persian Church's relation with the *Malankara* Church. He says: "even in Taprobane (Ceylon) an island in further India, where Indian sea is, there is a church of Christians, with clergy and a body of believers, but I know not whether there be any Christians in part beyond it. In the country called Male (Malabar), where the pepper grows, there is also a church, and at another place Calliana, there is moreover a bishop, who is appointed from Persia. In the island again, called the island of Dioscorides (Socotora), which is situated in the same Indian sea, and where inhabitants speak Greek, having been originally been colonists sent thither by the Ptolomies who succeeded Alexander in Macedonian, there are clergy who receive their orders in Persia and are sent on to the island there is also a multitude of Christians." Cosmos Indicopleustes was referring to the Mar Thoma Church, which was the earliest Christian church in India that also admits the Mar Thoma Church's episcopal supervision by the Persian Church. Moreover, the presence of the Persian Crosses in the Churches at Kottayam and Mylapore with *Pahlavi* inscriptions, affirms the argument of Cosmos in connection with the relationship of the Mar Thoma Church to the Persian Church. See, J.W. McCrindle ed.,

Syrian Christian merchants migrating to Kerala in 823 CE. They were accepted as Christian brethren from Persia by the *Malankara* Church, as in the case of Thomas of Cana.

The ties with the Persian church were two-tiered – the *Malankara* Church accepted episcopal supervision by Persian bishops and adopted the East Syriac liturgy in its worship. The episcopal supervision entails the mutual recognition of each other as churches, and the *Malankara* Church's acceptance of the oversight of Persian bishops. The mutual relation between the *Malankara* Church and the Persian Church were considered mutually beneficial by both the churches. According to Mingana, "in the year 823. the Syrian Fathers, Mar Sapor and Parut with the illustrious Sabrisho came to India and reached Kullam".[120] The then king of Venad[121] granted them the land for the construction of a Church and a town.[122]

It is difficult to assess the extent to which the links of the *Malankara* Church with the Persian Church served to further church unity efforts. But the ties do reflect the *Malankara* Church's openness to accept other churches and its ability to adopt considered suggestions from the churches, with which it has good relations. It had no hesitation in accepting the Persian Church as part of the "One, Holy, Catholic and Apostolic Church" and to receive episcopal oversight from the

---

Christian Topography of Cosmos An Egyptian Monk, Book III, (Cambridge: Cambridge University Press, 1897), 119.

120 A. Mingana, *The Early Spread of Christianity in India* (Manchester: Bull of John Rylands Libraray, 1926), 45.
Alfonso Mingana (1878–1937) was a Persian theologian and a historian, who collected many ancient documents on eastern Christianity.

121 *Venad* was a princely state in Kerala. The earliest reference about this kingdom is found in the Teressapalli copper plate in 849 CE. It was during the 12th century that the Venad Kingdom merged with the Ay Kingdom and later it became part of the Travancore kingdom.

122 *Ibid*. This act of the King serves as an illustration of the *Malankara* Church's high social position in the kingdom of *Venad*. It also illustrates the church's relation with the Persian Church. The Mar Thoma Christian's had a prominent role in trade and commerce in the southern coasts of India. The high social positioning of the Christians motivated the king to issue certain privileges and rights to them. He issued the *Teressappalli copper plate*, which contains several rights and privileges to the Christian community. This was executed by Ayyan Atikal Thiruvadikal of *Venad* during the reign of Stanu Ravi varman (844–885). See, A. Sreedhara Menon, *A Survey of Kerala history*, *op.cit.*, 85; K.K. Kuruvilla, *A History of the Mar Thoma Church and Its Doctrines* (Madras: CLS, 1950) 2.

Persian bishops. The historical basis was that both churches had the same founder – the Apostle Thomas.[123] For instance, the *Malankara* Church accepted the Persian Church's decision to elevate the Bishopric of Rewardastir as a Metropolitanate, for providing additional episcopal oversight to the *Malankara* Church in 410 CE.[124] This arrangement continued until the Seventh Century CE, when Patriarch Isho-Yahb II (628–643) appointed a Metropolitan for India separately.[125] The church submitted to the episcopal oversight of the Persian bishops until the 15th century.

A Nestorian nexus?

An assessment of the impact the Persian Church's doctrines had on the *Malankara* Church cannot ignore the influence the teachings of Nestorius (ca. 386–451) started to have on the Persian Church after its relations with the Indian church strengthened.[126] The Nestorian teaching was that there were two distinct persons in the incarnate Jesus Christ – one human and other divine. The *Malankara* Church was uncritical of the Nestorian teaching, when the Persian Church became Nestorian in 498 CE.[127] The Indian church allowed its members to be passive participants

---

123 The episcopal oversight and the interchangeability of priests between different churches are still an unresolved question in many of the churches in the world. See, "Interchangeability of Ministers Between the Church of England and the Member Churches of the EKD – The Present Legal Position", In: *Visible Unity and Ministry of Oversight – The Second Theological Conference held under the Meissen Agreement between the Church of England and the Evangelical Church in Germany,* (West Wickham: Church House Publishing, 1996), 5–8; Reinhard Frieling, *Amt – Laie – Pfarrer – Priester – Bishof – Papst* (Goettingen: Vandenhoeck and Ruprecht, 2002), 66–101.

124 T.V. Philip, *East of the Euphrates: Early Christianity in Asia, op.cit.,* 116.

125 *Ibid.*

126 Nestorius (386–451) was the bishop of Constantinople during 428–431 CE. He hesitated to call St. Mary as *Theotokos* instead he called her – *Christotokos* (Mother of Christ) – against the faith affirmation of the undivided Church. It was in this context that Cyril of Alexandria in the Council of Ephesus in 431 CE declared St. Mary as *Theotokos* as she bore Jesus Christ, who is divine and human. This led to the rejection of Nestorius's teachings.

127 The "Church of the East", the "Persian Church", the "Assyrian Church", and the "Babylonian Church" are the names of the church, which established at the side of the river Tigris. This church believes that Mar Addai was the founder of those churches. Mar Addai was a disciple of St. Thomas, who sent Mar Addai to the east. They followed the east Syrian rite of "Addai and Mari", of the 4th century. It is believed that at the Synod of Markabtha in 424 CE., this church declared independence and became

in the Nestorian teachings by following the Persian liturgy, without removing the Nestorian elements in it.

This was because the *Malankara* Church's leaders were not conscious of the ambiguities involved in the Nestorians' Christological teachings. They were also not conscious of the responsibility they had to provide guidance to the church folk in conformity with the teachings and doctrines of the undivided Church of the Nicene Creed. The *Malankara* Church thus followed the Nestorian teaching blindly, like in the case of adopting "caste" solidarity with the Brahmanical Hindus, as mentioned in the previous chapter.

So, was the *Malankara* Church Nestorian? Did it deviate from its stated autonomous nature by deciding to adopt Persian liturgy in its worship? I would submit that it is the church's core ecumenical nature that came to the fore in its ties with the Persian Church and later with the Nestorian Persian Church. For instance the Decree XIV of the Synod of Diamper says:

> Wherefore the Synod knowing that this Bishopric is full of books written in Surian (Syrian) tongue by Nestorian heretics and Persons of other Devilish Sects, which abound with Heresies, Blasphemies, and false doctrines, doth command in virtue of obedience, and up on pain of Excommunication to be *ipso facto* incurred, that no person of what quality and condition so ever, shall from henceforward presume to keep, translate read or hear read to others any of the following books.[128]

In that process, the *Malankara* Church failed to keep the doctrines of the church unaltered, as it uncritically adopted the Persian liturgy as its own. It is evident that

---

an autocephalous church. This church did not participate in council of Ephesus as it was being influenced by the Nestorian teaching. When Cyrilian formula – *mia physis tou theiou logou sesarkomene* – formulated, the Persians rallied under Nestorius and his disciple Theodore of Mopsuestia. Later, Bar Saumo and Narsai, who were exiled from the Roman Empire, became their leaders in propagating ideas of Theodore of Mopsuestia and Nestorius. His Christological position was that Christ has two *kiane* (*physis* or nature rather in the abstract), two *qnome* (an individual *kiana* that exists by itself; more or less *hypostasis*) and one *parsopa* (*prosopon*: the sum total of the individual notes and qualities of a *quoma*). The union of *kiane* in Christ is according to *quoma* (*Monophysitism*) and the union is according to *parsopa*. This theological position was not in conformity with the teachings of the undivided church. See, Placid J. Podipara, *The Thomas Christians, op.cit.*, 36–62.

128 "Act III, Decree XIV of the Synod of Diamper", In: Michael Geddes, *A Short History of the Church of Malabar Together with the Synod of Diamper* (London: Prince's Arms in St. Paul's Church yard, 1694), In: George Menacherry ed., *Indian Church History Classics, The Nazranis, op.cit.*, 64–65. K.N. Daniel, *Udayamperoor Sunnahadosinte Kanonukal* (Malayalam), *op.cit.*, 1–221.

Nestorian books used to be circulated in the *Malankara* Church in those times. Moreover, the liturgy also contained certain references with a distinctly Nestorian tone. The *Acts and Decrees of the Synod of Diamper* reported: "In the book of Prayer for the Great Lent, it is frequently said that there were two persons, a Divine and Human in Christ".[129] It is thus logical to assume that the Persian Church's Nestorian teachings did have a bearing on the *Malankara* Church's liturgical life. But it was not a Nestorian Church, as Menezis and Portuguese friar Gouvea suggest.

Biased historical account

Indeed early historical references have imputed a Nestorian character to the *Malankara* Church. This generalization was grounded on a biased narration of history by Alexis De Menezis and Antony Gouvea, which was endorsed by Milne Rae, Claudius Buchanan, Michael Geddes, L.W. Brown and others. They affirm that after the first four centuries, the *Malankara* Church became Nestorian.

However, it would be appropriate to consider the following questions to find the position of the *Malankara* Church during this period. I would submit here that the historians did not properly understand the so-called Nestorianist references within the *Malankara* Church's liturgy. Moreover, it is fair to say that the Nestorianism has not be appreciated and accepted as such by the Mar Thoma Christians. After all, at a time when the means of communication were rudimentary, how could the Bishop of Persia, sitting miles and miles away from India, effectively exercise his power and control over an Indian church and impart wholesale the Nestorian doctrines?

The autonomous nature of the *Malankara* Church is evident in the statement of Mingana. He says: "When in AD 345, the question came up on organizing the churches of the Persian Empire under the prelate of Seleucia Ctesiphon, the prelates of Persia stood aloof. They asserted that they were from the Apostle Thomas, and so they would not be under the Chaldean Church."[130] Therefore historians, who consider the *Malankara* Church as a Nestorian church may be subscribing to

---

129 "Act II, Decree XV of the Synod of Diamper", In: Michael Geddes, *A Short history of the Church of Malabar together with the Synod of Diamper, op.cit.,* 66.
130 A. Mingana, *The Early Spread of Christianity in India* (Manchester: Bull of John Rylands Libraray, 1926), 23. Also cited In: A.M. Mundadan, *Indian Christians Search for Identity and Struggle for Autonomy, op.cit.,* 12.

Gouvea's opinion that was reflected in his travel records, which were considered authentic ancient records.

Gouvea was a Portuguese Augustinian friar in Goa under Archbishop Alexis De Menezis (1559–1617).[131] Menezis wanted to put an end to the ties of the *Malankara* Church with the Persian Church and to bring it under the Roman Catholic Church, as mentioned in the previous chapter. With this in mind, the Archbishop branded practices of the *Malankara* Church, adopted from Hindu customs, as heathen.

Besides, he found fault with the old Syriac literature, worship and practices and branded all these records as Nestorian.[132] Being preoccupied by the directive of Archbishop Menezis, Gouvea wrote his biased account called *Jornada* first in Persian[133]. Three years later, in 1603, he wrote in Portuguese a narrative of the tour of Menezis in Malabar and his account of the Synod of Diamper. This was the earliest book available for non-Indians as references on the *Malankara* Church and its practices.

But S.H. Moffett has spoken of the real status of the *Malankara* Church, while considering its ties to the Persian Church. He affirmed that the *Malankara* Church "was not a daughter church of the Persian hierarchy. It already had a long history of its own".[134] In the light of the report of Theophilus the Indian, Moffett affirms that "at least 200 years before Cosmos, it had already begun the indispensable process of accommodating Christian practice in Indian ways".[135]

This is a well-considered statement of Moffett on the *Malankara* Church. In truth, the Mar Thoma Christians living among the Hindus and other religious communities outside welcomed with open arms whoever came from abroad, without

---

131 Alexis de Menezes was the Portuguese Archbishop of Goa. He convoked the Synod of Diamper on June 1599. The Synod of Diamper played a major role in changing the church history of Kerala. The synod convened after a prolonged power struggle spread over five months between Menezes and the Archdeacon of the *Malankara* Church. After the Synod Menezes visited most of the *Malankara* Churches, with a view to Latinize them by obliterating and erasing all their indigenous customs and practices.

132 See, "Act II, Decree XV, Act II, Decree XV, of the Synod of Diamper", In: Michael Geddes, *A Short history of the Church of Malabar together with the Synod of Diamper, op.cit.,* 64–67.

133 The book was written in a Portuguese perspective with facts mixed with biased interpretations, which aimed at praising achievements of Alexis de Menezes.

134 S.H. Moffett, *A History of Christianity in Asia, Vol. I, op. cit.,* 269.

135 *Ibid.*

inquiring about their precise doctrinal or church position. A number of Roman Catholics[136] also visited India during this period and the *Malankara* Church accepted them without any hesitation.

Therefore, it is logical to believe that while acknowledging the episcopal oversight of the Persian bishops over the church, the *Malankara* Church kept its autonomy under the leadership of the office of the Archdeacon.

An archdeacon and prince

Both in the Eastern Orthodox and the Eastern Catholic Churches, an Archdeacon was a senior deacon of the diocese, and he has the responsibility of assisting the bishop and directing the clergy. But in the Western church – Roman Catholic and Anglican Churches – it is the senior clergy office, just below the bishop.[137]

However, in the *Malankara* Church, the Archdeacon was the *jathikkukarthvyam*[138] (governor of a community – a title) and the "prince of all Christians" in Malabar. He was the representative of the Persian bishop, the leader of the clergy in the *Malankara* Church and had the privilege of representing the Christian community to the local monarchy. His office was hereditary in nature.[139] Being the head of the *Malankara* Church, he exercised all temporal and church administrative

---

136 Roman Catholic priests also visited India during the medieval period. John De Monte Corbino (1247–1328), the first Roman Catholic missionary bishop in China, who visited India on his way to China and stayed in India for thirteen months. He held that India is a place "wherein stands the Church of St. Thomas". Jordanius, another Roman Catholic bishop was sent by Pope with a "Papal Bull" to Christians in Quilon in 1330. John De Marignoli of Florence also spent more than a year in Quilon, India. He refers the existence of a Latin communion at Quilon in 1338. See, G.T. Mackenzie, *Christianity in Travancore*, (Travancore Government Press, 1901), 10ff.

137 The office of the Archdeacon is not in practice in both the Roman Catholic and the *Malankara* Church. But this office played an important function during the 10, the 11 and the 12th centuries in the Roman Catholic Church. This office was stopped in the *Malankara* Church since 1653. This office is currently present in the Anglican Church.

138 *Jathikkukarthavyam* means the head of the "caste". This was a *malyalam* title denotes the one, who is the lord of, or who is responsible for the community. See, A.M. Mundadan, *Traditions of the St. Thomas Christians, op.cit.*, 145–146.

139 In all other church traditions, other than the *Malankara* Church, the office of the Archdeacon was an elected one, not a hereditary one.

powers, including selection of seminarians, appointment of priests and held temporal power over the church properties.

The earliest evidence on the office of the Archdeacon of India is "a letter of Patriarch Timothy (780–826) to the Archdeacon of India".[140] In this letter the Patriarch wrote to the Archdeacon "about the right norms to be followed in the ordination of the priests, bishops, metropolitans and patriarch".[141] While the Persian Metropolitan had the right to send his own prelates to the *Malankara* Church, the continuance in governance was secured by the indigenous Archdeacon. Says A.M. Mundadan:

> "The foreign metropolitans, for the most part, exercised the powers of order only, which included a blessing of the foundation stones of churches; consecration of churches and altars, ordination of clerics ... the government of the church was left to the Archdeacon".[142]

No foreign bishop was in a position to impose their theological position without the proper consent and support of the Archdeacon, who represented the community in the local kingdom. This obviously provided a standard of autonomous existence of the *Malankara* Church in India that ran contrary to the Synod of Diamper's claim of a Nestorian nexus.

The analysis presented thus far indicates the application of the *Malankara* Church's guiding principle of ecumenism – when it engages with the Persian Church. The same principle was followed, when the Roman Catholic Church and the Antiochian Church came into contact with the *Malankara* Church during the 15th and 17th Century CE.

Foiling imperialist designs

The period of the discovery of Vasco Da Gama's trade route from Europe to India in 1498 up to the *Malankara* Church's "Coonen Cross Oath" in 1653 could be taken as a phase for the Roman Catholic imperialistic project to annex the *Malankara* Church. It eventually led to the fragmentation of the church into two – one

---

140 E.R. Hambye, "Some Eastern Evidence Concerning Early and Medieval Christianity in India", In: *Indian Ecclesiastical Studies,* 9, (Sept/1970), 185–193.

141 A.M. Mundadan, *Traditions of the St. Thomas Christians, op.cit.,* 145–146.

142 A.M. Mundadan, *Indian Christians Search for Identity and Struggle for Autonomy, op.cit.,* 16.

faction loyal to the Roman Catholic Church and other to the *Malankara* Church.[143] The Portuguese sought to use the *padroado*[144], a Papal Bull delegating the Pope's administrative powers on local churches to the Kings of Portugal and Spain, to further its imperialistic mission in India.

Hand in hand with the Roman Catholic Church, they hoped that a change of church loyalty of the *Malankara* Church could be achieved through systematic involvements and by condemning the Indian church's ecumenical practices and relations with the Persian Church. They branded the *Malankara* Church's openness outlook as unchristian and proposed a plan to "correct it" by implementing the Roman Catholic doctrines in the church. For the Roman Catholics, the *Malankara* Church appeared as an abode of Nestorian heretics, superstitions, and heathen customs and practices, as we have mentioned already. The attitude of the Portuguese, as Mundadan says, was "always motivated by a sense of superiority about their form of Christianity"[145] and to which the Mar Thoma Christians "had to conform in order to be perfect Christians".[146]

The *Malankara* Church did show its openness to the Portuguese as they did to all churches and other religious communities in India. It believed that "both

---

143 The discovery of Vasco Da Gama's trade route from Europe to India in 1498 was of great significance in the history of India. It was followed by another expedition of the Portuguese king under the leadership of Alvarez Cabral, with 33 ships and 1500 men to India in 1500. They were not well received by the local king and the Arab merchants at Calicut. Being humiliated by the Arab traders and the King of Calicut, Alvarez Cabral moved to Cochin, where he was received by the local king. This eventually led to a confrontation and wars between the king of Cochin and the King of Calicut. Portuguese supported the king of Cochin. Several wars fought between the kingdoms of Cochin and Calicut during 1503 and 1504. Under the leadership of Alfonso De Albuquerque (1509–1515), the Portuguese won the battle against the Zamorin of Calicut in 1513 and established firmly the Portuguese power in India. Since then the Portuguese made a systematic attempt to Romanize the Mar Thoma Church. See, A.M. Mundadan, *Indian Christians Search for Identity and Struggle for Autonomy, op.cit.*, 35.

144 There was an existing treaty of Pope with the Kings of Portugal and Spain, known as *Padrodo* by which the Pope delegated his power administration of the local churches to the Kings of Portugal and Spain. The Papal Bull dated, 8th January 1854 of Pope Nicholas V by which the Portuguese king Alfonso V got this special privilege. The Portuguese power in India have done what all possible for them to increase the numerical strength of the Roman Catholics in the country. Also. See, *Ibid.*, 193.

145 *Ibid.*, 33.

146 *Ibid.*

were Christians and both belonged to the universal church".[147] Based on this, the *Malankara* Church extended full co-operation and support to the Roman Catholic Church. This helped the Portuguese to establish a firm foothold in Kerala, despite the opposition from the local ruler of Calicut.[148] The Portuguese governor, Alfonso De Albuquerque (1453–1515), made Goa in India, the Capital of the Portuguese settlement in Asia.[149]

Side by side with this, with the establishment of the Portuguese empire in the East, the Portuguese programme was to bring Roman Catholicism to the East and to bring the *Malankara* Church under the Pope. As the Roman Catholic agenda of bringing the *Malankara* Church under the jurisdiction of the Pope was highly visible, the Archdeacon of the *Malankara* Church and other leaders devoted a considerable amount of time to critically evaluate the Portuguese actions. This created an apprehension in the *Malankara* Church about the Portuguese's vigorous Latinization agenda in India.[150] This feeling of apprehension was aggravated when

---

147 *Ibid.*
148 The Zamorin was the ruler of Calicut, which was a port in Kerala. He adopted a hostile attitude to the Portuguese at the instigation of Muslims, who were afraid that their trade monopoly was being threatened by the new comers. In such a context, the Mar Thoma Christians' offer of alliance to the Portuguese was politically significant as they were powerful and fairly prosperous community in Kerala. Moreover, there were trained soldiers among the Mar Thoma Christians in large numbers. M. Geddes writes: "They also had the monopoly in pepper trade. The Mar Thoma Christians had supplied with an army of 50,000 Gunmen to the King of Cochin. The significance of this is so obvious, that the King of Cochin granted the permission to the Portuguese to build their forts in Cochin and Cannanore. It helped the Portuguese to establish their political power in Kerala." See, Michael Geddes, *A Short History of the Church of Malabar Together with the Synod of Diamper, op.cit.*, 48; C.P. Mathews and M.M. Thomas, *The Indian Churches of St. Thomas, op.cit.*, 29.
149 Alfonso De Albuquerque was the second Portuguese Governor in India. He captured Goa in India in 1509.
150 The Portuguese believed that the Roman Catholic Church was the only Church in the world and therefore their vision of the Church was a Church, which should acknowledges the supremacy of the Roman Pontiff, the Pope and the doctrines of the Church. Therefore, they considered it was their duty to teach the *Malankara* Church Roman Catholicism and to put the *Malankara* Church under the jurisdiction of the Pope. This led to the confrontation between the *Malankara* Church and Roman Catholic Church. C.B. Firth noted the following differences between the *Malankara* Church and the Roman Catholic Church in teachings and traditions: 1. The Roman Catholic Church stood for the authority of the Pope over the church while, the *Malankara* Church considered the Patriarch of the East as its head. 2. On questions of sacraments,

a Diocese of the Roman Catholic Church was founded in Cochin by converting sizeable numbers of *Malankara* Church members and of other religions to the Roman Catholic Church.[151]

The Roman Catholic strategy was first, to control missionary endeavours of the *Malankara* Church and second, to ban the Persian Bishop's visit to India. The missionary efforts of the Roman Catholic Church started with the sending of Francis Xavier (1506–1552), a missionary, to India in 1542 CE by the Pope.[152] Having sensed the future of the Roman Catholic Church in India, Francis Xavier requested John III, the king of Portugal, to start an inquisition court in Goa[153] and the opening of Roman Catholic Seminaries to teach candidates for priesthood.

This move opened the doors to both the Franciscans and Jesuits to start educational institutions in India. They hoped that by "infiltrating into the (Mar Thoma) community, they would get a few among them as candidates for ministry and thereby a way would be opened to influence the Mar Thoma Community to accept the Roman Catholic faith".[154]

Moreover, the Roman Catholic Church did everything possible to suspend the visits of Persian bishops to India and to pressurize the *Malankara* Church to seek alternative arrangements for its much-needed episcopal oversight, as it had no

---

the *Malankara* Church practices confirmation along with baptism against the Roman Catholic practice of confirmation. 3. The *Malankara* Church serves the consecrated bread and wine separately to the communicants in the sacrament of the Holy Communion. 4. The *Malankara* Church's priests are allowed to marry. 5. *Malankara* Church does not follow the doctrine of purgatory. 6. *Malankara* Church does not practice the veneration of saints. C.B. Firth, *An Introduction to Indian Church History, op.cit.*, 69–88.

151 A. Sreedhara Menon, *A Survey of Kerala History, op.cit.*, 164.

152 Francis Xavier was a Jesuit Spaniard, who graduated at the University of Paris. He arrived at Goa in 6th May 1542 and started missionary work among Indians. His Jesuit house in Goa became a popular missionary order in India. It is reported that there were 349 Jesuits in India in 1584. See, Wicki. J., ed., *Documenta Indica XIII*, 766, cited In: Joseph Thekkedath, *History of Christianity in India, Vol. II, op.cit.*, 6; C.B. Firth, *An Introduction to Indian Church History, op.cit.*, 55–68.

153 Francis Xavier wrote a letter dated 10th of November 1545 to John III of Portugal requesting to establish an inquisition court in India. The inquisition court was started at the capital of the Portuguese settlement in India, Goa in 1500. See, K.K. Kuruvilla, *Mar Thoma Church and its Doctrines, op. cit.*, 4.

154 *Ibid.*, 4; A. Sreedhara Menon, *A Survey of Kerala History, op.cit.* 164.
It was during this period, the Roman Catholic missionaries – Jesuits, Franciscans, Dominicans and Augustinians – established their houses in India.

indigenous bishops.[155] The Portuguese thought that such a situation would force the *Malankara* Church to approach the Roman Catholic Church for a bishop. The efforts of the Portuguese and the missionaries presented to the Pope a situation ripe for making bold steps to bring the *Malankara* Church under his control.

The Pope sent the Archbishop, Alexis De Menezis (1559–1617), to India "to take possession of the Bishopric"[156] and he established his headquarters in Goa in 1592. The rest, as they say, is history, which we have already explained in detail regarding the Synod of Diamper that brought the *Malankara* Church under the direct control of the Pope. This led to widespread unrest within the Mar Thoma Christians, which culminated in the Coonen Cross Oath.

The relationship with the Jacobite Antiochian Patriarch is yet another instance when the *Malankara* Church's ecumenical outlook showed up. The church did not hesitate to approach the Patriarch for the dedication of the first Mar Thoma metropolitan. The Patriarch assigned Mar Gregorios of Jerusalem, who with the help of the Dutch political power, consecrated Mar Thoma I (1653–1660) in 1663, marking the start of a long-standing ecumenical relationship.

---

155 For instance, the Syrian Roman Catholic Patriarch Abdiso sent two bishops – Mar Joseph and Mar Ellia – to India. When they arrived in India, they were not greeted well by the Portuguese as they were Syrians. It was Mar Joseph, who introduced auricular confession, confirmation and extreme unction in the *Malankara* Church for the first time. Mar Joseph later accepted the Nestorian faith and on this pretext, the Jesuits and the Portuguese sent him back to Lisbon. See, C.P. Mathew and M.M. Thomas, *The Indian Churches of St. Thomas, op. cit.*, 30.

156 Alexis De Menezis was appointed as the Archbishop of India by Pope in 1594. In a Brief Pope, Clement VIII, commanded him "to take the possession of this Church and Bishopric; so as not to suffer any bishop or prelate coming from Babylon to enter therein as has hitherto been the custom". See, James Hough, *The History of Christianity in India, Vol. II*, (London: R.B. Seeley and W. Burnside, 1839), 2.

Chapter IV
A Reformed Church of the Orient

The hierarchical and legalistic structures of the Papacy and the Roman Catholic Church gave rise to widespread resentment, which led to the European reformation in the 16th Century. The *Malankara* Church had its own series of reforms in the 19th Century CE, which though was not in reaction to any episcopal or ecclesiastical structural tensions.[157]

On the contrary, the reforms were a result of confrontations within the church against traditionalism, as represented by remnants of Roman Catholic and Antiochian influences, in efforts at two different levels to modernise the *Malankara* Church's outlook. The first resulted from a struggle by those who stood fiercely for the *Malankara* Church's ecumenical outlook and second, by those who sought to imbibe fresh ideas from the Church of England and the Church Missionary Society (CMS).

The reforms were spearheaded by Palakunnathu Abraham Malpan (1796–1845)[158] and Kaithayil Geevarghese Malpan (1800–1855)[159] and were aimed, among other things, at regaining the autonomous position enjoyed by the *Malankara* Church prior to the Synod of Diamper (1599) and to position it as a contemporary church. The reformists sought to instil an evangelical fervour

---

157 The *Malankara* Church's autonomy and independence were eroding since the Synod of Diamper in 1599 and it reached at its peak at the Synod of Mulanthuruthy in 1875. This synod authorised the Patriarch of Antioch to exercise the spiritual and temporal authority over the *Malankara* Church. This led a schism within the church inevitable. Those who upheld the autonomy and independence of the *Malankara* Church (Reform group) felt that it was a departure from the church's tradition.

158 Abraham Malpan (1796–1845) was an ordained priest and a Syriac professor at the *Malankara* Church's Theological seminary, Kottayam, who led the reform movement in the church. Reforms started in the church by the sanction of the then Metropolitan and by the approval of the general body, met on December 3, 1818. See, K.N. Daniel, *Maankara Sabhayum Naveekaranavum* (Malayalam), Vol. I, (Tiruvalla: K.N. Daniel, 1949), 68.; Zac Varghese and Mathew A. Kallumpram, *Glimpses of Mar Thoma Church History op.cit.*, 24; P.M. Thomas, ed., *Mar Thoma Sabha Directory*, Revised Edition, *op.cit.*, 94–95.

159 Kaithayil Geevarghese Malpan (1800–1855) was another reform leader in the *Malankara* Church. See, *Ibid.*, 104–105.

in the *Malankara* Church and this effort was managed in cooperation with the Church of England's Church Missionary Society (CMS),[160] by way of a "mission of help" agreement formalised between then Metropolitan Dionysius I and the CMS missionaries in 1816. According to Philipose Mar Chrysostom, "Luther's Reformation emerged from a theological thinking, whereas ours was a protest in the context of certain practical situations in the church."[161]

The reforms in the *Malankara* Church were thus not a result of a systematic theological analysis as what happened in the western reformation. So how did the reform process come into the life of the *Malankara* Church? Was it the result of a deliberate attempt of the Anglican Church to establish a relation with an oriental Church? Or did Abraham Malpan and Geevarghese Malpan become easy preys to a strategic move of the Anglican missionaries and British resident Col. Munroe to place the *Malankara* Church under Anglican suzerainty? Or, were the reforms an effort to contemporize the *Malankara* Church with spontaneity and tradition, in order to revitalize it, as the reformers' claim?

Seeds of reforms

The seeds of reforms were planted when then Metropolitan Mar Dionysius I (1760–1808) welcomed the liturgical translation into Malayalam. However, it reached a new turn when Mar Dionysius IV (1825–1852) forbid the *Malankara* Church from receiving fresh ideas from and even having conversations with

---

160 The eevangelical zeal and enthusiasm to fight against moral corruption influenced a group of the Church of England's members in 1875. They were popularly known as British Evangelicals. Charles Grant (1746–1823), William Wilberforce (1753–1833) and others were chief promoters of this movement. They prepared the Anglican Church for mission. Their passion for mission led to the formation of the CMS in 1799 and to get legal sanction from the British parliament for its mission in India. The CMS mission started its mission in India in 1814. The *Malankara* Church's reform leaders decided to include the missionary work in the church with a view to contemporize it by incorporating the missionary zeal of the Protestant missions. With this aim of evangelization in India, the reform leaders started an indigenous missionary organization in India, – "Mar Thoma Evangelistic Association" – in 1888. This will be dealt with detail in the next chapter of this study. See, Andrew Walls, *The Missionary Movements in Christian History* (New York: Orbis Books, 1996), 240–258.

161 Jesudas M. Athyal, John J. Thattamannil, ed., *Metropolitan Chrysostom on Mission in the Market Place*, (Tiruvalla: Christava Sahitya Samithy, 2002), 37.

the Church of England's CMS missionaries. Those who stood for the continuation of the church's centuries-old ecumenist ideals of autonomy and openness were motivated enough to react against the Metropolitan's policy. The reforms within the *Malankara* Church during the 19th century can thus be understood as being partly a result of its wish to keep intact its age-old church traditions and partly a result of its ability to receive fresh ideas from the Church of England to contemporize it. The historical events that followed would corroborate these facts.

The important document for reconstructing the history of this period is Claudius Buchanan's book, *Christians Researches in Asia,* and a few other sources.[162] Buchanan's interpretation obviously has a certain Anglican bias, but its value as a historical document can't be overstated.

Buchanan's book lists three major reasons for the *Malankara* Church's reforms. First, the CMS missionaries inspired a new desire in Mar Thoma Christians to infuse missionary fervour in the life and witness of the church. This prompted the *Malankara* Church to institutionalise certain changes with a view to foster a mission-oriented programme of action.

Secondly, the need to revise and translate the Syriac liturgy became inevitable as the use of Syriac, a language totally unknown to the laity, was in use in the church. The laity welcomed the liturgical translation into Malayalam[163] and it was also accepted by then Metropolitan Mar Dionysius I (1760–1808). But one of his

---

162 Claudius Buchanan, *Christian Researches in Asia; with Notes of the Translation of the Scripture,* (London: Ward& Co. Paterson Row, 1849). Besides, this book, *Proceedings of the Church Missionary society for 1818–1819* (London: CMS College, 1819), A Sreedara Menon, *A Survey of Kerala History, op.cit.,* P.M. Thomas, ed., *Mar Thoma Sabha Directory, Revised Edition, op.cit.* "Abstract of a Brief History of the Syrians in Malabar Preserved among themselves as their Genuine History" In: *Appendix XVII,* in *Proceedings of the Church Missionary society for 1818–1819,* 317–319, "Extracts of Communication from the Rev. Benjamin Bailey and the Rev. Thomas Norton, respecting the Syrian Christians, In: *Ibid.,* 320–322; T.C. Chacko, *The Concise History of the Mar Thoma Church* (Malayalam), V Edition, (Tiruvalla: Episcopal Jubilee Institute, 2001), P. Cherian, *The Malabar Syrians and the Church Missionary Society, op.cit.*
Claudius Buchanan (1766–1815) was a minister of the Church of England and a missionary of the Church Missionary Society in India.
T.C. Chacko was a church historian, who wrote the history of the Malankara Mar Thoma Syrian Church.

163 *Letter of Benjamin Bailey to the Secretary of CMS* dt Nov 10, 1818, cited In: "Extracts of Communication from the Rev. Benjamin Bailey and the Rev. Thomas Norton,

successors, Metropolitan Mar Dionysius IV (1825–1852)[164], opposed the reforms and the liturgical revision, and suspended the translation work of the liturgy.[165]

The reform leaders appointed by Metropolitan Dionysius I and the CMS missionaries were not about to be restrained. They continued with the liturgical revision work in the light of the Scripture and the evangelical emphasis of the CMS.[166]

Third, the need to protect the autonomy and independence of the *Malankara* Church from the Antiochian Patriarchate also became inevitable, when the church was unofficially inclined to accept the temporal and spiritual authority of the Antiochian patriarch in 1836. This culminated in the Synod of Mulanthuruty (1875–76) where the *Malankara* Church became completely under the Antiochian Patriarchate. This will be dealt with at length in the following analysis of this study.

Reforms and the CMS

The reforms in the *Malankara* Church started in the context of its dependence on the Syriac language for liturgy and doctrines and resulted in efforts to translate the liturgy into Malayalam. The Metropolitan and the *Malankara* Church felt that the

Respecting the Syrian Christians", In: *Proceedings of the Church Missionary society for 1818–1819, op.cit.*, 321.

164 Cheppatt Philipose Mar Dionysius (1781–1855) or Dionysius IV was the Metropolitan of the *Malankara* Church from 1825–1852.

165 Mar Dionysius III had given approval of revising the liturgy to Abraham Malpan with a view to restore the church's spirituality, prior to the 16th century. See, Zac Varghese and Mathew A. Kallumpram, *Glimpses of Mar Thoma Church History* (New Delhi: Kalpana Printers, 2003), 24; K.N. Daniel, *Malankara Sabhayum Naveekaranavum,* (Malayalam), *op.cit.*, 68–69.

166 It was during this period the customs and practices of the *Malankara* Church were a mixture of the Roman Catholic, the Antiochine, the Persian, and the indigenous. They found that some practices of the *Malankara* Church were inconsistent with the Christian faith, and for instance; the ethical conduct of the clergy, the practice of considering the celebration of sacraments as a source of income, and so on. Moreover, the celebration of the liturgy which was written in Syriac found to be unknown language to the laity. It made a context for the translation of the liturgy and reforms in the light of the Scripture, inevitable. So the then Metropolitan appointed a committee to translate the liturgy into the vernacular. However, the moves in between eventually led to the suspension of the revision of the liturgy committee. But both reform leaders continued the translation of the liturgy. They celebrated the Holy Qurbana with the revised translated liturgy in their respective parishes in Maramon and Kollad, in 1836, without the permission of the then Metropolitan.

assistance from the CMS missionaries is fundamental for the fulfilment of those efforts. It is clear that Metropolitan Dionysius I understood the dire need for church members to understand and appreciate the liturgy in the language they speak and he felt the assistance of CMS missionaries was imperative in this regard. Claudius Buchanan also points to the church's requirement for theological education and teachings, after the Synod of Diamper and subsequent events had led to a certain corruption of the *Malankara* Church's convictions that had stood the test of time for centuries.

Three major points that have a bearing the *Malankara* Church's reform context can be drawn from a conversation that Claudius Buchanan had with then Metropolitan Dionysius I in 1806. First, the lack of proper teaching within the church was evident. Says Buchanan:

> The doctrines of the Syrian Christians are few in number, but pure, and agree in essential points with those of the Church of England; so that although the body of the Church appears to be ignorant, and formal, and dead, there are individuals who are alive to righteousness, who are distinguished from the rest by their purity of life, and are sometimes censured for too rigid a piety. In every church, and in many of the private houses, there are manuscripts in the Syriac language; and I have been successful in procuring some old and valuable copies of the scriptures and other books, written in different ages and in different characters.[167]

Secondly, leaders of both the *Malankara* Church and the Church of England had the vision for maintaining a future positive relationship. For instances, after his visit of the Kandanad Church,[168] Buchanan had come to realise the strategic significance of the Church of England's relationship with the *Malankara* Church to counter the undue influence of the Roman Catholic Church in India. This was evident in this Buchanan statement: "Since my coming amongst this people, I had cherished the hope that they might one day unite with the Church of England."[169]

Buchanan presented his desire to have a close relationship before the Metropolitan, making it clear that by such a relationship, the clergy of both the churches might be permitted to preach in their churches in India.[170] The then Metropolitan of the *Malankara* Church, in response to Buchanan's opinion, remarked:

---

167 Claudius Buchanan, *Christian Researches in Asia; with Notes of the Translation of the Scripture, op.cit.*, 62.
168 Kandanad Church was the cathedral Church where the *Malankara* Church's Metropolitan resided.
169 Claudius Buchanan, *Christian Researches in Asia; with Notes of the Translation of the Scripture, op.cit.*, 64.
170 *Ibid.*, 65.

"I would sacrifice much for such a union: only let me not be called to compromise anything of the dignity and the purity of the Church."[171]

Thirdly, the Metropolitan was aware of the need to keep the autonomy of the *Malankara* Church by introducing reforms in the church. This was reflected in his words to Buchanan:

"The Bishop confessed that some customs had been introduced in the latter centuries, which had no connection with the constitution of the church and might be removed without inconvenience."[172]

The visit of Buchanan to the then Metropolitan succeeded in getting the CMS missionaries the permission to start a mission among the Mar Thoma Christians.

Historically, the Metropolitan's decision to approve the *Malankara* Church's relationship with the Church of England in response to Claudius Buchanan's visit, without having any consultation with the Jacobite Patriarch of Antioch, points to the fact that the church was not under the foreign church. It also reflects the autonomy and ecumenical outlook of the Malankara Church.

British resident Col. Munroe (1810–1819),[173] a staunch evangelical,[174] also did everything possible to assist the *Malankara* Church. He invited the CMS missionaries to start mission work among the Mar Thoma Christians in 1814, in line with Buchanan's understanding with Dionysius I.[175] Col. Munroe hoped that "a respectable body of native clergy could be procured for the propagation of Christianity among"[176] the people of other religions.

---

171 *Ibid.*

172 *Ibid.*, 65–66.

173 Col. Munroe was the then British resident in Travancore and Cochin from 1810–1819.

174 Evangelical means belonging to, agreeable or consonant to, the gospel, or the truth taught in the New Testament.

175 Col. Munroe had a plan to found a college for the education of the *Malankara* Church clergy and laity in Kerala. He induced the ruler of Travancore for a free gift of land and money for the construction of the college. The king of Travancore granted INR 20000 and a land at Kallada in Quilon district for the specific purpose of promoting education among Christians. See, A Sreedara Menon, *A Survey of Kerala History, op.cit.,* 279; P.M. Thomas, ed., *Mar Thoma Sabha Directory,* Revised Edition, *op.cit.,* 41–44.

176 *Proceedings of the Church Missionary society for 1818–1819,* (London: CMS College, 1819), 169. See, P. Cherian, *The Malabar Syrians and the Church Missionary Society, op.cit.,* 26.
P. Cherian was a judge of the High Court of Travancore and a historian in Kerala.

The CMS missionaries extended full support to contemporize the *Malankara* Church by imparting missionary consciousness. They also felt the need for reforms within the Mar Thoma Church to equip it for missionary work in India. The pioneering missionaries, Thomas Norton, Benjamin Bailey, Joseph Fenn and Henry Baker arrived in Kerala in 1816 and prepared the ground for reforms and they were well received by the Metropolitan[177] and the church.[178]

The effect of the CMS missionaries work in India was twofold. First, Metropolitan Mar Dionysius IV (1825–1852) feared that it would tilt the church towards the western reforms. This was indeed a reflection of an underlying apprehension among Mar Thoma Christians that Metropolitan Dionysius I had entered into an understanding with Buchanan that was essentially against the autonomy of the church.[179]

Meanwhile, Mar Dionysius III made "a strategic move", as A.M. Mundadan puts it, by the requesting the Patriarch of Antioch to send a bishop to Kerala to counter the growing power of the Anglicans among Mar Thoma Christians.[180] However, "this strategy misfired"[181] when Mar Athanasius, the prelate from Antioch, apparently put forward his claim as the Metropolitan of the Mar Thoma Church.[182]

---

177 Metropolitans Mar Dionysius II (1816–1817) and Mar Dionysius III (1817–1825) had kept close relation with the CMS missionaries. However, their successor Dionysius IV (1825–1852), did not follow the same policy of friendship with the new CMS missionaries especially when Joseph Peet, who came to Kerala after Benjamin Bailey, Joseph Fenn, and Henry Baker. See, T.C. Chacko, *The Concise History of the Mar Thoma Church* (Malayalam), V Edition, (Tiruvalla: Episcopal Jubilee Institute, 2001), 73–74.

178 Thomas Norton was the first CMS missionary to India, who came to Kerala in 1816. Benjamin Bailey was a CMS missionary to work among the Mar Thoma Christians came to Kerala in 1816. He was a Seminary Professor. He founded a printing press at Kottayam. He made two dictionaries for the *Malayalam* language. He translated the Bible into *Malayalam* and the Book of Common Payer into *Malayalam*.
Joseph Fenn was a CMS Missionary who came to Kerala in 1818. He was also a Professor at the *Malankara* Church Seminary at Kottayam. Henry Backer was a CMS missionary and an educationalist came to Kerala in 1819.

179 *Proceedings of the Church Missionary society for 1818–1819, op.cit.*, 169; P. Cherian, *The Malabar Syrians and the Church Missionary Society, op.cit.*, 26.

180 A.M. Mundadan, Indian *Christians Search for Identity and Struggle for Autonomy, op.cit.*, 118.

181 *Ibid.*

182 Mar Athanasius declared the consecration of Mar Dionysius IV (1825–1852) as invalid on November in 1825. This eventually forced Mar Dionysius IV to approach the civil authorities for the expulsion of Mar Athanasius from Kerala. On the basis of

Reforms fuel confrontation

The CMS missionaries followed an attitude of missionary paternalism by implementing liturgical and custom changes without the prior consent of the then Metropolitan.[183] The paternalistic attitude of the CMS missionaries and Col. Munroe (1810–1819) turned the context of reform into one of confrontation. The missionaries found that many practices were not in line with the evangelical fervour that they sought to impart and decided to banish them, tracing those practices to the Roman Catholic Church. However, they failed to see the fact that such practices are cherished by the Jacobite Church of Antioch also.[184]

They also hoped that the church could easily be transformed by means of a sound education, circulation of the Bible, use of the translated copy of the Book of Common Prayer[185] and the spread of the evangelical doctrine.[186] With this intention, they translated the "Book of Common Prayer" into Malayalam and used it for Sunday public worship services at the Old Seminary Chapel.[187] Inevitably, this strained the relationship of the Metropolitan Dionysius IV with the CMS

Mar Dionysius IV's plea the Travancore civil government expelled the foreign bishop, Mar Athanasius from Kerala. See, Justice Ormsby's Statement in the "Judgment of the Royal Court of Malabar, Seminary Case", Kottayam: *Archives,* Mar Thoma Theological Seminary Archive, 1889. Also cited in C.P. Mathew and M.M. Thomas, *Indian Churches of St. Thomas, op.cit.,* 59; A.M. Mundadan, Indian *Christians Search for Identity and Struggle for Autonomy, op.cit.,* 118.

183　The *Malankara* Church witnessed the demise of four Metropolitans during the first two decades of the twentieth century. Mar Dionysius I, passed away in 1808. He was succeeded by Mar Thoma VII (1808). But he died on July, 4, 1809 and he was succeeded by Mar Thoma VIII (1809–1816), and Mar Thoma IX (1816–1817) and when he died in 1817, Mar Dionysius III, (1817–1825), became the Metropolitan. He was friendly with the missionaries and the work of Abraham Malpan, whom he authorize to take leadership in the revision of liturgy and other literary work. See, K.N. Daniel, *Malankara Sabhayum Naveekaranavum,* (Malayalam), *op.cit.,* 68–69.

184　The practices and customs of the *Malankara* Church that condemned by the CMS Missionaries were: the celibacy of clergy, adoration of images, auricular confession, veneration of saints, prayer for the dead, and prayer for St. Mary.

185　In a letter to Benjamin Bailey, Col. Munroe wrote: "the translation of the English liturgy is another object of primary importance; for I think if it were well translated, it might without any difficulty be substituted in all churches for their present form of worship". Cited In: P. Cherian, *The Malabar Syrians and the Church Missionary Society, op.cit.,* 192.

186　*Ibid.,* 84–85.

187　*Ibid.,* 194.

missionaries. The missionaries' acts overstepped the boundaries of religious neutrality and their agreement with Metropolitan Dionysius I. They did not care to study the importance given by the church to tradition, religious ethos, signs, symbols, rituals, practices and liturgical elements when the new liturgy and practices were introduced without the consent of the Metropolitan.[188] The missionaries failed to see the place of traditions in the *Malankara* Church before bringing every customs and practices into the mould of the rule of the Scripture.

On the other hand, Mar Dionysius IV (1825–1852), unlike his predecessors, was unfriendly to the missionaries. He was against missionary paternalism and decided to confront the missionaries and even Abraham Malpan, for his efforts to revise the liturgy.[189] He was not in favour of reforms within the *Malankara* Church.[190]

Conversely, the new missionaries were hasty in implementing reforms without seeking the support of the Metropolitan.[191] As a reaction to the Metropolitan, the Anglican Bishop Daniel Wilson of Calcutta (1832–1858) approached Mar Dionysius IV in 1835 and suggested six points for the Metropolitan's consideration, in order to make peace between CMS missionaries and the Metropolitan.[192]

---

188 The missionaries' anti-Catholic and strong protestant fervour blinded them to see the rich heritage in the *Malankara* Church's liturgy, ideas and customs. C.B. Firth, *An Introduction to Indian Church History, op. cit.*, 176–170.

189 Zac Varghese and Mathew A. Kallumpram, *Glimpses of Mar Thoma Church History* (New Delhi: Kalpana Printers, 2003), 24; K.N. Daniel, *Malankara Sabhayum Naveekaranavum,* (Malayalam), *op.cit.*, 68–69.

190 *Ibid.*, 25.

191 Joseph Peet, and W.J. Woodcock – two second batch CMS missionaries – boldly criticized the Mar Thoma Church's rituals and practices without realizing the authority of the Metropolitan in the church. See, Juhanon Mar Thoma, *Christianity In India and a Brief History of the Mar Thoma Church, op.cit.*, 20.

192 Six Points are: 1. as a general rule, the Metropolitan should ordain only those candidates, who passed through the Seminary at Kottayam and obtained certificate of proficiency and good conduct. 2. Accounts showing the produce of the land and other property belonging to the church, should be submitted annually to the British Resident, so that there might be no misappropriation or loss. 3. A permanent endowment should, if possible, be instituted for the uncertain dues realized on the occasion of various ceremonies such as marriages and baptisms and funerals for the needs of the clergy. 4. Schools should be established in connection with every parish church. 5. The clergy should expound the Gospel each Sunday during divine service. 6. Prayers should be in Malayalam, not in Syriac. See, C.P. Mathew and M.M. Thomas, *The Indian Churches of Saint Thomas, op.cit.*, 66–68.

In response, the Metropolitan convened a Synod at Mavelikara in 1836, on the pretext of considering the proposals of the Anglican Bishops, but with the real intention to suspend the CMS "mission of help" and stop the reforms in the church. The Synod unanimously rejected the proposals of Bishop Daniel Wilson (1832–1858)[193] and decided as follows:

"… We, the Jacobite Syrians, being subject to the supremacy of the Patriarch of Antioch, and observing as we do the liturgies and ordinances instituted by the prelates sent under his command, cannot deviate from such liturgies and ordinances and maintain discipline contrary thereto …"[194]

By this declaration, the church officially accepted Orthodox West Syrian Liturgy and discipline.[195] Besides, it decided that, "the Syrian traditions and liturgy are not to be changed or modified".[196]

The Metropolitan was under no obligation at that point to continue the relationship with Anglican Bishop or CMS missionaries. Nevertheless, the Mavelikara Synod, decided to surrender its autonomy before the Antiochian church.

This led to the third schism in the history of the *Malankara* Church. One group decided to continue the reforms within the church and to keep its autonomy and

---

193 It is true that the Metropolitan had any moral or legal obligation to give assurance to the Anglican bishop about the norms of ordination or any other matters of the Church, including the accounts as he was not under any obligation to the British resident or CMS missionaries. These attitudes of the missionaries were considered by the people as their deliberate plan to poke in to the affairs of the *Malankara* Church and an occasion to show their superiority complex. See, "Mavelikara Padiyola", In: Appendix C, In: P.M. Thomas., ed., *Mar Thoma Sabha Directory, Revised Edition, op.cit.*, 89–91.

194 *"Mavelikara Padiyola"* (Decisions of the Synod of Mavelikara, held on 18th January 1836), appendix C, P.M. Thomas, ed., *Mar Thoma Sabha Directory, op.cit.*, 89–91. Also See, *Official Transactions of the Decisions of the Mavelikara Synod in 1836*, cited In: P. Cherian, *The Malabar Syrians and the Church Missionary Society, op.cit.*, 390–391; Also See, *Resolution of the Synod of Mavelikara of 1836, held at the St. Mary's church*, In *www.syrianchurch.org/st.gg/mavelikara_padiyola.htm*, visited on 2nd January 2011;
K.J. Gabriel, *Gurumukhathuninnum Part 1* (Malayalam), (Kottayam: M G F, 1998), 91. K.J. Gabriel is a scholar and currently a Metropolitan (Gabriel Mar Gregorios) in the Malankara Orthodox Syrian Church.

195 *Ibid.*

196 *Resolution of the Synod of Mavelikara of 1836, held at the St. Mary's church.* In *www.syrianchurch.org/st.gg/mavelikara_padiyola.htm* visited on 2nd January 2011; "Mavelikara Padiyola" In: Appendix C, P.M. Thomas., ed., *Mar Thoma Sabha Directory, Revised Edition, op.cit.*, 89–91.

independence from Antiochiene Patriarch. The second group decided to establish an alliance with the Jacobite Patriarch of Antioch, while the third group decided to have a communion with the CMS missionaries.[197]

Reforms in faith and practice

Abraham Malpan and Geevarghese Malapan, who spearheaded the reforms, were convinced that the only way forward for the *Malankara* Church in its quest for autonomy and independence was to continue the liturgical translation and reject unscriptural practices in the church. They wanted to make the liturgy and worship meaningful to its participants for glorifying God, and insisted on translating the Syriac liturgy into *Malayalam*. They advocated the removal of prayers to the saints and prayers for the dead as those practices "deteriorated to such an extent that people believed that irrespective of how a person led his life, the priest could, through appropriate rituals, ensure eternal life for him".[198]

They wanted to reform the *Malankara* Church from within without joining the Anglican Church. Efforts against the amalgamation of the *Malankara* Church with any other denominations were visible in the church from 1836, when the claim of the Patriarch of Antioch was known,.[199] The words of L.W. Brown help us to see

---

197 *Ibid.*, L.W. Brown, *Indian Christians of St. Thomas, op.cit.*, 139–140; Being humiliated by decisions of the Synod of Mavelikara, the CMS missionaries continued their mission work among the Mar Thoma Christians separately. Concerning the question of the administration of properties, which jointly operated by the Metropolitan and the CMS missionaries, the then Resident appointed arbitrators, consisting of the representatives from the government, the Metropolitan and the CMS missionaries. They announced their award, dividing the property into two lots – one to the CMS missionaries for the sole benefit of the Mar Thoma community and the other to the Metropolitan in 1840. The CMS mission has started a separate Anglican Church and later it elevated as the Anglican Diocese of Travancore and Cochin in 1878. When the Church of South India was formed in 1948, the Anglican diocese of Travancore and Cochin merged into the CSI. Currently it is the *Madya* Kerala Diocese of the CSI. See, *Ibid.*, 139; Juhanon Mar Thoma, *Christianity In India and a Brief History of the Mar Thoma Church, op.cit.*, 22.

198 Jesudas M. Athyal, John J. Thattamannil, ed., *Metropolitan Chrysostom on Mission in the Market Place, op.cit.*, 37.

199 Since 1836, the reform leaders neither subscribed the decisions of the Synod of Mavelikara nor joined with the Anglican Church. They stood for the church's autonomy. See, P. Cherian, *Malabar Syrians and Church Mission Society 1816–1840,*

the viewpoints of reformers for not joining the Church of England. He says: "It was clear to Abraham Malpan that there was no prospect of widespread acceptance in the church of the reformed ideas that he had accepted from the missionaries and yet he had no desire to separate himself from the Church of his fathers".[200] When the CMS missionaries invited Abraham Malpan to join them, offering a huge salary, he refused the offer and remained in the church, determined to reform it from within.[201] However, the reformers were mistakenly considered by Mar Dionysius IV as Anglican agents.

The basic differences between Mar Dionysius and the reformists were seen in their views of the goal to modernize the church. While Mar Dionysius IV aimed at the adoption of the west Syrian liturgy and canon into the Malankara Church, the goal of the reformers was the removal of unscriptural practices, liturgical translation into Malayalam and church modernisation, based on Western theological insights.

Philipose Mar Chrysostom comments on Abraham Malpan's reforms as a "protest initiated by Western theological insights against the practices in his own church; he did not discard eastern theology to adopt a Protestant theology".[202] With this end, the reformists revised the liturgy for the first time in the *Malankara* Church. This is indeed also the first time the liturgy was revised in any of the Oriental churches in India.

---

op.cit., 390–391; C.P. Mathew, M.M. Thomas, *The Indian Churches of Saint Thomas*, Revised Edition, op.cit., 68–69; John R.K. Fenwick, *The Malabar Independent Syrian Church, op.cit.*, 24.

200 L.W. Brown, *Indian Christians of St. Thomas, op.cit.*, 141.
   Majority of Indian historians share the aforementioned view. See, K.K. Kuruvilla, *Mar Thoma Church and Its Doctrines, op.cit.*, 14; T.C. Chacko, *The Concise History of the Mar Thoma Church* (Malayalam), op.cit., 80–81.

201 Zac Varghese and Mathew A. Kallumpram, *Glimpses of Mar Thoma Church History,* op.cit., 38; T.C. Chacko, *The Concise History of the Mar Thoma Church* (Malayalam), op.cit., 80–81; P.M. Thomas, ed., *Mar Thoma Sabha Directory, Revised Edition, op.cit.*, 47.
   Abraham Malpan's reply to the CMS missionary, Peet, was that "It is better to stay in one's humble kitchen than living in somebody else's golden mansions". Quoted in Zac Varghese and Mathew A. Kallumpram, *Glimpses of Mar Thoma Church History, op.cit.*, 38. However the source of the statement is not mentioned in it.

202 Jesudas M. Athyal, John J. Thattamannil, ed., *Metropolitan Chrysostom on Mission in the Market Place, op.cit.*, 42.

Malayalam liturgy

The major liturgical changes made by Abraham Malpan in 1837 were aimed at restoring the autonomous nature of the church, with a liturgy that had a distinctly oriental identity. The three major revisions in the liturgy were the rejection of the idea of Holy Mass as sacrifice, the rejection of the emphasis on representative priesthood and the adoption of the royal priesthood of all baptised. The idea of Mass as a sacrifice was common in Anglo-Catholic and Roman Catholic traditions.[203] The liturgical revision removed the word, "sacrifice", from wherever it expressed the idea that the sacrifice of Christ is being repeated. The idea of offering (Qurbana) was instead emphasised, restoring the Oriental liturgical understanding.

On a different front, the clergy had come to be treated, in the Roman Catholic tradition, as representatives of God. The ordination of priest was believed to have given them mystical powers to pass on the divine sacramental grace to the participants and the authority to be celebrants. So the priests had the authority to pardon sins, to bring about substantive transformation in the elements – from bread and wine to body and blood – and to repeat the sacrifice of Christ in the Holy Mass.

The reform tradition[204] emphasises the priesthood of all believers. The reformists did not see the Mass either in repeated sacrificial terms, or as a one-for-all offering of Jesus Christ. For the reform tradition, priests are representatives of the people of God, called and anointed by God in the church for the administration of the word and sacraments. They have the authority to exercise the ministry of the Word and Sacraments. That authority had priestly, prophetic and administrative dimensions, as described in the Scripture.[205]

Two other changes made in the liturgy were on the use of incense and an emphasis on the invocation of the Holy Spirit.[206] The first one was aimed at removing

---

203 P.M. Thomas, ed., *Mar Thoma Church Directory, op.cit.*, 45–47.
204 The term "Reformed" denotes a type of Protestantism developed in Switzerland by Zwingli and John Calvin in 16th century. Later it had its roots in Europe and else where. They are active in the World Alliance of Reformed Churches, which includes the Presbyterian and Congregational with their headquarters in Geneva. They also share the basic teachings of Protestant Reformation as propounded in Martin Luther's writings in 1520. The word, "reform tradition" used in this study, is in a general sense of all churches that holds the reformation ideals of Martin Luther, not in the sense of the "Reformed Church Tradition" in its strict sense.
205 See, *Constitution of the Mar Thoma Syrian Church of Malabar, op.cit.*, 1–5.
206 P.M. Thomas, ed., *Mar Thoma Church Directory*, Revised Edition, *op.cit.*, 45–47.

the misconception, which was widely current among the people that incense "is something which effects reconciliation with God"[207]. This was understood widely as something that happens automatically or magically. Secondly, invocation is considered as the moment when the Holy Spirit comes upon both the elements in the Holy Qurbana and the communicants and therefore creates a moment of consecration.[208] This was considered as the crux of the oriental-Indian liturgy prior to the Roman period in the church and it was reinstated through the revision of the liturgy.[209]

Besides this, the reformers brought about three major alterations in the customs and practices of the *Malankara* Church. They decided to start administering bread and wine separately rather than dipping the bread in wine and administering as such, going back to the Eastern tradition. Secondly, the Antiochian and Roman Catholic practice of auricular confession was done away with. The third major

---

207 K.K. Kuruvilla, *Mar Thoma Church and its Doctrines, op.cit.*, 32; P.M. Thomas, ed., *Mar Thoma Church Directory,* Revised Edition, *op.cit.*, 45–47.

208 Eastern liturgies in general uphold this view. However, in the Roman Catholic tradition holds that the words of Institution as the moment of consecration because the efficacy is given to the words of Christ. The words of institution come after the invocation of the Holy Spirit in the revised liturgy of the Roman Catholic Church in India.

209 The major liturgical revision in this line could be summarised as follows: First "all prayers for the saints were omitted". Second, "all prayers for the dead were omitted". Third, a prayer before receiving the communion, "Thee I am holding Who holdest the bounds, Thee I am grasping Who orderest the depths, Thee O God, I place in my mouth" is removed to affirm the church's non-subscription of the theory of transubstantiation. Fourth, in another prayer the priest used to say "we offer Thee this unbloody sacrifice for Thy whole Church all over the world." In this prayer, the word 'prayer' was substituted for "unbloody sacrifice" with a view to avoid the idea of the repetition of Jesus Christ's sacrifice in each sacrament celebrations. Fifth, the prayer containing "live sacrifice" to be altered to "we submit the sacrifice of grace, peace and praise". Sixth, the prayer "this Qurbana is sacrifice and praise" was removed. Seventh, another prayer, "the Holy Spirit purifies the sensor" was removed. Eighth, the rubrics "that the sensor to be blessed" was removed. Ninth, the prayer "let this bread be made life-giving body" was changed to "Let the Holy Spirit, bless this bread to be the body of Christ and those who accept it and may receive it the absolution of their sins and for the attainment of eternal life". Tenth, another prayer "you are the fiery rock which was placed on the grave of our Lord" was changed to "You are the fiery rock which the builders rejected but on examination is found precious".
See, Abraham Malpan, and Kaithayil Geevarghese Malpan revised the *Malankara* Church's liturgy in 1836, In: P.M. Thomas, ed., *Mar Thoma Sabha Directory,* Revised Edition, *op.cit.*, 46–47.

reform was the decision to celebrate the Holy Qurbana in the new Malayalam liturgical order.[210]

Another major liturgical revision was done in 1927,[211] which gave centrality to the words of institution, removed all monophysitic references and emphasised the royal priesthood of all believers. Certain customs like *nercha*[212] or special offerings and such other practices, which have resemblance to the Hindu *vazhipadu*[213] offering were also discarded during the reforms. This revision will not be dealt with at length in this study, being outside its scope.

Decisive steps for reforms

Two major pragmatic moves were taken by Abraham Malpan and Geevarghese Malpan to implement the reforms. As the first step, the reformers requested Mar Dionysius IV (1825–1852) to review his position on reform. But when the Metropolitan rejected the request, they identified 24 faith practices that needed corrections to be sent to the British Resident for action.[214] Second, the reformers sought the feasibility of consecrating a bishop from within the reform sympathisers to lead the church in the path of reform. Reformers found in Abraham Malapan's

---

210 P.M. Thomas, ed., *Mar Thoma Church Directory,* Revised Edition, *op.cit.,* 45–47.

211 Ibid., 46–47; K.K. Kuruvilla, *Mar Thoma Church and its Doctrines, op.cit.,* 32–36. The monophysitic references entered in to the *Malankara* Church's liturgy when the church adopted west Syrian liturgy of the Antiochian church. The emphasis of the Holy Qurbana as mystery or *Raza* is emphasised. *Raza* is a Syriac word meaning mystery. This word is derived from the Persian word and from the same root as the Sanskrit word for mystery is *rahasyam.*

212 The *nercha* is an offering to the church. For instance devotees bring their offerings in kind or in money or calf or sheep, to the church and pray for healing or for other blessings.

213 In Hinduism, there are different kinds of offerings, in which temple devotees can bring articles in kind or money to the temple and pray for healing or blessing. Devotees can offer fireworks, food, *uruvazhipadu* or offering calf to the temple for favours. See, A. Sreedhara Menon, *Cultural Heritage of Kerala: An Introduction,* (Cochin: East-West Publication, 1978), 17.

214 This incident in 1836 is called as the Trumpet Call of the Reformation in the Malankara Church. See those 24 demands in Appendix B, In: P.M. Thomas., ed., *Mar Thoma Sabha Directory, Revised Edition, op.cit.,* 82–89.

nephew – Mathew[215] – a new prospect for the reforms within the church. They sent him to Mardin, the erstwhile seat of the Patriarch Syrian Orthodox Church of Antioch, to study under the Jacobite Patriarch.

Why did Abraham Malpan seek the support of the Antiochian Patriarch if he stood for church autonomy? The move could have been either to overthrow Mar Dionysius IV and to reinstate the reforms, with the support of the Patriarch, or to keep the age-old church's policy of mutual recognition and ecumenical relation with Antioch, or both. When the Patriarch of Antioch consecrated Mathews Mar Athanasius (1842–1877) in 1842 in Mardin and authorised him to lead the *Malankara* Church, rejecting the plea of Mar Dionysius IV, the dream of the reformers came to fruition. However, this created a fresh civil court litigation on the question of who – Mar Dionysius IV or Mathews Mar Athanasius – the legitimate Metropolitan of the *Malankara* Church was. The Travancore Government Civil Court made it clear in 1852 that Mar Athanasius was, in law as well as in fact, the Metropolitan of the Mar Thoma Church.[216]

The reformers thus succeeded in installing a reform sympathiser as the *Malankara* Church's Metropolitan. But the crisis within the church escalated to an all-out confrontation between two factions within the church.

While the reformers managed to get the Metropolitan consecrated by the Patriarch of Antioch, a strong group of church members rallied under Mar Dionysius IV, which the Patriarch of Antioch could not ignore. So the Patriarch sent Yuyakim Mar Coorilose from Antioch in 1846[217] to investigate the problem within

---

215 Being impressed by the leadership qualities and intellectual capacity of Mathew, the Patriarch consecrated him as the bishop and commissioned him as the Metropolitan of the *Malankara* Church. L.W. Brown commented on the theological and intellectual calibre of Mathews Mar Athansius as "the most able *metran* the Christians of St. Thomas Christians ever had". See, L.W. Brown, *Indian Christians of St. Thomas, op.cit.* 143.
See, A.M. Mundadan, *Indian Christians Search for Identity and Struggle for Autonomy, op.cit.*, 118–120.

216 When Mathews Mar Athanasius reached Kerala, the then Metropolitan did not recognize his authority and therefore, Mathews Mar Athanasius forced to approach the civil authorities of Travancore to secure legal standing for his office. In the light of the *staticon,* which authorize him to take the office of the bishop in India by the patriarch of Antioch, the King of Travancore pronounced a judgment in favour of Mathews Mar Athanasius and asked all Mar Thoma Christians to follow him. The King also allowed both Metropolitans to lead the church jointly. See, A.M. Mundadan, *Indian Christians Search for Identity and Struggle for Autonomy, op.cit.*, 118–120.

217 It was when the King of Travancore pronounced a judgment in favour of Mathews Mar Athanasius, Mar Dionysius IV, took a measure to approach the Patriarch of

the *Malankara* Church, in response to a request by Mar Dionysius IV. He made an abortive attempt to take the Metropolitanate from Mathews Mar Athanasius, which only widened the gulf between the two factions.

As another move from the followers of Dionysius IV, Joseph Pulikottil, a priest of the church, who belonged to the non-reform section, was sent to Mardin and the Patriarch Yakkub III of the Antiochian church consecrated him as Mar Dionysius V (1865–1909) in 1865. Instead of accepting Mar Dionysius V as the Metropolitan, Mathews Mar Athanasius retaliated by consecrating Thomas Mar Athanasius (1877–1893) as his successor in 1868.[218]

The Patriarch of Antioch noted that the act of Mathews Mar Athanasius to consecrate his successor was effectively the rejection of his authority over the *Malankara* Church. This prompted his direct intervention in the *Malankara* Church's affairs. Having received a formal invitation from Mar Dionysius V (1865–1909) to chair the Synod, Mar Peter III, a Jacobite Patriarch of Antioch, came to Kerala in 1975. He anathematised Thomas Mar Athanasius (1877–1893), the then Metropolitan, and moved a petition in the civil government to withdraw the recognition accorded to the Metropolitan.[219] Fed up by petitions from the church, the civil government issued a proclamation on 4 March, 1876:

> "Any apparent connections with appointments relating to the Syrian Church, which proclamations issued under times and circumstances now altered may seem to indicate, will henceforth be avoided."[220]

Antioch to declare Mathews Mar Athanasius' *staticon* null and void. To enquire this, the Patriarch sent Yuyakkim Mar Coorilose to India as his deputy. It was during this time, Mar Dionysius IV got ill and he requested the civil government to proclaim Mar Coorilose his lawful successor. Civil authorities did not accept his plea. Instead, the Government of Travancore and Cochin pronounced that Mathews Mar Athanasius is lawful Metropolitan of the church. Mathews Mar Athanasius was proclaimed as the Metropolitan of the *Malankara* Church in Travancore on July 28, 1852 and in Cochin on 4 October 1852 by orders of the civil government of Travancore and Cochin. L.W. Brown, *The Indian Christians of St. Thomas, op.cit.*, 142–143.

218 The zeal of Mathews Mar Athanasius towards reforms did create a suspicion among the conservative section within the church. When he consecrated the son of Abraham Malpan, Thomas, this suspicion was mounted at large among the people. This resulted in a loss of popular support to his successor, Thomas Mar Athanasius. See, L.W Brown, *The Indian Christians of St. Thomas, op.cit.*, 145; C.B. Firth, *An Introduction to Indian Church History, op.cit.*, 175–177.

219 L.W. Brown, *The Indian Christians of St. Thomas, op.cit.*, 146.

220 *Proclamation in Case III, III,* No. 205, 38, 39. *Tiruvalla*: Mar Thoma Sabha Archives. Also cited In: L.W Brown, *The Indian Christians of St. Thomas, op.cit.*, 146.

Besides, the government made it clear that all disputes were to be settled in the law courts.[221] This enabled the Patriarch to go ahead and convene a synod without any impediments from the civil authorities.

The Patriarch convened a Synod in Mulanthuruthy in 1876,[222] which C.B. Firth was to describe "a master-stroke of policy".[223]

The Synod decided to "adhere closely with the West Syrian doctrinal, liturgical and Church disciplinary norms and resolved a registered deed to be executed in this regard and presented to the Patriarch, declaring the official adherence of this Indian church with the Patriarch accepting his jurisdictional claims".[224] These decisions were taken unilaterally as the reformers led by Thomas Mar Athanasius boycotted it. Mulanthuruthy abandoned the autonomy of the *Malankara* Church and accepted the supremacy of the Patriarch of Antioch over the *Malankara* Church.[225]

On the basis of the Synod decisions, Mar Dionysius V (1865–1909) filed a case in civil court on March 4, 1889, claiming that he and fellow trustees were the lawful owners of the Church. Mar Dionysius V pleaded the court to bring under

---

221 The proclamation of the civil government enabled the Patriarch to act against Thomas Mar Athanasius without incurring any legal impediments. Thus Mar Dionysius V got an opportunity to bring the church under the patriarch of Antioch during the synod at Mulanthuruty in 1876. See, *Ibid.*, N.M. Mathew, *Malankara Sabaha Charithram*, Vol. II, (Malayalam) (Tiruvalla: Mar Thoma Episcopal Jubilee Institute, 2007), 98.
    N.M. Mathew is a church historian in Kerala.

222 Wolfgang Hage, "Reformatoriches Christentum in Orientalischem Gewand Die Mar Thoma Kirche in Indien", In: Peter Gemeinhardt und Uwe Keuhneweg, ed., *Patristica et Oecumenica*, (Marburg: N.G. Elwert Verland, 2004), 196.
    Patriarch Peter Ignatius III, visited England before he set out his travel to India to ensure co- operation of the Anglican church and government for his goal to bring *Malankara* church under the Antiochine Patriarchate.

223 C.B. Firth, *An Introduction to Indian Church History*, *op.cit.*, 175.

224 Official website of the Malankara Orthodox Syrian Church, *www.malankaraortho doxchurch*.in. accessed on April, 18, 2011.
    T.C. Chacko, *The Concise History of the Mar Thoma Church*(Malayalam), *op.cit.*, 137; L.W Brown, *The Indian Christians of St. Thomas*, *op.cit.*, 146; C.B. Firth, *An Introduction to Indian Church History*, *op.cit.*, 176.

225 The Mulanthuruthy Synod adopted the west Syrian church's faith, liturgy, episcopacy, church polity and church discipline.

his control the ownership of the Seminary in Kottayam and the other assets of the Church.[226] Both sides argued on their own grounds at the court.[227]

The Royal Court verdict in 1889 came in favour of Mar Dionysius V (1865–1909), resulting in a considerable church property loss. However, Justice Ormsby, the only Christian judge in the three-member judicial panel who heard the case, pronounced a judgement in favour of the reformers. In his judgement, he said:

> "My conclusion, on the whole, is that it is not made out that the imposition of hands by Antioch is essential to the consecration of a Metran of Malankara which is itself an independent and coeval Church."[228]

The judge thus upheld the *Malankara* Church's position of being an independent and autonomous Indian church, making a split of the church inevitable. The two

---

226 *O.S No. 439,* M.E 1054 (1879), *Alapuzha civil court, Kerala,* Mar Thoma Syrian Church Archives, Tiruvalla.

227 The argument of Mar Dionysius V, who was the Plaintiff in the Law suit in the civil court of Alapuzha was that the *Malankara* Church had been under the jurisdiction of the Jacobite Patriarch of Antioch. Consequently, the consecration of Thomas Mar Athanasius, who was the defendant by Mathews Mar Athanaius, without the sanction of the Patriarch, was not only irregular but also invalid. Therefore the defendant was not a bishop and so had no title to administer the property of the Church. However, on the other hand, it was argued, on behalf of Thomas Mar Athanasius of the Reform party that while *Malankara* Church had connections with the Jacobite Patriarch since the separation from the Roman Catholic Church in 1665, nevertheless it was an independent Church that throughout this long period of two centuries several Metropolitans had been consecrated by their predecessors in the *Malankara* Church itself, and that this was done without the sanction or even knowledge of the Patriarch of Antioch. See, *Judgment of the Royal Court of Malabar, Seminary Case, Kottayam: Archives,* Mar Thoma Theological Seminary Archive, 1889.
Thomas Mar Athanasius' arguments are in conformity with the findings of T.I. Varghese. T.I Varghese is a Church History Professor at the Orthodox Theological Seminary, Kottayam. He made a book review on I. Daniel's book titled, "The Syrian Church of Malabar" and in it he writes that: "the Syrian Christians of Malabar had deep connections with the Antiochene Patriarch from 1665 is also historically untrue. Because this connection was developed and deepened only from the middle of the 19th century in the Syrian Christian Church and the transition of the Syrian Christian Church purely as a West Syrian Church tradition was ascribed only from the Synod of Mulanthuruty in 1876 and not before". See, T.I Varghese, Introducing the Book of I Daniel, Syrian Church of Malabar in *Indian Church History Classics, The Nazranis, op.cit.,* 29.

228 *ibid.*

factions started fresh life journeys under the names, "Malankara Mar Thoma Syrian Church"[229] and "Malankara Jacobite Syrian Church" in 1889.[230]

However, this was not the end but the beginning of another fresh struggle within the "Malankara Jacobite Syrian Church" on the question of whether the Patriarch, or Mar Dionysius V had the real authority over the "Malankara Jacobite Syrian Church". That dispute is still unresolved after several vicissitudes of litigations and struggles.[231]

Faith practices and ecclesiology

There is no concrete primary material available on the faith practices and ecclesiology of the *Malankara* Church during the first four centuries of the Common Era. But on the basis of secondary and other sources, it can be surmised that St. Thomas established seven churches in India. These churches exist even today. From the Fifth Century to 15th Century, the *Malankara* Church's faith practices were in conformity with the Persian Church.

---

229 Malankara Mar Thoma Syrian Church as it is commonly called as Mar Thoma Church.

230 In the meantime, Sree Moolam Thirunal of Travancore (1885–1925), who was the then King of Travancore personally made an effort to reconcile both sides. However, both sides stood for their positions. Mar Dionysius V acknowledged the authority and jurisdictional claims of the Patriarch as well as his demand to stop the reforms. Thomas Mar Athanasius, preferred to stand for reforms, independence and autonomy of the church.

231 Mar Dionysius V did not execute the registered deed, even after the victory in court, in compliance with decisions of the synod of Mulanthuruthy in 1876. It was a violation of what they have decided, and the patriarch expected that would take place soon. Knowing that the Patriarch was deceived by Dionysius V, he consecrated six bishops of his own accord without the consent of the Malankara Orthodox Syrian Church and of Dionysius V, taking from each of the newly consecrated bishops registered deed, to ensure and strengthen their dioceses. This eventually led another schism within the "Malankara Orthodox Syrian Church" inevitable and thus "Malankara Orthodox Syrian Church" and "Malankara Syrian Orthodox Church" or "Jacobite Syrian Christian Church" came in 1912. The former has its head quarters in Kottayam, Kerala and the latter acknowledges the Patriarch of Antioch as its supreme head and its headquarters is at Mulamthuruthy, Kerala. Another schism occurred within the "Malankara Orthodox Syrian Church", when a group joined with the Roman Catholic Church in 1930, as "Uniates" known as "Syro-Malankara Catholic Church".

On the basis of the data available, the following faith practices and ecclesiology can be identified currently.

Malankara Mar Thoma Syrian Church (Mar Thoma Church) is an Oriental non-Chalcedonian wing of the undivided Church, because it stands in continuity with the Oriental Church going back through the medieval period of the Persian Church to the fathers and martyrs of the early Church. It embodies Eastern canon of the Scripture, the Nicene Creed, the three-fold ministry and seven sacraments, as well as structures its life and worship around those pillars.[232] With regard to the ecclesiology of the Mar Thoma Church, it shares the undivided church's stand that the church is a communion of salvation, revealed to the world through the Trinitarian mystery. The church "firmly held the orthodox faith regarding the mysteries of Trinity, the Incarnation and the Eucharist".[233] Its life is characterized by its participation in the witness, worship and service.

The Mar Thoma Church stands in apostolic succession, of which the three-fold apostolic ministry of bishops, priests and deacons is a central expression.[234] The foundation of the faith and practices of the Mar Thoma Church has been based on the undivided church's ecclesiology.

There is no evidence of a centralized administration, or a bishop to look after the early converts to Christianity, during the first four centuries in India. Since the fifth century, there have been evidences of an episcopal supervision of the *Malankara* Church by the Persian bishops. The Church governance has been characterized by the episcopal leadership of the Persian bishops through the Archdeacon, the clergy

---

232 Regarding the sacraments and ministry, K.K. Kuruvilla and Juhanon Mar Thoma shares the view that the *Malankara* Church "administered only three sacraments, namely, Baptism, Eucharist and Ordination" prior to the Synod of Diamper. Since their writings are secondary sources, which is not in conformity with the tradition of the undivided Church. Juhanon Mar Thoma, *Christianity in India and the Mar Thoma Church, op.cit.*, 11.; K.K. Kuruvila, *Mar Thoma Church and Its Doctrines, op.cit.*, 8; *Constitution of the Mar Thoma Syrian Church of Malabar,* English Version, (Tiruvalla: Mar Thoma Press, 2002), 1.

233 Joseph Thekkedathu, *History of Christianity in India,* Vol. II, *op.cit.*, 30.

234 "The Church accepts as its goal and function to be the repository of the divine doctrines revealed by Jesus Christ and proclaimed by His Apostles: to maintain these doctrines in their purity, to promote the spiritual life of its members through the administration of sacraments and by the ministry of the Word; to make disciples of all nations by the proclamation of the Gospel to the whole world, and through the administration of holy sacraments in the name of the Triune God." See, *Constitution of the Mar Thoma Syrian Church of Malabar,* English Version, (Tiruvalla: Mar Thoma Press, 2002), 1–2.

and laity in the early phases, and later by the leadership of the metropolitan, bishops, clergy and laity. The church's administrative system has been independent. In church administration and life, the role of the members of the church has been decisive. Important decisions have been taken at the *pothuyogam* or *Palliyogam* (general body of the parish).[235] This will be dealt with in detail in the next chapter of this study.

With regard to the training of the candidates for ministry, the Mar Thoma Church followed a *gurukula system*[236] in which a candidate for the ministry was send to live with *Malpans*[237] for his theological formation in the seminary. In this process, they maintained an intimate relation between the community and ministerial formation.[238]

---

235 *Palliyogam* or *pothuyogam* is the general assembly of the church, in which the parish representatives and the clergy of the parish are members. It is presided over by the priest. The daily administration of the parish is carried out by decisions of the *palliyogam* or *pothuyogam*. Moreover, powers such as the spiritual welfare of the parish, financial administration and issuing approval of the candidates to the ministry are vested in it. See, Mathew Vellanikal, "Perspective on the Identity of St. Thomas Christians" In: Kuncheria Pathil ed., *Mission in India Today*, (Bangalore: Dharmaram Publications, 1988), 95.

236 *Gurukula* System of education was a concept associate with the pursuit of education in ancient India. *Guru- Kula* means teacher's family. It is a place where the teacher resides and teaches his students. A student has to serve the teacher for many years by living with the family of the teacher, to convince him about his discipline, knowledge, sincerity, level of intelligence and so on. The history of this system of education can be traced from *Vedic* times. In *Upanishads* also mentions various *gurukulas*. In this system, the *guru* (teacher) does not take any fees from the student. However after the students' study, he would offer a *gurudhakshina*, which may be monetary as his gesture of respect, gratitude and acknowledgement to the teacher. Before the Romanization, the Mar Thoma Church also practiced this system of learning to equip its clergy for the church.

237 *Malpan* is the Syriac word meaning teacher.

238 The adaptation of Hindu and Buddhist elements from Indian culture, and its transformation into a vibrant basis for faith and morals, without contradicting God's revelation through Scripture and Tradition, is a typical contribution of the Mar Thoma church to the world. See, George A Maloney, "The Heritage of Eastern Christian Spirituality", In: Kuncheria Pathil ed., *Mission in India Today, op.cit.*, 134.

The Mar Thoma Church wants its members to have an evangelical fervour, but within the framework of the corporate life and liturgical devotion of an Oriental church.[239]

These analysis supports the thesis that is supports not merely the particular view on ecumenism – autonomy and openness – of the church, but my thesis as a whole on the Mar Thoma Church's ecumenical nature and its desire to contemporize the church with the Catholic Church of the Nicene-Constantinople Creed.

---

239 *Ibid.*, 97–98. A.M. Mundadan, *Indian Christians search for Identity and Struggle for Autonomy, op.cit.*, 122.

Chapter V
Autonomous Church Reaches Out

The 19th Century CE was an era of revival, reform and regeneration of churches worldwide. The Anglo-Catholic revival "Oxford Movement" of the 1830s in England and their "Tracts for the Times" initiatives to spread the movement's ideals created enormous enthusiasm for sending out missionaries to India and other parts of the world. The missionary zeal also spread to the reform movement of the Mar Thoma Church and the need to do mission work was felt within the church from the last decade of the 19th Century.

During this phase, the Mar Thoma Church asserted its autonomy, while spreading its mission from its original "high-caste" base to a rural and "low-caste" population, in line with its "openness" outlook of ecumenism. This was a fitting response to the Western Protestant and Anglo-Catholic charge that the Mar Thoma Church was not mission-oriented. This also revived its ecumenical relations with other churches in India.

A new beginning

The defeat in the court did not sap the morale of reform leaders and the then Metropolitan, Thomas Mar Athanasius.[240] However, the sudden demise of the Metropolitan on August 10, 1893, left the Mar Thoma Church without a Bishop, putting it in a thorny situation.[241] According to John Fenwick, "without bishops, the reform movement might either have petered out, or have been reorganised on a different

---

240 The failure in the court case led to a loss of church property to the Mar Thoma Church. Consequently, the Metropolitan lost his residence at the theological seminary, Kottayam. See, N.M. Mathew, *Malankara Mar Thoma Sabha Charithram* (Malayalam), Vol. II, (Tiruvalla: Mar Thoma Episcopal Jubilee Institute of Evangelism, 2003), 141; *Circular Letter of Thomas Mar Athanasius Metropolitan to the Vicars of the Mar Thoma Syrian Church of Malabar,* Dt. M.E. 1053, Thulam 8, Kottayam; Zac Varghese Kanisserril, Mathew A. Kallumpuram, *Glimpses of the Mar Thoma Church History, op.cit.,* 81.

241 *Malankara Sabhayile Episcopaciyum Mar Thoma Sabhayile Stanabhisheka Shusrooshakalum,* (Malayalam), (Tiruvalla: Mar Thoma Syrian Church, 1975), 31, 32; N.M. Mathew, *Malankara Mar Thoma Sabha Charithram* (Malayalam), Vol. II, *op.cit.,* 143.

ecclesiastical basis".[242] But the timely help of the Metropolitans of the Malabar Independent Syrian Church (MISC) helped clear the clouds over the Mar Thoma Church's longevity.

The MISC accepted the request of the representative assembly of the Mar Thoma Church for help in consecrating Titus I in 1893,[243] amidst the threat to disrupt the consecration by a vested group within the Malankara Orthodox Syrian Church. Joseph Mar Athanasius (1883–1898) and Geevarghese Mar Coorilose V (1892–1935)[244],

---

242 John R.K. Fenwick, *The Forgotten Bishops, op.cit.*, 586.

243 It was when the meeting of the Mar Thoma Church's clergy, which met after the funeral of Thomas Mar Athanasius at Maramon in 1893 that they decided to call a representative assembly. This was scheduled to be held at Niranam on October 7 and 8, 1893 with the purpose of selecting a Metropolitan. Titus Kathanar (1843–1910) of the Palakunnathu family was unanimously selected as the candidate to become the Metropolitan. (The *Kathanar* is the *Malayalam* word used to denote the Mar Thoma Church's priest.) Kovoor Iye Thoma Kathanar (1842–1917), the then Vicar General of the Mar Thoma Church (The Mar Thoma Church's Vicar General is the principal deputy of the bishop of a diocese, who has the executive power over the entire diocese, on advice of the bishop. This is the highest office that a married clergy of the Mar Thoma Church could occupy) and Punnathra Chandapilla Kathanar (1844–1931) were authorised to make arrangements for the Titus's consecration. The meeting also authorised them to request the MISC Metropolitans – Joseph Mar Athanasius (1883–1898) and Geevarghese Mar Coorilose V (1892–1935) – to consecrate the episcopal candidate as the *Ramban* and the bishop at Kottayam cheriapalli, which is an ancient church in Kerala, on 14th January, and 18th January 1894, respectively. (*Ramban* is the order of a monk-priest in the Mar Thoma Church. The monk priests are eligible for the office of the bishop in the Mar Thoma Church. The Mar Thoma Church's Constitution says: "although according to the Bible, *Episcopa* may be a married person, it is deemed necessary to continue the ancient custom, requiring *Episcopas* of the Malankara Mar Thoma Syrian Church to be celibates and therefore persons nominated for Episcopal candidature, shall be celibates".) See, *Constitution of the Mar Thoma Syrian Church of Malabar, op.cit.*, 11.

244 Geevarghese Mar Coorilose V (1892–1935) was the Metropolitan and Joseph Mar Athanasius (1883–1898) was the Suffragen Metropolitan of the MISC, who had the legitimate episcopal authority to consecrate a bishop as per the canon of the Mar Thoma Church. There were several occasions in the Mar Thoma Church, when the MISC's Metropolitans consecrated the church's Metropolitan and vice versa. For instance, prior to Titus I Metropolitan's episcopal consecration in 1894, when Metropolitan, Punnathra Mar Dionesius (1817–1825) passed away without consecrating his successor, the MISC Metropolitan, Mar Philoxinos (1811–1829), consecrated Mar Dionesyus IV (1825–1852) as the Mar Thoma Church's Metropolitan in 1825.

MISC metropolitans, led the consecration service on 18 January, 1894.[245] The district magistrate of Kottayam, as well as civil and police authorities, had taken all necessary steps to prevent any disruption of this sacred consecration and the enthronement of the Metropolitan of the emerging reformed Mar Thoma Church.

This sealed the issue of the church's Apostolic succession once for all.

The effect of this consecration on the Mar Thoma Church was startling. The laying-on-of-hands by the MISC's Metropolitans, at the consecration of Titus I, cemented the Mar Thoma Church's unbroken chain of connectivity with the St. Thomas apostolate, and this in turn continued the church's creedal marks – unity, catholicity and apostolicity – in its oriental liturgical use and evangelical principles. Besides, the Mar Thoma Church was stirred up with enthusiasm to continue a special kind of conciliar fellowship with the MISC, which will be dealt with later.[246] The high general enthusiasm around the consecration event prompted the Metropolitan and leaders of the church to devote considerable time to assert its legitimate independent existence, which they envisioned correctly, would blend seamlessly with its historic autonomous nature.

Autonomy asserted

The Mar Thoma Church adopted four guidelines to uphold its autonomy, independence and ecumenism, after the consecration of Titus I. First, it affirmed its evangelical and eastern liturgical footing to assert its historical autonomy and independence. For instance, during the three decades from the 1860s, the Mar Thoma Church was somewhat open to the concept of evangelisation. The church considered the feasibility of starting indigenous mission fields in India. Second, it was decided to set up

See, C.P. Mathew, M.M. Thomas, *The Indian Churches of Saint Thomas,* Revised Edition, (New Delhi: ISPCK, 2005), 58; Zac Varghese Kanisserril, Mathew A. Kallumpuram, *Glimpses of the Mar Thoma Church History, op.cit.,* 91–92; N.M. Mathew, *Malankara Mar Thoma Sabha Charithram* (Malayalam), Vol. II, *op.cit.,* 148–149.

245 John R.K. Fenwick, *The Malabar Independent Syrian Church,* (Nottingham: Groove Books, 1992), 34; Joseph Daniel, "Most Rev. Joseph Mar Koorilose – A Metropolitan Who Makes A Difference", In: *Joseph Mar Koorilose Valiya Metropolitan Silver Jubilee Festschrift 2011,* (Thozhiyoor: Episcopal Silver Jubilee Festschrift, 2011), 89–95.

246 John R.K. Fenwick, *The Malabar Independent Syrian Church,* (Nottingham: Groove Books, 1992), 34; Joseph Daniel, "Most Rev. Joseph Mar Koorilose – A Metropolitan Who Makes A Difference", In: *Joseph Mar Koorilose Valiya Metropolitan Silver Jubilee Festschrift 2011,* (Thozhiyoor: Episcopal Silver Jubilee Festschrift, 2011), 89–95.

schools for strengthening the Mar Thoma Church's social responsibility to provide education to all communities irrespective of religion or caste.[247]

Third, it was decided to introduce a democratic administrative system in the church. Metropolitan Titus I Mar Thoma identified the fact that the Mar Thoma Church's passion of mission decreases when people's participation in the church's mission, including administration, was restricted to the clergy alone. So he searched for a possibility to include the laity in the church's administration and introduced a democratic administrative set-up for the Mar Thoma Church by founding a management committee[248] and a general body,[249] with both clergy and laity as members.[250]

Fourth, it was the Mar Thoma Church's intention to strengthen relations with other churches with a view to fulfil a vision of a *Bharath* (Indian) *Church*[251] as promoted by the National Missionary Society (NMS), India's first indigenous inter-denominational missionary organisation. It was within the *Bharath Church* context that the promotion of a deeper relationship with the Church of England, the MISC and other churches began to develop as the church's dominant vision, although its concepts of apostolicity, independence and autonomy of the Indian church remained unhampered.

The historicity of the guidelines followed by the Mar Thoma Church in furthering its ecumenical principles is indisputable. But how far have those policies helped the church to assert its autonomy and independence in its life and work? What practical steps have the Mar Thoma Church taken to extend its age-old policy of openness to other denominations and to other religious communities?

Dedicated to Indian mission

The focus on the mission field that was India led the Mar Thoma Church to form an indigenous mission organisation called the *Mar Thoma Suvishesha Prasanga Sangham*, or the Mar Thoma Evangelistic Association (MTEA), in 1888. It was for the first time an Indian church took the initiative on its own to start a mission

---

247 *Ibid.,* 160.
248 Currently the "management committee" is called *Sabha Council,* which means "Church Council".
249 Currently the Mar Thoma Church's "General Body" is called *Pradhinidhi Mandalam.*
250 N.M. Mathew, *Malankara Mar Thoma Sabha Charithram* (Malayalam), Vol. II, *op.cit.,* 156.
251 *Bharath* is the Sanskrit name for India. It means the land of *Bharatha,* a renowned sage of India.

organisation just for indigeneous mission activities. In 1905 was started the *Mar Thoma Sunday School Samajam*, which aimed for Sunday Bible classes regularly for children. The *Mar Thoma Suvishesha Sevika Sangham*, (Mar Thoma Gospel Women's Association) which is a women's auxiliary wing of the church, started in 1919. The *Mar Thoma Sannadha Suvishesha Sangham* (Voluntary Evangelistic Association) was formed in 1924, and the *Mar Thoma Yuvajana Sakhyam* (Mar Thoma Youth League) an auxiliary organisation for youths in 1933.[252]

The initial step of the church towards the mobilization of its members was motivated by its openness to receive the CMS mission's ideas and strategies for mission, together with the church's oriental liturgical base. It was at this point that the Mar Thoma Church addressed its growing passion for evangelism.

A vision was transformed into specific action, when one clergy and 11 laymen of the Mar Thoma Church assembled for retreat and prayer at Kallissery, near Tiruvalla, on September 5, 1888. This meeting eventually marked the beginning of the *Malabar Mar Thoma Syrian Evangelistic Association* which is a pioneering indigenous missionary organisation in India. The main objective of the MTEA "shall be the propagation of the Gospel among the non-Christian and the deepening of the spiritual life of Christians..."[253] The task before the Mar Thoma Church after the formation of the MTEA was to integrate the eastern liturgical base of the church to the new found evangelical fervour.

When liturgy met evangelism ...

The Mar Thoma Church's integration task was twofold – integration of the eastern liturgical and evangelical faith of the CMS as well as the integration of the church and mission to create a church with a missionary zeal. The Mar Thoma Church's vision combined the "evangelical faith and experiences within the framework of corporate life" with the "liturgical devotion of an Eastern Church".[254] Therefore, the MTEA

---

252 Although the ancillary organizations of the church play a leading role in the life and witness of the church, its separate study is not included in this study as it would not serve the purpose of this study. But the role of women in the church will be analyzed in this study.

253 *The Malabar Mar Thoma Syrian Christian Evangelistic Association Memorandum and Articles of Association,* as amended in 1106 Malayalam Era., Reprint, (Tiruvalla: TAM Press, 1960), 3–6.

254 Malabar Mar Thoma Syrian Evangelistic Association was a registered organization under the Indian Companies Act VI, under the Travancore Regulation I, of 1882, in 1904. C.P. Mathew, M.M. Thomas, *Indian Christians of Saint Thomas, op.cit.,* 98.

had to assert its independence to western missionary societies and churches in thought and action.[255] The Mar Thoma Church's highly eastern liturgical basis led the church to devote time for integrating first the church's sacramental life and missionary consciousness in its teachings and subsequently the integration of the church and the MTEA. As to the leaders of the Mar Thoma Church, the church's integration with the MTEA was a dominant concern as it faced the independent existence of western missions and churches.[256] Many western mission agencies were separated from their respective churches. For instance, Thomas Mar Athanasius, the then Metropolitan, wholeheartedly supported the integration process.[257] Besides, MTEA leaders like Thomas Kottarathil[258], Mathai Edavanmelil, and Yohannan Kottoorethu were loyal churchmen and had been known for their efforts to amalgamate their missionary spirit and eastern liturgical ideals in their thoughts and actions.

The church employed two methods for integrating the missionary spirit and eastern liturgical deals. It started an educative phase to edify the church whereby it prepared teachings on "mission" and "eastern liturgical practice" for Sunday

---

255 The main outcome of the evangelical awakening of the eighteenth and the nineteenth centuries was the rise of modern missionary movements in Europe. Most of such missionary organizations including the CMS were voluntary societies independent of the church. These institutions considered themselves as separate institutions concerned with Christian missions in overseas.

256 The separation of the church from mission and the mission organization's reluctance to work under the direction of the church was a phenomenon in the early part of the nineteenth century and the first half of the twentieth century. William Anderson says: "The missionary enterprises regarded itself as a separate institution concerned with Christian operations overseas within, on the fringe of, in certain cases even outside, the existing Christian bodies; and, in accordance with its understanding of its nature, it developed its own independent organizational structure within or alongside of the organized churches". See, Wilhelm Anderson, *Towards a Theology of Mission*, (London: SCM Press, 1955), 15; C.P. Mathew, M.M. Thomas, *Indian Christians of Saint Thomas, op.cit.*, 104–105.

257 George Alexander, "Malankara Mar Thoma Suvishesha Prasangha Sanghom" (Malayalam), In: George Alexander, ed., Maramon *Convention Sathabhdhi Valyam* (Malayalam), (Tiruvalla: Mar Thoma Evangelistic Association, 1995), 160–302.
Rev. George Alexander is a clergy of the Mar Thoma Church. He was the General Secretary of the MTEA during 1981–1987 and he wrote a concise history of the MTEA since its inception in 1995.

258 Thomas Abraham Kottarathil was a clergy of the Mar Thoma Church, who was one among the twelve instrumental in the formation of MTEA.

worship services and convention meetings etc. Convention meetings were to conclude with the Holy Qurbana, explaining the Mar Thoma Church's paramount importance for the eastern liturgy. On another front, constitutional efforts were made to safeguard the church's integration with the MTEA by providing checks and balances. For instance, the third annual meeting of the MTEA made a decision that "the report of all meetings of the MTEA shall be submitted to the Metropolitan".[259]

Church's centrality in mission

The intention of this decision was to bring all proceedings of the MTEA before the Metropolitan for his perusal and approval. This was later included as a clause in the MTEA constitution. Similarly, the Mar Thoma Church's sacramental life made its oriental liturgical faith vibrant and the church's constitution made its liturgical observances obligatory.[260] C.P. Philipose (1868–1948),[261] the first General Secretary of the MTEA, helped the Mar Thoma Church keep the balance of these two elements by integrating missionary spirit and oriental liturgical piety in the MTEA's mission praxis.

Accepting decisively and consciously the joint responsibility for the Mar Thoma Church's missionary task, in contrast to the CMS administrative pattern[262], was a significant manifestation in its growing self-understanding that the church must be put at the centre of all mission work. This self-understanding of the church

---

259 *Report of the third meeting of the MTEA,* M.E. Dhanu 27, 1064, (February 7, 1889).
260 The Mar Thoma Church's Constitution states: "The ministry of Deacon, Priest, and Episcopa, rites of the church viz., Church Dedication, Church Consecration, Holy Baptism, Holy Communion (Qurbana), Holy Matrimony, unction of the Sick, funeral services, and observance of Sunday, Lents and Dominical Feasts shall not be abolished at any time".
    See, Declaration, Part I, *Constitution, Mar Thoma Syrian Church,* (Tiruvalla, Mar Thoma Church, 2002), 1.
261 C.P. Philipose (1868–1948), a clergy of the Mar Thoma Church was the first general secretary of the MTEA and he served the organization for fifty years. See, Alexander Mar Thoma, *The Mar Thoma Church: Heritage and Mission, op.cit.,* 58; P.M. Thomas, ed., *Mar Thoma Sabha Directory* (Malayalam), Revised III, *op.cit.,* 108–109.
262 The Travancore Mission of the CMS was an independent mission agency and therefore it was not under the Anglican Diocese of Cochin. See, Stephen Neill, *Creative Tension* (Duff Lectures), (Edinburgh: Edinburgh Press, 1959), 86.

had its debt to the "church and mission" paradigm of the ecumenical movement during 1910–1938.[263] These paradigm changes were undertaken by the global ecumenical movement in three phases, as given below:

The first phase saw the Edinburgh World Missionary Conference's vision of mission being put into action by the institution of the International Missionary Council" (1921)[264], the "Life and Work Movement" (1925) and the "Faith and Order Movement" (1927).[265] In the second phase, the global ecumenical movement, through the Jerusalem World Missionary Conference of 1927, saw a paradigm

---

263 Causes of the mission paradigm changes in the contemporary ecumenical movement were legion. However, two causes deserve special concern. They were the World Missionary Conference in Edinburgh in 1910 and the defeat of Russia in the Russo-Japanese war in 1904. (William Richy Hogg, *Ecumenical Foundations, op.cit.*, 130.) The Edinburgh Conference was the culmination of series of mission gatherings to expedite the missionary co-operation "to evangelize the world in this generation". The Edinburgh's proposal for a continuation committee virtually sowed seeds for the institutional expressions of the ecumenical movement of which paradigm changes emerged in the light of emerging contexts. (Brian Stanly, *The World Missionary Conference Edinburgh, 1910, op.cit.*, 28.) Consequently, plans were chalked out to establish ecumenical institutions aimed to bring missionary, ecclesiastical and social concerns separately for the church and mission. The defeat of Russia in the Russo-Japanese War in 1904 and the World War I (1914–1919) created a social context in the Asian countries that Asian countries could be seen in equal terms with the European countries. This new social context helped the "younger church" members to raise their voice for the equality in the mission fields and subsequently gave way to a new paradigm to view the "younger churches" and "older churches" without distinction. It was a departure from the earlier paradigm which had been guided by the objective that the "Christian west" ought to be engaged in converting the "heathen east", through the media of mission societies and English language.

264 Hereafter referred as IMC.

265 M.M. Thomas, *Recalling Ecumenical Beginnings*, (New Delhi: ISPCK, 1987), 63; Kenneth Scott LaTourette, "Ecumenical Bearings of the Missionary Movements and the International Missionary Council", In: Ruth Rouse and Stephen Charles Neill (ed.), *A History of the Ecumenical Movement 1517–194*, (Geneva: WCC, 1986), 355.

shift in the equal treatment of "younger churches" and older churches".[266] And, the Madras Conference of 1936 emphasised the centrality of the church in mission.[267]

In line with the aforementioned world ecumenical developments, leaders of the MTEA, especially the Metropolitan, Thomas Mar Athanasius, and C.P. Philipose took necessary precautions to avoid, in its organizational pattern, the possible division of the church- mission dichotomy as it appeared in western missionary societies.[268] A joint committee was constituted by the decisions of both the Mar Thoma

---

266 The Jerusalem meeting of the IMC showed a tendency to treat east and west equally with recognition of the presence of other faiths in mission fields in India. Superiority and missionary paternalism, as has already been indicated was a common missionary feature during the first decade of the twentieth century in India. However, the Jerusalem IMC conference helped to integrate the "younger church's" voices, which brought a visible change from the earlier mission paradigm. "What the Jerusalem conference discovered was that an indigenous church in Asia or Africa was not essentially different from any other church, in other part of the world, of which Jesus Christ is the head". See, T.V. Philip, *Edinburgh to Salvador, Twentieth Century Ecumenical Missiology. A Historical Study of the Ecumenical Discussions on Mission, op.cit., 33; Jerusalem Meeting Report, (JMR),* Vol. 1, (Oxford University Press, London 1928), 342–43.

267 A progression of the isolation of mission from the church was achieved at the IMC's Madras Conference in 1938, where the church became the locus of its mission. It was Henry Kramer's book "The Christian Message in a non-Christian World" helped the IMC to revive the Church's importance in mission. To Henry Kremer "the Church is emphatically reminded that it alone of all human institutions in the world is founded on divine commission. This however, can only be effectively done when the church becomes conscious in a new way of its mission in the "Christian" and the "non-Christian world, because it is being founded on a divine commission". (Henry Kramer, *The Christian Message in a Non-Christian World* (London: The Edinburgh Press, 1938), 1–13.) The church's centrality in mission in the context of growing secularism added fuel to the unity process of different denominations. This eventually resulted in the formation of the "World Council of Churches" in 1948. William Richey Hogg observes that the "Madras [conference] made the Church its central concern and a new sense of its reality runs through every statement produced there. As never before had been possible, the members of the churches saw the church universal partially disclosed in their midst. In a day when many regarded the historic Church as an unnecessary appendage to the Christian sprit, Madras meeting brought a new awareness of the church's importance." William Richy Hogg, *Ecumenical Foundations*, (Harper and Brothers Publication, New York, 1952), 297–298. Thus the Madras Conference concluded that the Church and mission are inseparable.

268 *Report of the third meeting of the MTEA,* M.E. Dhanu 27, 1064, (February 7, 1889); *The Malabar Mar Thoma Syrian Christians Evangelistic Association: Memorandum*

Church's general body and the MTEA's management committee in 1924 to make a further study on the relation between the church and the MTEA.

The committee was asked to submit a report to the Metropolitan in 1924. This was done to make sure that the integration of both the Mar Thoma Church and the MTEA could be carried out without any hindrance.[269] It submitted a report that was approved by the MTEA's managing committee and the Mar Thoma Church's general body.[270] This provided a constitutional framework to avert any possible friction between the Mar Thoma Church and the MTEA in future. The constitution of the MTEA made it mandatory for a report of the whole proceedings of its general body to be submitted to the Metropolitan for his approval. The constitutional intervention not only made it possible for the church and the MTEA to work in mutual cooperation, but made the church have effective control in the decision-making process of the MTEA.

Thus, long before the "church and mission" integration became a guiding principle in the global ecumenical movement leading to the 1961 New Delhi integration of the IMC with the "World Council of Churches", that concept had already appeared in the Mar Thoma Church's life and mission praxis. The "evangelical-oriental liturgical" and "church-mission" integration stood in contrast to the organisational pattern of the missionary enterprises in the West. This was an example of the Indian church's assertion of autonomy and independence, as it took its own chosen path in the new missionary context.

It is appropriate to conclude this discussion by looking at the question of how the Mar Thoma Church considered its existence in the light of the Gospel, while remaining in India's pluralistic society. It is believed that St. Thomas established the church in India, but there was no authenitic historical data to prove whether the church was caste-specific and catered to the spiritual needs of a caste-conscious society that included the "outcaste" or "lower caste" people of India. On the other hand, the Indian concept of ecumenism of living with differences, or unity in diversity, could have created a degree of harmony and unity. Thus the Mar Thoma Church's new mission policy to start mission work among "outcastes" could be seen as a departure from its centuries-old mission policy in a caste-conscious Indian society.

---

and Articles of Association, as Amended in 1106 M.E (1931), reprinted *op.cit.,* 1–12; Cited In: P.M. Thomas, *Mar Thoma Sabha Directory,* Reprint. *op.cit.,* 150.

269 *Annual Report of the Mar Thoma Syrian Church,* 1924, Tiruvalla.

270 George Alexander, "Malankara Mar Thoma Suvishesha Prasangha Sanghom" (Malayalam), In: George Alexander, ed., *Maramon Convention Sathabhdhi Valyam* (Malayalam), *op.cit.,* 168–169.

An Incarnation mission model

The "Incarnation model of mission" may be defined as a Christian mission model to adopt Jesus Christ's major life and mission engagements in the church's mission. The Incarnation of God through Jesus Christ invites the Church "to become living members of Christ's earthly community (Church) and to begin a life of service to others".[271] This would bring a new social order, in which, God's kingdom values dominate.[272] The new social order is not limited by any earthly institutions, and even by the Church. The Mar Thoma Church's mission, therefore, is to witness the message of incarnation – identification of God with the people and harsh world realities. However, as we have seen, the Mar Thoma Church's caste-conscious history seems to be an obstacle in its path to carry out its incarnation mission among the "outcastes". Therefore, the Mar Thoma Church's mission policy makers, during the last decade of the 19th Century CE thought that a change in the Mar Thoma Christian culture could be achieved through an internal cathartic process of renewal and regeneration. This was thought to be essential for accomplishing a broader outlook on mission, especially to extend Mar Thoma Church's mission among the "outcastes".

Renewal through revival

The leaders of the MTEA believed that to effect relevant cultural changes, there should be a spiritual revival through which the Mar Thoma Church's members might change themselves according to the incarnation value system. This could be achieved through the church's renewal in the light of the gospel within the oriental Church's liturgical premise. The church leaders suggested three means to achieve the renewal goal – conducting revival meetings, founding mission fields among "outcastes" and starting secular schools.

Revival meetings are regular Bible teaching meetings held annually at each parish of the Mar Thoma Church and at diocesan and regional levels, before the *Maramon Convention*.[273] The revival meetings primarily conducted by teachers

---

271 David J. Bosch, *Transforming Missions, Paradigm Shifts in Theology of Missions,* (New York: Orbis Books, 1992), 10–11.

272 Orlando E. Costas, "Christian Mission in the America," In: James A. Scherer and Stephen B. Bevans, ed, *New Directions in Mission and Evangelization- Theological Foundations* (Marknoll, New York: Orbis Books, 1994), 9.

273 The "Maramon Convention" is one of the largest annual Christian evangelistic conventions in the world. It started in1895 under the auspices of the MTEA. In the month

and preachers of the Word are aimed at educating the church. The Mar Thoma Church and the MTEA encouraged regular revival meetings, or "conventions", to be conducted in parishes every year. The season of conventions ends every year on the sand bed of the river Pamba, at Maramon, in Kerala, which has come to be known as *Maramon Convention*. Former MTEA general secretary KT Jacob,[274] in his article, "Maramon Convention Origin and Growth", in the book, *Maramon Convention Centenary Volume* (Malayalam), claims that the message from the Mar Thoma Church's convention was the major reason for the church's focus on spiritual revival of its members in its early contemporisation efforts.[275]

Revivalism in the church was effected through two phases. In the first phase, which could be termed evangelisation phase, the "lower caste" communities were sought to be drawn in to the church. Revival preachers, including converts from other religious, were encouraged to speak at the annual convention in different parishes.[276] This practice still continues.

These conventions, as M.M. Thomas says, is "where the spiritually revived received stability and nurture through preaching and teaching of the scripture".[277] These conventions brought converts from "lower caste" communities and other church members together under the Mar Thoma Church's roof, which was uncommon during the time.[278] The emerging new social context within the church enabled them – Mar Thoma Church members and new converts – to reap religious and social returns of mutual acceptance from interactions with each other.

In the second phase, the revival meetings inspired Mar Thoma Christians to turn to the gospel with a burning conviction, which led the church to intensify its mission to spread the Gospel message. Former vicar-general K.E. Oommen,

---

of February every year on the sand bed stretches of river *Pamba* at *Maramon*, Kerala, the convention convenes for a period of one week.

274 K.T. Jacob was a priest of the Mar Thoma Church, who served as a missionary, a managing committee member of the MTEA and the Clergy Trusty of the church.
See, K.T. Jacob, "Maramon Convention Uthbhavavum Valarchayum" (Malayalam), In: George Alexander, ed., Maramon *Convention Sathabhdhi Valyam* (Malayalam), *op.cit.*, 58–74.

275 *Ibid.*, 60–61.

276 K.E. Oommen, "M.T & E.A. Schools", In: *Mar Thoma Schoolukal (Malayalam), op. cit.*, 1–3.

277 C.P. Mathew, M.M. Thomas, *The Indian Churches of Saint Thomas*, Revised Edition, *op.cit.*, 104–105.

278 K.T. Jacob, "Maramon Convention Uthbhavavum Valarchayum" (Malayalam), In: George Alexander, ed., *Maramon Convention Sathabhdhi Valyam (Malayalam)*, *op.cit.*, 61.

whose son became the Metropolitan, Philipose Mar Chrysostom Mar Thoma, portrayed the influence of the revival meetings on the church:

> They had come to set a very high value of the daily reading and study of the Bible and also to accept the Bible as the primary authority in the doctrinal matters... In public worship ... on Sundays and other holidays, a sermon came to be an inevitable part of the service.[279]

It is evident that the revival meetings instilled a special importance for keeping personal piety among the church members. Including sermons at the corporate worship could be seen as an instance to support the church's new emphasis on spontaneity and to interpret the Bible in the light of the contemporary context.

K.T. Jacob provides extensive information about the nature of revival meetings as these conventions were open to all communities, including "outcastes". Considering the Mar Thoma Church's revival, most conventions defended the message of love and solidarity with the "outcastes". K.T. Jacob shows that there was a significant affirmation of the message of equality and evangelisation in sermons and songs in *Malayalam* during this period. For instance a convention's closing song had the following words: "Destroy caste distinction; take the flag of love; take the flag of the King Jesus' Gospel; elevate the flag with celebrations".[280] The MTEA, as L.W. Brown says, is "a society with very small beginnings which steadily permeated the whole church with a sense of responsibility for evangelism ..."[281]

A critical analysis shows a certain lack of ecclesiological and liturgical emphasis in the annual conventions at the parish, regional and diocesan levels and the Maramon conventions. This lack of emphasis is one major reason for the outflow from the Mar Thoma Church to the Brethren and Baptist churches, in the early decades of the 20th Century, and later to the Pentecostal and other independent groups.

It was evident that the church found it difficult to connect effectively its traditional oriental liturgical piety with the major changes in its evangelical revival context. This resulted in some less-informed preachers criticising the church's "mixing" of evangelical faith with its oriental liturgical moorings. Instead they wanted to emphasise spirituality based on individualistic pietism, over and above the oriental liturgical positioning.

This provided a space for some of the church members to try and water down its liturgical corporate worship base. This eventually developed into tension within the

---

279 *Ibid.*
280 *Ibid.*, The song was written in Malayalam and the translation is an independent English translation of the writer.
281 L.W. Brown, *The Indian Christians of St. Thomas*, *op.cit.*, 149.

church between its liturgical heritage and the new-found revivalism, which emphasised adult baptism, speaking in tongues and the second-coming of Christ.[282] This
tension prepared a ground for churches such as Baptist and Brethren to work among
the Mar Thoma Church members since the last decade of the 19th century.[283] Added
to this with other reasons were to result in a fresh schism within the church in 1961.[284]

The Mar Thoma Church continues to struggle with all those sectarian tendencies in the name of church-centred evangelicalism.[285] Since our study is designed
to be in line with the openness outlook of the Mar Thoma Church, this concern is
not dealt with at length in this study.

Ecumenism revived

Casteism in India[286] – which can be defined as the accordance of status to human
beings based on the "castes" in which they were born –was looked upon with
approval by the Mar Thoma Church as it was dominantly prevalent in the society
at that time. Professions, trade and work were caste-dependant and caste-based. A

---

282 C.P. Mathew, M.M. Thomas, *The Indian Churches of Saint Thomas*, Revised Edition,
      op.cit., 102–103; N.M. Mathew, *Malankara Mar Thoma Sabha Charithram* (Malay-
      alam), Vol. II, *op.cit.*, 174–175.
283 *Ibid.*, 168–170.
284 Having influenced by evangelicalism, some members of the Mar Thoma Church
      showed reluctance to integrate evangelical and eastern liturgical base in the church.
      They gave more emphasis on evangelicalism. This led to an internal struggle within
      the church and later the friction resulted in a schism in the church and subsequent for-
      mation of the St. Thomas Evangelical Church in 1961. Its headquarters is at Manjadi,
      Tiruvalla, Kerala.
285 C.P. Mathew, M.M. Thomas, *The Indian Churches of Saint Thomas*, Revised Edition,
      op.cit., 102–103.
286 Indian historians generally believe that the *Brahmin* migration to Kerala was domi-
      nant during the 8th century. This migration prepared a ground for the development of
      "Casteism" – "high caste", "lower caste" and "outcast" – in Kerala Society. Owing
      to the high entrepreneur nature of the Mar Thoma Christians, the local rulers gave
      Christians "high caste" positions. They granted special grants to them in 825 CE,
      which made them to have had equal social status with the "high caste" communities.
      This new elevated social position blinded the church to see the deplorable plight of
      "lower caste" communities. It was in this context that the work of the MTEA among
      the "lower caste" communities was significant. It was a departure from the church's
      previous mission policy and especially among the "lower caste" communities. See,
      A. Sreedhara Menon, *A survey of Kerala History, op.cit.*, 80–84.

poverty of aspiration was deliberately encouraged within the "lower castes". No one ever crossed caste boundaries; they were well defined and demarcated.

The Mar Thoma Church did not, somehow, foresee in "casteism" a potential danger for the propagation of the message of Gospel, although it stands against the incarnation principle of fellowship and equality of human beings. The crux of incarnation is the belief that God identifies with and is one with all kinds of people, irrespective of gender, class and colour. However, the Mar Thoma Church's new missionary consciousness helped it identify with the "lower caste" communities and start missions among them.

A new, strong and self-reliant missionary spirit and a will to work among the "lower caste" communities, formed the content of the MTEA at this stage.[287] This resulted in the inauguration of various mission fields among these communities in Kerala. These included the Othara mission in Central Travancore (1889), South Travancore Mission (1893), Sea Coast Mission (1903), North Travancore Mission (1905), Palghat Mission, (1924), Mukkola Mission (1935) and Guruvayoor Mission (1955). The Mar Thoma Church sent missionaries to these centres.

Currently the church has "56 mission fields spread over 17 states and two Union territories of India"[288] and "more than 750 mission personnel including missionaries, evangelists and *ashram* members"[289] working in these mission fields.

The conscious assertion of the Mar Thoma Church's inclusive evangelistic conviction thus reflected in the mission endeavours of the MTEA that included all communities under the incarnation message of the Gospel.

Mission strategy

The MTEA's mission strategies were personal evangelism, conventions and education, which were manifested in two phases. In the Keswick Spirituality phase[290],

---

287 See, Ninan Koshay, *Caste in the Kerala churches,* (Bangalore: The Christian Institute For The Study of Religion and Society, 1968), 23–24.

288 *Circular letter of C.K. Mathew, the General Secretary of the MTEA to all parishes,* dt April 17, 2011.

289 *Ibid.*

290 The Keswick Movement, which emphasised the winning souls to Christ by personal conversion, began in England as a series of conventions in 1874 by Hannah Whitall Smith and Robert Pearsall Smith and others. It emerged as a subsequent movement to the holiness movement that emerged in the United States of America in 1870. See, Donald W. Dayton, *The Higher Christian Life: A Bibliographical Over View* (New York: Garland Publishing, 1985), 23; David Bundy, "Keswick and the Experience of

the emphasis was on evangelisation for personal conversion and personal piety, while the incarnation mission phase provided an atmosphere for people to live as authentic human beings. The Mar Thoma Church's *ashrams* that developed since 1940 aimed to further the incarnation mission concept.

The Keswick mission strategy was dominant during the early decades of the 20th Century CE. The influence of Keswick spirituality on the Mar Thoma Church's mission could be seen in the following excerpts of church historian Alex Thomas:

> Keswick spirituality, which emphasized winning souls to Christ by personal conversion, began shaping the self-understanding of Mar Thoma Christians during the last decades of the 19th Century. It encouraged them to spread the gospel to people in an effort to lead them to a personal conversion to Christ. The influence of Keswick spirituality came to the Mar Thoma Church through revivals promoted by CMS missionaries such as Rev. Sabine Baring Gould, Rev. G. Karney, V.D. David, and L.N. Wordsworth, creating a passion for evangelism and holy living.[291]

It was clear that Keswick spirituality had an upper hand within the Mar Thoma Church's mission activities. The church missionaries emphasized individual conversion, holy living and immediate salvation for those accepting Jesus Christ as Saviour. In chapter III of his dissertation on the North Kanara Mission, Alex Thomas states that the early mission strategy of the church focused on the Keswick spirituality in many instances.[292] The Annual Report of the MTEA provides relevant information on the praxis of its mission strategy.

> On 20th *Makaram,* two public meetings were conducted at the market place at Vizhinjam, one at 10 a.m. and another at 5. p.m. Many people gathered from different places. In the afternoon some Hindu houses were visited and the gospel imparted. On 24th, a few were specially contacted and they gave themselves to the Lord. At night a meeting was held for the *Parayas.* They renounced sin and the devil and publicly accepted Jesus. More than 80 were present. On 25th, a meeting was held in a church near *Aaranmula,* and another one for the non-Christians who expressed interest in the Gospel.[293]

Evangelical Piety," In: Edith L. Blumhofer and Randall Balmer, eds., *Modern Christian Revivals*, (Urbana and Chicago: University of Illinois Press, 1993), 118; Charles Price and Ian Randall, *Transforming Keswick*, (U.K: OM Publishing, 2000), 15; E.H. Johnson, *The Highest Life: A Story of Shortcomings and a Goal* (New York: A.C. Armstrong and Son, 1901), 42–43.

291 Alex Thomas, A *Historical Survey of the North Kanara Mission of the Mar Thoma Church,* Dissertation, Boston, University of Boston, 2003, 71–72.

292 *Ibid.*

293 *17ᵗʰ Annual Report of the MTEA,* M.E. 1083 (1906), 16–17.

The objective of the mission, as is evidenced by this report, is to spread the message of the Gospel among non-Christians, especially to the "outcastes" and invite them for conversion into the Christian faith. While engaging in the mission, the church has always been alert in instructing its evangelists to spread the Gospel message, without condemning other religious cultures. The evangelists preached on Sundays at streets and circulated tracts which contain Christian messages. Besides, regular public conventions were organised by the evangelists to teach non-Christians messages from the Bible regularly.

Acts of social emancipation

The Mar Thoma Church considers solidarity with the acts of social emancipation as part of its mission. Evangelists preached against social discrimination and tried to create social and political awareness among the people to fight for equality and social justice. The missions stood for the abolition of slavery and untouchablity[294] in India's social system. The church provided Christian fellowship to those who converted to Christianity and joined the church.

Although it is difficult to assess the extent to which the mission strategy may be useful for the "outcaste" community's social emancipation, it nevertheless opened new possible choices. There were several instances in which the church's missionaries and evangelists identified with the "lower castes" with a view to encourage those "castes" to consider themselves equals with other communities. The Mar Thoma Church's evangelists in North Travancore ate in the houses of "lower caste" converts, against the social practice of those times.[295] M.A. Thomas

---

294 Untouchability was a socio-religious practice of ostracizing the India's "outcaste" communities by segregating them from the main stream by the *Brahmanical* Hindu social customs and rules. The socio-religious rules prevented them to approach or touch the "high caste" communities. In principle it was believed that the "outcaste" communities' approach or touch would pollute "high castes" members. So the socio-religious rules prevented the "outcaste" to use public roads, enter the temples, and public places. The Constitution of India prohibited this practice and made it punishable if any Indian being treated discriminately on the basis of his religion, language or race. See, Joseph Daniel, "Socio-Religious Impact of the Temple Entry Proclamation (1936) on Christian Community in Travancore", Unpublished B.D. Thesis, Kottayam: Mar Thoma Theological Seminary, 1994, 8–20.

295 M.A. Thomas, "Mar Thoma Church's Approach to Other religions and Mar Thoma Church's Socio-Political Involvement", In: *Mar Thoma Sabha Saradhikal* (Malayalam) (Tiruvalla: Mar Thoma Church Publication, 1993), 6.

explains another instance, which illustrates how the Mar Thoma Church established the right of "outcastes" to use public roads in Kerala.[296]

"There was an instance of an "upper caste" Hindu leader beating up a converted Christian at Valakom, in the district of Ernakulam in Kerala, for his refusal to leave the road. The Mar Thoma Church fought it out and made the Hindu leader apologise publicly.[297] It was also reported that the Travancore Government prohibited Chacko Sasthri, an evangelist of the Mar Thoma Church, from preaching the Gospel for three months as he organised the *Ezhava* community to fight for social equality".[298]

Mission work and a newly-envisioned social system that upheld social justice and human rights propagated by church evangelists expedited the influx of converts to the Mar Thoma Church. For example, 85 people belonging to the *pulaya* community were baptised by K.T. Thomas, a priest of the church at Othara near Tiruvalla in the Central Travancore Mission by 1891.[299] Similar congregations were formed from among converts in *"Pularikadu, Idayaranmula, Iravallipra, Anaprampal, Vengaza, Vettikonam, Perissery and Niranam"*[300] before the close of the 19th Century. The number of the converted-Christians in the church reached 2,543 in 23 congregations in 1910.[301] The Central Travancore Mission established 45 congregations and 39 schools by 1935.[302]

As can be seen from the reports of the MTEA, the Mar Thoma Church's membership and the congregations grew constantly over 60 years from 1889.[303] The North Travancore mission had 20 congregations and 13 schools in 1935.[304] Starting

---

296 *Ibid.*, "Outcastes" were forbidden to use Kerala public roads and Hindu religious temples until 1936. The Temple Entry Proclamation of the Travancore in 1936 by the local king of the princely state of Travancore opened all temples and roads to the "outcastes" in Kerala. See, Joseph Daniel, "Socio-Religious Impact of the Temple Entry Proclamation (1936) on Christian Community in Travancore", Unpublished B.D. Thesis, Kottayam: Mar Thoma Theological Seminary, 1994, 8–20.

297 M.A. Thomas, "Mar Thoma Church's Approach to Other religions and Mar Thoma Church's Socio-Political Involvement", In: *Mar Thoma Sabha Saradhikal* (Malayalam) (Tiruvalla: Mar Thoma Church Publication, 1993), 6.

298 J.W. Gladstone, *Keralathile Protestant Chritumathavum Bahujanaprastanagalum* (Malayalam), (Trivandrum: C.D – Siddi Publications, 2004), 262.

299 A.T. Philip, *The Mar Thoma Church and the Kerala Society, op.cit.*, 47.

300 *Ibid.* 47–48.

301 *23rd Annual Report of the Mar Thoma Evangelistic Association*, 1911, (Tiruvalla: MTEA Office, 1911), xv.

302 *Ibid.*

303 *Annual Reports of the Mar Thoma Evangelistic Association*, 1948.

304 *Annual Report of the Mar Thoma Evangelistic Association*, 1937.

from zero in 1908, the South Travancore Mission membership level and congregation numbers had reached 2000 members and 23 congregations by 1949.[305] This trend has been continuing in all mission fields.

Several evangelists and priests were trained from among the new converts, as a result of the efforts of the missions. P. Chacko, a member of the Kumbanadu congregation, became a member of the legislative assembly of Travancore and Kerala.[306]

What motivated the "lower caste" communities to join the Mar Thoma Church and to form new parishes were the Christian idea of fellowship and the offer of free salvation, together with their social position as the members of the Mar Thoma Church. The conversion rate of "lower castes" to the church was higher than that of the "higher castes" because of this. The numerical growth of the "lower-caste" communities in the church is indeed significant, but what was more important was the change in a predominantly "high-caste" church's mission perspective to consciously become more inclusive.

However, the true significance of the Mar Thoma Church's stand has not been appreciated in its local parishes. Higher conversion rates during 1910's led to a higher percentage of Mar Thoma Church membership in local parishes. But, in most parishes, the traditional Mar Thoma Church members opposed the admission of the converts from "lower caste" communities as members with full constitutional rights and privileges in their local parishes.[307] This discriminated the newly converted members within the church.

To resolve this deadlock, the Mar Thoma Church decided to form *Puthusabha*[308] congregations within the Mar Thoma Church under the supervision of the

---

305 M.M. Thomas was a regular visitor to the South Travancore mission field and he appreciated the progress of the church's mission among the "lower castes". He says: "I joined a youth team in regular visit to a locality of "low caste" Hindu residence to preach Christ to them."
See, M.M. Thomas, "My Pilgrimage in Mission", In: *N.C.C Review,* Vol. CIX, (October, 1989); M.M. Thomas, "My Pilgrimage in Mission", In: *International Bulletin of Missionary Research,* 13, No. 1 (1989), 28–31.

306 P. Chacko was a member of the Kerala Legislative Assembly during 1947, 1954 and 1960–1965. Being a high school teacher, he dedicated his life for social reforms and the upbringing of "lower caste" communities. He was a member of the "All Indian Congress Committee", which is the national political party since 1885. He also held several coveted posts in the Government of Kerala.

307 P.J. Thomas, *Mar Thoma Church and Its Message, op.cit.,* 42–43.

308 *Puthusabha* is a Malayalam word, which means "New Church".

MTEA, bereft of constitutional privileges entitled to the local parishes.[309] This arrangement continued till 1979 when the Church's general body decided to elevate *Puthusabha* congregations into the status of full-fledged parishes, with all constitutional rights and privileges entitled to regular church members.[310] But discrimination prevails within the church and this will be dealt with later.

Educating the 'outcastes'

Besides preaching the gospel to the "outcastes", attention was given by the Mar Thoma Church for their educational and economic progress.[311] The history of education in Kerala during the last two centuries would show the contributions of the Mar Thoma Church. The Western missionaries, churches and religious organisations were in the forefront of education.[312] Before the British period (1800–1947), each Kerala region[313] had its own system of education. Residential *Vedic* schools were popular during the Ninth, Tenth and 11th centuries CE. Admission in these schools to study subjects such as science, Sanskrit, philosophy and "*vedas*" was restricted to Brahmin students. Non-Brahmin students learned the language from *ezhuthupallikoodam*[314] (old-style elementary village school). However, the "lower caste" and the "outcaste" children were denied the right to education.[315]

---

309 Parishes entitle to send representatives to the *Mandalam* (General Body) in proportion to its number of members in the parish. For instance, those parishes with 100 to 2000 members have to send one representative and similarly members from 2001 to 5000, two representatives, and those with membership exceeding 5000, three representatives. Clause 77, *Constitution, Mar Thoma Syrian Church of Malabar, op. cit.*, 30

310 *The Minutes of the General Body of the Mar Thoma Syrian Church,* held on 9, May 1979, VJT Hall, Tiruvalla.

311 C.P. Mathew, M.M. Thomas, *The Indian Churches of Saint Thomas*, Revised Edition, *op.cit.*, 106.

312 K.K. George, George Zacharia and Ajith Kumar, "Grants-in-Aid" *Policies and Practices Towards Secondary Education in Kerala,* (New Delhi: National Institute of Educational Planning and Administration, 2002), 1.

313 During the British period, Kerala comprises of three Kingdoms – Travancore, Cochin and Malabar.

314 The *ezhuthupallikoodam* is a *Malayalam* word, which denotes school. Earlier the schools in Kerala were called as *Ezhuthupallikoodam* or *ezhuthupalli* or *pallikoodam*. It is significant that the *Malayalam* word for church is *palli* and the name for the school has its debt to the church *(palli)* as it attached to the church and it is called *pallikoodam*.

315 *Ibid.*, 1–2.

The beginning of modern education in Travancore had its debt to the issue of a Royal Order in 1817, by the then Travancore ruler, Queen Gouri Parvathi Bai (1815–1829), under the direction of the British resident, Col. Munroe. The Royal Order held that "the state should defray the entire cost of education of his people".[316] The Government started English and district schools in 1839.

T. Madhava Rao (1828–1891), the *Diwan* of Travancore, took special interest in starting vernacular schools during 1862–1874.[317] His educational plan of 1865–1866 enabled private agencies to start schools using grant-in-aid[318] from the government. Within a period of 20 years the number of schools increased from 20 to 1,388.[319] The total number of students enrolled had risen to 57,314 by 1893–1894.[320] It was during this period that the Mar Thoma Church also entered the field of elementary education by founding schools. K.E. Oommen (1881–1984) states that the reason for starting schools under the auspices of the church was "the desire of its members to read the Bible".[321] He says:

People had Bibles and they wanted to read but there were only very few people who could read and write. So they wanted their children to learn to read the Bible at home. Hence primary schools were started wherever possible with the grant-in-aid system. It resulted in the church beginning several schools in various places. The church has shown great enthusiasm to start English schools also with a view to equip children to read the commentaries of the Bible. The church appointed a school inspector to look after the ones started and to persuade and help people to start new schools and to secure the grants-in-aid for them.[322]

316 Cited In: *Ibid.*, 3.
317 A. Sreedhara Menon, *A Survey of Kerala History, op. cit.*, 280–281.
318 The Elementary Education Act of 1880 in the British Parliament made the elementary education in Great Britain compulsory. On the pretext of this Act, Rama Varma Vishakam Tirunal (1880–1885) of the Travancore, being a British subject, promoted elementary education to his subjects. Besides, he encouraged private agencies to start elementary schools. For this, he set apart a fund – "Grants-in-Aid" – for the promotion of elementary education. The "Grants-in-Aid" system encouraged to construct school building by providing one-third of the cost of construction to the private school managements in Travancore.
319 K.K. George, George Zacharia and Ajith Kumar, *Grants in Aid Policies and Practices Towards Secondary Education in Kerala, op.cit.*, 4.
320 *Ibid.*, 3–4.
321 *Ibid.*, 1–3.
322 *Ibid.*, A. Sreedhara Menon, *A Cultural Heritage of Kerala,* 2nd Ed., (Madras: V. Subramanyam, 1996), 163; Malabar Gazetteer (Malayalam), Vol. 3, Madras, 147.

The Mar Thoma Church started schools to provide learning to read and meditate the Bible with the assistance of commentaries through the medium of English and in vernacular, and provide elementary education to the converts from the "lower castes".[323] The Mar Thoma Seminary High School was started in Kottayam in 1896 and the Syrian Christian Seminary School, Tiruvalla in 1902. Several other lower primary and upper primary schools were started during this period. The Mar Thoma Church had 65 schools including primary and high schools by 1910.[324]

The Mar Thoma Church opened its schools for the education of "lower caste" communities.[325] It was only in 1904 that the Travancore government took upon itself the responsibility to provide education to all children irrespective of caste and religion.[326] Although the Government of Travancore's Education code of 1910 enabled the "lower caste" children to study at schools, teachers belonging to the "upper caste" were reluctant to teach them. The active government intervention started to ensure education to them only after 1914.[327] However, the Mar Thoma Church enrolled "lower caste" and "outcaste" children in the church's schools since its inception, ignoring the objections of the "upper caste" teachers and students.

The founding of schools which could impart education to the "lower caste" communities was Mar Thoma Church's most effective step in its effort to practice ecumenism in India's wider community. For example the history of the lower primary school at Keerampara in Kerala testifies this: "It aimed at providing education to the converts from the "lower castes" in the church".[328]

"Schools admitted children from "lower caste" and taught them along with the "high caste" Hindus and Christians and thus it provided an atmosphere to integrate children, who were of different religious and caste groups, together in an atmosphere of Christian fellowship".[329]

---

323 K.E. Oommen, "M.T & E.A. Schools", In: *Mar Thoma Schoolukal* (Malayalam), *op. cit.*, 1–3, 89.

324 *Mar Thoma Schoolukal Charitra Samkshepam* (Malayalam), *op.cit.*, 1–159. This book contains a concise history of the M.T. Church's schools.

325 The "lower caste" communities – Ezhavas, Channars, and the "outcaste" communities such as *Pulayas, Parayas, Vetas* – were not allowed to study with "high-caste" children at schools in Kerala until 1910.

326 K.K. George, George Zacharia and Ajith Kumar, "Grants-in-Aid" *Policies and Practices Towards Secondary Education in Kerala, op.cit.*, 5.

327 *Ibid.*

328 K.E. Oommen, "M.T & E.A. Schools", In: *Mar Thoma Schoolukal* (Malayalam), *op. cit.*, 89.

329 *Ibid.*

Thus the initial phase of the Mar Thoma Church's mission endeavours demonstrate that the Church integrated evangelical faith, Eastern liturgical faith, mission centre planting, retreat from "casteism" and an incarnation-oriented mission in its distinctive ecumenical way. We shall now briefly examine the Mar Thoma Church's constitutional history in order to see whether and how far the spirit of the Mar Thoma Church's constitution cherished its broader outlook.

Democratic church polity

The broader outlook of the Mar Thoma Church could be seen in the reorganisation of its administrative set-up in a democratic way, which is considered as a pioneering attempt among the Mar Thoma Christians in India. It is now appropriate to enquire how the traditional aspect of the Church's oligarchic administrative set-up gave way to the adoption of a democratic constitution. What is attempted here is a historical interpretation the Mar Thoma Church's broader outlook to integrate western democratic church polity with its Episcopal polity as reflected in its constitutional history.

The Mar Thoma Church's democratic administrative system is a basic administrative feature, and as such the church expects it to be sharply implemented in its social existence. It is in continuity with the Mar Thoma Church's evangelical emphasis, spirit of liberal individualism and Episcopal polity.[330] Western education through mission and schools, that made known the spirit of liberal individualism and individual responsibility to the Mar Thoma Church, created a viable atmosphere for the Metropolitan and its leaders to come into positive interaction with Western democratic principles.

The Mar Thoma Church's administration from the time of the Mar Thoma I (1653–1670) to the time of Thomas Mar Athanasius (1877–1893) was oligarchic.[331] The administration of a local parish rested with the vicar ordained for the parish and the treasurer from a dominant family for life. The governance of the Church was under the control of the Metropolitan. However, within the Mar Thoma Church's reform context, the then Metropolitan, Thomas Mar Athanasius, started a clergy council to assist him in the church's administration in 1876.

---

330 "Mar Thoma Bharana Samvidhanam" (Malayalam), In: P.M. Thomas, ed., Mar Thoma Sabha Directory, op.cit., 128–131.
331 T.C. Chacko, Malankara Mar Thoma Sabha Charithram (Malayalam), op.cit., 191.

This marked the beginning of a shift in the administrative set-up of the church towards a democratic line. Meetings of the clergy were arranged regularly in the following years.

Thomas Mar Athanasius' successor, Titus I, moved an idea of forming a church managing committee'[332], and a *samastalochana sabha*,[333] (general body) which comprises of both clergy and laity, for the Mar Thoma Church's general administration. He authorised the then Vicar-General, Ipe Thoma Kathanar, to organise and convene a *samastalochana sabha* to discuss the Mar Thoma Church's administrative set-up. The meeting was held in Tiruvalla in 1896, when the general body elected a managing committee from among clergy and laity, with the Metropolitan presiding. Another meeting of the *samastalochana sabha* was held at Kozhencherry in Kerala in the same year to study the draft constitution, which was prepared in 1895 in which both, democratic and Episcopal polity were included.[334]

Within four years the Mar Thoma Church organised a new administrative set-up for parishes and the message had been carried to the local parishes. The *samastalochana sabha* representing clergy and laity from 47 parishes was held at *Maramon* in May 21, 1901, and this meeting adopted the new Constitution.[335] The church also made necessary and relevant revisions in the Constitution.

The Constitution defines the Mar Thoma Church's administrative set-up in the parish, dioceses and centres. Its central administrative set-up consists of the Metropolitan, the Episcopal Synod,[336] the *Prathinithi Mandalam*[337] (council of

---

332 It is called the "Sabha Council".
333 *Samastalochanasabha* is a Malayalam word meaning "General Consultative Assembly" and its present constitutional form is *sabha Pradhinidhi Mandalam* (general assembly of the church).
334 "Mar Thoma Bharana Samvidhanam" (Malayalam), In: P.M. Thomas, ed., *Mar Thoma Sabha Directory, op.cit.*, 128–131.
335 N.M. Mathew, *Malankara Mar Thoma Sabha Charithram*, Vol. II, *op. cit.*, 158.
336 The episcopal synod of the church helps the Metropolitan in the general administration. It approves decisions of the *prathinidhi mandalam* and the *diocesan assemblies*. Matters pertaining to the clergy and the revision of the liturgy are rest with the Episcopal synod. See, *Mar Thoma Syrian Church of Malabar Constitution*, Revised, English Version, (Tiruvalla: Mar Thoma Syrian Church, 2002), 28–29.
337 The *prathinidhi mandalam* consists of the Metropolitan, bishops, vicars generals, representatives of the clergy and parishes, representatives of the Mar Thoma Church's recognised institutions, representatives of those who have become the church members as a result of its missionary work and persons nominated by the Metropolitan. A significant feature of the legislative assembly is that 65 percent of its members are from laity and the rest from among the clergy. The *prathinidhi mandalam* elects the

representatives) and the *Sabha Council* (church council).[338] The constitution also defined an elaborative administrative set-up for the parish and the dioceses. The Metropolitan[339] is the Church's head and Bishops assist him.

With the assistance of the episcopal synod and the *sabha council*, the Metropolitan formed the Dioceses. He is the president of all the Mar Thoma Church's administrative offices and the ex-officio trustee.[340] M.M. Thomas summarises the nature of the constitution as follows:

> It was therefore a revolutionary change when the Mar Thoma Church adopted a democratic constitution based on adult franchise and made the officers of the *idavakas* (parishes) and of the church elective and converted monarchical episcopacy in to a constitutional one.[341]

The Mar Thoma Church's democratic administrative set-up, as we have seen, is a mix of episcopal polity and democratic system. The episcopal polity approves a hierarchical form of church governance with chief authority over a church resting in the Metropolitan together with democratic participation by the people. However, the Mar Thoma Church's episcopacy is constitutional in nature, which necessitates more than 75 percent votes of the *Prathinithi Mandalam*, from the clergy and the laity separately. This is mandatory for a candidate to get elected as a Bishop.[342]

---

secretary, lay trustee, and clergy trustee. It decides all administrative and spiritual matters including annual report, accounts and budget while it is in session once a year. See, *Constitution of the Mar Thoma Syrian Church of Malabar, op.cit.,* 29–49.

338 The *sabha council* is the executive body of the *prathinidhi mandalam*. The metropolitan, bishops, the senior vicar general, trustees and secretary are ex-officio members of the council, besides the elected members from various dioceses, and the members of the *prathinidhi mandalam*, for the tenure of three years. The council has the power to implement the decisions of the *prathinidhi mandalam* which are approved by the Synod and confirmed by the Metropolitan.
   Sabha council is the Mar Thoma Church's executive body. See, *Ibid.,* 49–54.

339 The senior most bishop is installed as the metropolitan from among the church's bishops. *Ibid.,* 3.

340 *Ibid.,* 3–4.

341 C.P. Mathew, M.M. Thomas, *The Indian Churches of Saint Thomas, Revised Edition, op.cit.,* 111.

342 *Ibid.*

Chapter VI
Project for Indian Evangelisation

The Mar Thoma Church's history during 1905–1948 moved in tandem with that of Indian Christianity and the global ecumenical movement.[343] Different European mission agencies had started operations in India since the early 18th Century CE. To fight against "casteism" and social inequalities, the missionaries felt that

---

343 The ecumenical movement was an outcome of the evangelical awakening in the western protestant churches, during the 18th and the 19th centuries. The modern evangelical awakening had its root in German pietism, which was a movement that arose in the Lutheran church as a reaction against the sterility of the then prevailing Lutheran orthodoxy in Germany by the end of seventeenth century. Having been influenced by the spirit of evangelical awakening many European churches including the Moravians considered missionary work as Church's primary responsibility in the world. In consequence, several protestant missionary movements –the Tranquebar Mission (1706), the Basel Mission and the Church Missionary Society sent its missionaries to India. King Frederic IV of Denmark took the responsibility to send missionaries to India. He sent two German missionaries, the Saxon Bartholomaeus Ziegenbalg (1682–1719) and Henrich Pluetschau of Malchenburg (1677–1746) to India. See, Gerhard Rosenkranz, *Die Christliche Missionsgeschichte und Theologie,* (München: Christian Kaiser Verlag, 1977), 164. The Baptist Missionary Society had its beginning in India by the arrival of William Carey (1761–1834), its founder missionary in Calcutta in 1793. The Serampore Mission (1793) and the Church Missionary Society (1799) also sent its missionaries to different countries including India. The missionaries started philanthropic activities as part of their mission work in their mission fields. The missionaries felt that if Christian fellowship achieve there would be better prospects for accomplishing social goals. Apparently there emerged missionary co-operation between different mission societies in the mission fields. The result was the unity and mutual acceptance of missionaries in mission fields. These societies and movements became pioneer movements for modern ecumenical movement. Ruth Rouse succinctly articulates this international mission phenomenon as "they were not ecumenical in objective. Each had some specific aim of its own-missionary work or social reform but though not ecumenical in aim, they were ecumenical in result". See, Ruth Rouse, "Voluntary Movements and the Changing Ecumenical Climate", In: Ruth Rouse and Stephen Charles Neill, eds., *A History of the Ecumenical Movement 1517–1948, op.cit.,* 309–310; J.W. Gladstone, *Protestant Christianity and People's Movement in Kerala,* Dissertation, Hamburg: University of Hamburg, 1983, 1–15.

co-operation with the British colonial power and other missionary movements was inevitable in India. This thinking prepared the ground for co-operation between missions in India. The missionaries started to get together for prayer and discussions on problems in their mission fields.

One such meeting was held in the late 19th Century, when Anglican, Baptist and Congregationalist missionaries attended a meeting in Henry Martin's pagoda in Hooghly, Calcutta.[344] The non-partisan nature of those meetings was described by Pearce Carey as follows:

> "… As the shadow of bigotry never falls upon us here, we talk sweet counsel and go together to God's House as friends".[345]

Such meetings discussed matters such as comity and mission co-operation. However, the rise of Indian nationalism against British colonialism and missionary paternalism motivated Indian Christians to focus more on indigenous missionary societies, with evangelization of India by Indians being the guiding principle.

Mission with a mandate

The National Missionary Society, a group of different denominations in India founded in 1905, is India's first indigenous missionary organisation. The society has the mandate for evangelization from the synods of the Mar Thoma Syrian Church, the Church of South India, the Church of North India and other protestant churches.[346]

The founding of the NMS was the culmination of the process of Indian Christian nationalism that began during the last decades of the 19th Century CE. Is Mar Thoma Church's mission outlook the result of its broader outlook towards nationalism? Could the church's first cross-cultural mission in North Kanara be seen as its institutional expression of missionary co-operation for an indigenous mission?

Since the middle of the 19th Century, a crisis of identity among Christians in India had been felt in the context of western imperialism as nationalist Indians believed that the agenda of Western colonialists was to convert Indians to the Christian faith and disintegrate the Indian culture.[347] Politically, nationalism

---

344 Henry Martin Pagoda was a pre-Muslim period (1526–1857) ruin site of a Hindu temple, which is situated in between Saraswati and Hoogli at Serampore, in Calcutta, India.

345 Pearce Carey, *William Carey*, London 1923, In: Ruth Rouse, *Ibid.*, 311.

346 *www.national-missionary-society-of-india/part1.com*, visited on 13th March 2011.

347 This statement was not applicable to all British missionaries, especially to the Oriental scholars like William Jones (1746–1794), and Charles Wilkins (1749–1836),

appeared as a result of widespread "impatience to British rule and an aspiration towards *swaraj,* or self rule"[348], and the Indian National Congress (1885), a political organization, adopted *swaraj* as its watchword to oust British imperialists.

British missionaries considered Indians as uncivilised and superstitious and they embarked on a "civilization" effort by imposing Western culture through English education. The intention of British missionaries was reflected in the words of Alexander Duff (1806–1878).[349] He says:

> "... to increase and multiply Christians is to increase and multiply the only class of truly staunch and loyal subjects of the British crown".[350]

Being British evangelicals,[351] as we have seen, the CMS missionaries also followed the same cultural imperialist attitude[352] in their efforts for the conversion of Indians to Christianity and their reforms in the Kerala society.

But historian George Thomas says:

> "... for a traditional (Indian) society, in which politics and religion existed in sanctioning the values in one another, the degrading of its own religion was the most humiliating. But that was exactly what the colonists and the missionaries performed in the nineteenth century in India."[353]

---

who unearthed the past cultural glory of India and they maintained a high regard to the Indian sacred texts and Indian spirituality. This will be dealt with in details in the following section of this study.

348 *Ibid.,* 248.

349 Alexander Duff (1806–1878) was a Scottish Presbyterian missionary, who began his work in Calcutta in 1830. His contribution on western education in India was commendable.

350 Kaj Baago, "Book Review of Colonialism and Christian Missions", by Stephen Neill, London, 1966, In: *Indian Church History Review,* (December, 1967), 165. R.C. Majumdar, *An Advanced history of India,* Reprinted, (London: Macmillan and Company Limited, 1953), 818.

351 The British evangelicalism was a movement in the Church of England during 1860s and 1870s. This was an offshoot of the evangelical zeal and enthusiasm of a group of members of the Church of England to fight against moral corruption. They were known as British Evangelicals. Charles Grant (1746–1823), William Wilberforce (1753–1833) and others were chief promoters of this movement. They prepared the Church of England for mission.

352 The superiority complex of the British missionaries about their continent and culture was evident in their mission work. So they considered that it was their responsibility to civilize the east by implanting the western culture in the east.

353 George Thomas, *Christian Indians and Indian Nationalism 1885–1950*, (Frankfurt: Verlag Peter D. Lang, 1979), 46.

This resulted in the reaction of educated Indians against the imperialistic attitude of western missionaries. Political and religious nationalism started getting asserted against western Christian missions and British imperialism. Religiously, the Arya Samaj (1875), the Ramakrishna Mission (1896) and such other socio-religious organisations, which upheld Indian nationalism, culture and religious ethos, were founded in India to counter imperialism.

In contrast to the British missionary attitude, the Serampore Mission that mostly consisted of Scottish missionaries and the German-origin Basel Mission had a positive attitude to Indian culture and religion. They wanted to revitalise the Indian culture and languages and allowed Christian values to be assimilated into Indian culture.[354] The Basel mission[355] sought to revitalise the *Malayalam* language and culture. Missionaries attempted to study Indian culture and India's languages with a view to revitalise it.

William Ward, part of the Serampore Trio, says:

"We have carefully avoided everything which might anglicise the converts. We have made no changes in their dress, their names, their food, their language and their domestic habits".[356]

---

354 David Kopf, *British Orientalism and the Bengal Renaissance, The Dynamics of Indian Modernization 1773–1835* (Los Angles: Berkeley, 1969), 80–94; Tara Chand, *History of the Freedom Movement in India*, Vol. II, (New Delhi: Publication Division: Ministry of Information and Broadcasting, 1967), 180–185.

355 The Basel Evangelical Missionary Society commonly known as the "Basel Mission" was formed by a group of Christians – both clergy and laymen – belonging to the Reformed Church of Basel and the Lutheran Church of Wurtenberg at Basel in 1815. This was in the context of the fall of Napoleon at Waterloo in the same year. They decided to start a seminary for the training of missionaries at Basel with an intention to train missionary candidates of the Dutch and British missions. The East India Company Act of 1813 at the British Parliament enabled the Basel Mission, along with other missionaries to send its missionaries to India and they reached in India on 12th February, 1834. The main areas of their activities were in Malabar, which is on the southern coast of India and in North Karwar, which is situated in the present Karnataka state in India. The Basel Mission made lasting imprints on India by the introduction of clock manufacturing and printing press as well as the literary contributions such as the *Kannada*-English Dictionary, English-*Malayalam* Dictionary, *Malayalam* grammar text and so on.

356 David Kopf, *British Orientalism and the Bengal Renaissance, The Dynamics of Indian Modernization 1773–1835, op.cit.*, 261.

The result was the development of a consciousness among Indian Christians about the rich heritage of Indian culture and about their responsibility to spread the Gospel. This eventually helped the growth of nascent nationalism in India. Both educated Indians and Indian Christians, who were influenced by Indian nationalism, came to regard western missions in India as icons of western imperialism around the last decades of the 19ᵗʰ Century and the early decades of the 20ᵗʰ Century. It was at this point that the Indian Christians began to "uphold the conscious assertion of Indian rights and ethos against those of the west in politics, society and religion".[357]

The protest of Indian Christians against western missionary paternalism became apparent as they made conscious attempts to start indigenous churches, independent of western missionary control: *Christo samaj* in Calcutta by K.C. Banurji (1847–1907)[358] in 1887 and The National Church of India at Madras by Puleny Andy (1831–1909)[359] in 1886 were the outcome of such efforts. Both movements aimed at "uniting the various denominations, and having one united church as suited to the national peculiarities and instincts of the people".[360]

It was in this context that the NMS was founded by V.S. Azariah (1874–1945)[361], K.C. Banurji, K.T. Paul (1876–1931)[362] and others in Serampore in 1905. This could be seen as the culmination of the desire of Indian Christians to form an indigenous mission organization from different denominations. The NMS upholds three

---

357 George Thomas, *Christian Indians and Indian Nationalism 1885–1950, op.cit.*, 146.
358 Kali Charan Banurjee (1847–1907), a practicing lawyer by profession was an illustrious Brahmin convert to Christianity in 1864. He was also a pioneer in the Indian Christian movement and Indian nationalism.
359 Pulney Andy (1831–1909) was a convert from "high caste" Hindu community in Trichnopoly near Madras to Christianity in 1863. He studied at London, from where he was being influenced by Christianity, liberalism and nationalism. He was a pioneer in the Indian Christian movement.
360 *A collection of Papers Connected with the Movement of the National Church of India,* (Madras: Cosmopolite Press, 1893), 7; George Thomas, *Christian Indians and Indian Nationalism 1885–1950, op.cit.*, 79; Kaj Baago, *Pioneers of Indigenous Christianity*, (Madras: Christian Literature society, 1969), 7–11.
361 Vedanayagam Samuel Azariah (1874–1945) was a nationalist Indian Christian and the first Anglican Bishop of the Dornakkal Diocese of the Anglican Church in India. He also served as the first general secretary of NMS.
362 K.T. Paul (1876–1931), the first general secretary of the YMCA in India, was an Indian Christian and an ardent follower of Mahatma Gandhi. He was the first treasurer and later a General Secretary (1909) of the NMS. See, Gerald H. Anderson ed., *Biographical Dictionary of Christian Missions*, (Michigan/Cambridge: Wm B. Eardmanns, 1999), 521.

principles: "Indian leadership", "indigenous methods" and "Indian money".[363] Delegates from five denominations from seven political divisions of India[364] and Ceylon gathered during the meeting.[365] As for the leaders of the NMS, "the evangelistic concern was the manifestation of patriotism"[366] and they held the conviction that the mission of churches in India was "primarily the responsibility of Indians and that for the fulfilment of this mission, indigenous methods are to be adopted".[367] They decided to send letters to all Christian denominations seeking support to NMS, stating:

> "We stand between a hundred million of our fellow countrymen without Christ, and the Christian community could be aroused to give them the Gospel".[368]

The Mar Thoma Church, as part of its indigenous missionary initiative directed the MTEA to support fully the mission policy of the NMS in 1905. The Mar Thoma Church joined with the NMS in achieving its aim, as Banurji Harnam Singh and Sathianathan, Christian leaders in India, in their joint letter to fellow Christians confirmed:

> "To awaken in our people a national consciousness, to create in them a sense of true patriotism, and to unite in the cause of the evangelisation of the country the Indian Christians of all denominations and provinces, it has been placed in the hearts of many of our brethren to organise a National Missionary Society of India..."[369]

After having felt the need for missionary work in India, the Mar Thoma Church decided to support it, and it is well-reflected in these words of Alexander Mar Thoma:

> "As a completely Indian Church, the Mar Thoma Church appreciated this stand, and actively participated in the NMS from the beginning".[370]

The church's decision led it to work together with the NMS in North Kanara.

---

363 "The Constitution of the National Missionary Society of India", In: *The National Missionary Intelligencer*, Vol. X, No. 3 (March/1916): 40; V.S. Azariah, *India and the Christian Movement* (Madras: The Christian Literature Society of India, 1936), 95; George Thomas, *Christian Indians and Indian Nationalism 1885–1950, op.cit., 146; The First Twenty Five Years of the National Missionary Society*, 1905–1930, *op.cit.*, 4.

364 Seven political divisions of India during the British rule were Assam, Bengal, Bombay, Burma, Madras, Punjab and United Province.

365 *The First Twenty Five Years of the National Missionary Society*, 1905–1930, *op.cit.*, 2.

366 George Thomas, *Christian Indians and Indian Nationalism 1885–1950, op.cit.*, 146.

367 Alexander Mar Thoma, *The Mar Thoma Church: Heritage and Mission, op.cit.*, 94.

368 Donald Fossett Ebright, *The National Missionary Society of India, 1905–1942: An Expression of the Movement toward Indigenization within the Indian Christian Community, Dissertation*, Chicago, IL: University of Chicago, 1944, 94.

369 Cited In: *Ibid.*, 80.

370 Alexander Mar Thoma, *The Mar Thoma Church: Heritage and Mission, op.cit.*, 94; N.M. Mathew, *Malankara Mar Thoma Sabha Charithram*, Vol. II, (Malayalam),

Missionary joint venture

The decision of the MTEA in 1905 to start joint missions with the NMS[371] resulted in the "North Kanara Mission", the church's first joint mission outside Kerala. Earlier, in seeking the support of the church, NMS wanted "to secure the co-operation of the oldest and in many ways the most important community in the land".[372] In the light of the Mar Thoma Church's positive response, the NMS included the Mar Thoma Church in its mailing list.[373]

The Mar Thoma Church, in turn, decided to invite NMS organizing secretary K.T. Paul with the intention of understanding from him the goals of the missionary body.[374] Paul arrived in Kerala in 1906 and conveyed its aims to the Mar Thoma Church.

These developments resulted in the church deciding to venture into a joint mission work with the NMS. The executive of NMS accepted the offer "with joy … After many inquiries and negotiations, a part of the North Kanara District of the Bombay Presidency was finally fixed in September 1909 as the field for the Syrians and appeals made to send missionaries".[375] It was originally a Basel Mission field, about to be taken over by the NMS from the German mission by an agreement in September, 1909.[376]

A final agreement between the NMS and the Basel Mission was reached in 1912. This gave NMS the responsibility for the Karwar, Ankola, Supa, and Halyal taluks, as well as the northern part of the Yellapur taluk, which together comprised the North Kanara mission field, where the Mar Thoma Church and the NMS started their first joint mission outside Kerala.[377] Consequently in 1910, the Mar

---

  op.cit., 166; *The First Ten Years of the National Missionary Society,* 1905–1915. P.M. Thomas ed., *Mar Thoma Sabha Directory*, (Malayalam), *op. cit.*, 144.

371 17th *Annual Report of the Evangelistic Association* for the year 1905, 2–3.
372 *The National Missionary Intelligencer*, Vol. X, No. 2, (February/1916), 135.
373 Alex Thomas, *A Historical Survey of the North Kanara Mission of the Mar Thoma Church, Dissertation, op.cit.*, 121.
374 Donald Fossett Ebright, *The National Missionary Society of India,* 1905–1942: *An Expression of the Movement toward Indigenization within the Indian Christian Community, Dissertation, op.cit.*, 134; See, Alex Thomas, *A Historical Survey of the North Kanara Mission of the Mar Thoma Church, op.cit.*, 123.
375 *The National Missionary Intelligencer*, Vol. X, No. 3 (March/1916): 138; Donald Fossett Ebright, *The National Missionary Society of India,* 1905–1942, *op.cit.*, 134.
376 *Report of the Basel Mission in South Western India,* 1912, 63.
377 The official documents of the Evangelistic Association termed this mission as "Foreign Mission". However, Alex Thomas referred it as a "cross-cultural" mission. See,

Thoma Church sent P.S. Mathai, P.O. Philip, and P.T. Varghese[378] to North Kanara as the church's pioneering missionaries. P.O. Philip became the general secretary of the NMS in 1917.

North Kanara, having an area of about 3,976 square miles, was part of British India (1858–1947). As a backward district, the North Kanara region was predominantly a "lower caste" Hindu area. The Roman Catholic missionaries were pioneers, who had mission centres there since the 16th Century. They were followed by the Basel Mission, which started their mission work at Honavar and Karwar in the region in 1834.

Initially, the Mar Thoma missionaries joined the Basel missionaries in their work, while they learned the regional *Konkani* and *Kannada*[379] languages.[380] They involved themselves in efforts such as education through the Basel Mission School,[381] work against "castiesm" and evangelism.[382] The evangelists worked hard to alleviate the "caste system" and prostitution.

Religiously sanctioned temple prostitution had roots in India's "caste system".[383] Alex Thomas says: "The evangelists reckoned this as a social evil and appealed for its eradication".[384] The concerted long-term efforts of the missionaries created awareness among the women-folk and it eventually helped the society to abandon

Alex Thomas, *A Historical Survey of the North Kanara Mission of the Mar Thoma Church, op.cit.*, 141.

378 *22nd Annual Report of the Evangelistic Association for the year 1909–1910*, 9. P.T. Varghese was an ordained minister of the Mar Thoma Syrian Church.

379 *Konkani* and *kannada* are two South Indian languages.

380 Donald Fossett Ebright, *The National Missionary Society of India, 1905–1942: An Expression of the Movement toward Indigenization within the Indian Christian Community, Dissertation, op.cit.*, 135; *22nd Annual Report of the Evangelistic Association for the year 1909–1910*, 9.

381 Basel Mission School at Honowar was founded in 1905. The mission handed this school to the Mar Thoma Church in 1919. Since then, the management of this school has been under the Mar Thoma Church.

382 Alex Thomas, *A Historical Survey of the North Kanara Mission of the Mar Thoma Church, op. cit.*, 124–144.

383 See, J.H. Hutton, *Caste in India: Its Nature, Function, and Origins, op. cit.*, 140. In India, girls, who dedicated to Hindu temples were known as *devadasis*. They lived in temple premises and worked as temple prostitutes for "high-caste" people.

384 Alex Thomas, *A Historical Survey of the North Kanara Mission of the Mar Thoma Church, op.cit.*, 124.

this practice.[385] George Thomas summarizes the role of the Mar Thoma Church in its joint actions with NMS by citing the "*The First Ten Years of the NMS*":

> Abraham Mar Thoma (1880–1947), the Metropolitan of the Mar Thoma Syrian Church, characterized this effort to organize and utilize indigenous talents "towards the evangelization of the dear old land of India" as an epoch-making event in the missionary history of India" because he held that "if India's millions are to be reached and won for Christ, it will be by India's sons".[386]

What Abraham Mar Thoma underlined was the church's policy of autonomy and independence that had stood the test of time. The church was quicker in striving towards the goal of indigenous mission in India as a result of its experience of autonomy and independence from the first century onwards. It upheld the independence from western mission leadership as part of the substance of Indian nationalism and the new independent identity of the nation.

The Mar Thoma Church-NMS missionary joint venture had a serious nationalistic implication in that an awareness was created among members of the church as also the missionary society on the need to banish caste-ridden consciousness. For the church, the effect of this partnership turned intense as the nationalistic mission strategy of the NMS turned into a church agenda.

In 1940, the Mar Thoma Church developed the North Kanara mission field into an *ashram* (monastery). This reflected yet again the church's open outlook that took Indian spirituality and nationalism seriously. The church regarded *ashram* spirituality as an Indian way of searching God. It started similar *ashrams* during the middle of the 20th century, which merits further study.

---

385 *An Interview with J. Abraham, the former principal of St. Thomas High School Honavar, at his residence in Honavar on July 31, 2001.* Cited In: Alex Thomas, *A Historical Survey of the North Kanara Mission of the Mar Thoma Church, op. cit.,* 130.

386 George Thomas, *Christian Indians and Indian Nationalism 1885–1950, op. cit.,* 149.

Chapter VII
Blending Hindu, Christian Ascetism

The outlook of openness that the Mar Thoma Church has followed since its inception meant the church could accept, embrace and internalize the monastic traits that prevails in other religions as well as in other Christian denominations. This was dealt with in some length in the previous chapter that describes how this openness helped the church develop an indigenous mission culture that gave rise to a partnership with NMS in the North Kanara Mission. That mission was to later take the form of an *ashram,* that effectively mixed concepts from the Hindu, Roman Catholic and Protestant monastic movements.

This chapter reviews the historical evolution of the *ashram* movement in the Hindu, Roman Catholic and Protestant streams and how the church was able to synthesise the ascetic principles in these streams to develop its own brand of monasteries.

The *ashram* movement, as we mentioned in the last chapter, started in the church as it found in that concept an Indian way of communicating the message of the Gospel. The movement could be seen as another example of the church's ability to adapt major Indian religious life experience in its missionary praxis. The Mar Thoma Church's *ashram* movement also drew copiously from the Indian Christian monastic tradition.

Sadhana path to salvation

Closely linked with the concept of *ashram* life, as understood by the Mar Thoma Church, is the Hindu way of life to salvation. India's *ashram* concept may be defined as "a spontaneous community of seekers (of truth), or disciples gathered around a spiritual leader called a *guru,* who points a way to salvation".[387] It has

---

387 Helen Ralston, *The Construction of Authority in the Christian Ashram Movement / La Construction de l'autorité dans le mouvement des ashrams chrétiens.* In: *Archives des sciences sociales des religions. N. 67/1, 1989. pp. 53–75. doi: 10.3406/ assr.1989.1370,* In: *www.perSee.fr/web/revues/home/prescript/article/assr_0335– 5985_1989_num_67_1_1370* visited on 4th April 2011.

its root in the Brahmanical Hinduism's *ashrama* theory that refers to a way of life characterised by meditation, asceticism, and spiritual living in all stages of life – *Brahmachaari, Grahystyasrama, vanaprasta* and *sanyasa*.[388]

The Sanskrit word, *ashrama,* refers to the home of a small religious community of Hindus, who spend their lives in meditation, austerities and imparts their teachings and the experience of the Absolute to disciples. *Sadhana* is considered the means to the realisation of the *ashrama* life. It refers to a "course of spiritual discipline or teaching leading to the fulfilment or realisation of life". Helen Ralston shows that there is a similarity in all religious traditions at this point.

"The spiritual guides of Christian tradition, as well as the *gurus* of the Indian tradition formulate for their disciples common or particular *sadhanas*".[389]

So an *ashram* offers certain *sadhanas*, which are prescribed by *gurus,* around whom an *ashram* is constituted. India's *Upanishad*[390] tradition considers the *guru,* or teacher, as a medium through whom God reveals himself to the disciples. In India's ancient *gurukula,* or teaching, system, groups of pupils sit near the *guru* to learn from him the *Brahman* or ultimate knowledge. Max Weber shows that in India's Hinduism, a *guru* is regarded more than a teacher, spiritual guide and *Brhaman's* prototype, who leads the disciple to God, the *guru* could be deified as a living God.[391]

---

388 *Brahmachaari, Grahystyasrama, vanaprasta* and *sanyasa* are four stages of human life stratification in the light of the *varna ashrama dharama* – a Brahmanical Hindu way of life. The *Brahmacharya* refers to a way of life under the tutelage of the *Brahman* or Ultimate Reality during the period of 14 to 20 years of age as practiced in the Brhmanical Hinduism. The *Brahmacharya* also refers to the self-imposed celibacy, a prerequisite for being a member of the *Bramacharya aashrama* way of life. The *Grihastyasrama* refers to the family life, usually in between 24 to 48 years of age. The *vanaprasta* refers to the third stage of the *varna asrama dharma* – elder advisor. The *sanyasa* refers to an ascetic way of life and it is observed after 72 years of age.

389 Helen Ralston, *The Construction of Authority in the Christian Ashram Movement / La Construction de l'autorité dans le mouvement des ashrams chrétiens, op.cit.*

390 The Sanskrit word *Upanishad* is derived from three Sanskrit words – *upa* (near), *ni* (down), and *shad* (to sit). The *Upanishadic* period constitutes the *veda-anta,* which means the end of Vedas, which are the sacred texts of the *Brahmanical* Hinduism. It is the last part of Vedas. The *Vedas* are *Rig Veda, Yajur Veda, Sama Veda* and *Atharva veda.* The *upanishad* also contains the conclusion of *vedic* teachings.

391 Max Weber, *Religion of India: The Sociology of Hinduism and Buddhism,* (New York: Oxford University Press, 1958), 319.

The *ashrama sadhanas* are closely linked with three *margas* as mentioned in *Sreemath Bhagavat Geetha*[392] – *karma marga, bhakti marga* and *jnana marga* – as ways to reach salvation. The *karma marga* refers to the selfless path of ritual actions, or path of obligations; the *bhakti marga* refers to path of devotion, or love for a personal God; and *jnana marga* refers to the use of meditative concentration preceded by a systematic ethical and contemplative training for supra-intellectual knowledge.[393] The systematic ethical and contemplative training is known as *yogas* and it is explained in the second century *Yoga Sutras* of the India's Patanjali.[394]

However, India's *ashram* culture faded by the arrival of Muslims and by the establishment of the Delhi Sultanate (1206) and Mughal Empire (1526) and during the subsequent Portuguese (1498); Dutch rule (1610) French rule (1674); and British rule (1857) in India. By the middle of the 18th Century CE, western Orientalist scholars[395] seem to have been obsessed with learning and translating India's sacred religious texts and history of Indian culture.

The recovery of India's past glory by Orientalist scholars from Europe during the period of Warren Hasting (1773–1785) up to Lord Amhest (1823–1828) of the British Empire, helped to revive the Indian civilization and culture, which we have already dealt with earlier.[396] British education served as a means to convey India's

---

392 *Srimad Bahgavat Gita* is a sacred book of the Hindus.
393 *http://www.britannica.com/EBchecked/topic/304137/jnana-marga.* Visited on 4th, April 2011.
394 The *Yoga sutra* is a foundational text for the India's *yoga* philosophy and techniques. The Sanskrit word *yoga* refers to physical, mental and spiritual disciplines. These are considered to be the pre-requisites for attaining salvation. The salvation can be achieved through the practice of three ways – *karma marga* (Way of work), *jnana marga* (Way of knowledge) and *bhakti marga* (Way of Devotion) as is explained in the *Bhagavat Gita*.
395 Orientalist scholars were European scholars, who felt that India's past achievements were examples of rich cultural heritage and civilization of India. The prominent orientalist scholars were William Jones (1746–1794), Charles Wilkins (1749–1836) and Max Mueller, (1823–1900). They studied Indian culture and religions and appreciated Indian religion and culture in the light of their research. They translated the sacred texts of Hinduism into vernacular. In their research, they found India's golden age of Indian culture, religion, language, literature, schools of philosophy, arts and architecture. See, George D. Bearce, *British Attitude towards India (1784–1858),* (London: Oxford University Press, 1961), 20–25; S.L. Kaeley, V.K. Bhandari and et. all, *Indian History and Culture; op.cit.,* 356–357.
396 David Kopf, *British Orientalism and the Bengal Renaissance, The Dynamics of Indian Modernization 1773–1835, op.cit.,* 31, 39.

rediscovered history and culture to educated Indians through mission schools and colleges.

This resulted in an Indian Renaissance of the high culture of *vedic* religion and a resurgence of the *"ashram* movement" in the 19th and 20th centuries. There were several neo-Hindu reform movements such as *Brahmo samaj* (1828) and *Arya Samaj* (1875) founded to reform the Hindu society. Helen Ralston observes that leaders and followers of these socio-religious movements "stimulated the revival of the *ashram* mode of life"[397] through their *ashrams* such as: Sri Ramakrishna Mission (1897) by Sri Ramakrishna Paramahamsa (1836–1886); and his disciple Swami Vivekanda (1862–1902); *Santhinikethan Ashram*(1901) by Rabindra Nath Tagore (1861–1941); *Aurobindo Aashram* (1927) by Aurobindo Ghosh (1872–1950); and *Satyagraha ashram* (1915) by Mahatma Gandhi (1869–1948).[398]

The *"ashram* movement" aimed to reform the Indian society without repudiating their religion and culture by *sadhanas* in the *ashram life*. The Christians subsequently founded similar Christian organisation – *christo samaj* – in 1887 for the "propagation of Christian truth, the promotion of Christian union, and the welfare of Indian Christians".[399]

Passion for *ashrams*

A higher interest of the Hindu *ashram* way of life during this period was attributed to a passion for the *ashram* way for the Indian Christians as well. The a*shram* way of life and nationalism were accorded equal acceptance among Indian Christians. This led to the founding of several Christian *ashrams* during the early decades of

---

397 Ralston Helen. *The Construction of Authority in the Christian Ashram Movement, op. cit.,* 57–58.

398 Paul Pattathu, *Ashram Spirituality: A Search into the Christian Ashram Movement against its Hindu Background* (Indore: Satprakashan Sanchar Kendra, 1997), 4; K.V. Varghese, *A Vision for Wholeness: Ashrams and Healing in India,* (Delhi: CMAI/ISP-CK, 1999), 1–2; K.V. Varghese, *Hirannadiyude Thheram Thedi,* (Malayalam), (Tiruvalla: CLS, 1993), 15–16; Helen Ralston, *Christian Ashrams: A New Religious Movement in Contemporary India* (Lewiston/Queenston: The Edwin Mellen Press, 1987), 15–22; George Thomas, *Christian Indians and Indian Nationalism 1885–1950: An Interpretation in Historical and Theological Perspective op.cit.,* 14, 28–35.

399 Benjamin Russal Barber, *Kali Charan Banurji, Brahmin, Christian, Saint,* (Madras: 1912), 48; George Thomas, *Christian Indians and Indian Nationalism 1885–1950, op.cit.,* 75.

the 20th Century CE in India. Direct historical evidence in support of this conclusion comes from several recent studies conducted by Helen Ralston, Paul Pattathu and K.V. Varghese.[400]

Christian *ashrams* that have drawn lessons from the Hindu *ashram* life representations can be categorised into the Protestant Christian *ashrams* and the Catholic *ashrams*. The Protestant Christian *ashrams* are evangelical social service and action-oriented *ashrams*. Examples of this category include *Christukula ashram* (1921) in Tiruppattur in Tamil Nadu founded by Jesudasan and Forrestor Paton (1891–1970) and *Kristavashram* in Kottayam (1940) by Sadhu Mathaichen (1885–1971). The Catholic *ashrams* refers to catholic contemplative and monastic oriented *ashrams*, like *Saccidananda ashram* (1950) in Santhivanam at Kulittalei in Tamil Nadu.

It was in this context, from the early decades of the 20th Century that the church got obsessed with finding new ways of communicating the Gospel to Indian society by means of indigenous mission strategy.

The NMS made its first proposals for Protestant *ashrams* in 1912.[401] As the church's new enthusiasm to find indigenous methods of evangelisation was gathering momentum, when Abraham Mar Thoma Metropolitan, (1880–1947) who supported indigenous missions, became the Mar Thoma Church's missionary bishop in 1917. George Thomas observes that Abraham Mar Thoma's support "to organise and utilize indigenous talents" for the evangelisation of India was an "epoch-making event in the missionary history of India".[402]

He became instrumental in changing the Mar Thoma Church's mission strategy in India from a mood of western evangelicalism to that of indigenous evangelism. What is significant in the mission policy adopted by Abraham Mar Thoma was that it considered the Hindu *ashrama* way of life as the most suitable indigenous method of evangelisation in India.[403] Thus a spirit of indigenous mission, discarding western mission strategy, gave rise to the *ashram* movement in the Mar Thoma Church, parallel to the church's mission work at other levels.

---

400 *Ibid.*

401 M.M. Thomas, *Acknowledged Christ of Indian Renaissance, op. cit.*, 276; Robin H. Boyd, *An Introduction to Indian Christian theology, op.cit.*, 87–88.

402 George Thomas, *Christian Indians and Indian Nationalism 1885–1950, op.cit.*, 149.

403 C.K. Mathew, "Suvishesha dauthaym Aashramagaliloode" (Malayalam), In: *Mar Thoma Sabha Saradhikal* (Malayalam), (Tiruvalla: Mar Thoma Syrian Church Publication, 1993), 30–134.

The Mar Thoma Church's *ashram* movement owed its debt also to the intellectual and spiritual sermons of Stanley Jones (1884–1973), who was a close friend of the Mar Thoma Church and a regular "Maramon convention" speaker from 1920 onwards. Alex Thomas argues that he introduced to the church a "Kingdom of God" model of Christian community life.[404] The "Kingdom of God" model refers to the formation of a Christian community, which redeems "all areas of life – economic, social and political"[405]. This model was the emphasis in mission engagements in India's villages. Stanley Jones emphasized the same motivations current among the Mar Thoma Church's leaders to form an *ashram* community that is suited to India's peculiarities – social, political and economic discriminations.

The Mar Thoma Church's passion for *ashrams* during the 1930s was reflected in the church owning the maximum number of such Christian institutions in the country. The Mar Thoma Church *ashrams* that mushroomed were *Christudasa Ashram* at Palaghat, Kerala (1928); *Ashram* at Perumbavoor, Kerala (1931); *Christhu Mitra Ashram*, in Ankola, North Kanara (1940); *Christu Panthi Ashram* in Sihora, Madhya Pradesh (1943); *Christiya Bandhukula* in Satna, Madhya Pradesh (1947); and *Christhu Santhi Sanghom,* in Nepal (1952).

When the Mar Thoma Church's a*shrams* were formed, the influence of Christian monasticism was self-evident. Former MTEA general secretary C.K. Mathew describes the Indian Christian *ashrams* as a synthesis of the Indian Hindu culture's "ashram vision" and the Christian monastic movement's ideals.[406] Christian monasticism's major ideals of "chastity, obedience and poverty" were synthesised with the Hindu *ashram* way of life.[407]

Christ, the true guru

However, the Mar Thoma Church was conscious of keeping its independent identity while it formed *ashrams*. There were certain major differences between the characteristic features of Mar Thoma Church a*shrams* and the Protestant and Hindu *ashrams*. The Hindu *ashrams* give central position to the *Acharya,* or guru, in

---

404 Alex Thomas, *A Historical Survey of the North Kanara Mission of the Mar Thoma Church, op.cit.,* 143.
405 *Ibid.,* 145.
406 C.K. Mathew, "Suvishesha Dauthaym Aashramagaliloode" (Malayalam), In: *Mar Thoma Sabha Saradhikal (Malayalam), op.cit.,* 131–132. C.K. Mathew, a Mar Thoma Church clergy, is the current general secretary of the MTEA.
407 *Ibid.*

their *ashrama* system, against the central position given to "Jesus Christ, the true guru". Second, unlike the Hindu and the Protestant *ashrams*, which were either for men or for women, the Mar Thoma Church's *ashrams* consist of both male and female members, who live together in separate buildings in the same campus. Thirdly, both the Hindu and the Protestant *ashrams* preserve their autonomy and independent administrative set-up but the Mar Thoma Church's *ashrams* function under the aegis of the church and the MTEA.[408]

The Mar Thoma Church *ashrams* share the general objectives of Protestant Christian *ashrams* which have evangelistic, medical, educational, social and economic development aims.[409] *Ashram* members include priests, evangelists, doctors, nurses, and para-medical workers. However, over the last two decades, the number of celibate a*shram* members has steadily declined. Currently the Mar Thoma Church has only three *ashrams* such as: *Christudasa Ashram, Christu Mithra Ashram* and *Christu Panthi Ashram.* Surprisingly, *Christu Panthi Ashram* is the church's only celibate *ashram* with a significant membership.

Observes former Ecumenical Christian Centre founder-director M.A. Thomas (1913–1993): "Though they are not opposed to conversion that is not the dominating motive of these *ashrams.* They emphasise love and service."[410] *Ashrams* provided places where people of different faiths could come and study the Gospel in an Indian *gurukula* way of atmosphere. A sense of unity with all of creation, devotion to God, obedience, renunciation, poverty and chastity are the main features of the Mar Thoma Church *ashrams.*

The Mar Thoma Church thus owes the Hindu and Protestant *ashram* movements for the salient features that it imbibed from them while setting up their own *ashrams.* Its approach to the Hindu and ecumenical ideology has been based on an attitude openness and broadness, which can be traced back to the time of the church's founding. The same openness is obvious also in the church's sociopolitical involvements.

---

408 *Ibid.*, Helen Ralston, *The Construction of Authority in the Christian Ashram Movement, op. cit.*, 62.

409 Helen Ralston, *Christian Ashrams: A New Religious Movement in Contemporary India, op.cit.*, 80–84; Alex Thomas, *A Historical Survey of the North Kanara Mission of the Mar Thoma Church, op.cit.*, 182; K.V. Varghese, *A Vision for Wholeness, op.cit.*, 52–55.

410 M.A. Thomas, "Mar Thoma Church's Approach to Other Religions and Mar Thoma Church's Socio-Political Involvement", In: *Mar Thoma Sabha Saradhikal* (Malayalam), (Tiruvalla: Mar Thoma Syrian Church Publication, 1993), 3; Joseph Daniel, *One Family under Heaven: Response to Paradigm Shifts in Ecumenism* (New Delhi: ISPCK, 2008), 112–113.

Chapter VIII
A Church For The People

The start of Mar Thoma Church's *ashram* movement reflected its active involvement in the socio-religious realms of Indian villages, which itself was a natural extension of an attitude of openness that it followed from the beginning. Such an experiment made the church aware of the hard realities of the socio-religious base of "Bharat", or the India in villages. As a follow-up, the church has become conscious since the 1930s of the need for concerted action by joining hands with all sections of people, irrespective of caste or creed. The church got involved in the 1930s in the joint struggle by the Ezhava (Hindu), Muslim and Christian communities in Kerala for gaining proportionate representation in the government and public sector.

The church silently supported the Nivarthana (abstention) Movement, that saw the Ezhavas, Muslims and Christians unitedly agitating against the government to ensure adequate representation in the Legislative Assembly. The agitation was in protest against the Legislative Reforms Act of 1932, which did not safeguard the interests of these groups.

The Abstention Movement was a concerted agitation of the *Ezhava*, Christian and Muslim communities against the lack of representations in the Travancore for different religious and caste communities in the Legislative Assembly and jobs in the government offices.[411]

Community	Population	No. of Officers
Tamil *Brahmins*	45,868	509
Nairs	690,495	469
Christians	1172,934	413
Ezhavas	661,367	32
Muslims	261,367	14

Fig. 1: Gazetted officers in government service in Travancore in 1929[412]

---

411   A. Sreedhara Menon, *Kerala and Freedom Struggle,* (Kottayam: D. C. Books, 1997), 98.
412   George Jacob, *Religious Life of the Ilavas of Kerala*, (New Delhi: ISPCK, 1995), 71.

The Figure 1, above, on gazetted officers in government service in 1929 is self-explanatory about the discrimination in providing government jobs to the Muslim, Christian and *Ezhava* communities. It shows the distribution of gazetted officers decreases in a social hierarchical order, starting with the "high caste" Tamil *Brahmins* to the socially-backward Muslims. The distribution was disproportionate to their populations in the kingdom of Travancore.

George Mathew, a noted Indian social scientist, argued that there were phenomenological reasons for the mobilisation of the three communities. First, the Muslims, the *Ezhavas* and the Mar Thoma Christians – comprising of the Roman Catholics and the Orthodox – could not gain access to the Travancore government jobs in proportion to their population and education. Second, community-based movements started mushrooming in Travancore. These movements, including the Ezhava *Sree Narayana Dharma Paripalana Yogam* (SNDP), felt the need to mobilize their respective communities politically to gain their due social status.[413] The Mar Thoma Church members joined hands with these groups in the struggle for proportionate representation.

M.M. Thomas claims that these community-based organisations in Travancore were inspired by the Mar Thoma Church's pioneering historic acts of emancipation, namely the Coonen Cross Oath and reforms. Hindu communities such as *Nairs* and *Ezhavas* mobilized their communities to fight for social emancipation, drawing strength from the above acts.[414] The community-based movements such as *Nazrani Jathyaikya Sangham*, (1866)[415] and *Sree Narayana Dharma Parpipalana Yogam* (1903)[416] were subsequently formed to safeguard their community's interests. Agitations were organised to gain their rights such as the right of proportionate entry into civil services and due representation in the Legislative Assembly.

It was when this new rebellious communal agitations were gathering momentum in Travancore that Sri Chitra Thirunal Balarama Varma (1931–1949), the then ruler of Travancore kingdom, reconstituted the Assembly under the Legislative Reform Act of 1932–1933. The right to vote was determined on the basis of

---

413 George Mathew, *Communal Road to Secular Kerala, op. cit.*, 20–48.
414 M.M. Thomas, *Abraham Malpante Naveekaranam Oru Vyakyanam*, (Malayalam), (Tiruvalla: TLC, 1979).
415 *Nazrani Jathyka Sangahom* was a Syrian Christian organization in Kerala.
416 SNDP is the organization that formed in 1903 for the empowerment of the backward *Ezhava* community in Kerala by Sri. Narayana Guru (1856–1928). He was a socio-religious reformer in Kerala.

property rights and it consequently enabled the "high caste" Hindus to monopolise the electoral seats as before.[417]

This sparked a joint agitation of Christians, Muslims and *Ezhavas* for political rights. An "All Travancore Political Conference"[418] met on 17 March, 1933 in Trivandrum and decided to boycott elections.

> The important resolution on abstention was that the members of the various political organisations of Christians, Muslims and *Ezhavas* should abstain from taking part either by voting or by standing as candidates in elections or by accepting nomination to the reformed legislative bodies so long as the government did not provide for the equitable representation in the legislature in election of all concerned communities, proportionate to their population.[419]

The Mar Thoma Christians, including members of the Roman Catholic, Orthodox and Mar Thoma Church, supported the move.[420] A mass meeting was organised in Tiruvalla, near the Mar Thoma Church's headquarters, on 14 March, 1933, and an abstention resolution was unanimously passed. But elections were held under prohibitory orders on 1 April, 1933.[421]

Community	Population in Hundred Thousands	Seats in the Legislative Assembly (48) and Council (22)
Christians	16.04	10
Ezhavas	08.09	03
Nair	08.68	36
Other *Savarnas* (including *Brahmins*)	04.79	15
Muslims	03.53	03
Depressed Classes	09.17	01
Europeans	(587)	2

---

417 A. Sreedhara Menon, *A Survey of Kerala History, op.cit.*, 283.
418 All Travancore Political Conference was a meeting of the joint Christian, Muslim and *Ezhava* community to protest against reforms of the government for providing more favours for the "high caste" Hindus. It was formed in Trivandrum at 17th December 1932.
419 George Mathew, *Communal Road to Secular Kerala, op. cit.*, 93.
420 A Report published in *Dasan* on December 31, 1932, which reported the participation of the Muslims, the Christian in the All Travancore Political Conference meetings. *Ibid.*, 92.
421 *Ibid.*

Community	Population in Hundred Thousands	Seats in the Legislative Assembly (48) and Council (22)
Total	50.30	70

Fig. 2: Results of general elections held on 1 April, 1933[422]

In Travancore, the Legislative Assembly membership had been the monopoly of the "high caste" Hindus – *Brahmins* and *Nairs* – since the assembly was constituted in 1888. Figure 2 shows the disproportionate representation of the various communities in the Assembly after the passing of the Legislative Reforms Act in 1932. As can be read from the figure, relatively few candidates from the Christian, Muslim and other depressed communities, which totally constituted 70 per cent of population, got elected in the general election as those communities abstained from voting. This reflected the success of the *Nivarthana* movement that cut across religious and communal divides.

The *Nivarthana* Movement started in Travancore in 1933, when the government's plan for the Legislative Reform Act by then *Diwan* (head of government) C.P. Ramaswamy Ayer (1879–1966)[423] was known. The protest entered a new phase with the Joint Political Congress[424] agitation against the government's reforms under the leadership of T.M. Varghese (1886–1961), a Mar Thoma Church member. Says George Mathew:

> "From June 1933, when elections were held, till February 1938, the Joint Political Congress of the Abstention Movement kept aflame the political awakening of the state".[425]

However, this resulted in a backlash from the "high-caste" *Nair* community, which met in Trivandrum and passed a resolution against the *Nivarthana* Movement. The "high caste" groups joined hands with the government to suppress the movement. This was met with an intensification of the Joint Political Congress' agitation against the social discrimination.

---

422 History of Freedom Movement Part II cited, In: *Ibid.*, 94.

423 C.P. Ramaswami Ayer (1879–1966) was an advisor of the King of Travancore and he was instrumental for constitutional changes in the princely state of Travancore. He was an admirer of autocracy and an apologist of British rule in India.

424 All Travancore Political Conference assumed a new name – "All Travancore Samyukta Rastriya Congress" or "Joint Political Congress" in 1932.

425 George Mathew, *Communal Road to Secular Kerala, op. cit.*, 94.

The Travancore Christians met for a three-day conference at Kozhencherry[426] on May 9, 1935, and passed a resolution moved by T.M. Varghese, urging the government to dissolve the Legislative Assembly.[427] The conference concluded with a meeting of the "Joint Political Congress", in which C. Kesavan (1891– 1969), an *Ezhava* leader, publicly "challenged Ramaswamy Ayer's repressive rule in Travancore ... It declared the rights of the subaltern classes and called for a relentless battle to achieve those rights".[428]

C. Kesavan stunned the government in his speech by stating that *Ezhava*s would leave the Hindu fold,[429] which led to his arrest and trial for sedition. Although the Mar Thoma Church's members – T.M. Varghese, K.T. Thomas and George Joseph – appeared at the court as C. Kesavan's advocates, he was convicted and sentenced for two months imprisonment and fined INR 50,000.

Church stands for the people

The leaders of the church decided to make a specific choice for standing in favour of the concerted agitations of the Hindu, Muslim and Christian struggle against autocracy. In a bold move, the Mar Thoma Church expressed solidarity with the struggling communities by inviting noted Ezhava leader C.V. Kunjiraman (1879–1949)[430] to speak at the Maramon convention in 1936. At the convention, Kunjiraman also hinted that the *Ezhava*s would leave Hinduism and join Christianity.[431] In the context of the agitations, C.V. Kunjiraman's speech at the Maramon convention, the

---

426 Kozhencherry is the cradle of the Mar Thoma Church's reforms and majority of its population are members of the Mar Thoma Church.

427 N.M. Mathew, Malankara *Mar Thoma sabha Charithram*, (Malayalam), Vol. III, *op.cit.*, 72.

428 "Kozencherry Address' a milestone: Baby", In: *The Hindu*, 11, May 2010. "The Hindu" is an India's National Daily.

429 George Mathew, *Communal Road to Secular Kerala, op.cit.*, 95.

430 C.V. Kunjiraman was a prominent *Ezhava* community leader in Kerala.

431 The *Ezhava* leaders showed a gesture to join in the Mar Thoma Church. But the church's Metropolitans – Titus II and Abraham Mar Thoma – were not in favour of giving membership to them in the church. They were against adding the numerical strength of the church through political moves. This has been the church's centuries-old policy on conversions. The church affirms a proper conversion of beliefs a prerequisite for membership in the church.
Interview with Joseph Mar Thoma, Metropolitan, Sinai Mar Thoma Church, London, dated 17th March 2013.

Christian lawyers' gesture to take *vakalath* for (appear in court on behalf of) C. Kesavan and a hint of the threat of conversion in the speeches of the *Ezhava* leaders, forced the government to accept the demands of the *Nivarthana Prasthanam*.[432] Accordingly, a public service commission was appointed by the King in 1935 to ensure fair representation for all communities in public services on the basis of "efficiency combined with preference on communal basis".[433] This also led to the government opening up temples to all Hindus, irrespective of caste. This decree by the Travancore King in 1936 has come to be known as the "Temple Entry Proclamation".[434]

The joint struggle for socio-political emancipation of the Christian, Muslim and *Ezhava* communities thus served as a catalyst to break up the "upper caste" Hindu monopoly in the socio-political and socio-religious realms of Travancore. The Commissioner's report on franchise and delimitation was submitted to the government on 16 August, 1936, and the government passed orders to extend voting rights to elect representatives to the assembly to all Travancore citizens, who paid INR1.00 or more as tax.[435] The success of the *Nivarthana* Movement enabled all Joint Political Congress candidates to win the election held in May 1937 under the new franchise rule. The elected candidates chose T.M. Varghese as the Deputy President of the Legislative Assembly.

The Metropolitan and the leaders of the Mar Thoma Church, without hesitation joined hands with "lower-caste" communities, and were convinced of their needs – constitutional reforms and freedom. They also came to consider *Diwan* C.P. Ramaswamy Ayer as a symbol of autocracy and an enemy of Travancore's merger with the Indian Republic.

The church stood for the Indian union, after India's independence on 15 August, 1947. The Metropolitan and the leaders of the church decided to confront the decision of the *Diwan* not to unite Travancore state with the Indian Federal Union. It was within this consciousness of constitutional reforms and India's freedom struggle that the church's approach to the emerging Indian Union took shape. Zac Varghese states that the Mar Thoma Church metropolitans "Abraham Mar Thoma and

---

432   N.M. Mathew, *Malankara Mar Thoma Saba Charitram, Vol. III, op.cit.*, 73.
433   A. Sreedhara Menon, Kerala and Freedom Struggle, *op.cit.*, 100.
434   See, Joseph Daniel, *Socio-Religious Impact of the Temple Entry Proclamation on the Christian Community in Travancore*, unpublished B.D. Thesis, *op.cit.*, 25–30.
435   George Mathew, *Communal Road to Secular Kerala, op.cit.*, 96.

Titus II gave sound leadership during the independence struggle at local and national level by their speeches".[436]

'Responsible government' stir

The agitation for 'responsible government' was part of the Indian National Congress agenda to overthrow the British regime in India. After the Haripura session of the Indian National Congress in 1938, it was decided that separate political organisations should be formed in princely states for the agitation for responsible government. The term, 'responsible government' refers to a democratic government for the people of India. To achieve this goal, the Joint Political Congress joined hands with the "Travancore State Congress"[437] on 4 July, 1938, that led people in the struggle for freedom and the establishment of a responsible government in the princely state of Travancore.[438]

The concept of "responsible government" proposed by the Indian National Congress, appeared to the Mar Thoma Church as a major step towards the concept of "responsible society" discussed by the world ecumenical movement in the 1930s, which became a programme of the World Council of Churches in the Amsterdam (1948) and Evanston (1954) general assemblies.[439]

Church and 'responsible society'

It was during the period between the Stockholm Conference of the Life and Work Movement in 1925 and the formation of the WCC in 1948 that the socio-political and ethical concerns of Europe received much attention in ecumenical discussions. The ecumenical movement analysed these in the context of fascism, communism and capitalism, which resulted in the articulation of the "responsible society"

---

436 Zac Varghese and Mathew Kallupuram, *Glimpses of Mar Thoma Church History, op. cit.*, 134.
437 The Travancore State Congress was a political organisation aimed at protecting "the interest of the minorities and establish responsible government in the state". See, *Resolution of the Joint Meetings of the Citizens of Trivandrum*, February 16, 1938.
438 See, George Mathew, *Communal Road to Secular Kerala, op.cit.*, 97.
439 Christine Lienemann-Perrin, "Leitvorstellungen im Ökumenischen Rat der Kirchen zur politischen Verantwortung der Kirche, In: *Die politische Verantwortung der Kirche in Südkorea und Südafrika*, (München: Chr.Kaiser, 1992), 465–466.

concept, described as a socio-ethical criterion to evaluate critically the existing social, ethical and political structures.

In the global ecumenical scenario, this criterion made possible a critical evaluation of both communism and capitalism.[440] The concept of "responsible society" accepted at the WCC General Assembly in Amsterdam proved to be the key concept in the ecumenical programmes of the WCC in more than two decades of ecumenical socio-ethical thinking. The post-World War II context of the disorder in the world, cold war, and the oppressive political structures were put in the crucible of this concept during this period.

The Evanston Assembly made clear that ...

> "... responsible society is not an alternative social or political system, but a criterion by which we judge all existing social orders and the same time a standard to guide us in the specific choices we have to make. Christians are called to live responsibly, to live in response to God's act of redemption in Christ in any society, even within the most unfavorable social structures."[441]

The concept of "responsible society" aimed at "a free and democratic society, where all citizens are guaranteed freedom and where those holding political authorities are responsible to the electorate".[442] In this process for the formation of a responsible society, the churches' role in society was fundamental.

The leaders of the Mar Thoma Church adopted this concept as a criterion to analyse the contemporary socio-political context of Travancore. By this criterion, the church critically analysed the existing socio-political system of the princely state of Travancore. In that analysis, the Metropolitan and the leaders of the church felt that the autocratic regime was against the criterion of the "responsible society". Therefore the church decided to support the struggles of the people for the responsible government in Travancore.

It was during this time the Travancore State Congress started agitations for a responsible government in the state. Amidst these agitations, T.M. Varghese and E.M. John represented the Mar Thoma-Jacobite interests[443] and A.J. John upheld Catholic interests in the organisation. The *Diwan* and *Nairs* came to be the

---

440 *Ibid.*, 465–466.
441 *Social Questions – The Responsible Society in a World Perspective, A Report of the Evanston Assembly, Section III, op.cit.*, 4.
442 Carl-Henric Grenholm, "Responsible Society". In: Nicholas Losskey and others eds., *Dictionary of the Ecumenical Movement*, (Geneva: WCC Publication, 2002), 980–981.
443 George Mathew, *Communal Road to Secular Kerala, op.cit.*, 101.

defenders of the independent Travancore state. They also tried to propagate a rumour that the State Congress was a Christian organisation, which was not true.

The reason behind this political move was to apply the policy of "divide and rule". However, T.M. Varghese won the support of the *Nair* community leader and freedom fighter, Pattam Thanu Pillai (1885–1970).[444] Mannathu Padmanabhan (1877–1970), a leader of the *Nair* community. The *Diwan* "accused *Nairs* who joined the State Congress of being just a handle of Varghese's axe".[445]

Abraham Mar Thoma's leadership

It was in this context of the *Diwan*'s "divide and rule" policy that Abraham Mar Thoma Metropolitan made a speech, which put a spoke in the wheel of the *Diwan*'s intention to create a division between Hindus and Christians. The following excerpt from Abraham Mar Thoma's speech, at the centenary celebration of the church's reformation at Trivandum in 1938 is typical of the Mar Thoma Church's approach to other religions and the then political developments:

> Father, as we are one, they should be one as well ... This unity is essential not only for Christians but also for all castes and communities. *Nairs, Ezhavas, Brahmins,* backward community people, other Hindus, Muslims and Christians belong to a common brotherhood of man. If anyone is trying to split us for political expediency, it is unfortunate. Christians should take a leading role for religious harmony and understanding. We should make our non-Christian friends understand that we have no hidden political motives in our spiritual activities and evangelistic work. It is our failure that they misunderstand us, and it is our responsibility to put it right. If anyone spreads the rumour that Christians are interested in mass conversion for giving them an advantage over others, it is just a wicked propaganda. We should expose the falsehood of these allegations and demonstrate our traditional loyalty and patriotism to our royal family ...[446]

That speech confirmed the ecumenical relationship between the Mar Thoma Church and different religious communities over several centuries. It underlined the church's age-old position of religious harmony and the stand to react against any bid to destroy social harmony and freedom.

---

444 Pattam Thanu Pillai (1885–1970) was the chief minister of Kerala during 1960–1962.
445 George Mathew, *Communal Road to Secular Kerala, op.cit.*, 101.
446 Cited In: Zac Varghese and Mathew Kallupuram, *Glimpses of Mar Thoma Church History, op. cit.*, 134–135; N.M. Mathew, *Malankara Mar Thoma Sabha Charithram,* Vol. II, *op.cit.*, 232–233.

When this new agitation against responsible government was gathering momentum in Travancore, C.P. Ramaswamy Ayer banned the activities of the State Congress in 1938 and police repression followed. It was in this context that Abraham Mar Thoma gave another sensitive speech in favour of the agitators at his episcopal silver jubilee celebrations at the Trivandrum Law College hall in 1943.

> Christians all through their history had to face difficulties and challenges from the Roman Emperors to the present time. But none of them destroy the church ... Please remember that martyr's blood is the seed of the church. If ever we are put through such trials and tribulations we have the courage to face such challenges boldly; I am sure that the young people of our land will volunteer for such an eventuality. These are challenges affecting the members of all religions. And we should fight it together. Although I am getting old and I am not all that well, you can be rest assured that I will be in the frontline with you to fight any divisive action against religious freedom, which we have been enjoying in this land for generation.[447]

The speech reflected the Mar Thoma Church's unrest against C.P. Ramaswamy Ayer's communalist strategy of "divide and rule", while at the same time brought out its long-term support to the Travancore State Congress' freedom struggle.

Bold, open support for Congress

Not only did Abraham Mar Thoma identify with the forces that stood against C.P. Ramaswamy Ayer's intention to destroy communal harmony in Kerala society, he openly supported T.M. Varghese, Pattam Thanu Pillai and other State Congress leaders despite the government's prohibitory orders against supporting the State Congress. He even visited prisoners in jail.

The prisoners included K.C. Mammen Mappila, the editor of the *Malayala Manorama* daily, who wrote against C.P. Ramaswamy Ayer's autocracy and his political moves to avert the Travancore state's merger with the Indian union.[448] In his autobiography, K.M. Mathew, chief editor of India's circulated regional daily, *Malayala Manorama,* wrote:

---

447 *Ibid.*, 233–234; Zac Varghese and Mathew Kallupuram, *Glimpses of Mar Thoma Church History, op.cit.*, 135–136; Varghese K.A, *Abraham Mar Thoma Thirumeni,* Third Edition, (Tiruvalla: 1959), 28.

448 K.M. Mathew, *Ettamathe Mothiram* (Autobiography), (Kottayam: Malayala Manorama, 2008), 269–272.

Abraham Mar Thoma was the only one who comforted us during the time when the people feared to even whisper against CP. We will not forget Maratte Thirumeni, who later became Abraham Mar Thoma, his visit to our father in jail and his spiritual inspiration ... Thirumeni was the then Bishop of Titus II. It is important to know that Abraham Mar Thoma's visit to our father in jail was at a time when all religious heads were hesitant to meet our father. Maratte Thirumeni, together with K.C. Chacko, who is my father's brother, met Deenabandhu C.F. Andrews and informed him about the problem in our bank (Quilon Bank) and requested him to involve in the matter. Maratte Thirumeni had a deep friendship with our father. We still remember the resolution that was passed at the Mar Thoma Church General Assembly against the autocratic rule of C.P.[449]

K.M. Mathew's testimony about the Metropolitan shows his open support to the agitators against the autocratic rule of the *Diwan.* In expressing solidarity with the agitators and visiting the detainees, the Metropolitan was openly daring the autocratic government despite the clear possibility of getting arrested.

In another instance, Abraham Mar Thoma wrote a letter dated 11th August, 1947 to K.A. Mathew citing Ramaswamy Ayer's reluctance to join the Indian union and the need to evoke Indian nationalistic feelings among the Travancore citizens, who were demanding the Travancore "state's perfect union with India".[450] The church also supported the Travancore State Congress move, as we noted earlier, and decided to fight for the establishment of a responsible government in Travancore.

Yet C.P. Ramaswamy Ayer announced that "Travancore would set itself up as an independent sovereign state" under the British declaration of the "Lapse of Paramountcy"[451] on 11 June, 1947, which permitted local rulers to decide either to join the Indian Union or Pakistan or remain independent state.

---

449 *Ibid.*, 270. An independent translation of the author from the Malayalam book *"Ettamathe Mothiram".*

450 *Letter of Abraham Mar Thoma to Mr.K.A. Mathew, 60 Finborough Road, London, SW10, dt 11th August 1947.*

451 The "Lapse of Paramountcy" refers to a statement issued by the British administration on 12th May 1946 about the rights and privileges of the Indian states after the transfer of power from the crown to the Indian government. The statement say that the British administration could not and will not in any circumstances transfer paramountcy to an Indian government. Based on this the rights of the states, which follow from their relationship to the crown no longer exists and all rights and privileges surrendered by the states to the British power will return to the state. Relying on this, the Diwan made an attempt to declare the state of Travancore a sovereign, independent republic on 15th August 1947.

151

Call for responsible government

The violent people's agitations seeking C.P. Ramaswamy Ayer's resignation for a transition from autocracy to democracy and Travancore's union with the Indian union resulted in the Mar Thoma Church Council passing a resolution:

> The Council feels that the situation in Travancore should be viewed in relation to the rest of India and demands first of all the establishment of a Government fully responsible to the legislative elected on the basis of a wide Franchise. Only such a Government should consider and make decisions on the future status of Travancore in relation to the Indian union now coming into being.[452]

The church's strong disapproval led to the spreading of a rumour that Abraham Mar Thoma would be arrested.[453] But C.P. Ramaswamy Ayer did not dare to arrest him in the face of concerted Hindu, Muslim and Christian protests.[454] Forced by the agitations and the church's strong position for freedom, C.P. Ramaswamy Ayer resigned from the office of *Diwan* on 14 August, 1947. The King issued a proclamation of responsible government and subsequently the Travancore state joined with the Indian union. This marked the successful conclusion of the protests for the Travancore responsible government, in which the Mar Thoma Church and other religious communities played an active part.

The Mar Thoma Church's bold stance to be part of the responsible-government agitation highlighted its willingness to update its ecumenical outlook in tune with the global ecumenical movement. It showed that the church's failure in the court case of 1889 did not dampen its determination to remain autonomous. The church's ecumenical response also brought into the spotlight the socio-religious predicament of India's "outcaste" communities.

The missionary, social and political responses during the first part of the 19th Century were thus natural extensions of its ecumenical outlook. But the church's ecumenical outlook continued to manifest in its praxis as it engaged in full-communion agreements with other churches, which is the subject matter of the next chapter.

---

452 *Annual Report of the Mar Thoma Syrian Church,* 1947.
453 M.A. Thomas, "Mar Thoma Church's Approach to Other Religions and Mar Thoma Church's Socio-Political Involvement", In: *Mar Thoma Sabha Saradhikal* (Malayalam), *op.cit.,* 9.
454 N.M. Mathew, *Malankara Mar Thoma Sabha Charithram,* Vol. II, *op.cit.,* 234–235.

Chapter IX
Church Unity in Action

There is a reason to believe that the Mar Thoma Church has an ecumenical *avant la lettre* – the church had started an ecumenical way of corporate living well before the theoretical formulations on ecumenism were articulated. This is evident while reviewing its church unity engagements and its ecumenical history. An insight into the Mar Thoma Church's church unity engagements – which started even before ecumenical thoughts took institutional shape at the international level – would potentially be of a considerable historical and ecumenical benefit.

The next important stage in the church's life and work was its search for a dynamic participation in inter-communion relationships with other denominations at the national and the international levels and in the modern ecumenical movement. In its formative phase, after the loss of the case in the British royal court in 1889, the Mar Thoma Church sought deliberate ecumenical engagements with the MISC and "occasional inter-communion"[455] relations with

---

455 The "Occasional Inter-communion" refers to an agreement between the Mar Thoma Church and the CIBC (Church of England) in 1937 that permitted the members of both the churches to receive the communion from the Altar of the other. Consequently, both churches granted permission to their clergies to officiate sacraments in the other church, whenever any need arose, in 1957.

See, "Resolution of the Mar Thoma Syrian Samudayalochana sabha, 1936; Resolution 4, Episcopal Synod of the Church of India, Burma, and Ceylon, 1933", In: C.E. Abraham. ed., *Mar Thoma Syrian Church and the Church of India and the Church of south India,* (Tiruvalla: Mar Thoma Church, 1968), 5.

There were different terms used by the Anglican Church to denote the relation between churches, based on the nature of its relation with the other church. Those terms were "occasional Inter-communion", "full Communion" and "Inter-communion". The Lambeth Conference 1958 endorsed a paragraph in the Report of the Committee on "Church Unity and the Church Universal", which refers to the use of terms "full communion" and "inter-communion" and recommends accordingly that where between two Churches, not of the same denominational or confessional family, there is unrestricted *communio in sacris* including mutual recognition and acceptance of ministries, the appropriate term to use is "full communion" and that where varying degrees of relation other than "full communion"

the Church of India, Burma and Ceylon[456] (CIBC) of the worldwide Anglican communion.

This "occasional inter-communion" relationship paved the way for future church unity engagements with member churches of the Anglican communion. This chapter tries to unearth the history of the Mar Thoma Church's ecumenical praxis that progressed in two phases. The period relevant here is roughly 1816–1961, during which the church developed its ecumenical relations with the MISC, Church of England (Anglican Church), World Council of Churches (WCC), Christian Conference of Asia,[457] National Council of Churches in India[458] and the Kerala Council of Churches[459]. The crowning glory of this period was the Mar Thoma Church's leadership in the WCC's General Assembly meeting in New Delhi in 1961, which incidently also brought out Metropolitan Juhanon Mar Thoma's ability as an organiser par excellence.

Ecumenism to the rescue

It was the *Malankara* Church's ecumenical outlook that came to the rescue, when the church found itself in a thorny situation right after Metropolitan Mar Thoma VIII (1809–1916) passed away without consecrating a successor. The predominant understanding among the *Malankara* Church leaders is to see themselves as bearers of the same episcopal succession line of the Antiochian Patriarchate. This

---

are established by agreement between two such Churches, the appropriate term is "inter-communion".

"Resolution 14, "Church Unity and Church Universal – Full Communion and Inter – Communion", Lambeth Conference, 1958", In: *www.lambethconference.org/resolutions/1968* visited on 17th October 2011.

456 The Church of India, Burma and Ceylon was known as the Church of England's churches in India, Burma and Ceylon before 1927. Under the provision of the Church of India Act 1927, the Church of India dissolved and became part of the "Church of India, Burma and Ceylon" in 1927.

See, *Indian Church Act, 1927* (17 & 18 Geo.V, Chapter 40), United Kingdom, 209–219; *Indian Church Measure 1927* (17 & 18, GeoV, No. 1), United Kingdom, 1927; Noel Davis, Martin Convoy, *World Christianity in the 20th Century*, (London: SCM Press, 2008), 133–134.

457 Hereafter referred as CCA.
458 Hereafter referred as NCCI.
459 Hereafter referred as KCC.

means that they do not see the need to approach Antioch or any other foreign bishop to continue their episcopal lineage.

It was this understanding that prompted the church to turn to the Malabar Independent Syrian Church (MISC), which also shares the same apostolic succession lineage, in their hour of need, instead of running to Antioch. At the same time, this awareness of a shared succession lineage from the Antiochian Patriarchate does allow the church to accept and respect the spiritual and ecclesiastical leadership of the Antiochian Patriarch, while keeping the church's core autonomous and indigenous nature.

So, when Mar Thoma VIII passed away, the church selected Ittoop Kathanar of Kunnamkulam as the Metropolitan designate and invited MISC Metropolitan Mar Philoxinos (1811–1829) to consecrate Ittoop as the Metropolitan of the *Malankara* Church. MISC's timely help averted clouds of suspicion, when Mar Philoxinos consecrated Ittoop Kathanar as Pulikottil Joseph Mar Dionysius (1816–1817) Metropolitan on March 22, 1816.[460] The move to seek the MISC's assistance to consecrate a Metropolitan was a practical one but it also resulted in the melting down of *Malankara* Church's feeling of bitterness towards the MISC.

Bishops' bid for authority

The formation of the MISC is associated with an abortive attempt made in 1787 by Mar Thoma VI to merge the *Malankara* Church with the Roman Catholic Church by severing the then existing relationship with the Antiochian Church. Mar Thoma VI (1765–1802) had earlier received a re-consecration from Antiochian Bishop Mar Gregorios, in the presence of Mar Ivanios, another Antiochian bishop, and received the title Dionysius in 1770. This gesture of Mar Thoma VI was with a view to establish further church unity engagements with the Antiochian church. So, why did Mar Thoma VI attempt to reunite the *Malankara* Church with the Roman Catholic Church? Was it to sideline the Antiochian Church?

Mar Thoma VI's (1765–1808) effort was to become the sole Metropolitan of the Mar Thoma Christians and he suspected that Antioch wanted to have authority

---

460 Juhanon Mar Thoma, *Malankara Sabhayile Episcopaciyum Mar Thoma Sabhayile Stanabhisheka Shushrooshakalum,* (Malayalam), (Tiruvalla: T.A.M. Press, 1975), 11; George Mathew, "Thozhiyoor Sabhayum Mar Thoma Sabhayum", In: *Malalnkara Sabha Tharaka* (September/ 1994), 19.

over the *Malankara* Church through the two bishops[461], Mar Gregorios and Mar Ivanios sent by the Patriarch.

Mar Thoma VI (1765–1808) "wished to reunite all Christians of St. Thomas and he was determined to be their Metropolitan".[462] He also showed a positive gesture to keep the unity of the church with its separated brethren of the Roman Catholic Church.[463] For instance, a letter of the Carmelite Vicar Apostolate of Verapoly to *Propaganda* dated 7 May, 1787, says that Mar Dionysius I (1765–1808)[464] was willing to make his submission to the Roman Catholic church, on condition that he be recognized as the Metropolitan of all Mar Thoma Christians in Malabar, not only his own flock but also the Mar Thoma Christians in communion with Rome.[465]

However, this move of the Metropolitan eventually led to strains in the church's relation with the Antiochian bishops sent by the Patriarch. The relation became worse, when the *Malankara* Church Metropolitan violated the agreement that "he agreed to give a daily salary of one *rasi pannam*[466] per person"[467] to the Antiochian bishops. This move of the Metropolitan was a pragmatic one to sideline the Antiochian church and its bishops and to establish unity with the Roman Catholic Church. This was indeed a departure from the church's centuries-old policy of safeguarding its autonomy and independence from the Roman Catholic Church.

On the other hand, the Antiochian bishops tried to counter the Metropolitan's move by consecrating a new Metropolitan, without the *Malankara* Church Metropolitan's consent. Both bishops were concerned about the impact of the proposed

---

461 John. R.K. Fenwick, *The Malabar Independent Syrian Church* (Nottingham: Grove Books, 1992), 16; Three Syrian Orthodox Antiochine Bishops – Mar Baselios, Mar Gregorios and Mar Ivanios – came to the *Malankara* church, in response to the request send by the latter through Dutch colonists. They were not well received by the then Mar Thoma VI (1765–1808). Having annoyed by the Mar Thoma VI's attitude, the Antiochine Bishop Mar Gregorios consecrated Mar Koorilose I (1772–1802) in 1772 without consulting Mar Thoma VI.

462 L.W. Brown, *The Indian Christians of St. Thomas, op.cit.*, 122.

463 *Ibid.*, 16. See, G.T. Mackenzie, *Christianity in Travancore*, Note No. 98, *op.cit.*, 140.

464 Mar Thoma VI (1765–1802) received a re-consecration from the Antiochian Bishop Mar Gregorios, in presence of the Mar Ivanios and received the title Dionysius in 1770. This gesture of Mar Thoma VI could be seen as his effort to establish further church unity engagements with the Antiochian church.

465 G.T. Mackenzie, *Christianity in Travancore*, Note No. 98, *op.cit.*, 140.

466 *Rasi panam* was the then currency of Travancore and Cochin State of India.

467 *Mannanam Malayalam* 3/MS Mill 192, Papers of W.H Mill, Bodleian Library, Oxford, 47.

unity between the *Malankara* Church and the Roman Catholic Church in India. So the Antiochian Bishop, Mar Gregorios decided to find a suitable Mar Thoma Metropolitan candidate "... to uphold the faith and traditions of the church at any cost".[468]

However, the bishops did not foresee in the act of consecration a potential danger for the loss of popular support to the new Metropolitan, Mar Koorilose I (1772–1802). The non-approval of the *Malankara* Church forced Mar Koorilose to move towards Thozhiyoor in India and founded a new church by name "Malabar Independent Syrian Church" (MISC) in 1772.[469]

The *Malankara* Church considered the Antiochian bishop's act of consecration as an attempt to secure his authority over the *Malankara* Church. Writing in 1972, Metropolitan Juhanon Mar Thoma said: "It is not obligatory for the Mar Thoma Church to accept the supremacy of the Antiochian Patriarch, from whom Mathews Mar Athanasius (1842–1877) received consecration, during the reformation of the Malankara church".[470]

It is therefore known that a substantial antipathy of the *Malankara* Church towards the MISC can be ascribed to the act of the Antiochian bishops to establish their supremacy over the *Malankara* Church. However, both the churches were aware of their common historic episcopacy from the Antiochian church. This helped them to accept each other and also served as the basic point of reference for their church unity engagements. This also helped them to extend mutual administrative and liturgical assistance whenever there was a need.[471]

We shall now briefly examine the Mar Thoma Church's church unity history in order to see how far the church cherished its inter-communion relationship with

---

468 P. Varghese, *Reunion Efforts of St. Thomas Christians of India (1750–1773): A Historical Critical Analysis of the Contemporary Documents, op.cit.*, 10.

469 Historians are not unanimous on the actual date of consecration of Mar Koorilose I (1772–1802). According to L.W. Brown, the consecration was taken place on 28th November 1772; See, L.W. Brown, *The Indian Christians of St. Thomas*, (Cambridge: Cambridge University Press, 1956), 130; P Varghese suggests the date much earlier as 1767. See, P. Varghese, *Reunion Efforts of St. Thomas Christians of India (1750–1773): A Historical Critical Analysis of the Contemporary Documents*, (Trissur: Marymatha Publications, 2008), 11; P. Cherian suggests the date of consecration of Mar Koorilose I on 1770. See, P. Cherian, *The Malabar Syrians and the Church Mission Society, op.cit.*, 55.

470 Juhanon Mar Thoma, *Ormakalum Kurippukalum*, (Malayalam) *op.cit.*, 143.

471 Administrative and liturgical assistance agreement of both churches will be dealt with in detail in the following analysis of this study.

the MISC as an extension of its ecumenical outlook, even before the term inter-communion[472] came to be widely accepted in the modern ecumenical movement.[473]

Full communion with the MISC

The historical context prepared a way to realise the need for church unity engagements for both the Mar Thoma Church and the MISC. This happened before church unity was defined or explained in a logical and doctrinal way internationally. The sudden demise of Pulikottil Joseph Mar Dionysius Metropolitan (1816–1817) a few months after his consecration, in November, 1816, left the church again without a bishop.

This incident again led the *Malankara* Church to benefit from the historic common episcopacy shared with the MISC. During this time, the *Malankara* Church accepted the MISC Metropolitan as the *Malankara* Church's Metropolitan and this was ratified by the then British resident, Col. Munroe (1810–1819) in 1816.[474] This act showed up in a positive light the *Malankara* Church's openness in accepting a bishop of another church as its Metropolitan.

Despite the animosity that had built up between the *Malankara* Church and the MISC, the mutual help extended by both these churches during critical points is now history.

---

472 The Mar Thoma Church has inter-communion relation with the MISC. Thus both churches consider the sacraments of the other valid.

473 Although, most of the 20th century ecumenical debate was centred on the question of inter-communion between churches, the earliest agreement in this direction was reached only in 1931 between the Anglican Church and the Old Catholic Church. The Bonn Agrement was considered as one of the earliest agreements between churches for inter-communion relationship in the history of the church unity engagements. See, "Old Catholic Church 167 – Statement Agreed Between the Representatives of the Old Catholic Church and the Churches of the Anglican Communion at a Conference held at Bonn July, 2, 1931", In: G.K.A Bell, *Documents on Christian Unity, Third Series 1930–1948* (London: Oxford University Press, 1948), 60; Warren C Platt, "Intercommunion Between the Episcopal Church and the Polish National Catholic Church: A Survey of Its Development", In: *Internationale Kirchlicke Zeitschift* 82, (1992), 142–165.

474 R.N. Yesudas, *Colonel John Munro in Travancore*, (Trivandrum: Kerala Historical Society, 1977), 28.

Essential points for full communion

Two essential common agreements for the unity of both the *Malankara* Church and MISC can be recognized. An agreement which mutually acknowledged and accepted the orders, sacraments and ministry of both the churches was reached on the basis of the shared historic episcopacy derived from the Antiochian church. The two churches also agreed to provide mutual administrative assistance in the event of an administrative deadlock, despite the fact that neither church had authority over the other.

The inherent awareness in both churches of their common apostolic heritage led them to greet with enthusiasm the agreement to recognize mutual orders and sacraments. Its effect was startling. In the Mar Thoma Church's episcopal consecrations, the MISC's Metropolitans started to serve as co-celebrants, and vice versa.[475] The possibility of attaining further church unity and progress through this

---

475 The MISC's Metropolitan, Geevarghese Mar Philoxinos's (1811–1829) consecration of Pulikkottil Mar Dionysius (1816–1817), Punnathra Mar Dionysius (1817–1825), and Cheppatt Mar Dionysius (1827–1852) could be seen as the MISC's helping and ecumenical gesture to the *Malankara* Church in times of their need. The same nature of Christian love and concern was reciprocated by the *Malankara* Metropolitan, Mathews Mar Athanasius (1842–1877) by consecrating Joseph Mar Koorilose IV (1856–1888) in 1856. The Mar Thoma Church's Metropolitan, Titus II (1899–1944) in association with the then Suffragan Metropolitan Abraham, Mar Thoma (1944–1947) consecrated the MISC's Metropolitan, Kuriakose Mar Koorilose VI (1935–1947) on January 1936. The MISC's Kuriakose Mar Koorilose (1935–1947) participated in the consecration of the Mar Thoma Church's Juhanon Mar Theomtheos (1937–1976) and Mathews Mar Athanasios (1937–1973) in 1937. The Mar Thoma Church's Metropolitan, Juhanon Mar Thoma (1947–1976) with the assistance of the Mar Thoma Church's bishop Mathews Mar Athanasios consecrated the MISC's Metropolitan, Geevarghese Mar Koorilose VII (1948–1967) in 1948. The MISC's Geevarghese Mar Koorilose VII (1948–1967) was a co – celebrant at the bishop's consecration of the Mar Thoma Church's bishops – Alexander Mar Theophilus, (1953–2000) Thomas Mar Athanasius (1953–1984), and Philopose Mar Chrysostom (1953 –) in 1953. The Mar Thoma Church's Metropolitan consecrated the MISC's Paulose Mar Philoxinos (1967–1977) in 1967. The Mar Thoma Church's Metropolitan, Alexander Mar Thoma (1976–2000) consecrated the MISC's Mathews Mar Koorilose as Metropolitan in 1978. The Mar Thoma Church's Metropolitan, Alexander Mar Thoma (1976–2000) consecrated MISC's Joseph Mar Koorilose (1986 –) as Metropolitan in 1986.
See, Joseph Daniel, "Most. Rev. Joseph Mar Koorilose – A Metropolitan Who Makes a Difference", In: *Joseph Mar Koorilose Valia Metropolitan's Silver Jubilee Festschrift*, (Thozhiyoor: MISC, 2011), 89–95.

networking of practical ecumenical engagements led to a full communion relation between the churches in 1893. It is significant that this inter-communion relation was achieved, even before the first organic model of church union of India – local union of Presbyterians in South India – materialised in 1901.[476] Although the full communion relation between the churches cannot hide the differences in doctrines and rites between the churches, these differences do not affect the shared common apostolicity that is the essential element for inter-communion.

Administrative assistance

The Mar Thoma Church's administrative assistance to the MISC has a long and continuous history. It was within the context of the Antiochian Patriarch's claim over the MISC's jurisdiction and especially the Patriarch's Indian deputy, Yoakim Mar Koorilose's (1846–1876) efforts to acquire a civil court verdict to establish his claim on the MISC that the Mar Thoma Metropolitan assisted the MISC by providing an affidavit declaring the MISC's autonomy and independence[477] at the British civil court. Mathews Mar Athanasius' affidavit says:

"I affirm that the church and its properties belong to the Metropolitan of Anjoor (MISC) and his community alone and that church is an independent church, to which the Antiochian Patriarch or his associates, or the Mar Thoma Metropolitan of me have no administrative authority over it."[478]

---

476 Alexander Mar Thoma, *The Mar Thoma Church Heritage and Mission, op.cit.*, 92; C.B. Firth, *An Introduction to Indian Church History, op.cit.*, 238. From the last decade of the nineteenth century onward different mission agencies and their Indian denominations felt the need for a unity of churches in India over against denominationalism, to solve common problems of the Indian churches. Consequently, decennial conferences of missions and the European churches in India begun in Allahabad in 1872. Since then the unity negotiations received desired results in India. The Presbyterian churches in South India achieved a local union of Presbyterians in 1901. This was the first definitive achievement of churches unity in India. In Madras decennial conference of 1902 formally accepted the principle of comity. By this agreement each mission agreed to keep their territorial integrity and agreed to avoid encroachments from other missions. These conferences had a positive effect on the church union negotiations and church union movements in India. See, C.B. Firth, *An Introduction to Indian Church History, op.cit.*, 233–247.

477 Juhanon Mar Thoma, *Malankara Sabhayile Episcopaciyum Mar Thoma Sabhayile Stanabhisheka Shushrooshakalum*, (Malayalam), *op.cit.*, 26.

478 *Ibid.* This is an independent English translation of the author.

The church funded the MISC to meet the court expenses and the MISC defended its autonomous and independent position at the British lower court at Palaghat in Kerala and the British high court in Madras.[479] The British high court upheld the lower court's decision in 1862 and ruled that the MISC "was independent and that neither the Patriarch of Antioch nor his delegate had any authority over it".[480]

The consequence of this verdict was the development of a conscious stand of the MISC's Metropolitan, Joseph Mar Koorilose (1856–1888), to build a special relation with the Mar Thoma Church, even in matters of administration. In his will to his successor Joseph Mar Athanasius (1883–1898), he says:

Although the *Thoziyoor church* and the *Malankara church* are independent, both churches are moving together in mutual consultation and in mutual help, and therefore, in times when you have doubt on church administrative matters, you should seek the advice and opinion of the Malankara Metropolitan, who was and is not submissive to any foreign allegiance, and move together with him mutually.[481]

As is explicit in this quote of the MISC Metropolitan, the MISC church did look for a permanent relation with the Mar Thoma Church. The mutual trust of the Metropolitans of both the churches was looked upon with much value by the Mar Thoma Church in the matter of administrative assistance. For instance, the Mar

479   It was a time when Yoakim Mar Koorilose (1846–1876) came to India by the advice of the Antiochian Patriarch in 1846 to pacify the non- reform group, who were unwilling to accept Mathews Mar Athanasios (1842–1877) in the *Malankara* Church. Yoakim Mar Koorilose instigated his followers to build separate churches for non – reform groups in India. It was when the MISC's Metropolitan died in 1856, Yoakim Mar Koorilose made a claim over the MISC. Having sensed his desire to bring MISC under the Antiochian church, Mathews Mar Athanasius consecrated the MISC's Metropolitan, Joseph Mar Koorilose IV (1856–1888) in 1856. Thus he curbed the move of Yoakim Mar Koorilose. John Fenwick commented about this consecration: "defended the church's independence from Patriarch".
John. R.K. Fenwick, *The Malabar Independent Syrian Church, op.cit.*, 29. Juhanon Mar Thoma, *Malankara Sabhayile Episcopaciyum Mar Thoma Sabhayile Stanabhisheka Shushrooshakalum*, (Malayalam), *op.cit.*, 26.

480   Extract from the British High Court verdict, in Madras, cited In: John. R.K. Fenwick, *The Malabar Independent Syrian Church, op.cit.*, 29.

481   The citation is an independent translation of the author. The aforesaid will was of Alathur Joseph Mar Koorilose (1856–1888), who gave this will to his successor Joseph Mar Athanasius (1883–1898) in 1883. Juhanon Mar Thoma, *Ormakalum Kurippukalum* (Malayalam), *op.cit.*, 140; *Interview with the Joseph Mar Koorilose, the Metropolitan of the MISC*, dated 17 July 2011.

Thoma Metropolitan convened a general body of the MISC to elect its Metropolitan, after Metropolitan Geevarghese Mar Koorilose (1892–1935) died of a heart attack, without consecrating his successor in 1935. The MISC general body, in turn, expressed their wish to elect a candidate nominated by the Mar Thoma Metropolitan. Filled with happiness, as John Fenwick writes, "with tears in his eyes"[482], Mar Thoma Metropolitan declared his nominee, K.M. Kuriakose, and he was consecrated as the MISC's Metropolitan.

Fenwick adds that "no episcopal election has been conducted in such a peaceful atmosphere since 1935".[483] Besides consecrating Metropolitans for the MISC, the Mar Thoma Church took the initiative to draft a constitution for the MISC, by appointing a constitution draft committee, which consisted of C.M. John,[484] V.T. Chacko[485] and A.G. Mathew,[486] in consultation with MISC members K.C. Varghese[487] and Cheeran Varghese. The new drafted constitution for the church was approved in 1948 by the MISC. In the MISC's constitution, there is a provision, which recognizes their relation with the Mar Thoma Church and it says:

> If the church's regular administration becomes difficult, by reason of the provisions of this constitution or by the reason of any other matters, follow the tradition of the fathers and the current practice of the church by acting in consultation with the sister (Mar Thoma) church's Metropolitans and may take appropriate decision in the matter by following their advice.[488]

The constitutional provision, which approves the historic relation of the MISC with the Mar Thoma Church, is considered a milestone, representing the progress of the relationship between the churches. It shows that the Mar Thoma Church's relation with the MISC is defined by the MISC's formal acceptance of facts of the mutual co-operation and assistance in administrative matters between the two churches.

---

482 John Fenwick, *The Malabar Independent Syrian Church, op.cit.*, 37.
483 *Ibid.*
484 C.M. John was a priest of the Mar Thoma Church and he was later consecrated as Juhanon Mar Thoma Metropolitan in 1947.
485 V.T. Chacko was a priest of the Mar Thoma Church.
486 A.G. Mathew was a lawyer.
487 K.C. Varghese was a priest and Cheeran Varghese was a lay member of the MISC.
488 *Article 21, Constitution of the Malankara Independent Syrian Church, Thozhiyoor,* 10. It is an independent translation of the author of Constitution of the MISC, which is written in *Malayalam.*

MISC's scepticism on reforms

It becomes evident in this study's evaluation of the Mar Thoma Church's relation to the MISC over the years that the church leaders are uncritical of the doctrinal and ritual position of the MISC. But they do not encourage members to remain passive participants in the doctrinal life that is evident in its liturgy. They are aware of the doctrinal and ritual differences[489] inherent in the church's relation with the MISC.

While the MT Metropolitans desired the progress of its full communion relationship with the MISC, they looked upon the MISC's doctrinal position as serving the cause of Antiochian tradition. So they looked for an inclusion of reform principles in the MISC's life and mission.[490] However, the MISC has had a sceptical attitude to the Mar Thoma Church's reforms in faith and practices. The Mar Thoma Church upheld its reform principles such as: removal of all mediatory prayers including prayers to the Blessed Virgin Mary, to the saints and the prayers for the church triumphant; removal of icons and pictures from the church and the discontinuation of the auricular confession.

However, these doctrinal teachings are not included in the church's agenda to reach a doctrinal consensus with the MISC in its ecumenical journey.[491] The common historic episcopacy has been considered as the connecting link of both churches. For instance, the Mar Thoma Church held that nothing prevents it from engaging in a full communion relationship with the MISC, as both the churches share the common historic episcopacy.[492] Considering the common historic episcopacy and the lack of codified doctrines of both churches, both the churches took a position to accept the sacraments and ministry of each other, without engaging in a serious discussion on doctrinal matters. This gesture may be viewed as the Mar Thoma Church's reluctance to engage in a serious discussion on doctrinal matters with the MISC. This attitude has invited criticisms as well.

---

489 The MISC follows an Antiochian doctrinal tradition, which upholds the prayer for the church triumphant, auricular confession, prayers to the Blessed Virgin Mary, and the intercession of saints.

490 Juhanon Mar Thoma, *Ormakalum Kurippukalum (Malayalam), op. cit.*, 144.

491 The Mar Thoma Church following a policy of the non- inclusion of doctrinal matters in its unity engagements with the MISC. This policy is in conformity with the conviction of the world ecumenical movement. The earlier conviction of the ecumenical movement was that "the service unites and the doctrines divide". So pioneers of the ecumenical movement avoided doctrinal matters in the ecumenical discussions initially. But this policy was changed since the formation of the Faith and Order Movement.

492 Juhanon Mar Thoma, *Ormakalum Kurippukalum* (Malayalam), *op. cit.*, 144.

An ecumenist and a priest of the Mar Thoma Church, M.J. Joseph, wrote in 1981 that engaging in a meaningful dialogue with the MISC during the last two centuries has helped dialogue and an encounter in favour of maintaining full communion relations of both churches against doctrinal and ritual differences.[493] He went on to observe: "It is mandatory that both churches should journey long distances from the pattern of extending helping hands at the time of each other's need to reach further unity levels".[494]

The Mar Thoma Church's special communion relation with the MISC led other sections of the St. Thomas denominations, which are not in communion with the Mar Thoma Church, to be cautious in engaging with the MISC, as it appeared to them as the Mar Thoma Church's sister church. This generated a concern among leaders of the MISC about its future ecumenical engagements with other denominations in India. The crux of their apprehension was translated in the MISC Metropolitan's act of consecrating his successor Cyril Mar Baselios Metropolitan himself in 2001, going against convention. It could also be seen as the MISC's deliberate move to strengthen their ecumenical relationship with other St. Thomas denominations in India as well.[495]

Even though the Mar Thoma Church was able to keep its communion relationship with MISC, it should search for a conciliar form of ecumenical praxis to support MISC's vision to engage in ecumenical relation with other churches in Kerala and to further its full-communion relation with the MISC by engaging in discussions on doctrinal matters.

The Mar Thoma Church's ecumenical nature is based on effective church unity movements. The church cherished its ecumenical vision even before the flowering of the modern inter-communion relations.[496] The success of its full communion relation with the MISC motivated the church to start fresh discussions with the Anglican Church towards inter-communion relations.

---

493 M.J. Joseph, "Ecumenism Mar Thoma Sabhayude Bhavi Veekshanan" (Malayalam), In: M.J. Joseph ed., *Church Unity: Response of the Mar Thoma Church*, (Manganam: St. Augustine Study Centre, 1981), 40–46.

494 *Ibid.*, 42; M.J. Joseph, *Ormakalude Theruveedhiyil*, (Malayalam), (Tiruvalla: CSS, 2010), 220–221.

495 *Interview with Joseph Mar Koorilose, Metropolitan, Valia Metropolitan of the MISC*, dt 17 July 2011.

496 The Bonn agreement of the Anglican Church with the Old Catholic Church in 1931, which we have referred previously, was a guiding principle in the world church unity movements. This agreements supported sacramental unity, while the doctrinal differences exists.

Chapter X
Proactive Ecumenism

The Bonn Agreement of 1931 between the Old Catholic Church – an ancient denomination that keeps the undivided Catholic faith without accepting the infallibility of the Pope as decreed by the First Vatican Council of 1870 – and the Church of England presented new vistas for the Mar Thoma Church to enter into formal ecumenical agreements for full communion. This agreement opened up ample space for the oriental Indian church to engage in communion relationship with the Church of England, which belongs to the Western Anglo-Catholic tradition. This became possible even while the churches stuck to their different theological and liturgical stances.

The relationship between the Mar Thoma Church and the Church of England does go back a couple of centuries to 1816, when the first band of Church Missionary Society (CMS) missionaries from England officially started their "mission of help", with the intention of helping the Indian church to be contemporised. That relationship has continued since then as both the churches stayed in cooperation at different levels in their corporate lives. The Bonn Agreement, however, paved the way for the Mar Thoma Church and the Church of England to take those ties to a higher plane of formal communion status.

The ties with the Church of England did lead to churches of the Jacobite tradition attacking the Mar Thoma Church for its susceptibility of getting influenced or even merged with the English church at some point. And, as we have seen, the Church of England's chaplain, Claudius Buchanan, did convey his desire to have a relationship with the Indian church even in his maiden visit to the *Malankara* Church. Abraham Malpan, Geevarghese Malpan and other early reformers of the church kept positive and progressive ties with the CMS missionaries and the Church of England. But they never had an intention to merge the Indian church with the Church of England, a fact that history will vouch for.

Developing ties that bind

But is survival the major underlying factor that is prompting the Mar Thoma Church to keep its ties with the Anglican Church – the umbrella term that came to be used for all erstwhile branches of the Church of England in the Commonwealth that later became independent churches? Or, did the Mar Thoma Church consider ecumenism as its defining mark, even while it struggled for survival? This chapter makes an attempt to know why and how the Indian church's proactive openness to the Anglican Church and to other churches is positively related to its fundamental ecumenical praxis. It was after the 19th Century that the Mar Thoma Church became interested in a close relationship with the Church of England's CMS missionaries.[497] The continuance of the Mar Thoma Church reforms after the church became independent in 1889 attracted the CMS missionaries, as they viewed the Indian church as a positive target of their "mission of help". The CMS thus had enough justification for its efforts to further help the church, although the Mar Thoma Church held on to its traditional moorings and remained negative on the question of merging with the Anglican Church, as desired by the CMS missionaries.

Besides the CMS, the Church of England and the British colonial administration did foresee in the Mar Thoma Church a potential scope for the continuance of their existing relations, which we have already highlighted. This developing relationship appeared to the Mar Thoma Church as an added strength in its existence.

But the church faced a two-fold challenge. Having failed to get a favourable court verdict, it had to defend its position of autonomy and prove its self-sufficiency in integrating the liturgical and evangelical elements together. Secondly, the Indian church was searching for ways to confront the Brethren Church's aggressive proselytising methods without diluting its inherent nature of openness to other churches. These challenges helped create a favourable context for church unity engagements with the Church of England.

Missionary ties to inter-communion

The relationship between the Mar Thoma Church and the Church of England progressed in two phases. In the first phase (1816–1936), the CMS missionaries cooperated with and assisted in the Indian church's mission work in Travancore-Cochin area, while in the second (1936–1961), the relationship moved to new level of formal agreements to have "occasional inter-communion" and later "full

---

497 L.W. Brown, *Indian Christians of St. Thomas, op.cit.*, 141. Majority of historians of both European and Indian Church share the above mentioned view. See, K.K. Kuruvilla, *Mar Thoma Church and Its Doctrines, op.cit.*, 14; T.C. Chacko, *The Concise History of the Mar Thoma Church* (Malayalam), *op.cit.*, 80–81.

communion". The "full communion" relationship allowed members to share the Eucharist in both the churches.

The missionary co-operation phase saw CMS missionary preachers being invited regularly to lead the Mar Thoma Church's Bible conventions.[498] For instance, the CMS missionary, Thomas Walker (1859–1912), "a fiery preacher"[499] was the main speaker of the Mar Thoma Church's annual Maramon Convention regularly from 1899 to 1912, until his death.[500] The CMS attitude towards the Mar Thoma Church is self-evident in the letter of Thomas Walker to his wife on 15th February 1900, from Maramon, in Kerala. He says:

> "The MarThomites are ardent in faith and therefore the CMS needs to consider a joint conference … with the Mar Thoma Church."[501]

It should be understood that the Mar Thoma Church was always open to receiving the CMS missionaries' opinion on its mission activities and respected those opinions. In 1893–1894, the church discussed the feasibility of extending the Mar Thoma Church's missionary activities beyond the central Travancore area through its missionary wing, MTEA. The then CMS missionary archdeacon asked the Mar Thoma Church to reverse or modify the MTEA constitution to facilitate the launch of a mission field in North Travancore area, which was in the same geographical territory of the CMS mission. Although this proposal was against the MTEA's

---

498 K.T. Jacob, Maramon Convention: "Utbhavam Valarcha", In: *Maramon Convention Sadabhti Valyam* (Malayalam), *op.cit.*, 58–74.

499 *The People of Dohnavur to the Home Secretary, CMS, Touring the Tinnavely Diocese,* 1 February 1947, *Tinnavely Box, 1, Special Collections,* Bishop College, Calcutta, India; See, Dyron B. Daughrity, *Bishop Stephen Neill: From Edinburgh to South India,* (New York: Peter and Lang, 2008), 97.
   Thomas Walker (1859–1912) was a Cambridge scholar and a CMS missionary at Tinnavely. He arrived in Kerala in 1894, to work among members of the Anglican Church. He took Bible classes and sermons at the Mar Thoma Church's convention meetings at *Maramon*, and his close association with the *Maramon* convention made him known as *Maramon Wlaker Sayip* by the local people of Kerala. Bishop Stephen Neill was another speaker at the Maramon convention. See, J.C. Kurudamannil, "Maramon Conventionile Prabhashakarum, Paribhashakar-um", In: *Maramon Convention Sadabhti Valyam* (Malayalam), *op.cit.*, 81–97.

500 It is reported that Thomas Walker addressed the Mar Thoma Church audience three-times a day at various meetings that were scheduled at the *Maramon convention. Ibid.*

501 *Letter of Thomas Walker to Mrs. Walker, dated* 15th *February 1900, Maramon,* India. J.C. Kurudamannil, "Maramon Cnnventionile Prabhashakaurum Paribhashakarum, (Malayalam)", In: *Maramon Convention Satabhdi Valyam,* (Malayalam), *op.cit.*, 84.

decision to keep comity principles in relation to other missions,[502] the Mar Thoma Church accepted his appeal and started its mission in North Travancore in 1901.[503] The Mar Thoma Church's acceptance of the archdeacon's proposal was attributed to the historical broad relationship that existed with the Anglican-CMS missionaries. As the mutual relationship of the Mar Thoma Church and the CMS missions began to mature, the manifestations of this relationship in different parts of Kerala meant people started being aware of these ties. The growing enthusiasm for missionary co-operation between the churches is also evident in these words of M.M. Thomas:

"When the Jacobite Syrian Christians who heard the gospel"[504] from the MTEA evangelists in North Travancore and those who "attended the preaching and prayer meeting were excommunicated, they approached the CMS for help. It was on the persuasion of the latter that the Association decided to start to care pastorally for evangelically-minded Christians".[505]

In an article in *Malankara Sabha Tharaka*, the official church magazine of the Mar Thoma Church, Eli Koshy Karimparambil commented on the arrival of CMS missionaries F.S. Nicholson and Sara Mackibbin to Keral in 1894. Eli Koshy, who had seen the missionaries, wrote that Anglican priest T.K. Kuruvilla could have adviced the visitors to meet the then Metropolitan, Titus I (1894–1909), to enquire on the feasibility of starting their mission work under the auspices of the Mar Thoma Church in Kerala.[506] George Alexander, former general secretary of the MTEA, reported that the then Anglican Bishop, E.N. Hodges (1890–1904), directed the women missionaries to see the Metropolitan and discuss the practicability

---

502 MTEA has taken a decision not to start a mission field within the jurisdiction of the other mission agencies in India.
503 George Alexander, "Malankara Mar Thoma Suvishesha Prasangha Charithra Samgraham" (Malayalam), In: *Maramon Convention Satabhdi Valyam*, (Malayalam), *op.cit.*, 185. The Mar Thoma Church followed a policy to keep the principle of comity in the mission fields. MTEA took policy not to start mission fields in the other Christian dominated areas. The MTEA was reluctant to start a mission work in North Travancore area as it was dominated by the Jacobite Church members.
504 C.P. Mathew and M.M. Thomas, *The Indian Churches of Saint Thomas, op.cit.*, 108; *Vadakkan Thiruvitamkur Suvishesham*, (Malayalam), (Tiruvalla: History Publication Committee, 1950).
505 *Ibid.*
506 Eli Koshy, "Nooramathe Vayasil Ezhuthiya Lekhanam" (Malayalam), In: *Malankara Sabha Tharaka*, (April/(2005), 13–14; N.M. Mathew, *Malankara Mar Thoma Sabha Charithram*, Vol. II, (Malayalam), *op.cit.*, 166.

of starting work under the Mar Thoma Church.[507] The Metropolitan, before permitting them to start work in Kerala, sought the advice of the then CMS President and Anglican Bishop E.N. Hodges on their appointment as missionaries patronised by the Mar Thoma Church.[508] The mutual recognition policy of both churches had thus manifested itself already by the beginning of the 20th Century.

Both churches not only considered their mutual relation as inviolable, but also tended to engage each other to promote common programmes for cementing the existing relationship. Members of both the churches started a union Bible convention in Mallappally, a *taluk* (administrative division) in Kerala, in 1922. It is still jointly conducted by the members of the Mar Thoma Church and the CSI.[509]

It is obvious that the Mar Thoma Church kept a positive relationship with the CMS missionaries. The church also established an equally positive relation with the British government authorities in India as well. During this phase, the British government authorities noted the Mar Thoma Church's positive ties with the Church of England's CMS missionaries, and they encouraged it.

Ferguson, the then Malabar collector of the British government, encouraged the MISC Metropolitan to officiate in the consecration of the Mar Thoma Church Metropolitan in 1893–1894, when the Jacobite faction of the Mar Thoma community openly discourged it.[510]

The propensity among the Mar Thoma Church leaders and the Anglican CMS missionaries was thus to see themselves as partners in the common missionary task in India and to seek its improvement through the common use of spiritual and doctrinal resources of the traditional Mar Thoma Church in India and the rich missionary tradition of the CMS. In that process, they believed that it was essential to remove obstacles and contradictions, at least within the MTEA. This was to make mutual acceptance of missions to be a decisive motivating element in the missionary co-operation phase by keeping their own functional independence and autonomy in India. This developed into stronger co-operation in the mission

507 George Alexander, "Malankara Mar Thoma Suvishesha Prasangha Charithra Samgraham" (Malayalam), In: *Maramon Convention Satabhdi Valyam, (Malayalam), op.cit.,* 176.

508 *Ibid.*

509 V. Titus Varghese, "Convention Yogangal – Oru Thirinju Nottam" (Malayalam), In: *Mallappally Union Christian Convention, Golden Jubilee Memorial Volume,* (Mallappally: Mallapaly Union Christian Convention, 1981), 9–12; "Mallappali Union Christian Conventionte Charithra Samkshpam", In: *Ibid.,* 13–20.

510 N.M. Mathew, *Malankara Mar Thoma Sabha Charithram,* Vol. II, (Malayalam), *op.cit.,* 150.

field and raised the question of the nature and quality of the historic relationship between the Mar Thoma Church and the Church of England.

The Mar Thoma Church also adopted some of the Church of England doctrines. For instance, in the presidential address on the occasion of Mar Thoma Church Metropolitan Titus II's (1909–1944) silver jubilee in 1924, Anglican Bishop Charles Hope Gill (1905–1925) made it clear that not only was there a close similarity in the spiritual matters of the missionary wing of the Church of England and the Mar Thoma Church, the Indian church could draw on the Anglican Church's faith and doctrine as found in its "Book of Common Prayer" and in its "Articles of Faith".[511]

The Anglican doctrines such as the acceptance of the Nicene-Constantinople Creed, Faith in the Holy Trinity – Father, Son and the Holy Spirit – the resurrection of Jesus Christ, the sufficiency of the Holy Scriptures for salvation, the authority of the Church, ministry of the church, the sacraments and traditions of the church are in conformity with the doctrines of the Mar Thoma Church.[512]

By this way, the Mar Thoma Church hoped to continue being part of the historic Mar Thoma church tradition that they cherish and cultivate a contemporary Mar Thoma ethos, that upholds both tradition and reform elements together. The contemporary Mar Thoma Church tradition is a participatory and composite one sustained by spiritual, liturgical and reform values of the traditional Mar Thoma and other Eastern churches, on one hand, and those of the Anglican Church, on the other, all within a distinctly Indian setting. The leaders of both churches have devoted considerable amount of time to nurture it by signing a formal agreement, signifying their missionary and doctrinal common nature in 1937.

This agreement, signed between the Mar Thoma Church and the Anglican Church, represented by the Church of India, Burma and Ceylon, also had the provision of "occasional inter-communion" between both churches.

The agreement can be considered as a positive corollary to the Mar Thoma Church's missionary co-operation with the CMS, followed by an unrelenting cordiality with the Church of England, which bore more missionary rewards. Occasional inter-communion permitted members to receive communion from the altar

---

511 Summary of the Presidential Address delivered by Bishop Dr. Gill on the Silver Jubilee celebration of the Mar Thoma Metropolitan, Kottayam, 1936. See, T.C. Chacko, *Malankara Mar Thoma Sabha Charithra Sangraham*, (Malayalam), *op.cit.*, 243–244.

512 Thirty Nine Articles of Faith, the Church of England In: *http://www.churchsociety. org/issues_new/doctrine/39a/iss_doctrine_39A_intro.asp* visited on 15th December 2011; *The Constitution of the Mar Thoma Syrian Church of Malabar*, (Tiruvalla: Mar Thoma Church, 2002), 1–3.

of the other. The mutual agreement on membership permitted the churches to issue membership to members of both churches, by authorisation from bishops. In the search for full communion relation with the Anglican Communion, the Mar Thoma Church succeeded in reaching an agreement for "occasional inter-communion" with the Church of India, Burma and Ceylon (CIBC).[513]

Anglican Church in India

The Anglican presence in India dates back to 1608, when the English East India Company, founded as a British trading company by Queen Elizabeth I's (1533–1603) Royal Charter in 1600, got a permission to establish a warehouse at Surat in India from India's Mughal Emperor, Jahangir (1605–1627). From that time, the British missionaries and the Anglican chaplains started arriving in India from time to time. However, it was only in 1813 that the East India Act of the British Parliament opened India for mission work, together with the authorisation to establish a Church of England Diocese at Calcutta.

Thus the first Anglican diocese was established in Calcutta in 1814. Subsequently, Anglican Dioceses were formed in Madras in 1834, Bombay in 1837 and Travancore-Cochin in 1879, with the episcopal authority derived from the Church of England.[514]

The Indian Church Act 1927 of the British Parliament and the Indian Church Measure of 1927 made a provision for the dissolution of the legal union between the Church of England in India.[515] Under this provision of the Church of India Act 1927, the Church of India was dissolved and became part of the Church of India, Burma and Ceylon (CIBC) in 1927.

It was when the points of the Bonn Agreement between the Anglican Church and the Old Catholic Church was accepted by the CIBC in 1932,[516] that a fresh discussion on "occasional inter-communion" relation between the Mar Thoma Church and the CIBC surfaced in discussions between the leadership of both

513   Hereafter referred as CIBC. India was divided into India and Pakistan during India's independence in 1947. Consequently, the Church in Pakistan became a CIBC member, and thus it is renamed as Church of India, Pakistan, Burma and Ceylon (CIPBC).

514   Noel Davis, Martin Convoy, *World Christianity in the 20th Century,* (London: SCM Press, 2008), 133–134.

515   *Indian Church Act, 1927* (17 &18 Geo. V, Chapter 40), United Kingdom, 209–219; *Indian Church Measure 1927* (17 &18, Geo V, No. 1), United Kingdom, 1927.

516   "Details of Acceptance of the Bonn Agreement by Churches of the Anglican Communion", In: *WEF/File 8, Archive of the Lambeth Palace,* 27th August 1971.

churches. The agreed points in a joint statement of the representatives of the Anglican Church and the Old Catholic Church in Bonn on 2 July, 1931 says:

1. Each communion recognizes the catholicity and independence of the other and maintains its own.
2. Each communion agrees to admit members of the other communion to participate in the sacraments.
3. Inter-communion does not require from either communion the acceptance of all doctrinal opinion, sacramental devotion, or liturgical practice characteristic of the other, but implies that each believes the other to hold all essentials of the Christian faith.[517]

The expounders of this new model for church unity – the Anglican and the Old Catholic Churches – agreed that "if two churches are in agreement on the essentials of doctrine and church order, even wide divergence in interpretation and practice ought not hold them apart".[518] This agreement was beneficial to both the Mar Thoma Church and the CIBC to leave questions relating to their historical baggage, as the two churches belonged to the eastern and western church traditions. Therefore, the two churches decided to utilize opportunities for making use of the statement's spirit of the non-requirement of full agreement on every details of their doctrinal and sacramental position as a precondition for their discussions on inter-communion.

The effect of this was that the CIBC's episcopal synod, which met in 1933, set up a committee with Bishop E.A.L. Moore (1925–1937)[519] as the convenor to study the Mar Thoma Church's faith and order position, in order to find the feasibility for starting "occasional inter-communion" with the Mar Thoma Church. The committee's formation was likely to have resulted from the 1930 Lambeth Conference's authorization to the bishops of the CIBC to go ahead with "the task

---

517 "Old Catholic Church 167 – Statement Agreed Between the Representatives of the Old Catholic Church and the Churches of the Anglican Communion at a Conference held at Bonn July, 2, 1931", In: G.K.A Bell, *Documents on Christian Unity, Third Series 1930–1948, op.cit., 60;* Report of the Meeting of the Commission of the Anglican Communion and the Old Catholic Churches held at Bonn on Thursday, July 2, 1931, London, 1931/32, cited In: Routh Rouse and Stephen Neill, *A History of the Ecumenical Movement,* Vol. I, (1517–1948, *op.cit.,* 470; Harald Rein, *Kirchengemeinschaft: Die Anglikanisch – Altkatholisch – Orthodoxen Beziehungen von 1870 Bis 1990 Und Ihre okumenische Relevanz,* (Bern: P. Lang, 1993), 173.
518 Routh Rouse and Stephen Neill, *A History of the Ecumenical Movement,* Vol. I, (1517–1948), *op.cit.,* 470.
519 Bishop E.A.L Moore was the fourth Anglican Bishop of Travancore – Cochin Diocese during the period of 1925–1937.

of working out in detail the principles which are embodied"[520] in the South Indian Church union scheme.[521]

The Mar Thoma Church's Metropolitan, Titus II (1909–1944), its Suffragan Metropolitan, Abraham Mar Thoma (1917–1947), and CIBC's Bishop E.A.L. Moore were only applying the churches unity principles in faith and order with a view to enter into a new phase of "occasional inter-communion" relationship and to enhance the unity of both churches with a common Eucharistic fellowship. They expedited the committees' agenda to examine the faith and order of both churches, independently.

It was reported that …

"… after consideration and investigation, they came to the conclusion that there was no bar to inter-communion between the two churches on doctrinal grounds".[522]

The CIBC committee reported to the church's episcopal synod with their recommendation that "the committee was fully satisfied that there was no solid ground for refusing to recognise the Mar Thoma Orders, and that the "form" used in the Mar Thoma Church was adequate"[523] for entering into an "occasional inter-communion" between both the churches. At the general council of the CIBC in 1935, a decision was taken to "appoint a committee to carry on official negotiations"[524] with the Mar Thoma Church and authorised Bishop E.A.L. Moore to make necessary steps to further the process. If that common agreement was to happen, Bishop Moore was authorised to enter into an agreement on "occasional inter-communion" with the Mar Thoma Church, in consultation with the other CIBC bishops, without referring the matter again in the general council, for their mandate.

Consequently, a joint committee was formed by both churches under the Mar Thoma Metropolitan and Bishop Moore. The committee unanimously took a decision that …

"… there was no bar in respect of order, worship and doctrines to the formal establishment of the measure of intercommunion, known as 'occasional inter-communion', between the two churches".[525]

---

520 *Resolution 40, e. Church Union – South India, Lambeth Conference Archives 1930 – Resolution, www.lambethconference.org/resolutions/1930* visited on 10th October 1911.
521 "Resolution 4, Episcopal Synod of the Church of India, Burma, and Ceylon, 1933", In: C.E. Abraham. Ed., *Mar Thoma Syrian Church and the Church of India and the Church of south India,* (Tiruvalla: Mar Thoma Church, 1968), 5.
522 *Ibid.,* 5–6.
523 *Ibid.,* 6.
524 *Ibid.*
525 *Ibid.*

The Metropolitan included this as an agenda at the church's *samasthalochana sabha* meetings during 5–6 May 1936 that resolved to authorise him to implement the "occasional inter-communion" relation with the CIBC's Travancore-Cochin Diocese with two notes.[526]

1. On occasions when for reasons not involving breaches of rules the members of a church are not able to participate in Holy Communion in their own church, they may be admitted to Holy Communion in the other church and they may partake of the same.
2. Each church may allow its members to partake of Holy Communion on special occasions from the other church, even though there is nothing standing in the way of the members receiving communion from their own church.[527]

The Mar Thoma Church's resolution at first pointed out that both churches are in agreement on the questions of faith and order. However it did not try to explain the common agreed points in particular and therefore acted upon in accordance with the remarks of the CIBC. Having received the Mar Thoma Church's favourable decision, Bishop Moore acted according to the authorization given by him by the CIBC's general council of 1935 and "authorisation was solemnly promulgated in St. Paul's Cathedral, Calcutta, on 4 April, 1937".[528]

The "occasional inter-communion" relation between both the churches was greeted with enthusiasm in the Mar Thoma Church. This relationship revealed to the Mar Thoma Church the recognition of its catholicity, and on its self-determined independent and autonomous existence, the possibility of attaining more ecumenical progress through its persistent ecumenical engagements with the ecumenical movement and above all its self-understanding as the "bridge church" that connects both the eastern and the western church traditions. This had an element of relevance in the ecumenical movement, the details of which have been highlighted in the next section.

The Anglican Church's acknowledgement of the Mar Thoma Church's faith, order and ministry, and the agreement on "occasional inter-communion" created a viable atmosphere for the Mar Thoma Church leaders to have a positive interaction with the Anglican Church. This led to the Anglican Church allowing members of the Mar Thoma Church into its own fold, where the Indian church had no parishes.

---

526 *Resolution of the Mar Thoma Syrian Samudayalochana sabha,* May 5, 6, 1936, Tiruvalla.
527 *Ibid.*
528 *Ibid.*

Agreement on membership

The mutual agreement on membership, together with new provisions for a close relationship between the Mar Thoma Church and the Anglican Church, was the result of the new historical context of the migration of the Mar Thoma Church members to other countries. The outflow from Kerala had been affecting the corporate life of the church since 1930.

When the British colonists allowed their subjects to migrate to other British colonies, the Mar Thoma Church members started migrating to Malaysia and to other Indian cities, looking for better prospects. The migration started in 1912 and intensified after 1930s.[529] Those migrant church members organised worship centres, on the advice of the Metropolitan.[530]

By 1950s, the Mar Thoma Church members had spread widely in Malaysia, Singapore and Indian cities. This placed a burden on the church leaders to provide a comfortable pastoral and episcopal oversight for its members in these distant lands, resulting in a context that moved the Mar Thoma Church to take initiatives to strengthen the existing ties with the Anglican Church.

In response to an initiative by Metropolitan Juhanon Mar Thoma, the representatives of both Anglican and Mar Thoma Churches met at Tiruvalla in Kerala during 18–19 August, 1957, and reiterated that …

> "… each church recognises the catholicity and independence of the other and maintains its own, and that inter-communion does not require from either church the acceptance of all doctrinal opinions, sacramental devotion or liturgical practice, characteristic of the other, but implies that each believes the other to hold all essentials of the Christian faith".[531]

This meeting agreed upon nine "Rules of Comity"[532] based on the Bonn Agreement and decided to find feasibilities for the full communion relation between churches. An addendum to the preamble and "rules of comity" approved by the Mar Thoma Church and the CIPBC says:

> With reference to the addendum to the Record, the committee, while recognizing that further study of the implications of mutual participation in the consecration of

---

529 *Interview with T.M. Mathew, Mar Thoma Syrian Church, Singapore,* dated 12 November 2011.

530 *Kalpana of the Titus II to T.N. Koshy, the first vicar of the Malaya – Singapore,* dated 1936.

531 C.E. Abraham, ed., *The Mar Thoma Syrian Church, and the Church of India, and the Church of South India, Mar Thoma Church, op. cit.,* 6–7.

532 *Ibid.,* 7–9.

Bishops may still be desirable, resolved to record its considered opinion that in view of the information already before it and the measure of inter-communion now proposed to be recognized analogous to that between the Anglican and Old Catholic Churches, the implementation of such mutual participation in consecration need no longer be delayed.[533]

The desire of both the churches to implement inter-communion and episcopal participation in the bishop's consecrations on the basis of the Bonn Agreement is visible. The "occasional inter-communion" between both the churches helped them to progress the mutual relations between the churches in the later period. Besides the existing "occasional inter-communion" agreements, there was agreement in both churches on the following:

1. Members of the Mar Thoma Church may be granted membership in an Anglican parish by the Anglican bishop, with the permission of the MT Metropolitan in places where a Mar Thoma parish does not exist, and vice versa.
2. The Mar Thoma Church's members may receive the Anglican episcopal supervision in places where the Mar Thoma Church has no parishes and vice versa.
3. A change of membership from one church to another will be permitted only with the consent of the authorities concerned of both the churches.[534]

As can be seen in these points, the Mar Thoma Church tended to feel more comfortable in receiving pastoral care and episcopal supervision from the Anglican Church in places where it had no parishes. However, its real significance was in the implied equal ecclesiological status of the Mar Thoma Church and the Anglican Church as reflected in the move to allow Anglican "bishops of provinces or of missionary dioceses of the Anglican communion to exercise episcopal supervision over the clergy and laity of the Mar Thoma Syrian Church on the request of the authorities of the church"[535], which was in compliance with the Lambeth Conference 1948 decision

---

533 "Preamble and Rules of Comity, A.(C), an addendum; in Anglican Mar Thoma Conversations August 1957", In: *Ibid.*, 4–5.
534 *Ibid.*
535 The Anglican Church's position on the question of validity of the celebrant in the Eucharist and ordination was well defined in the Lambeth Conference in 1958. The Report of the Committee of the Lambeth Conference of 1958 on "church unity and church universal" says that "Anglican's conscientiously hold that the celebrant of the Eucharist should have been ordained by the bishop standing in the historic succession, and generally believe it their duty to bear witness to this principle by receiving Holy communion only from those who have thus been ordained". See, *The Lambeth Conference 1958, The Encyclical Letter from Bishops together with Resolutions and*

176

and vice versa.[536] The Lambeth Conference 1958, Resolution 44, approved the relation of the Anglican Church with the Mar Thoma Syrian Church and says:

> The Conference notes with interest the discussions now in progress between the Church of India, Pakistan, Burma and Ceylon and the Mar Thoma Church. It recommends that, before these discussions are brought to a conclusion, other churches, provinces, and dioceses of the Anglican Communion which are concerned with relations with Mar Thoma Christians should be taken into consultation so that if possible a common agreement may be reached by all authorities concerned.[537]

The most significant development of this phase was the agreement on Comity and the subsequent full communion agreement with the CIPBC. This agreement led to the opening of fresh consultations with the Anglican Communion churches in other parts of the world. The Mar Thoma Church considered those agreements as the church's success in its way towards the realisation of unity, as envisaged in the Nicene-Constantinople creed. It was in this context that under the leadership of Metropolitan Juhanon Mar Thoma, the Mar Thoma Church's General Assembly in 1961 adopted a resolution, requesting ...

> "... the episcopal synod to take necessary steps for mutual participation in the episcopal consecration of bishops in the Church of India, Pakistan, Burma and Ceylon (CIPBC) and the Mar Thoma Syrian Church".[538]

The full communion between both the churches materialised, when the 1968 Lambeth Conference's Resolution on "Relations with other churches – Reciprocal Acts ..."[539] formulated the terms and conditions for it.

Reports, Part 2, (London: SPCK, 1958), 2; Oliver S. Tomkins, ed., *The Third World Conference on Faith and Order, Lund, 1952,* (London: SCM, 1953), 52–53.

536 *Lambeth Conference Report, 1948,* Part II, 72; Roger Coleman, ed., *Resolutions of the Twelve Lambeth Conferences, 1867–1988,* (Toronto: Anglican Book Centre, 1992), 78.

537 "Resolutions from 1958, Resolution 44, Lambeth Conference Report, 1958", In: *www.lambethconference.org/resolutions/1958,* visited on March 14, 1958.

538 *Resolution No. 9, Minutes of the Mar Thomas Syrian Church's General Assembly,* 1961.

539 "Resolution 47, Lambeth Conference, 1968", In: *www.lambethconference.org/resolutions/1968* visited on 17th October 2011. It says; "The Conference recommends that, where there is agreement between an Anglican Church and some other Church or Churches to seek unity in a way which includes agreement on apostolic faith and order, and where that agreement to seek unity has found expression, whether in a covenant to unite or in some other appropriate form, a Church of the Anglican Communion should be free to allow reciprocal acts of inter-communion under the general direction of the bishop; each province concerned to determine when the negotiations for union in which it is engaged have reached the stage which allows this intercommunion."

The Conference recommends that, where there is agreement between an Anglican Church and some other church, or churches, to seek unity in a way, which includes agreement on apostolic faith and order, and where that agreement to seek unity has found expression, whether in a covenant to unite or in some other appropriate form, a Church of the Anglican Communion should be free to allow reciprocal acts of intercommunion under the general direction of the bishop; each province concerned to determine when the negotiations for union in which it is engaged have reached the stage which allows this intercommunion.[540]

Full communion agreement

It was against this backdrop of a progression of relations with the Anglican Church that the Mar Thoma Church's general assembly resolved to authorise the Metropolitan to take steps to further the full communion agreements with the member churches in the Anglican Communion.[541] Consequently, full communion relations were established with the Anglican Churches in South Africa, Hong Kong, and Ireland in 1975, with the American Episcopal churches in 1980, with the Episcopal churches in Canada in 1983 and with the Anglican Church in Australia in 1991.[542]

---

540 "Resolutions from 1968, Resolution 47, Lambeth Conference Report, 1968", In: *http://www.lambethconference.org/resolutions/1968/1968-47.cfm*, visited on January 14, 2014.

541 *Minutes of the Mar Thoma Syrian Church's General Assembly*, 1971.

542 Juhanon Mar Themotheos, "Mar Thoma Sabhayum Athinte Prathyekathayum" (Malayalam), In: *Malankara Sabha Tharaka* Vol. 4, Makaram (Malayalam Era/116), (Feb/1928), 115–129. P.M. Thomas, ed., *Mar Thoma Sabha Directory, op.cit.*, 136; N.M. Mathew, *Mar Thoma Sabha Charithram*, Vol. III, (Malayalam), *op.cit.*, 145–146.

Chapter XI
A New Ecumenical Paradigm

The first major ecumenical step of the Mar Thoma Church during the second half of the 20th Century was an Encyclical from the Metropolitan in 1952, in which the episcopal synod affirmed its need "to declare its readiness to become part of the Church of Christ in India".[543] The Mar Thoma Church's engagements with the Church of South India (CSI)[544] and the Church of North India (CNI)[545] became significant in this regard.

In 1947, Protestant churches in India shed their individual existence and merged together to form the CSI. This led to a call from ecumenical movements in India for the need to have organic unity[546] movements in India. In this context, the

---

543 Juhanon Mar Thoma, Mathews Mar Athanasius, "A Call to the Churches of Christ in India", *Joint Statement of Juhanon Mar Thoma and Mathews Mar Athanasius to Indian Churches,* December 21, 1952, Tiruvalla.

544 Church of South India (CSI) is a united church of India by the merger of the CIPBC and Protestant Churches in South India, following the organic union model of church unity in 1947. This church is the second largest Christian church in India.
    See, J. Russel Chandran, "A Brief History and Interpretation", In: *www.csimkd.org/ History_of_csi_html.* visited on 6th June, 2012; K.M. George, *Church of South India – Life in Union, (1947–1997)* (New Delhi: CSS & ISPCK, 1999) 1–10; Rajaiah D. Paul, *Ecumenism in Action: A Historical Survey of the Church of South India* (Madras: CLS, 1972), 1–6.

545 Hereafter referred as CNI. The CNI is a united church of India, which came into being in 1971 by the merger of the CIPBC, United Church of Northern India, the Baptist Churches of Northern India, the Brethren Church in India, the Methodist Church and the Disciples of Christ denominations following the organic union model of church unity. This church is a major church in North India.
    See, "The Church of North India", In: *www.C.N.I.synod.org.* Visited on 6th June, 2012; J. Russell Chandran, *Joint Council of the Church of North India, The Church of South India and the Malankara Mar Thoma Syrian Church: A Brief Account of the History and Meaning of its Formation,* (New Delhi: ISPCK, 1984), 18.

546 "Organic unity" model refers to an ecumenical model for church unity. It subscribes the union of different denominational churches merged together to form one united church. Thomas Mar Athanasius, "The Concept of Church Unity", a Paper presented at the Consultation on *"Conciliar Unity"* at the St. Augustine Study Centre,

Mar Thoma Church's existing relation with the CIPBC,[547] that was working well, pushed the church to look for union with the united protestant churches in India. This chapter attempts to describe the history of Mar Thoma Church's church unity engagements with the CSI and CNI and explore how those engagements have helped it go forward and examine the conciliar fellowship model of unity. An attempt is also made to assess the effectiveness of this model of ecumenical praxis in its engagement with the CSI and CNI, the subsequent formation of the Joint Council of the CSI-CNI-Mar Thoma Church and the Communion of Churches in India (CCI).[548] The period relevant for the study in this chapter, is roughly 1961–2010, during which the conciliar fellowship model took institutional shape in the CSI-CNI-MTC Joint Council.

Defining conciliar fellowship

Conciliar fellowship is a model of church unity that combines the meanings of a traditional Old Testament "assembly"[549] called to plan a common action, the New Testament *ecclesia*[550] council that was called out for a special task and the "ecumenical councils" of Nicea, Constantinople and Ephesus aimed to defend the apostolic faith. It is therefore a form of church unity that strengthens God's given unity in "each place"[551] and in "all places"[552], thereby enabling the local churches to develop common structures in the form of "councils" for common mission and decision-making. This form of "communion" finds expression in the "common council", in the common confession of faith, in the celebration of the baptism and Eucharist and in the exercise of the Ministry. In this sense, the "common council" is a means of enabling local churches to express the unity of the "One Holy, Catholic and Apostolic

---

16ᵗʰ August, 1979, In: M.J. Joseph, ed., *Conciliar Fellowship* (Manganam: St. Augustine study Centre, 1979), 38–42.; Thomas F. Best, "Unity Models of", In: Nicholas Lossky and others ed., *Dictionary of the Ecumenical Movement, op.cit.*, 1173–1175.

547 For more details see the Chapter X, History of the Anglican Church in India, pp. 170ff.

548 Hereafter referred as CCI.

549 Psalms 83: 3, 68: 27.

550 St. Mathew 5: 22; Acts 4: 15.

551 Lesslie Newbigin, "Organic Union", In: Nicholas Lossky and others ed., *Dictionary of the Ecumenical Movement, op.cit.*, 1160–1161.

552 Lesslie Newbigin, "Unity of "All in Each Place"", In: Nicholas Lossky and others ed., *Dictionary of the Ecumenical Movement, op.cit.*, 1175–1178.

Church".[553] In a spatial sense, it refers to the "state of relatedness and its expression through everyday living, grounded on mutual co-operation and mutual trust"[554] of the churches.

It was against the backdrop of the discussions on the organic unity model as the best model of unity for the Indian churches that fresh discussions on a new model for unity – conciliar fellowship – surfaced in discussions of the WCC's General Assembly in 1961 and was adopted during the General Assembly in Nairobi in 1975.

The history of the development of a "conciliar model" of unity in the World Council of Churches could be traced from the "Toronto Statement in 1950" on "The Church, the Churches and the World Council of Churches".[555] Although the term, "conciliarity", did not find explicit expression in the document, an effort was made to explain the meaning of inter-church relationship in it. Consequently, the Faith and Order Commission's meeting at New Haven in 1957 initiated a study process on "The Nature of the Unity We Seek".[556] In the light of this meeting, the New Delhi Assembly (1961) came to regard "one fully-committed fellowship" as the goal of the ecumenical movement.

This enabled the "Faith and Order" meeting held at Bristol in 1967 to define the goal of the ecumenical movement in terms of "conciliar fellowship". This was the premise of the WCC Uppsala General Assembly's (1968) emphasis for the need to stress the "unity" of "all Christians" in "all places". Uppsala suggested that the WCC should work for a genuinely "universal council", comprising of members from all churches.[557] The idea for the formation of a "universal council" was taken up at the Faith and Order consultation in Louvain in 1971 and in Salamanca in Spain in 1973. Lukas Vischer, the then director of the "Faith and Order" secretariat, presented this idea for a "universal council" in the central committee of the WCC in 1969 with certain proposals for the founding of a universal council.[558]

553 *Ibid.*

554 Geogfrey Weinwright, "Conciliarity and Eucharist", In: *op.cit.*, 78–80.

555 "The Church, the Churches and the World Council of Churches: The Ecclesiological Significance of the World Council of Churches", In: *A Documentary History of the Faith and Order Movement: 1927–1963*, (St. Louis, Bethany Press, 1963), 167–176.

556 *Minutes of the Commission on Faith and Order, New Haven, 1957*, Faith and Order Paper No. 25, (Geneva: World Council of Churches, 1957) 11–28.

557 See, Norman Goodall ed, *The Uppsala Report 1968: Official Report of the Fourth Assembly of the World Council of Churches*, Section I, *op.cit.*, 19.

558 Lukas Vischer, "a Genuinely Universal Council...?", In: *The Ecumenical Review*, 22, (1970), 97–106.

In the central committee meeting of the WCC at Addis Ababa in 1971, the committee felt the need for the WCC to formulate the goal of the unity of the church in an accepted way of all member churches.[559] The Louvain meeting of the Faith and Order Commission in 1971 adopted it in the context of a concept, "Unity of the Church – the unity of the Mankind". The report of the 1971 consultation was titled "Conciliarity and Future of the Ecumenical Movement".[560]

These studies and discussions formulated a theoretical framework for the "conciliar fellowship" model at the Salamanca "Faith and Order" consultation in 1974 that discussed the question: "What unity requires?" Salamanca described its vision of one Church in terms of "conciliar fellowship" of united local churches. Each church should recognize other members and ministries of other denominations.[561] These discussions on "conciliar fellowship" led the Nairobi Assembly of the WCC (1975) to present conciliar model as a concrete model for church unity.[562]

Unity in diversity

Surprisingly, the Mar Thoma Church's understanding of church unity that aimed at keeping the individuality of churches, while maintaining full-communion relationships, was in line with the world ecumenical discussions on conciliar fellowship. The conciliar model appealed to the Mar Thoma Church as the church unity model that can keep unity in diversity. The model also called for the unity of the churches at the local and national levels, even as the individual churches kept their autonomy. Consequently, the Mar Thoma Church wanted to form a common council

---

559 *Central Committee of the World Council of Churches, Minutes and Reports of the Twenty fourth Meeting, Addis Ababa,* January 1971, (Geneva: World Council of Churches, 1971), 49; Aram Keshishian, *Conciliar Fellowship: A Common Goal,* (Geneva: World Council of Churches, 1992), 6–22.

560 *Faith and Order, Louvain, 1971, Study Reports and Documents, Faith and Order* Paper No. 59, (Geneva: World Council of Churches, 1971, 225–229.

561 Document III.1, "the Unity of the Church-Next Steps", In: Gunther Gassmann ed, *Documentary History of the Faith and Order 1963–1993,* Faith and Order paper No. 159, (Geneva: WCC Publication, 1993, 35–49.

562 See, *Ecumenical Collaboration at the Regional, National and Local Levels,* (Vatican: Secretariat for Promoting Christian Unity, 1980), 19; Emmanuel Lanne, "Conciliarity", In: Nicholas Lossky and others ed., *Dictionary of the Ecumenical Movement, op.cit.,* 235–236.

with the CSI and CNI to serve as a common platform for common mission[563] and decision-making for common programmes.[564] The church's advocacy for the formation of a common council of three churches could be seen as a step forward in its ecumenical praxis through the conciliar fellowship route – from its previous church unity engagements with the MISC, CIPBC and the Anglican Communion churches, when the question of a common council never came up. The church then focussed mainly on full communion relations.

The formation of the CSI-CNI-MTC Joint Council in 1978 was a significant manifestation of the conciliar model. It was the crowning glory of the Mar Thoma Church's ecumenical engagements with other Indian churches for generations. The cultural and social basis of these engagements was the broader outlook and the resulting ecumenical praxis, which we have amply discussed in the previous chapters.

Unfortunately, the vision of the Mar Thoma Church to launch new joint projects on evangelism, medical mission and education through the joint council did not materialise. There were hopes for ambitious projects, but that would have required commitment and mutual responsibility at local and national levels, which somehow seemed missing.[565]

Ecumenical engagement with the CSI

The unity movements in the Indian Protestant churches sparked the ecumenical engagements of the Mar Thoma Church with the CSI, although the progression towards this could traced back to 1816, when the church set out to have strong missionary ties with the CMS. Consequently, from the first decade of the 20th Century onwards, the Mar Thoma Church felt a sense of solidarity with the church unity engagements of the Protestant churches in India.[566] Besides, the church was inspired by its ecumenical

---

563 The suggested common mission agenda was the founding of a Joint Theological College for training both churches' clergy; adopting some mission fields jointly run by both the churches for the evangelization of India.

564 C.V. John, "Mar Thoma Sabhayum Aykya Sambrambhangalum" (Malayalam), In: M.J. Joseph ed., *Conciliar Fellowship*, *op.cit.*, 43–52; M.A. Paylee, "Sabhaikathinte Swabhavam", (Malayalam), In: *Ibid.*, 53–57; Thomas Mar Athanasius, "The Nature of the Conciliar Fellowship", In: *Ibid.*, 38–42.

565 Thomas Mar Athanasius, "The Nature of the Conciliar Fellowship", In: *Ibid.*, 40.

566 The Protestant church unity history in south India starts when a federal union took place between Presbyterian missions – the United Free Church of Scotland Mission, the American Arcot Mission of the American Dutch Reformed Church and the Basel

engagements with the Church of England's CIBC, CIPBC and MISC. Those ecumenical engagements boosted the Mar Thoma Church to widen its church unity engagements with the united Protestant churches and Orthodox Syrian churches in India.

An analysis shows that the Mar Thoma Church's unity discussions with the CSI were held in three phases. In the first phase (1919–1952), the church tried to educate its members with a view to equip itself for conciliar fellowship initially with the Church of England groups CIBC and CIPBC, and later with the CSI. The second phase (1953–1971) saw the church coming out publicly with its official pronouncement of its stance on church unity in the form of committee resolutions, reports and Joint Theological Committee resolutions. The above efforts culminated in the agreement reached between both the churches for a full communion relationship and the formation of a joint advisory council, in the third phase (1971–).

Preparing the church

Concerted efforts were made within the Mar Thoma Church towards priming its members ahead of the church unity engagements in India. The message was communicated through conduits such as the Metropolitan's circulars and the writings of church council and lay leaders in the *Malankara Sabha Tharaka*. The church affirmed the conciliar fellowship model in these moves, against the organic unity model proposed by the CSI and CNI in ecumenical engagements. The following analysis advances a hypothesis linking factors promoting the Mar Thoma Church towards the concept of conciliar fellowship. Here we try to explore why such an initiative for conciliar fellowship occurs in the Mar Thoma Church in its relationship with the CSI.

The new impulse from the church unity discussions between the Protestant churches in India since 1919 challenged members of the Mar Thoma Church to join in the church unity movements. But the mainline thinking of the Mar Thoma

---

Mission in 1901. A similar church unity process was taken place when the London Missionary Society churches, (Congregationalists) started unity engagements with the congregational churches of the American Board of Missions in South India and Jafna in Sri Lanka. This eventually led to the merger of the above two traditions forming a federal union in 1904. Followed by the success of these mergers both the Congregational and the Presbyterian traditions started a fresh discussion for the merger of both and was materialised by forming the South India United Church (SIUC) in 1908. See, J. Russell Chandran, ed., *The Joint Council of the Church of South India, The Church of North India and The Malankara Mar Thoma Syrian Church: A Brief account of the History and meaning of its formations, op.cit.,* 10.

Church was not in favour of the merger of churches for the sake of unity on the ground that it would indirectly force the churches to discard its individual autonomy and identity.[567]

The strength of the Mar Thoma Church's ecumenical relation with the MISC, CIBC and CIPBC in the past had become the mirror by which Mar Thoma Church could reflect its oriental liturgical, as well as ecumenical, potentialities. This enabled it to remain an independent church, upholding at the same time the new ecumenical paradigm of conciliar fellowship in its engagements with the Protestant churches.

The Mar Thoma Church's approach to church unity engagements with the CSI was mixed. The Protestant church unity efforts appeared distasteful to the Mar Thoma Church as a narrow Protestant church movement that excluded the Oriental churches. When the Mar Thoma Church received an invitation to the Protestant church unity meeting of Tranquebar in 1919,[568] it realised that the traditional Indian churches – the Malankara Jacobite Syrian Church and the MISC – were not invited.[569] This led to the Mar Thoma Church not participating in the talks. The Mar Thoma Church was also reluctant to join the unity discussions of the CSI as it would have hindered its relationship with the Jacobite Church.[570] It feared that the church's relation with the Protestant churches would likely retard the progress of its church unity aspiration with those Indian churches.[571] It was during this time that the Mar

---

567 *Reply Letter of Abraham Mar Thoma, C.P. Philipose and V.P. Mammen, to the invitation to join the church unity movement in 1919*, In: G.K.A. Bell, ed., *Documents on Christian Unity, 1920–1924, op.cit.*, 281–285; Juhanon Mar Thoma, Mathews Mar Athanasius, "A Call to the Churches of Christ in India," *Joint Statement of Juhanon Mar Thoma and Mathews Mar Athanasius to Indian Churches,* December 21, 1952, Tiruvalla.

568 Protestant church unity meeting of Tranqubar in 1919 decided to extend an invitation to the Mar Thoma Church to join with the church unity movements in south India. This meeting was the forerunner to the formation of the CSI in 1947.

569 The question of why the Indian Orthodox church's absence in the church unity discussion of the Protestant church unity movements during the first half of the twentieth century was that these churches belongs to the family of the Oriental Orthodox Churches.
See, H.S. Wilson ed., *Oriental Orthodox-Reformed Dialogue*, (Geneva: WARC, 1998); K.M. George, "Oriental Orthodox and Orthodox Dialogue", In: Nicholas Lossky and others ed., *Dictionary of the Ecumenical Movement, op.cit.*, 859–862.

570 T.P. Abraham, *Malankara Mar Thoma Sabha Noottandukaliloode (Malayalam)*, (Tiruvalla: CSS, 2012), 438.

571 *Ibid.*

Thoma Church started talks with the Malankara Jacobite Syrian Church in India, which led to the formation of the Union Christian College, Aluva.[572]

When 30 delegates of both the Anglican Church and the South Indian United Church (SIUC) met in Tranqubar in 1919 under the chairmanship of Bishop V.S. Azariah (1874–1945), to explore the possibility of an union of Indian Protestant churches, they decided to send an official invitation again to the Mar Thoma Church to join future church unity meetings with them.[573] It was in this context of a new invitation that the church had a rethink of its position. The then Suffragan Metropolitan, Abraham Mar Thoma (1880–1947), and two clergies – C.P. Philipose (1868–1948) and V.P. Mammen (1874–1952) – replied jointly, expressing their wish for common witness, while at the same time keeping the church's autonomous and independent existence as an Indigenous Indian entity.[574] But the church did not officially participate in the unity discussions of the Indian Protestant churches that finally led to the formation of the CSI. The same policy was adopted by the Mar Thoma Church, when it received an invitation to join the church unity discussions with the CSI in 1947.

---

572 The efforts of John R. Mott during his visit to India in 1912 was able to bring the Mar Thoma Church's Metropolitan, Titus II (1866–1944) and the Malankara Jacobite Syrian Church's Metropolitan, Mar Vattasseril Geevarghese Mar Dionysius (1858–1934) and some clergy together around one table for discussions in 1912. In this meeting a significant decision was taken for the founding of a union Christian school. This eventually led to an unofficial dialogue between the Mar Thoma Church and the Malankara Jacobite Syrian Church of India. The first phase of these discussions was done during 1912–1921. It was during these conversations of both the churches that they proposed to start a Union Christian College, in Kerala to symbolise the visible unity of the churches. This has dealt with the previous chapter of this study. Since then the Mar Thoma Church, the Malankara Orthodox Syrian Church and the Anglican Church "church unity" conversations continued during 1921–1940, without much visible results. Un-official Dialogue Group Discussions of the Mar Thoma Church and the Malankara Orthodox Syrian Church under the chairmanship of Paul Varghese (1922–1996) during the 1967–1980 led to the formulation of a common statement on "faith and order" of the both churches.

See, P.M. Thomas ed., *Mar Thoma Sabha Directory, op.cit.*, 139–140; C.V. John, "Mar Thoma Sabhayum Aikya Samrambhangalum" (Malayalam), In: M.J. Joseph, ed., *Conciliar Fellowship, op.cit.*, 43–52; Paul Varghese, M. Thommen, ed., *Orthodox – Mar Thoma Conversations: Some Papers and Statements from the Period 1968–70*, (Kottayam: 1971), 3.

573 *Ibid.*

574 "A Joint Letter of Abraham Mar Thoma, C.P. Philipose and V.P. Mammen", In: G.K.A. Bell ed., *Documents on Christian Unity 1920–4, op.cit.*, 281–285.

Thus the Mar Thoma Church was evidently not in favour of a merger with the CSI. For instance, when the Mar Thoma Church's general assembly in 1961 appointed a Theological Commission for finding feasibilities to further the existing relation with the CSI, the church made it clear in its terms of reference that the task of the commission was not to find feasibilities to reach the merger of the two churches, but to further the existing relations of the church with the CSI.[575]

It is not difficult to understand why the Mar Thoma Church did not favour a merger with the CSI. The church affirms the providence of its historical existence in India through centuries. That history brought about a confluence of three streams – the Syrian liturgical tradition, the Indian socio-cultural ethos and church reforms based on the primacy of the Word of God – which made up the substance of the church's identity. The Mar Thoma Church wants to safeguard that identity at all costs.

Secondly, the Mar Thoma Church was doubtful on the unresolved question of the validity of the ministerial orders of the CSI, as the CSI accepted the SIUC clergy, who were not ordained by the bishop's laying-on-of-hands.[576] CSI's acceptance of non-episcopal ordained ministers appeared to the Mar Thoma Church as a dilution of the tradition of ordination. This generated an ambiguity with regard to the episcopacy of the CSI to the church. I will return to this theme, but turn now to examine the Mar Thoma Church's treatment of the CSI invitation for merger, when the CIPBC merged with the CSI in 1947.

But the formation of the CSI did create an enthusiasm within the Mar Thoma Church on the possibility of more church unity engagements. The CSI union of churches from different Protestant traditions made the Mar Thoma Church's ecumenical engagements easier, as it had to deal with only one entity. This enthusiasm was primarily a result of the church's passion to work with other churches for the evangelisation of India, as well as to further the church's ecumenical praxis with

---

575 *Report of the Annual General Body of the Mar Thoma Church, on* May 16, 17, 1961, Mar Thoma Church office, Tiruvalla; See, Also cited In: T.P. Abraham, *Mar Thoma Sabha Noottandukaliloode,* (Malayalam), *op.cit.,* 596.

576 The SIUC had clergymen without Episcopal ordination. This was unacceptable to the leaders of the CIPBC and therefore they wanted the integration of the clergy within the CSI. They insisted that the laying-on-of- hands by the bishop for ordination is a requirement for the incorporation of a clergy into the three-fold ministry of the church. See, "Questions Raised by Lambeth Resolution 53, Lambeth Conference, 1948", In: C.E. Abraham, ed., *The Mar Thoma Syrian Church, the Church of India, the Church of south India* (Tiruvalla: Theological Commission of the Mar Thoma Church, 1967), 16–24. In: *The Report of the Metropolitan's Committee, 1953,* In: *Ibid.*

ecumenical institutions such as the NMS and National Council of Churches in India (NCCI), of which the member churches are from the different Protestant folds. The formation of the CSI in 1947 resulted in a situation that made it imperative for the Mar Thoma Church to take a decision on whether the "occasional intercommunion" relation, that existed with the CIPBC could continue with the CSI or not. Two concerns held back the Mar Thoma Church in copying its existing "occasional intercommunion" relation model with CIPBC for building relationship with the CSI. These concerns were the episcopal character of the CSI and its position on the validity of the clergy ordination – as some of the clergy members had no episcopal laying-on-of-hands in their ordination.

Concerning the episcopal character in the CSI, the CSI constitution says: "The CSI accepts and will maintain the historic episcopate in a constitutional form".[577] But as for its understanding about the nature and character of the episcopacy, the CSI continued to affirm that ...

"... this acceptance does not commit it to any particular interpretation of episcopacy or to any particular view or belief concerning orders of the ministry, and it will not require the acceptance of any such particular interpretation or view as necessary qualification for its ministry".[578]

The description of episcopacy in the CSI constitution is that...

"the CSI agrees that as episcopacy has been accepted in the church from the early times, it may be in the sense fitly be called historic and that it is needed for the shepherding and extension of the CSI. Any additional interpretations, though held by individuals, are not binding to the CSI".[579]

This constitutional interpretation of the episcopacy without defining its nature and character in clearer terms led to scepticism in the Mar Thoma Church about the episcopal character of the CSI. Meanwhile, the inclusion of the old SIUC clergy who were not duly ordained by a legitimate bishop remained an unresolved problem.

But the CSI constitution made it clear that in future "every ordinations of presbyters shall be performed by the laying-on-of-hands by bishops and presbyters and all consecrations of bishops shall be performed by the laying-on of-hands at least of three bishops".[580] This clause of the CSI constitution, thus, cleared the ambiguity about the nature and characteristic of ministry in the church. Such a context of

---

577 *Constitution of the Church of South India.*, Chapter II.
578 *Ibid.*
579 *Ibid.*
580 *Ibid.*

strong, autonomous, and self-reliant spirit as well as openness to the conciliar fellowship model, which has already been highlighted, formed the content of the Mar Thoma Church's position to start a fresh church unity discussion with the CSI.

The Mar Thoma Church decided to undertake a study on the nature of the episcopacy in the CSI on the basis of objections raised by the Lambeth Conference[581] 1948 over the "episcopal character" of the CSI, as a preliminary step towards finding the feasibility of entering into an ecumenical engagement with the CSI. The Metropolitan appointed a special committee to study and report on the question of the Mar Thoma Church's relation to the CSI in 1953.[582] In his written statement to the "Metropolitan's Special Committee of 1953"[583], he set five questions for in-depth discussion:

1. "What is the position of the CSI, with regard to Episcopacy?
2. If we enter into inter-communion with the CSI, shall we compromise in any way the Episcopal position we have been following?
3. What shall be our attitude to the orders of the old SIUC ministers, who have been accepted as ministers of the CSI, without Episcopal ordination (sic)?
4. What about the orders of the Bishops of the CSI, who have been consecrated since the inauguration of the CSI?
5. Should our courteous relationship with regard to the admission of members from the Anglican Church to the Mar Thoma Church be extended to the CSI?"[584]

---

581 "Unity of the Church – Suggestions relating to the Constitution of the Church of South India", *Resolution 53, The Lambeth Conference 1948,* In: *www.lambethconference.org/ resolutions/1948/.* The Lambeth conference 1948 raised six suggestions relating to the Constitution of the CSI and which will be dealt with the following section of this study. See, C.E. Abraham, ed., *The Mar Thoma Syrian Church, the Church of India, the Church of south India, op.cit,* 16–24.

582 *Order of His Grace Juhanon Mar Thoma, dated* 27ᵗʰ September 1950, in the Archives, Mar Thoma Theological Seminary, Kottayam. Also See, C.E. Abraham ed., *The Mar Thoma Syrian Church and the Church of India and the Church of South India, op.cit.,* 10;
Mar Thoma Church members of this committee were K.E. Oommen, C.V. John from the clergy and K.K. Kuruvilla, P.O. Philip, M.M. Thomas from the laity. See, *Report of the Metropolitans Committee 1953,* Tiruvalla, 15ᵗʰ July 1953, In: *Ibid.,* 10–31. Hereinafter this committee is referred to as the "Metropolitan's Special Committee of 1953". This committee's recommendation serves the basis for the Mar Thoma Church's "church unity" discussions with the CSI.

583 Hereafter referred as "M.S. Committee".

584 *Ibid.*

These five questions of Metropolitan Juhanon Mar Thoma set the basis for the official church unity discussions with the CSI. The significance of the Metropolitan's attempt in articulating these questions was that he sought to elucidate the constitutional position of the episcopacy in the CSI. As is clear in the scope of the above questions, he looked for clarity on the questions such as apostolic succession, ordination and ministry in the CSI, before a formal agreement of unity between the churches can be realized.[585]

Therefore, he considered that the task of the Metropolitan's Special Committee was to study the episcopal character, ordination and ministry of both the churches, and to interpret the constitutions of both the churches in an ecumenical context and aspirations and in such a way as to bring into a pragmatic consensus and thereby to exercise the full communion relation. I will turn now, to examine the church's treatment of these questions at its official church unity discussion phase (1953–1971) under the "Metropolitan's Special Committee", the "Inter Church Relations Committee"[586] and the "Theological Commissions".

In the history of the Mar Thoma Church's official discussions for full communion, the Metropolitan's Special Committee dealt with a steady stream of questions on the constitutional position of the churches' episcopacy, faith, ministry, sacraments and questions raised by the Lambeth Conference in 1948 on the episcopacy of the CSI.[587] The Mar Thoma Church's ecumenical encounters with other churches and ecumenical bodies form a dynamic force that guided the church to strive towards the goal of extending its full communion relations with the CSI.[588] In that process, the church viewed the above-mentioned questions of the Metropolitan on the basis of the Nicene Creed and its constitution.[589]

---

585 *Excerpt from the Kalpana of the Juhanon Mar Thoma Metropolitan and Mathews Mar Athanasius Episcopa*, (Malayalam) Dated March 21, 1953.

586 Hereafter referred as ICRC.

587 *Report of the Metropolitans Committee 1953*, Tiruvalla, 15th July 1953, In: C.E. Abraham ed., *The Mar Thoma Syrian Church and the Church of India and the Church of South India, op.cit.*, 10–31.

588 *Ibid.*, 10–31; "Report of the Inter-church Relations Committee of 1958", In: C.E. Abraham ed., *The Mar Thoma Syrian Church and the Church of India and the Church of South India, op.cit.*, 34–40.; "Prathi Nidhi Mandalam Resolution – 1958 regarding inter-communion with the Church of South India", In: *Annual Report of the Prathi Nidhi Mandalam of the Mar Thoma Syrian Church*, 1958, Mar Thoma Church office, Tiruvalla.

589 "Report of the Metropolitan's Committee, July 15, 1953", In: C.E. Abraham ed., *The Mar Thoma Syrian Church and the Church of India and the Church of South India, op.cit.*, 34–40.

It is interesting to note that in the Special Committee's discussion, the proposal in the "Metropolitan's Encyclical of 1952 … to be part of the Church of Christ in India" was not taken as a subject of importance, while the excerpts from it were used by the Committee to illustrate the stance of the Mar Thoma Church.

Why was the proposal in the "Metropolitan's Encyclical of 1952" for "Church of Christ in India" sidelined from the Metropolitan's Special Committee's discussions, while the CSI sought Mar Thoma Church's merger? Could it be the result of the Mar Thoma Church's tradition and constitutional position of assigning the supreme authority to the church's collective body of the Metropolitan, bishops, priests and laity, in defending the church's faith and practices? Or is it a departure from the stance of the Metropolitan Titus II (1866–1944) and Juhanon Mar Thoma (1893–1976) on church unity?

The sidelining of the Metropolitan Encyclical shows the Mar Thoma Church's character of assigning the supreme authority in decision-making to the whole body of the church that comprises bishops, laity and clergy.[590] On the basis of the canonical and the constitutional position of the churches' episcopacy, faith, ministry, sacraments and questions raised by the Lambeth Conference in 1948 on the "episcopacy of the CSI", the Metropolitan's Committee reached a few conclusions.

Ecclesiology

The Mar Thoma Church, in principle, accepts the authority of the church over matters of faith and practice and therefore it practices historic episcopacy.[591] The Mar Thoma Church affirms that episcopacy is an essential expression of the wholeness

---

590 More details see, Chapter II, 4.6. Faith Practice and Ecclesiology of the Mar Thoma Church, 57–59.

591 *Mar Thoma Sleehayude Edavakayakunna Malankara Suriyani Sabhayude Canon* (Malayalam) *[Canon of the Malankara Mar Thoma Syrian Church (English translation)], op.cit.*, 10–18; *Constitution of the Mar Thoma Syrian Church of Malabar, op.cit.*, 29–32; The Mar Thoma Church shares affirmations of the historic episcopacy by the Oriental Orthodox Churches, the Anglican Church, Old Catholic Church, and the Lutheran churches on varied dimensions. The Anglican and the Lutheran churches affirm the apostolicity of the whole church as God's gift and therefore, the apostolic succession does not confine to the three-fold apostolic ministry of the church alone, but it extended to the variety of means, activities and institutions of the church. Thus for them the apostolicity connects to the whole life of the Church – People of God –, who are being baptized in to the Church. But the three fold ministry is a central characteristic of the church.

and the historic continuity of the corporate life of the church[592] and where the "Catholic Church" is, "historic episcopacy and its effective maintenance are an expression of the Church's being".[593] The Mar Thoma Church stands in continuity with the apostolic succession, of which, the three-fold apostolic ministry of bishops, priests and deacons is a central expression.[594] This means that whatever the bishop is doing in word, sacraments, doctrines, and faith, must have continuity going back to the church fathers, the first 72 disciples, the Apostles, to the Apostle Thomas and to Jesus Christ.[595] Ministry of the church is also connected to the life of the church in relations to the Apostles and to the people of God.

Concerning the apostolic succession, the church insists that it is not something that the bishop enjoys as a personal possession in isolation with the Church, but in the Church as a whole.[596] Thus apostolic succession is in continuity with the

---

See, *The Report of the Conversations 1970–72 authorized by the Lambeth Conference and the Lutheran World Federation, Pullach Report* (London: SPCK, 1973) Paragraph 69–81.

592 *Ibid., 1*; *Report of the Metropolitan's Committee,* July 15, 1953.
The Mar Thoma Church's understanding of episcopacy is in conformity with the understanding of the Old Catholic Church on the basis of the above mentioned statement. For instance, the Statute of the Old Catholic Bishops United in the Union of Utrecht, affirms: "In continuity with its soteriological-Trinitarian foundation, the catholicity of the Church is expressed by those elements and processes which are signified by the term, "apostolic succession". This means that whatever the Church is doing in word and sacrament, doctrine and ministry, has and must have its origin, in space and time, in the mission of Jesus Christ, and the apostles operated by the Spirit. This includes pre-eminently the passing on of the ordained ministry by prayer and laying on of hands." *The Statute of the Old Catholic Bishops United in the Union of Utrecht,* (Beiheft zu IKZ/2001), 30.

593 *Report of the Metropolitan's Committee,* July 15, 1953.

594 *Mar Thoma Sleehayude Edavakayakunna Malankara Suriyani Sabhayude Canon, op.cit.,* 13–18; The Constitution, The Mar Thoma Syrian Church of Malabar, *op.cit.,* 17.

595 *Unpublished Liturgy of the Mar Thoma Episcopal Consecration, Amalogia,* (Tiruvalla – Poolatheen: Handwritten copy); See, St. Mathew: 16: 18–19; St. John: 20: 21–23.

596 The Mar Thoma Church follows the teaching of Irenaeus and he says that, "We should obey those Presbyters in the Church who have their succession from the Apostles and who together with succession in the episcopate, have received the assured charisma of the truth."
See, *Irenaeus, Against the Heresies* IV, xI, [xxviii] 2, 236. Also cited in Kallistos Ware, "Patterns of Episcopacy in the Early Church and Today: An Orthodox View", In: Peter Moore ed., *Bishops But What Kind?, op.cit.,* 12.

Trinitarian mystery of salvation, which brought the Church together with God.[597] This includes the passing on of the three-fold apostolic ministry of bishops, priests and deacons and laying-on-of-hands.[598] For instance, the apostolic authority is handed over to the bishop through the handing over of *staticon*, which is an authorisation certificate from the Metropolitan at the time of the bishop's consecration. It is the most significant sign of the unbroken apostolic authority, going back to the Apostle Thomas and Jesus Christ. It is an emphatic statement and the humble expression of an unbroken chain of succession of bishops.[599] It is the most emotionally moving part of the Episcopal consecration of the church.

The strength of the Mar Thoma Church's perspective on episcopacy is that unlike the Anglican Church in the past, it treats the apostolic succession in connection with the three-fold apostolic ministry and the apostolic life of the church on one hand, and on the other, unlike the Lutheran and reformed traditions, the episcopacy represents the visible centre of unity within the church. Thus the church affirms the validity of the ministry of the baptised people of God within the ordained ministry with a basic oneness, but within the three-fold form, the episcopacy has a special function of pastoral oversight in personal, collegial and communal ways[600] for witnessing and safeguarding the unity and catholicity of the church by presiding over the Eucharist in the church.[601]

---

597 *Mar Thoma Sleehayude Edavakayakunna Malankara Suriyani Sabhayude Canon,* *op.cit.,* 13–18.

598 *Ibid., Interview with Joseph Mar Barnabas,* dated 15 January 2013.

599 It was in the discussions of the Anglican Church on the question of the apostolic succession, there was a tendency to see the apostolic ministry from the perspective of the apostolic ministry of the church. However this stance has changed and currently holds a wholistic view that "refusing to wrest the apostolic ministry from the apostolic life of the whole people of God".
See, Mary Tanner, "The Anglican Position of the Apostolic Continuity and Apostolic Succession in Porvoo Common Statement", In: *Visible Unity and the Ministry of Oversight,* (West Wickham: Church House Publishing, 1996), 112–118.

600 A personal, collegial and communal dimension of the bishop refers to the bishop's authority in his diocese, his collegiality with other bishops and his connection with the Episcopal synod. See, The Constitution, *The Mar Thoma Syrian Church of Malabar,* *op.cit.,* 3–24.

601 The Porvoo Common Statement of the Anglican and Lutheran churches in 1992 shares the aforementioned oneness of the three-fold apostolic ministry. The statement affirms that episcopacy, apostolic succession, and apostolicity are relational. It connected to the life of the church in relations to the Apostles and to the people of God. Therefore, the statement finds the relational aspect of the apostolic ministry of the

The Mar Thoma Church affirms the connection between the Eucharist and the bishop, which is a dominant idea of all Orthodox Churches.[602] The presiding bishop of the Eucharist acts as a sign and sacrament of the Church's unity.[603] This idea of the Eucharistic unity of bishops has its debt to the teachings of Ignatius of Antioch. For him the bishop is "the one who presides at the Eucharist, acting as a living image of Christ, and so constituting the focus and visible centre of unity within the Church".[604] Ignatius therefore instructs:

> "Let that Eucharist be considered valid, which is celebrated by the bishop or the one whom he appoints. Wherever the bishop is, there let the people be".[605]

To keep this tradition in the church, the bishop consecrates the wooden block called *tabalitho*, which reminds the faithful on whose altar the priests celebrate the Eucharist. It is considered as a requirement for the priests to celebrate the Eucharist in the Mar Thoma Church's parishes or in any place of worship.

The three-fold task of the bishop in the church is shepherding, consecration and ordination.[606] The bishop is "the spiritual father and the chief shepherd".[607] He has

---

church with the oneness of three-fold ministry of the church. In this sense the Mar Thoma Church's understanding of episcopacy is in line with both traditions. See, Mary Tanner, "The Anglican Position of the Apostolic Continuity and Apostolic Succession in Porvoo Common Statement", In: *Visible Unity and the Ministry of Oversight*, (West Wickham: Church House Publishing, 1996), 112–113; Porvoo Common Statement, In: *www.anglicancommunion.org/.../docs/.../ porvoo_common_statement.pdf*, visited on 4th April 2013; *Edavakayakunna Malankara Suriyani Sabhayude Canon, op.cit.*, 13–18; Interview with *Joseph Mar Barnabas* dated 15th January 2013.

602 Kallistos Ware, "Patterns of Episcopacy in the Early Church and Today: An Orthodox View", In: Peter Moore ed., *Bishops But What Kind?*, (London: SPCK, 1982), 2–3.

603 The Constitution, *The Mar Thoma Syrian Church of Malabar, op.cit.*, 3–24; *Edavakayakunna Malankara Suriyani Sabhayude Canon, op.cit.*, 13–18.

604 *Ibid.*, 2.

605 *Letter of St. Ignatius to the Smyrneans,* Ch: 8–9; See, Archimandrite Kallistos Ware, *Communion and Inter-communion,* (Minnesota: Light and Life Publishing Company, 1980), 11–15.; J. Romanides, "The Ecclesiology of the St. Ignatius of Antioch", In: *The Greek Orthodox Theological Review,* VII (1961), 63–65.

606 In the Roman Catholic, the Anglican, the Lutheran, the Episcopal reform, and the Old Catholic churches, the sacrament of confirmation is assigned to the bishop. However in the Eastern Orthodox and Oriental Orthodox Churches, the priest can do the task of confirmation.

607 The Constitution, *The Mar Thoma Syrian Church of Malabar, op.cit.*, 6; *Mar Thoma Sleehayude Edavakayakunna Malankara Suriyani Sabhayude Canon, op.cit.*, 13–18.

the function to visit, teach and admonish.[608] The bishops thus form the leadership in the church.

The bishop is a teacher of faith and the link between the Church of the Apostles and that of the current time. During the time of the episcopal consecration, the episcopal candidate is being reminded by the Metropolitan that the bishop should follow the teachings of the apostles, St. Thomas, the first 72 disciples, St. Ignatius and all church fathers of the undivided church, including the current Metropolitan, who is in the long chain of the Metropolitans, currently sitting at the throne of St. Thomas.[609]

Thus, the church's episcopacy has its debt to the teachings of Ignatius of Antioch, Irenaeus, Cyprian of Carthage and other fathers. For Irenaeus, "the throne is the symbol of teaching".[610] In the parishes of the Mar Thoma Church, a chair is set aside exclusively for the bishop.[611]

In the matters of a proposition dealing with theological questions, the Mar Thoma Church's episcopal synod together with the whole body of the church – priests and laity – have their function to protect the church in truth and to guard it from errors. In the event of dealing with a theological proposal, the Mar Thoma Church constitution demands "the three-fourths majority of the laity and clergy of the general assembly, sitting separately, and simple majority in the house of bishops before it can become an act of the church".[612] Therefore, the Mar Thoma Church's episcopacy is a historic and constitutional episcopacy, which is also in conformity with the teachings of Cyprian of Carthage and Ignatius of Antioch: "Do not decide without the counsel of the Presbyterium and the consent of the people,"[613] said Cyprian to the bishops. And, "as the Lord was united to the

---

608 "Erste theologische Konsultation zwischen der Mar-Thoma-Kirche und den Altkatholischen Kirchen der Utrechter Union", Santhigiri Statement, In: *Internationale Kirchliche Zeitschrift,* 102, (Oktober – Dezember/ 2012), 315–320.

609 *Unpublished Liturgy of the Mar Thoma Episcopal Consecration, Amalogia* (Tiruvalla – Poolatheen: Handwritten Copy).

610 Irenaeus, *Demonstration of the Apostolic Preaching, 2.*

611 The above mentioned tradition can be seen in the Catholic, the Anglican, and the Eastern Orthodox traditions.

612 The Constitution, *The Mar Thoma Syrian Church of Malabar, op.cit.,* 6.

613 Cyprian of Carthage, *Letter to Ephesians 14: 4.* Cyprian of Carthage joined with Ireneus about the *charisma veritatis* endowed to the bishop, by virtue of their apostolic office, to proclaim the faith. But at the same time Cyprian reminded the basic principle that the bishop is in the Church. In this sense the authority to proclaim the truth, belongs to the Bishop grounded in his presiding role in the Eucharist. See, Kallistos Ware, "Patterns of Episcopacy in the Early Church and Today: An Orthodox

Father, and did nothing without him, neither by himself nor through the apostles, so should you do nothing without the Bishop and the presbyters",[614] Ignatius told the people. For instance, without the simple majority approval of the bishops in the episcopal synod, the house of the laity or clergy or both cannot impose their decisions in matters of faith in the church. Similarly, the episcopal synod by itself cannot impose its decision in matters of faith in the church.

This collective authority of the Metropolitan, bishops, clergy and laity holds good for the church to guard it from errors collectively. When the church acts collectively, the collective authority of the church provides tools and strategies for resistance to external coercion as well as to resist unilateral imposition of power and authority, by the Metropolitan, the episcopal synod, or the house of the laity or clergy or both together, in the church.

The analyses presented also suggests that the Mar Thoma Church accepts the importance of the local church's contexts and its importance in determining the most appropriate pattern of its episcopacy and church polity. In this, there seems an "Adiaphorist" attitude indirectly visible in the Mar Thoma Church's episcopacy and church polity. The "Adiaphorist" attitude was developed in the Church of England during 1560s.[615] The "Adiaphorists" suggested that "God had given no commands and it was right that local circumstances should be allowed to dictate the most appropriate pattern"[616] of church polity. However, the Mar Thoma Church's approach of giving importance to the local church and its local circumstances for defining its episcopacy and church polity is based on its oriental church moorings.

The importance given to the local church, gathered for Eucharist under a bishop is an oriental church's feature, and as such the Mar Thoma Church expects it to be sharply respected in its episcopacy, church polity and its ecumenical engagements.[617] The understanding of the Mar Thoma Church and of all other oriental churches about the visible Church "is rooted in St. Paul's manner of addressing

View", In: Peter Moore ed., *Bishops But What Kind?*, *op.cit.*, 18–19; *Cyprian, Letter* Iv, lxxiii.26.

614 *Ignatius of Antioch, Epistle to the Magnesians, vii, 1*; See, Ignatius of Antioch, *Epistle to the Philadelphians 7:* In: *www.earlychristianwritings.com/.../ignatius-philadelphians-lightfoot.*, visited on 12th January2013.

615 John Findon, "Developments in the Understanding and Practice of Episcopacy in the Church of England", In: *Visible Unity and the Ministry of Oversight, op.cit.*, 79–83.

616 *Ibid.*, 83.

617 *Constitution of the Mar Thoma Syrian Church of Malabar, op.cit.*, 1–8.

communities in various places: the Church of God which is in Corinth"[618] and in the teachings of St. Ignatius. Its territorial approach is that it centres on the "one Eucharistic community" in "one place". The local Eucharistic community, the prototype of which consists of the people gathered around their bishop, is the place where the One Holy Catholic and Apostolic Church presents itself.[619] This identified with the perception of the Church of Ignatius of Antioch.[620]

The local Eucharistic communities' liturgy represents their faith and life. The local church has a freedom to give importance to the local circumstances in its decisions, which are not contrary to the tradition and canon of the church.

Metropolitan's encyclical sidelined

In the light of the collective nature of the church in defending the faith of the church and the church's emphasis of the local church in defining its church polity, the sidelining of the "Metropolitan's Encyclical of 1952" proposal for the Church of Christ in India could be seen as an instance when the church's collective authority prevailed over the Metropolitan's.

This is obvious in the statement of Philipose Mar Chrysostom, Metropolitan, while commenting on the Mar Thoma Church members' response to the "Metropolitan's Encyclical of 1952". He admits that while bishops of the church had an "eagerness for church unity, this cannot be seen as the mainline thinking within the

---

618 Nicholas Lossky, "Orthodox Churches", In: *The Christian Church: An Introduction to the Major Traditions* Edited by Paul Avis, (London: SPCK, 2002), 3.
St. Pauls's view of the church was that the Church is a Body of Christ, which has both communitarian and Eucharistic dimension. (1 Corinthians 10: 16–17). St. Ignatius developed this idea and for him, church is a Eucharistic community under a bishop. It is the Eucharist that actualises the oneness of the church. Ignatius further distinguished the one bishop from *synedrion* or college of bishops and considered one bishop is the sign and the centre of the unity of the local church. In short, St. Ignatius gave importance to the local church and the unity of the church. See, Kallistos Ware, "Patterns of Episcopacy in the Early Church and Today: An Orthodox View", In: Peter Moore ed., *Bishops But What Kind?, op.cit.*, 1–24.
619 Nicholas Lossky, "Orthodox Churches", In: Paul Avis, ed., *The Christian Church: An Introduction to the Major Traditions* (London: SPCK, 2002), 3.
620 Ignatius of Antioch says: "where there is Jesus Christ, there is Catholic Church". Ignatius of Antioch, "Ad Smyrn.8, 2", In: *"Sources Chretiennes 10"* (French), Christian Source Resource Centre, Lyon, 162–163; Ignatius of Antioch, Ad Smyrn.8, 2: *Apostolic Fathers,* II/2, (Cambridge: Harvard University Press, 2003), 311.

church".[621] It is worth noting that the "Metropolitan's Encyclical of 1952" stands in continuity with the wish of the Metropolitan Juhanon Mar Thoma's predecessors. The point is that even if the Metropolitans were in favour of a united Church in India they did not use episcopal authority and power to implement that wish. Instead they presented the wish for the organic unity of the Indian churches before the church for its final decision. Commenting on reasons for sidelining this, Metropolitan Philipose Mar Chrisostom says:

"Our Church (Mar Thoma Church) too welcomed church unity in general, but is not yet prepared to shed our distinctive identity to become part of one united church. Therefore within the Church, there was little follow up action on the Encyclical".[622]

This is because when the proposal in the "Metropolitan's Encyclical of 1952" appeared before the episcopal synod, church council and the general assembly of the Mar Thoma Church, these bodies upheld the church's age-old position as an independent church in India – without hampering its conciliar fellowship with other churches.[623] This constitutional position of the Mar Thoma Church found its praxis in the major decision-making of its council and the General Assembly.[624]

The church considers its constitution and traditions as primary and found, in its collective wisdom, the proposal in the Metropolitan's Encyclical of 1952 as not in line with that. This understanding made them place the church unity discussions with the CSI and CNI within the framework of the church's constitutional guidelines to keep its autonomy and independence. This eventually led to the sidelining of the "Metropolitan's Encyclical of 1952's" proposal, as also the merger of the church with the CSI and the CNI.[625] This became evident when the CSI-CNI-MTC Joint Theological commission of 1974 recommended a common name for

---

621 Jesudas M. Athyal, John J. Thattamannil, ed., *Metropolitan Chrysostom on Mission in the Market Place, op.cit.*, 91.

622 *Ibid.*, 92.

623 *Annual Report of the Mar Thoma Syrian Church of Malabar*, 1968, the Archives, the Mar Thoma Church Office, Tiruvalla; *Annual Report of the Mar Thoma Syrian Church of Malabar*, 1961, the Archives, the Mar Thoma Church Office, Tiruvalla; *Annual Report of the Mar Thoma Syrian Church of Malabar*, 1975, the Archives, the Mar Thoma Church Office, Tiruvalla; *Annual Report of the Mar Thoma Syrian Church of Malabar*, 1984, the Archives, the Mar Thoma Church Office, Tiruvalla.

624 *Ibid.*

625 Juhanon Mar Thoma, Mathews Mar Athanasius, "A Call to the Churches of Christ in India", In: *Joint Statement of Juhanon Mar Thoma and Mathews Mar Athanasius to Indian Churches*, December 21, 1952, Tiruvalla.

the three churches, which the episcopal synod, church council and the general body of the Mar Thoma Church were reluctant to accept.[626]

On the other hand, the Metropolitan's Special Committee adopted the spirit of the "Metropolitan's Encyclical of 1952", which was the unity of Indian churches, as it addressed the question of the validity of the "order" of the CSI, in relation to the Mar Thoma Church. The position of the "Metropolitan's Encyclical of 1952" on church unity has the following accommodation:

"Do not insist on any one doctrinal emphasis about episcopacy and sacraments but willingly allow differences in doctrinal emphasis."[627]

In the light of these and the constitutional guarantee of the episcopacy in the CSI, the Metropolitan's Special Committee recommended that if the Mar Thoma Church enters into communion relation with the CSI, following the "form" of the "Bonn Agreement of 1931",[628] the church would not in "any way compromise its episcopal position"[629] and autonomous existence in India.

Finding a common ground in faith

The thought process of allowing doctrinal differences between churches could be seen in the Mar Thoma Church's attitude in dealing with the faith and practices of the CSI and CNI with a view to attain full communion relation with them. The task of the Metropolitan's Special Committee was to find a common ground in the faith of both the churches and to discover a solution to the objections raised at the Lambeth conference 1948 against the CSI constitutional provision on episcopacy and order.

---

626 *Annual Report of the Mar Thoma Syrian Church of Malabar,* 1975, the Archives, the Mar Thoma Church Office, Tiruvalla.

627 Juhanon Mar Thoma, Mathews Mar Athanasius, "A Call to the Churches of Christ in India", In: *Joint Statement of Juhanon Mar Thoma and Mathews Mar Athanasius to Indian Churches,* December 21, 1952, Tiruvalla.
It is important to note that the same principle was adopted in the Leuenberg statement in 1973 for the inter-communion relation with the reformed churches' tradition in Europe. This will be dealt with in details in the last section of this chapter.

628 For more details, see the Chapter IV of this study, in which the Bonn Agreement of the Old Catholic Church and the Anglican Church in 1931 has been dealt with in detail.

629 "Report of the Metropolitan's Committee, July 15, 1953", In: C.E. Abraham ed., *The Mar Thoma Syrian Church and the Church of India and the Church of South India,* op.cit., 34–40.

The Special Committee, after studying the constitutions of both the churches, reached the following conclusions on the faith of the churches:

1. Both the churches follow the faith affirmation in the Nicene Creed of the Catholic Church.[630]
2. Both the churches accept the authority of the Word of God.[631]
3. With regard to the adherence of their historic faith of the Catholic Church, both the churches consider themselves as part of the "One, Holy, Catholic and Apostolic Church"[632] as well as having a missionary agenda to "proclaim the historic faith of the Church".[633]
4. Both the churches accept historic episcopacy and two dominical sacraments.[634]

The committee came to the conclusion that since it contains essentially the same doctrines of the Trinity and the Nicene Creed, there is nothing on faith matters that prevents the Mar Thoma Church from entering into full communion relation with the CSI.[635]

Ministry and sacraments

The Metropolitan's Special Committee analysed the differences in ministry and sacraments between the two churches on the basis of the Mar Thoma Church's emphasis on apostolic succession, which encompassed the three-fold apostolic ministry and its emphasis on the seven sacraments. The analysis yielded not only information about the consensus that both the churches arrived at on ministry and sacraments but also, gave hints on differences that both the churches hold in their stance on ministry and sacraments. For instance, although the vocation of the ordained ministry and the episcopacy are affirmed by the CSI[636] and the Mar

---

630 *The Constitution of the Mar Thoma Syrian Church of Malabar, op.cit.*, 1–3; *The Constitution of the Church of South India,* Chapter II, *op.cit.*, 5.
631 *Ibid.*
632 *Ibid., The Constitution of the Mar Thoma Syrian Church of Malabar, Part I, I, op.cit.*, 1; Documents dealing with the relation between CSI and the Anglican Communion, 6, cited In: the *Report of the Metropolitan's Committee,* July 15, 1953, *op.cit.*, 11.
633 *Ibid.*
634 *Constitution of the Church of South India, Chapter II.* 5; *The Mar Thoma Syrian Church of Malabar Constitution* (English Version), *op.cit.*, 1–3.
635 *Ibid.*
636 *Constitution of the Church of South India, Chapter II, 7–8.*

Thoma Church, both the churches rejected the idea of "mediatorial priesthood". They affirm the royal priesthood of all believers. However, there are certain visible differences in the understanding of the ministry and sacraments of both the churches.

First is the fact that the Mar Thoma Church considers a priest's ordination by the bishop a requirement for the administration of the seven sacraments,[637] while the CSI considers the administration of sacraments by ordained ministers not part of its faith requirement, but just as a rule.[638] The Mar Thoma Church …

"… considers the administration of sacraments by an ordained minister or a bishop, as a matter of faith and as part of the 'spiritual conditions' necessary to be fulfilled for the validity of the sacrament …"[639]

on the basis of its canon.[640] The Mar Thoma Church also considers episcopal succession and the three-tier ministry as a central expression of the One Holy Catholic and Apostolic Church's life of *leitourgia, martyria* and *diakona* (liturgy, witness and service) and the unity of the Church.

Second, the Mar Thoma Church upholds the importance of the seven sacraments – baptism, confirmation, confession, Holy Communion, marriage, ordination and extreme unction (Öil salbung) – which are considered as the visible expressions of the invisible grace of God. It declares that the administration of seven sacraments is obligatory in the church and it "shall not be abolished at any time".[641] However, the CSI considers only two sacraments – Baptism and Eucharist – as obligatory.

Third, concerning the question of non-integration of ministers in the CSI, the Metropolitan's Special Committee came to a conclusion that it would be appropriate not to make a judgemental stand on the validity of the order and sacraments of

---

637 However, it was during 1950's, there was a small group of members of the Mar Thoma Church believe that what is needed in the validity of the sacraments is the promise of God. This stance was in conformity with the CSI position on sacraments. However, this is not the official position of the Mar Thoma Church. The Mar Thoma Chruch considers the laying-of-hands by a bishop for the ordination of a priest is a requirement to ensure the validity of his office.

638 *Constitutions of the Church of South India,* Chapter II, *7–8.*; Also In: the *Report of the Metropolitan's Committee,* July 15, 1953, *op.cit.,* 28.

639 *Report of the Metropolitan's Committee,* July 15, 1953, *op.cit.,* 11. *Ibid.,* 29.

640 *Mar Thoma Sleehayude Edavakayakunna Malankara Suriyani Sabhayude Canon* (Malayalam) [*Canon of the Malankara Mar Thoma Syrian Church* (English translation)], *op.cit.,* 23.

641 *The Mar Thoma Syrian Church of Malabar Constitution* (English Version), *op.cit.,* 1.

the CSI in the light of the guarantee that the CSI constitution provided.[642] There-fore the committee decided to give individual freedom to the faithful to use their discretion (conscience) to take an appropriate decision on the authority of a minis-ter celebrating the Eucharist. They were thus free to decide whether to partake of the Eucharist from ministers of the CSI without proper Episcopal ordination. The committee made it clear that …

> "… with regard to our attitude to the orders of the old SIUC ministers and others who have been accepted as ministers of the CSI without Episcopal ordination, we are of the opinion that without any sense of compromising the Mar Thoma position regard-ing the orders, the matter should be left to be decided by the individual members of the Mar Thoma Church."[643]

Although the committee's recommendations could be seen as a practical suggestion for inter-communion, emphasising the conscience of the individual member in the partaking of the Eucharist from the CSI, it revealed the say of all the baptised in the Mar Thoma Church – bishops, priests, deacons and laity – in the church's decision-making process.[644]

The Metropolitan's Special Committee is seen to have been no more than partly successful and the gulf between the Mar Thoma Church's standpoint of ministry and those of the CSI remained imperfectly bridged. It could only work around the roadblock to unity by extending the baton to the church members to choose whether they wanted to receive the Eucharist from a CSI minister, who was not ordained by the laying-on-of-hands by a bishop, or not, on the basis of the individual conscience.

Such a proposal was not in line with the collective authority of the church in de-fining its faith and order as the church has been practicing since the beginning. The committee overlooked its responsibility to uphold the fact that the fundamental faith and order of the church should be the same as that of the undivided Church. There is very little sense that the permission to exercise individual conscience might be employed within the church for the seeping-down of church unity en-gagements to the grass roots level of the church.

---

642 The CSI Constitution says: "It is a rule or order in the CSI that the celebration of the Eucharist shall be entrusted only to those who have by ordination received authority thereto." See, *Constitution of the Church of South India,* Chapter II, *op.cit.*, 7–8.

643 *Ibid.*

644 The eligible person to celebrate the Eucharist in the CSI and Mar Thoma Church is an ordained minister. In the light of this rule, the Mar Thoma Church came to the conclu-sion that, "in the above line of reasoning the non- unification of the ministry was not seen as an obstacle to inter-communion." See, *Ibid.*

However, the committee allowed the differences of the churches in doctrinal matters to be discussed at the grass root level. This opened a room for further discussions on church unity with the CSI at the local level.

Response to Lambeth concerns

The Mar Thoma Church believed that for the fulfilment of its search for church unity, a full communion relationship with the CSI was vital. But it saw questions raised by the Lambeth Conference 1948[645] as supporting fears over CSI's episcopacy and ministry. The Metropolitan's Special Committee avoided a judgemental stand on the episcopacy and ministry of the CSI in its analysis of the Lambeth Conference's objections. This led them to formulate conclusions to serve it as the basis for future church unity talks with the CSI.

Four conclusions can be identified from these discussions.

1. Concerning the lack of a constitutional rule for the confirmation of CSI's members by a bishop, the committee came to the conclusion that since the Mar Thoma Church does not have the practice of confirmation[646] of its members by the bishop, as in the case of the Anglican Church, it need not to be considered as a concern that directly affects the church.
2. In relation to the taking away of the constitutional guarantee of a bishop as the custodian to safeguard the faith and order in the CSI, the Metropolitan's Special Committee deemed it was not a valid concern for the Mar Thoma Church, as it considered the whole body of the church, being the guard of its faith and order.
3. Lambeth 1948 argued that "in deciding to be in communion with the non-episcopal churches, the episcopal position of the CSI is weakened".[647] Concerning this argument, the committee made the Mar Thoma Church's position clear by quoting the "Metropolitan's Encyclical of 1952" that the church, "does not want to make any judgement on the orders of the non- episcopal churches blessed by God".[648] Since the CSI maintains episcopacy – and the Mar Thoma Church is

---

645 *Report of the Metropolitan's Committee,* July 15, 1953, *op.cit.,* 16–24.
646 The Sacrament of Confirmation is administered immediately after the Baptism in the Mar Thoma Church. See, *Mar Thoma Liturgy on Baptism.*
647 *Report of the Metropolitan's Committee,* July 15, 1953, *op.cit.,* 18.
648 Juhanon Mar Thoma, Mathews Mar Athanasius, "A Call to the Churches of Christ in India", *Joint Statement of Juhanon Mar Thoma and Mathews Mar Athanasius to Indian Churches,* December 21, 1952, Tiruvalla.

not going to have communion with non-episcopal churches – nothing prevented it from extending its communion relation with the CIPBC to the CSI.

4. With regard to the fourth Lambeth objection of "receiving the non-episcopally ordained ministers of the uniting churches as ministers of the united CSI, the episcopal position of the CSI is compromised"[649], the committee took a stance here that since the Mar Thoma Church is entering into a relationship with the CSI as part of the "One, Holy, Catholic and Apostolic Church", the unity of the church is important. Therefore, the full communion relations "into which the Mar Thoma Church as a Church enters should be such as to treat the CSI as a corporate whole and not in parts".[650]

In the light of the above findings, the Metropolitan's Special Committee made it clear that, since the CSI constitution affirms constitutional historic episcopacy, there is nothing preventing the Mar Thoma Church from entering into full communion with the CSI. Second, if the Mar Thoma Church, enters into communion with the CSI, following the form of the "Bonn Agreement of 1931", the church "shall in no way be compromising"[651] its episcopal position.

Third, the question of the old SIUC ministers in the CSI was to be decided by the individual members of the church using their conscience.[652] Fourth, the committee recommended that the ministerial offices of the CSI be accepted as the part of true ministerial offices of the Catholic Church.[653] Fifth, it recommended the church to accept the CSI as part of the "Catholic" Church.[654]

It was in this context that the importance of the "Bonn Agreement" and the Mar Thoma Church's "occasional inter-communion" agreement with the Anglican Church in 1936 (CIBC), has been taken as a basis to formulate conclusions to materialise unity while keeping its doctrinal and ritualistic differences. The committee recommended entering into a communion relationship with the CSI, following a slightly modified "Bonn Agreement" formula, which has been highlighted several times already. The formula says:

(a) "Each communion recognizes the other as part of the One Universal Church.

---

649 "Questions Raised By Lambeth 1948", In: *Report of the Metropolitan's Committee,* July 15, 1953, *op.cit.,* 16–24.
650 *Ibid.*
651 *Report of the Metropolitan's Committee, July 15, 1953, op.cit.,* 29–30.
652 *Ibid.*
653 *Ibid.*
654 *Ibid.*

(b) Each communion agrees to admit members of the other communion to participate in the sacraments.

(c) Inter-communion does not require from either communion the acceptance of all doctrinal opinion, sacramental devotion or liturgical practice characteristic of the other but implies that each believes the other to hold all the essentials of the Christian faith".[655]

As is evident in this new formula, the committee made the modification of the "Bonn Agreement of 1931" only in the wording of its first clause, not in its contents.[656] The one universal Church refers to the "One, Holy, Catholic and apostolic Church". In the light of this, the Mar Thoma Church accepted the sacraments and ministry of the CSI.

Two significant points could be seen in this formula: One was the suggestion to continue the same church unity scheme, which permitted the Mar Thoma Church to enter into communion with the CIBC in 1936 and subsequently with the CIPBC in 1947, and the acceptance of the truth of the "local church" as part of the Catholic Church from within the oriental churches' understanding. The importance given to the local church, gathered for Eucharist under a bishop is an oriental church's feature, as have seen already in this study. The Mar Thoma Church expects it to be sharply respected in its church unity engagements with the CSI and other churches. The committee submitted the report and the recommendations on 15 July 1953, which the Metropolitan forwarded to the church council for action. The church council authorised the Mar Thoma Church's "Inter Church Relations Committee" (ICRC) to study and to report on the matter on 31 March, 1957.

Inter-Church Relations Committee

The Mar Thoma Church's Inter-Church Relations Committee (ICRC) reviewed the recommendations of the Metropolitan's Special Committee.[657] The ICRC had

---

655 *Report of the Metropolitan's Committee,* July 15, 1953, *op.cit.,* 30–31.
656 First Clause of the Bonn Agreement says: "Each communion recognizes the catholicity and independence of the other and maintains its own." "Old Catholic Church 167 – Statement Agreed Between the Representatives of the Old Catholic Church and the Churches of the Anglican Communion at a Conference held at Bonn July, 2, 1931", In: G.K.A. Bell, *Documents on Christian Unity,* Third Series 1930–1948, *op.cit.,* 60.
657 The "Inter Church Relations Committee" under the chairmanship of Thomas Mar Athanasius met at the Bishop's house in Chengannur on the 30th and 31st of July 1957 and discussed on the topic: Inter-communion between the Mar Thoma Church and the CSI.

two issues over the recommendations of the committee. The first was about the recommendation to accept the Eucharist from ministers not ordained by bishops. The second difficulty was the way in which the Mar Thoma Church looks at the problem faced by the CSI on the question of the non-episcopally-ordained SIUC ministers.

Although the ICRC did allow using individual discretion in participating in the Eucharist, it recommended the re-ordination of the priests from the SIUC by the laying-on-of-hands of the bishop and it was considered a necessary condition for the celebration of sacraments. Moreover, the ICRC made it clear that the integration of the ministry in the CSI was essential for full communion[658] relationship.

Despite these differences, the ICRC found sufficient unity in faith and order between both the churches and therefore advised to proceed with inter-communion[659] relation with the CSI, following the Metropolitan's Special Committee's communion formula, in which they added a clause for the integration of the ministry as a requirement. The rationale of the formula of the ICRC also encompassed the ecumenical nature of the Mar Thoma Church, which accepts the reality that there are theological and liturgical differences between the two traditions, but that these are not necessarily church dividing issues – they rather provide possibilities for unity of shared ministry and mission.

The Metropolitan's Special Committee's stance led to the ICRC also declaring its aim for full communion between the two churches, in which the freedom of each communion's doctrinal opinion and liturgical practices remain unaltered. Within this relation, both churches were to become inter-dependent while remaining autonomous. However the full communion formula,[660] together with a set of

---

See, "Report of the Inter Church Relations Committee, 1958", In: C.E. Abraham ed., *The Mar Thoma Syrian Church and the Church of India and the Church of South India, op.cit.*, 34–40.

658 Full communion relation of the Mar Thoma Church and the CSI refers to the mutual recognition of the other church as Catholic and apostolic and recommends for unrestricted *comunio in sacris* including the mutual recognition and acceptance of ministries.

659 Inter-communion between the Mar Thoma Church and the CSI refers to the relation of the both churches; in which each recognize the other church as catholic and apostolic. But in the inter-communion relations between both churches, there is no unrestricted *comunio in sacris*, including mutual recognition and acceptance of ministries. Since there were not duly ordained ministers from the SIUC in the CSI, the Mar Thoma Church had not fully recognized the ministry of the CSI.

660 The full communion formula of the "Inter Church Relations Committee" was: I. "Each communion believes the other and holds the essentials of the Christian faith and recognizes the other as part of the universal church.

"Rules of Comity",[661] was adopted by the ICRC and submitted to the Metropolitan on 22 February, 1958. The Mar Thoma Church's council adopted this document and forwarded it to the General Assembly for the final approval which came the same year. The CSI also adopted the formula and the "Rules of Comity". While the relationship between the two churches was progressing on the basis of the formula and the "Rules of Comity," the Mar Thoma Church General Assembly constituted a theological commission in 1961, to find feasibilities for a closer relation with CSI[662] at the grass root level – parish and diocese – for common witness. The General Assembly constituted another theological commission in 1967 to find the feasibility of establishing full communion with the CSI.[663] The CSI also constituted its theological commission, which had discussions with its Mar Thoma counterpart. The result was a joint theological commission of both the churches recommending a full communion

1. Each Communion agrees to admit members of the other communion to participate in the sacraments.
2. The Mar Thoma Church recognizes that among its members there are those who have objection to receiving Eucharist celebrated by a non- episcopally ordained minister of the CSI and those who do not have such objections.
II. The Mar Thoma Church respects those difference even as the CSI by its pledge (Constitution 2: 13) guarantees to respect the conscience of those who wish to receive Eucharist only from episcopally ordained ministers. III. Inter-communion does not require from either communion the acceptance of all doctrinal opinion, sacramental devotion or liturgical practice of the other."
See, "Report of the Inter Church Relations Committee, 1958", In: C.E. Abraham ed., *The Mar Thoma Syrian Church and the Church of India and the Church of South India, op.cit.*, 38.
661 "Rules of Comity" refers to a set of practical guidelines for the inter-communion between the churches in various situations like, students conference and clergy conference, in the places where one church is not there and the other church exist, and rules for the change of membership from one church to the other.
662 *Report of the Annual General Body of the Mar Thoma Church,* on May 16, 17, Tiruvalla; *Annual Report of the Mar Thoma Syrian Church,* 1962, Tiruvalla, 22, 25; See, T.P. Abraham, *Mar Thoma Sabha Noottandukaliloode,* (Malayalam), *op.cit.*, 596; "Report of the Mar Thoma Theological Commission – 1961", In: C.E. Abraham ed., *The Mar Thoma Syrian Church and the Church of India and the Church of South India, op.cit.*, 50–56.
663 ""Pradhinidhi mandalam" Resolution B.(g), of the Mar Thoma Syrian Church, 1967", In: C.E. Abraham ed., *The Mar Thoma Syrian Church and the Church of India and the Church of South India, op.cit.*, 63.

relationship, beginning a new phase of full communion relation with the CSI in 1971.[664]

Full communion

In 1971, the Mar Thoma Church and CSI agreed to have a full communion relationship.[665] By this agreement, both the churches recognized each other as churches in which the Scripture was rightly preached and the sacraments rightly administered according to the word of God. The churches also recognized their respective ministries, each other's baptism and Eucharist and authorised the sharing of the Eucharist among their members. The agreement committed the churches to an ongoing process of dialogue to make clear the understanding of the faith and practices of both churches and to foster the common witness and service.

---

664 *Letter of the CSI Moderator,* dated 27/4/1959, Archives, Mar Thoma Theological Seminary Kottayam.; *Letter of the Mar Thoma Church Secretary, to the Moderator of the CSI,* dated 2/6/1961, Archives, Mar Thoma Theological Seminary Kottayam.; *Reply Letter of the CSI Moderator to the Mar Thoma Church Secretary,* dated 31/8/1961, Archives, Mar Thoma Theological Seminary Kottayam. *Letter of the President of the Mar Thoma Theological Commission to the Moderator of the Church of South India,* dated 27/11/1967, Archives, the Mar Thoma Theological Seminary Kottayam; *Letter of the Moderator (Reply) to the President of the Mar Thoma Theological Commission,* dated 2/12/1967.

665 In the light of ICRC's recommendations, the Mar Thoma Church's *pradhinidhimandalam* (General Assembly) held on May 1958 resolved to "welcome and accept proposals for inter-communion between the Mar Thoma Church and the CSI as outlined above and to request the CSI Moderator to appoint representatives of the CSI to meet and confer with the representatives of the Mar Thoma church." The Synod of the CSI reported its joy over the recommendations of the Mar Thoma Church at its Synod meeting on September 1959. The Mar Thoma Church *pradhinidhimandalam* held on 16th and 17th May 1961 has appointed a theological commission to consider the possibilities of closer contacts with the CSI and if necessary enter into discussions with the theological commission appointed by the CSI. The Theological commission adopted the recommendations of the Inter Church Relations committee's aforementioned recommendations. The Mar Thoma Church's Theological commission recommended a full communion relationship with the CSI. A joint Theological commission of both churches met on April 1969, at Bangalore recommended the establishment of a full communion relation between two churches. The Mar Thoma Church's *pradhinidhimandalam* (general body) approved their recommendations on 4 and 5 May, 1971. Thus a full communion relation both churches came into being in 1971.

Two major decisions of the full communion agreement bear upon the progress of the Mar Thoma Church and the CSI in their mutual relation: They are the mutual recognition of the oneness in doctrines of both the churches and of its sacraments and ministry. For instance, both the churches agreed to participate in the episcopal consecrations[666] and to practice the concelebration of sacraments.[667] Second, both the churches agreed to set up an ad-hoc board with equal number of representatives from both churches "to explore ways and means of closer cooperation between the churches in matters such as theological training, evangelism, Christian education, general education, medical work and social actions".[668] The founding of an ad-hoc board, representing a common council, could be seen as a step to establish a council to make common decisions following a conciliar fellowship model.

The road to this deliberate agreement for full communion did have its own tensions and contradictions of views, but the Mar Thoma Church did not stray from its affirmation on faith, ministry and sacraments. The premise that underlies the agreement becomes clearer in later discussions of the joint theological commissions of the CSI, CNI and the Mar Thoma Church during 1974–1982.[669] We have already noted the differences in stances to the church unity model, which the Mar Thoma Church regards as an extension of the full communion relation with the CIPBC.

The Mar Thoma Church followed the model of conciliar fellowship in its relation with the CSI, which stood for an organic merger. The Mar Thoma Church has always tried to safeguard its autonomy in the church unity discussions. It was against a merger that would have an impact on its Oriental independent

---

666 *Minutes of the CSI – Mar Thoma Church negotiations for closer cooperation,* Bangalore, April, 1969. Also See, *Minutes of the Second Meeting of the Joint Theological Commission of the CSI-CNI.-Mar Thoma Joint Council at United Theological Collage,* Bangalore, 3, 4 June, 1975, Annexure 1.

667 *Ibid.*

668 The Mar Thoma Church's full communion agreement with the CSI seems to be step further than its communion relation with the MISC and the CIPBC.

669 *Minutes of the CSI – Mar Thoma Union Negotiations Commission,* held at Zion Hill Aramana, Kottayam on 17th May 1974; Archives, Mar Thoma Theological Seminary, Kottayam; V.P. Thomas, "The Nature of the Union of the Churches that we Seek", In: *Minutes of the Second Meeting of the Joint Theological Commission of the CSI-CNI-MTC* held at Ranson Hall of the United Theological College, Bangalore on 3rd and 4th June 1975, Annexure IV, 34–37; *Minutes of the First Meeting of the Joint Theological Commission of the CSI-CNI MTC,* held at the Community Service Centre, Kilpauk, Madras on 16th January 1975, Archives, Mar Thoma Theological Seminary, Kottayam.

foundations. It also did not want to do away with its individual existence or to deny its eastern liturgical and Indian cultural autonomous existence.

Seen from this perspective, the Mar Thoma Church's rejection of a common name for the three churches – Bharath Church of Christ – is understandable. I shall return to this theme later, and now turn to examine the Mar Thoma Church's church unity engagements with the CNI.

Engaging the CNI

It was in 1970 that six churches in North India – the Baptist Church, the Church of the Brethren, CIPBC, the Disciples of Christ, the Methodist Church and the United Church of North India – merged to form the CNI on 29 November 1970.[670] The Mar Thoma Church felt the need for a similar full communion agreement with the CNI in the same way as the church had with the CSI. The Mar Thoma Church's general assembly appointed a theological commission to study the possibility of entering into a full communion relation with the CNI in 1971.[671]

Since the ministry of the CNI was integrated at the time of its formation, there was no major theological concern that would have prevented the Mar Thoma Church to have a relationship with the CNI, except for the position of the latter on baptism.[672] But it was found that although the CNI approves adult baptism – in order to pacify those people who come from the Brethren Church – its position of baptism was in conformity with the Nicene Creed, which affirmed that "we acknowledge one baptism for the remission of sins".[673]

The CNI's constitution made it clear that it did not re-baptise persons, who were baptised in infancy. The joint theological commissions met at Nagpur on February 1973 and decided to recommend the Mar Thoma Church for a full communion relation with the CNI following the same formula and the "Rule of Comity" agreement with the CSI. The Mar Thoma Church's General Assembly unanimously approved the recommendations of the theological commission and authorised the

---

670 The Mar Thoma Church's Alexander Mar Theophilus was a co- celebrant at this opening service.

671 *Report of the Mar Thoma Theological Commission,* February 27, 1973; *Malankara Sabha Tharaka, op. cit.,* 5–9.

672 Because the Church of the Brethren was part of the CNI, the CNI permitted its members to delay the baptism till adulthood.

673 *Mar Thoma Syrian Church Liturgy,* 6th Edition, (Tiruvalla: Mar Thoma Church Publication, 2004), 26–27.

episcopal synod to take necessary steps for a full communion relation with the CNI in 1973.[674] We should note that the church's full communion relation with the CSI and CNI in its own way paved the way for the framing of a joint council of the three churches for conciliar fellowship updating with the world ecumenical movement which had adopted conciliar fellowship as a viable model for the unity of churches.

---

674 Item No. 19, *Minutes of the Mar Thoma Sabhapradhinidhimandalam*, 1st and 2nd May 1973.

Chapter XII
Conciliar Fellowship in Action

The Mar Thoma Church, CSI and CNI constituted a joint council in 1978 to discuss matters pertaining to a common mission and witness in India. The joint council aimed at reaching a common agenda for the evangelisation of India. The joint council was considered the beginning point of a long journey towards unity of churches in India and forming the "Bharat Church of Christ". The Mar Thoma Church's intention was to keep a conciliar fellowship within the "Bharat Church" as it continued its Oriental autonomous existence and liturgical traditions.

The Mar Thoma Church considers conciliar fellowship as akin to organic unity in the sense that it presupposes complete mutual commitment and mutual responsibility to materialise in its unity function in India. Consequently, with a view to form an appropriate council to represent the three churches, the CSI-CNI-MTC Joint Council was proposed by the CSI-Mar Thoma Church commission for union meetings on 17 May 1974. This led to the constitution of the Joint Theological Commission of the CSI, CNI and the MTC in 1975. The CSI-CNI-MTC Joint Council was subsequently formed in 1978, which was described as …

"… the visible organ for common action by three churches, which recognize themselves as belonging to the one Church of Jesus Christ in India, even while remaining as autonomous churches, each having its own identity of traditions and organisational structures".[675]

The joint council was expected to move forward in providing more visible expressions of their unity. With this aim, the joint council was renamed as "Communion of Churches in India" (CCI) in 2003.[676] An analysis of the impact of the joint council is relevant here.

---

675 *Preamble of the Constitution of the Joint Council of the CSI- C.N.I-M.T.C.*
676 "Communion of Churches in India" commonly known as the CCI is the successor of the Joint Council of the CSI-CNI-MTC. It came into being in 2003 as a new name for the Joint Council of the CSI-CNI-MTC. With the reality of the disagreement on the model for unity and the need to constantly be on the lookout for ways to define the nature of unity of the Joint Council of the CSI-CNI-MTC, it is expected that openness to common experience will be important in predicting the success in the Indian church union process. This led to a joint meeting of the executive committees of the CNI, the

The founding of the joint council and the CCI was a turning point in the evolution of the Mar Thoma Church's ecumenical engagements with the Protestant churches. They enabled the Mar Thoma Church to become part of the joint executive committee of the three churches, to organise and participate in common meetings of bishops, clergy, women and youth at the regional and national levels, and the occasional con-celebration of the Eucharist. During the CNI Episcopal consecration in 1970, Alexander Mar Theophilus, a bishop of the Mar Thoma Church was a concelebrant[677] of the Eucharist in the CNI's All Saints' Cathedral in Nagpur on July 4, 1978.[678] Joint liturgical celebrations, unity observance on the second Sunday in November every year and the use of a common lectionary are the visible expressions of the joint programmes of the three churches.

Critical reaction to organic union idea

For the Mar Thoma Church, the unity of the three churches was not an end in itself. It considered the move as a stimulus for the transformation of the CSI-CNI-MTC Joint Council as one for manifesting the conciliar fellowship model of unity of the three churches. At the same time, the Mar Thoma Church was also aware of the changes apparent in the church's autonomous structure in case the organic union model was adopted. The Mar Thoma Church also rejected a proposal for a joint theological college in Kerala.

The Mar Thoma Church's critical attitude to the CSI's stance on the above mentioned proposals and its openness to constitute the CSI-CNI-MTC Joint Council are positively related to its desire to keep its oriental liturgical tradition and

CSI and the Mar Thoma Church at Charalkunnu in Kerala on November 1999 during which it was resolved that the CSI- CNI-MTC Joint Council be replaced by the term, "Communion of Churches in India". This resolution was adopted by the three churches and the constitution of the council was amended accordingly. Thus the CCI officially inaugurated its function in 2003.

The Report of the Joint Meetings of the Executive Committees of the C.N.I. – CSI & M.T.C held at Charal Kunnu, Kerala, 11th–14th November 1999. (The writer attended the meeting by virtue of his vocation as the Chaplain to the then Metropolitan, Alexander Mar Thoma.)

677 "Report of the Mar Thoma Theological Commission, 1973", In: *the Annual Report of the Mar Thoma Pradhinidhi Mandalam,* 1 and 2, May 1973.

678 "CSI- CNI- Mar Thoma Joint Council Meeting at Nagpur", In: *Malankara Sabha Tharaka* (Aug/1978).

independence. The church has always asserted its central position – oriental liturgical base and reforms – and in doing so, it has proclaimed its normative tradition of autonomy and independence powerfully. In this sense, the Mar Thoma Church takes its own oriental liturgical identity to an extreme – not by moving away from its central stance on conciliar fellowship model of ecumenical engagements with other churches, but by intensifying the church's self-understanding of the oriental-Indian church tradition, as representing its core.

In that sense, the Mar Thoma Church could appear to other churches as one that did not welcome change, although it was open to fresh ideas and spontaneity. This was evident when the church rejected the recommendation of a common name – "Bharath Church of Christ"[679] – after a merger of the CSI the CNI and the Mar Thoma Church. At the same time, the church did bring in a critical as well as a win-win standpoint of its own to safeguard both the Mar Thoma Church and the CSI stances.

As I mentioned earlier, the Mar Thoma Church disowned the proposal in the "Metropolitan's Encyclical of 1952" to be an organic part of the "Church of Christ in India". The disagreement to a common name proposed by the joint theological commission was in line with that move within the Mar Thoma Church. This is evident in the introductory statement of Alexander Mar Theophilus (1913–2000), the then Suffragan Metropolitan of the Mar Thoma Church, at the "CSI-MTC Union Negotiations commission" in 1974 that ...

"... the resolution of the Mar Thoma Church regarding this matter is to consider ways of closer relationship between the two churches and not to make Union Negotiations".[680]

This statement of the Metropolitan was in the context of the CSI stand that the adoption of a common name for the three churches was an option in order to make the unity of the churches visible.

The Mar Thoma Church's Oriental liturgical tradition and Indian socio-cultural moorings are highly treasured within the church. The Mar Thoma Church leaders foresaw the possible damage which could develop around the ecclesiastical differences of the church to the CSI and the CNI at its praxis level in case of an organic merger. These three churches constituted the second largest Christian population in India. They belong to three different traditions – Oriental reformed, Anglican and Protestant – which makes a merger an impractical idea.

---

679 "Bharath Church of Christ" means "Church of Christ in India."
680 *Minutes of the CSI-Mar Thoma Union Negotiations Commission,* Held at Zion Hill Aramana, Kottayam on 17th May 1974.

What the Mar Thoma Church envisaged in its ecumenical engagements was not to have an organisational or administrative unity with uniformity of liturgical and other practices. On the contrary, what the church aimed for is suggested in the following quotation by V.P. Thomas, former professor of the Leonard Theological College, Jabalpur:

"But a search for a unity at a deeper level that at the same time will provide for whatever distinctiveness, which the component churches wish to preserve and which we hope would be enriching the total life of the church as a whole and helpful to the fulfilment of the mission of the church in India.[681]

As Thomas says,[682] the Mar Thoma Church did look for a permanent relation with the CSI and CNI. But it feared that any decision by the joint council against the decision of the individual churches may result in resentment and divisions.[683] So the Mar Thoma Church was not in a position to subscribe for a joint council having decision-making power over the individual churches.

The CSI stand on church unity with the Mar Thoma Church was made clear in the resolution of the CSI Synod: The synod notes with appreciation the work done by the joint session of the theological Commission of the CSI and the Mar Thoma Church. It expresses the hope for furthering conversations, which would lead to negotiations for organic union between the two churches.[684] But what the Mar Thoma Church envisioned in the union negotiations is oneness in Eucharistic fellowship and in common mission in India.

It was in this context of a clash of interest between the churches that the adoption of declarations leading towards a union of churches with the common name "Bharath Church of Christ" by the first meeting of the CSI-CNI-MTC Joint Theological Commission should be analysed.[685] Some of the Mar Thoma Church

---

681 V.P. Thomas, "The Nature of the Union of the Churches that we Seek", In: *Minutes of the Second Meeting of the Joint Theological Commission of the CSI-CNI-MTC* held at Ranson Hall of the United Theological College, Bangalore on 3rd and 4th June 1975, Annexure IV, 34–37.

682 V.P. Thomas was a clergy and a Principal at the Mar Thoma Theological Seminary of the Mar Thoma Church.

683 Lukas Vischer, *Conciliar Unity*, (Bangalore: Faith and Order and ECC Publication, 1978), 42.

684 *The Report of the Mar Thoma Theological Commission*, 1971.

685 The other recommendations were: First the unifying factor for full communion relationship of the churches is its faith in Jesus Christ and its expression through theological agreement, two dominical sacraments, historic episcopacy and the acceptance of the faith of the historic creeds – Nicea and Constantinople. Second the present theological

216

leaders in the theological commission were not critical of the move for a common name and for a common structure with authority, but most of the leaders were. And, most of the leaders asked church members not to be passive participants in following the joint council's recommendation for a common name.[686] The Mar Thoma Church feared that the new common structure and authority are significant as it may lead to the absorption of the smaller church by the majority tradition. This antipathy towards a common name and a sense of an overriding need to keep its traditional name worried the Mar Thoma Church leaders of the church on the legal implications of such a move. To ease the difference between the three churches, J.R. Chandran, former principal of the United Theological College, Bangalore, and a representative of the CSI in the joint theological commission, attempted to clarify the aim of the union in these words:

> What is envisaged in the union is not organisational or administrative unity with uniformity of liturgical and other practices, but rather an expression of organic unity, which would permit diversity of traditions and practices, which would highlight and bear testimony to the riches we have in Christ without obscuring or hindering the visibility of our unity in Christ.[687]

agreement of the three churches is sufficient warranty for growing together in unity. Third, "the growing together of the three churches needs to be expressed through structures". Fourth apart from the new structure they suggested for a Joint Advisory council of Bishops, clergy, and laity to consider issues connected with the life of the church, together with a Joint Advisory Council to safeguard the expression the diversities within the unity of the church. They also suggested a Bishops' conference.

See, *Declaration of the Joint CSI, C.N.I., Mar Thoma Theological Commission, Annexure VI, Ibid.*, 41–42. See, *Minutes of the First Meeting of the Joint Theological Commission of the CSI-CNI-MTC*, held at the Community Service Centre, Kilpauk, Madras on 16th January 1975.

686 M.A. Thomas and other ecumenists of the Mar Thoma Church were not in favour of adopting a common name for three churches. They advocated for the maintenance of a Joint Council of the CSI-CNI-MTC. They invited the churches to widen its ecumenical agenda by including the Indian churches, viz., Malankara Orthodox Syrian Church, Malankara Syrian Orthodox Church and the Roman Catholic Church in to the Joint Council.

See, M.A. Thomas, *Oru Pothunamam Avsyam illa*, (Malayalam), (Kottayam: Palathinkal Printers, 1983), 23; *Proposed Resolution*, No. 16, *Report of the Mar Thoma General Assembly*, 1984.

687 "J.R. Chandran's Proposal for CNI- CSI-MTC Joint Council Commission", Annexure V, In: *Minutes of the Second Meeting of the Joint Theological Commission of the CSI-CNI-MTC* held at Ranson Hall of the United Theological College, Bangalore on 3rd and 4th June 1975, 39.

Nevertheless, these descriptions suggest a significant change of perspective of the Mar Thoma Church on the common name proposal. For instance, while speaking at the seminar conducted by the Mar Thoma Church at St. Augustine's Study Centre Kottayam on "Conciliar Fellowship", Chacko George[688] observes, in the context of the preamble[689] of the CSI-CNI-MTC Joint Council:

> "The complete retention of the authority of the three churches and the organisational structures, which again means constitutional sovereignty or permanency of the individual churches, clearly rule out the formation and the creation of a common church or the One Church" …[690]

Besides, the general assembly of the Mar Thoma Church "has not taken any decision to constitute and become part of the 'One Church', composed of the CSI, CNI and the Mar Thoma Church. Therefore, the question of adopting a common name not arise."[691] Consequently, the Mar Thoma Church decided not to accept the common name proposal. This was made clear at the church general assembly during 4–5 May, 1976, which reiterated that:

1. "The proposed "Conciliar fellowship" is not for the formation of one united church;
2. The church's constitution shall not be defected, the constitutional sovereignty of the general assembly of the church and the rights of the parishes shall not be lessened, and there will not be any hindrance to continue the church's faith and order, celibate episcopacy and other traditions in the new proposed conciliar fellowship.
3. Just like in the worldwide Anglican Communion, the church aimed at the unity of three churches, while remaining as autonomous churches with sovereign administrative freedom."[692]

---

688 Chacko George was a renowned Kerala High Court Advocate and the Mar Thoma Church's former legal advisor.
689 The Preamble to the Constitution of the CSI-CNI-MTC says that three member churches of the Joint Council recognize themselves as belonging to the one Church of Jesus Christ in India, while remaining as autonomous churches. The Preamble permits each church to maintain its own identity, traditions and organizational structures. See, *Preamble, the Constitution of the "Joint Council of the CSI-CNI.-MTC"*, op.cit., 1–3.
690 Chacko George, "Constitutional Legitimacy of Adopting a Common Name for CNI, CSI and the Mar Thoma Church", In: M.J. Joseph, ed, *Conciliar Fellowship*, (Manganam: St. Augustine's Study Centre, 1979), 64;
   M.J. Joseph ed., *Church unity: Response of the Mar Thoma Church*, (Manganam: St. Augustine's Study Centre, 1979), 1–47.
691 *Ibid.*
692 *Circular Order of the Juhanon Mar Thoma Metropolitan, Circular*, No. 332, 1976. It is a translated version of the original text in the Malayalam vernacular by the

218

The significance of the general assembly decisions is that they articulated the Mar Thoma Church's stance of church unity from the context of church tradition and its relation with the Anglican Church. At the same time, in order to arrive at a win-win agreement in defining the nature of the unity, the Mar Thoma Church accepted a new terminology, which was called "organic oneness" that was a fusion of both the "organic unity" and "conciliar fellowship" models. This was as suggested by the joint committee of the three churches as a formula to define the meaning of the unity of the three churches.

It was agreed "not to describe the unity of the three churches as either organic or conciliar. It is actually both".[693] This led to the formulation of a new unity concept – "organic oneness" – which was acceptable to both the churches. "Organic oneness" is an abstract concept that refers to the Church's oneness, of which diversity and plurality are preserved.[694] It is "not interpreted in terms of monolithic uniformity but oneness which preserves the richness of diversity".[695] Although "organic oneness" attempts to convey an idea of the fusion of the three churches, it didn't effectively disguise the fact that what actually emerged in the end from

author. See, *Minutes of the Mar Thoma Sabha Pradhinidhi Mandalam,* 4th and 4th May, 1976.

693   Russell Chandran, "The Joint Council of the CNI- CSI- MTC", In: Russal Chandran, ed., *Joint Council of the Church of South India, The Church of North India and the Mar Thoma Syrian Church: A Brief account of the History and Meaning of its Formation,* (Delhi: ISPCK, 1984), 44–45.

694   The concept of "Organic Oneness" is akin to "Conciliar Fellowship". Russell Chandran formulates this concept of organic oneness, from the "Trinitarian" as well as the "Body of Christ" models, in which the Church's oneness reflecting the oneness of the Trinity, as well as the oneness of the "Body of Christ". This model of oneness recognizes plurality and diversity within the local churches. But its final goal is the merger of the churches. (See, Russell Chandran, "Celebrating the Festival of Unity", Appendix I, In: the *Report of the Joint Council Meeting of the Executive Committees of CNI-CSI & M.TC,* at Charalkunnu, on 11th–14th November 1999, 20–28) Russell Chandran himself admitted that the terminologies used by theologians and church leaders such as "organic unity" "conciliar fellowship" and "organic oneness" are "only different ways of expressing the already existing unity of the three churches". Russell Chandran, "Celebrating Festival of Unity", In: *Ibid.,* George Ninan, "The Working Paper of the Joint Council of CSI-CNI-MTC", In: *The Joint Council of the Church of South India, the Church of North India and the Mar Thoma Syrian Church of Malabar,* Appendix V, (Mumbai: Joint Council of the CSI-C.N.I.-M.T.C, 1999), 49–62.

695   Russell Chandran, "Celebrating the Festival of Unity", Appendix I, In: the *Report of the Joint Council Meeting of the Executive Committees of C.N.I. – CSI & M.T.C,* at Charalkunnu, on 11th–14th November 1999, in *Ibid.,* 20–28.

the protracted discussions was conciliar fellowship. This new concept can be considered as unity model starting with conciliar fellowship, but ultimately aimed at a merger to form a church with common name and common structure with authority.

The Mar Thoma Church's second critical reaction to the CSI was related to the founding of a joint theological college in Kerala. The then three CSI dioceses in Kerala and the Mar Thoma Church started discussions for the founding of a joint theological college in Kerala in the early 1960s. This created a division of leaders of the Mar Thoma Church, on one side, and those of the CSI, on the other, regarding questions such as the representation in the governing board of the proposed theological college, the question of whether or not the CSI dioceses should act as one unit or three units and on the question of raising finances for the college.[696]

Both churches took different positions to safeguard their interests. For instance, the CSI South Kerala diocese decided that "the draft constitution of the proposed theological college shall be accepted with two amendments".[697] One amendment proposed that "of the total membership of the governing board 1/3 will be from the Mar Thoma Church and 2/3 from the three dioceses of the CSI"[698], against the proposal of the Mar Thoma Church council of three bishops from the three dioceses of the CSI and three Bishops from the Mar Thoma Church.[699]

This power struggle led to discontentment among leaders of the Mar Thoma Church as it was considered a move by the CSI dioceses to dominate the proposed joint theological college's governing board. In view of the mounting differences, the joint committee found it difficult to proceed with the scheme.

In step with global moves

The Mar Thoma Church kept its ecumenical stance of openness and autonomy, by adopting some general principles of the world church unity agreements, in its relation with the CSI and the CNI. The full communion agreement also met requirements of church unity proposed by the Lambeth Conference. The *Lambeth Quadrilateral* of 1888 and 1920 made it clear that church unity requires acceptance of the authority of the scripture, affirmation of the two early creeds,

---

696 "Joint Committee resolution of three Dioceses of the CSI and the Mar Thoma Church", In: M.J. Joseph *Defender of Faith, op.cit.*, 365. "Eikya Aalochanakalum Oru Visadeekaranam", In: *Ibid.*
697 *Ibid.*
698 *Ibid.*
699 *Ibid.*

the acceptance of the baptism and Eucharist and of the historic episcopate. This is more evident when we compare the formula of the Leuenberg agreement (1973) of the Lutheran and Reformed churches in Europe for their full communion and the full communion agreement reached between the Mar Thoma Church and the CSI.

Leuenberg Agreement

In the analysis of the Mar Thoma Church's formula for the full communion agreement with the CSI and the CNI, there have been some features that share the formula of the Leuenberg Agreement.[700] Like the Mar Thoma Church's formula for the church unity between the CSI and the CNI, the Leuenberg Agreement ensures that it ...

> "... does not affect the validity of the confessions of faith to which the participating churches are committed. It is not to be regarded as a new confession of faith. It sets out a consensus reached on central points that make church fellowship possible between churches of different confessional positions".[701]

Secondly, the Leuenberg and the CSI-CNI-MTC formulas both acknowledge the important theological, liturgical and tradition differences between churches, but these differences are not church-dividing, but rather a gift to each other. Thus "there is reconciled diversity and visible unity".[702]

This is considered as the basic point, which brings churches together for full communion relation. Thirdly, both formulas celebrate the potential for shared mission and ministry as the two traditions grow closer. Fourthly, both formulas affirm that the pre-requisite for the unity of the church is agreement in the right teaching of the Scripture, and the right administration of the sacraments in essence.

There are basic differences between the traditions of the Mar Thoma Church, a reformed oriental church, and churches of other reform traditions. The reformation tradition churches emphasis the right teaching of the Gospel and the right administration of the sacraments, namely the baptism and Eucharist, as a pre-requisite for church unity. But the Mar Thoma Church considers the right teachings of the Scripture, the faith affirmations of the Nicene Creed and the right administration

---

700 Leuenberg Agreement was an agreement between the Churches that belong to the reform traditions in Europe on 16th March 1973. See, *www.leuenberg.net* visited on 14th March 2013.
701 37.b. "Continuing Theological Task", In: *Ibid.*
702 *Ibid.*

of the seven sacraments essential for its agreement for full communion with other church traditions. Therefore, with regard to the importance of Scripture and its relation to tradition and the Church, the Mar Thoma Church follows the stance of the Oriental churches.

The Mar Thoma Church shares the spirit of the Leuenberg Agreement with regard to the Eucharist that "in the Lord's Supper, the risen Jesus Christ imparts himself in his body and blood, given up for all, through his word of promise with bread and wine. He thus gives himself unreservedly to all who receive the bread and wine; faith receives the Lord's Supper for salvation, unfaith for judgement".[703] Both the formulas aimed at participating churches to be guided towards a common service and witness.[704]

---

703 *Leuenberg Agreement., Lord Supper, 18.*, In: *Ibid.*; *O.S No. 439,* of M.E. 1054 (1879), *Alapuzha civil court,* Kerala, in the Mar Thoma Syrian Church Archives, Tiruvalla.
704 37.b. "Continuing Theological Task", In: *www.leuenberg.net* visited on 14th March 2013.

Chapter XIII
Helming and Guiding
Global Ecumenism

As we have seen clearly in the previous chapters, the autonomous nature and open outlook of the Mar Thoma Church have been the pillars around which its ecumenical thinking has been built up over the years. At the same time, the Mar Thoma tradition that is rooted in the Oriental liturgical base has provided the pivot around which the church traversed in its ecumenical praxis. Broadly speaking, these two factors constituted the church's cognitive base within which ecumenical engagements and its ties with other religious communities emerged.[705]

The Mar Thoma Church's autonomous nature and open outlook also helped the church see itself as belonging to the traditional Indian socio-religious classes, which were custodians of Indian culture and religion, as well as of wealth and politics. The same factors served as the basis for the church's solidarity with the ecumenical movement at the national and international levels and in its ecumenical praxis during the 20th Century.[706]

These factors, along with the ecumenical vision of the Mar Thoma Church leadership, created a practical atmosphere for the church to constructively engage the modern ecumenical movement and search for a new ecumenical identity in India. The importance of the top church leadership, especially the metropollitans, cannot be overstated here.

Titus II, the motivator

The first Mar Thoma Metropolitan, in whom the Mar Thoma Church's modern ecumenical search found a viable national and international expression, was Titus II (1866–1944). The major ecumenical efforts of the Metropolitan were four-fold. First, he worked with the Serampore conference organised by John R. Mott in Calcutta in 1912. This conference was a follow-up meeting of the Edinburgh conference's continuation committee. In this meeting they dealt with challenges to Christian

---

705   *Ibid.*, 119.
706   *Ibid.*

ministry and the national leadership for mission in India.[707] This marked the Mar Thoma Church's official entry into the ecumenical movement of the 20th Century. This meeting was instrumental for the formation of the National Missionary Council (NMC)[708] in India, which was the forerunner of the National Council of Churches in India (NCCI).

Secondly, Titus II also worked for the unity of the Kerala churches – the Jacobite, the Anglican and Mar Thoma churches – following the Serampore Conference's spirit. This eventually resulted in the formation of a Union Christian College in Aluva, which is the visible expression of the three churches ecumenical engagements. Thirdly, he encouraged and sent the Mar Thoma Church's Suffragan Metropolitan Abraham Mar Thoma (1880–1947) to the early unofficial meetings organised by those three churches at the Union Christian College, Aluva in 1925 for furthering the ecumenical relation between the aforementioned churches in India.[709] Fourthly, it was during his Metropolitan tenure that the Mar Thoma Church came into an "occasional inter-communion" agreement with the Anglican Church in 1937. Motivated by the ecumenical spirit, he emphasised the need for the churches' unity in India, which is evident in his last circular letter to all parishes, dated 3rd July 1944. His circular letter says:

> Although our church is a small church, I firmly believe that we are an ancient church founded in A.D.52. Therefore our responsibilities are great. In India we are divided into church denominations. I wish for a united church in an independent and unified India. May our Lord give us grace to achieve this objective. Quarrels and arguments belong to the world, but reality is the paradigm of the world yet to come.[710]

This circular indicates the Metropolitan's singular and significant interest to see the Mar Thoma Church as a distinct traditional Christian church in India and to project itself as a leading player in the ecumenical movement in India. The letter explored the feasibility of the church taking leadership of the unity process through its rich and age-old apostolic traditions and resources. Thus Titus II held that church unity was the paradigm of the Kingdom of God, over and above the world paradigm of disunity. From this standpoint he argued for a united church in India.

---

707 T.C. Chacko, *Malankara Mar Thoma Sabha Charithra Sangraham* (Malayalam), *op.cit.*, 222.
708 Hereafter referred as NMC.
709 N.M. Mathew, *Malankara Mar Thoma Sabha Charithram*, (Malayalam), *op.cit.*, 196.
710 *Circular Letter of Titus II to all parishes, Circular No. 324,* 3 July, 1944. Tiruvalla.

Abraham Mar Thoma, the nationalist

The ecumenical quest and legacy for a united church in India of Titus II Metropolitan was passed down to Abraham Mar Thoma (1880–1947), who had been the suffragan Metropolitan of the church since 1917.[711] His consecration as the bishop on 27th December 1917 was a spectacular instance of ecumenism, with the participation of the MISC and the CIBC. In his Episcopal consecration, Geevarghese Mar Koorilose (1892–1935), the Metropolitan of the MISC, and Bishop Charles Hope Gill (1905–1925), the Anglican bishop of Cochin and Travancore, were co-celebrants.[712]

In analysing this gesture on the part of the Anglican and the MISC bishops in the Mar Thoma Church's episcopal consecration, it becomes clear that a practical unity between those churches was in force even before the doctrinal consensus and the official agreements were reached in 1937.

Abraham Mar Thoma's Christological base provided the content of his ecumenical engagements. He held that unity of humankind as expressed in the teachings of Jesus Christ is the basis of the Mar Thoma Church. From this standpoint he argued that, Christ is the centre of the Gospel and this truth needs to be communicated to all humanity through missionary work and through the participation in the peoples' socio-religious and political agitations to provide a feasible atmosphere for the implementation of the Gospel. Said Abraham Mar Thoma:

"Father, as we are one, they should be one as well. This unity is essential not only for Christians but also for all castes and communities, *Nairs*, Muslims, *Ezhavas*, *Brahmins*, backward community people, other Hindus, Muslims, and Christians who belong to a common brotherhood of man."[713]

This perspective of the unity of humankind made him the benefactor, who supported the concerted struggles of the people for autonomy and unity in India. Stanley J. Samartha affirms this as he says:

---

711 Sherwood Eddy, *Pathfinders of the World Missionary Crusade, op.cit.*, 155–160.
712 *Annual Report of the Mar Thoma Syrian Church of Malabar,* 1918; Zac Varghese, Mathew A Kallupuram, *Glimpses of Mar Thoma Church History, op.cit.*, 124.
713 Abraham Mar Thoma's Speech, Centenary Celebration of the Reformation of the Mar Thoma Church, Trivandrum, 1938, Cited in Zac Varghese, Mathew A Kallupuram, *Glimpses of Mar Thoma Church History, op.cit.*, 134–135.

"He was strong and outspoken in his protest against the autocratic and repressive measures of the state authorities, who tried to keep the state of Travancore separate and outside the union of India."[714]

Thus, Abraham Mar Thoma not only envisioned Christian unity but also infused a sense of nationalism and ecumenism, which encompassed the unity of other religious communities, into the modern history of India through his constructive participation in the joint Hindu-Muslim-Christian struggle for responsible self-government that we discussed earlier.

The result of this standpoint was two-fold: It enabled the church to engage with missionary and ecumenical movements, and also to join with the socio-political agitations in Kerala.

Juhanon Mar Thoma, the articulator

Juhanon Mar Thoma was the next Metropolitan, who became the torch bearer of the Mar Thoma Church's legacy that was initiated by Titus II and handed down to Abraham Mar Thoma. He began his episcopacy in 1937 and was convinced that the way of the Mar Thoma Church towards witnessing in the community was through strengthening its oriental liturgical base and openness and its relationships with other Indian religious communities. By writing books on those two areas, he established a solid theoretical ground for the typical autonomy and openness outlook of the church.[715]

The Metropolitan's leadership in the global, Asian and Indian ecumenical movement testifies his vision on ecumenism. He led the Mar Thoma Church's delegates at the WCC's first general assembly in 1948.

"His thoughtful statements expressed quietly and his impressive personality was appreciated at the WCC and so in the 1954 Evanston Assembly he was elected as one of the Presidents of the WCC."[716]

He was the chairman of the third General Assembly of the WCC and "guided the deliberations with distinction".[717] His leadership at the WCC and the national and international ecumenical bodies gave him a deeper sense of ecumenism that

---

714 Stanly J. Samartha, "Abraham Mar Thoma", In: Gerald H. Anderson, ed., *Biographical Dictionary of Christian Missions,* (Michigan/ Cambridge: William B. Eerdmans Publishing Company, 1999), 3.
715 Juhanon Mar Thoma, *Ormakalum Kurippukalum, op.cit.,* 190–202.
716 Zac Varghese and Mathew Kallupuram, "Metropolitan Juhanon Marthoma" (1893–1976), In: *Light of Life,* Volume 3/7 (July 2004).
717 *Ibid.*

helped the church to achieve a formal full communion agreement with the Anglican Church in 1961, with the CSI in 1971, and with the CNI in 1974.

Juhanon Mar Thoma's pre-eminence in the Asian and Indian ecumenical movement, as well as in the Mar Thoma Church's ecumenism efforts, were brought forth in his writings and life. He created an excitement of ecumenical thought within the church, and initiated a schema on the need for unity and support for the Indian ecumenical movement. This was done in the full awareness of the church's rich heritage of autonomy and openness and of its potential for the furtherance of church unity engagements within India and in the larger world ecumenical movement. His contribution in the church's engagement with the institutional expressions of the global, Asian and Indian ecumenical movements is evident in the whole ecumenical endeavours of the church during his tenure as the Metropolitan and therefore, it is not being elaborated here.

Institutional links

The Mar Thoma Church's ecumenical predilection is the major factor that has drawn it closer towards the institutional expressions of the national, regional and global ecumenical movement.

The church top leadership has had a great impact in its ecumenical efforts as they provided the momentum for the church's participation in the modern ecumenical movement. Metropolitans Titus II, Abraham Mar Thoma and Juhanon Mar Thoma, and other church leaders such as P.O. Philip, K.K. Kuruvilla, C.P. Mathew, M.A. Thomas and M.M. Thomas were among the stalwarts who promoted the spirit of ecumenism in the church. Juhanon Mar Thoma's letters to the members of the Mar Thoma Church through the *Sabha Tharaka* – the church's official monthly publication – used to express his wish regularly for the promotion of ecumenism. In one of his letters, he wrote that "the unity of the Syrian church ought to be achieved"[718] together with the church unity efforts in south India.[719] A new ecumenical spirit and a will to participate in the ecumenical efforts formed the content of the Mar Thoma Church's ecumenism during 1910–1961. This new spirit found expressions through two types of applications at the praxis level – the Mar Thoma Church's constructive participation in the ecumenical movement's institutional expressions such as National Council of Churches in India (NCCI),

---

718 "Letter of Juhanon Mar Themotheos", In: *Malankara Sabha Tharaka*, Vrichikam, 1122(Malayam Era), (December/ 1947), 175–178.

719 *Ibid.*

Christian Conference of Asia (CCA), World Council of Churches (WCC) and a call to the Church of Christ in India.

The National Missionary Council (NMC) was the first institutional expression of the ecumenical movement in India in which the Mar Thoma Church was a pioneer member. The ecumenical and the evangelical thought propensity current in the first decade of the 20th Century after the Edinburgh world missionary conference in 1910 had its influence on the missionary and ecumenical policies of the Mar Thoma Church. For instance, the church started a mission work in Ankola in 1912, jointly with the National Missionary Society (NMS) that we have discussed in a previous chapter. The Mar Thoma Church appeared to the NMS and the Indian Christian community at large as a traditional Indian church, having Indian cultural moorings, but with strong evangelical fervour.

This inspired the Mar Thoma Church to take the leadership of the missionary work in India. The NMS wanted to make use of the Mar Thoma Church's potential to evangelise India. It was during this period that John R. Mott held a meeting at Serampore in Calcutta in 1912 following the guidelines of the Edinburgh Conference.

The Mar Thoma Church leaders accepted John R. Mott's call at the Serampore conference for an Indian missionary council, as an institutional expression of ecumenism.[720] The church believed in its responsibility to participate in the process of developing an ecumenical outlook and the unity of different churches in India for missionary endeavours by Indians.[721] The Mar Thoma Church not only considered its loyalty to the Serampore conference's proposal for the National Missionary Council (NMC) as firm, but agreed to pledge its commitment to missionary co-operation with other mission societies in India. Two decisions of the conference – a decision to start a residential school, an icon of ecumenical praxis by the Indian churches, and the formation of a provincial representative council – were taken seriously by the Mar Thoma Church.[722]

---

720 This meeting was organised by the directives of the Edinburgh conference in 1910 for the promotion of unity at the national and regional levels. Ninan Koshy, *A History of the Ecumenical Movement in Asia*, op.cit., 54–55.

721 The Mar Thoma Church's missionary position as explained by Abraham Mar Thoma Metropolitan (1880–1947) was that, "If India's millions are to be reached and won for Christ, it will be by India's sons". This has already dealt with in the previous chapter of this study. See, *The first Ten Years of the National Missionary Society, 1905–1916*, op.cit., 16.

722 See, A.M. Pylee, "Mar Thoma Sabha Sabhaykkya Sambrambhangalil" in *Church Unity Response of the Mar Thoma Church*, (Manganam: St. Augustine Study Centre,

Icon of cooperation

The effect of the Serampore meetings resulted in the founding of a university accredited college[723] and the founding of the NMC. Having acknowledged the aforementioned decisions of the Serampore meeting, the leaders of the Anglican, Jacobite and Mar Thoma Churches sought to reach ecumenical engagements at the grassroots level. This led to the dream for a prestigious university college at Aluva in Kerala. The Union Christian College, Aluva, was established in 1921 by the official consent and support of the heads of the churches concerned in Kerala and the tireless efforts of the lay members of these churches such as C.P. Mathew (1896–1970), K.C. Chacko (1884–1947), V.M. Ittyerah (1895–1985) and A.M. Varkey (1892–1944).[724]

This could be seen as a visible institutional manifestation of the ecumenical relations of these churches at the grassroots level during this period. This institution served as a platform for the unofficial ecumenical meetings of the three churches in Travancore, viz., Malankara Mar Thoma Syrian Church, Malankara Jacobite Syrian Church and Anglican Church, starting from 1925.[725] This institution still stands as an icon of inter-church co-operation as it is jointly managed by representatives of the above mentioned churches.

The Mar Thoma Church played its part in the formation of the NMC and has been a member of the council since its inception in 1914.[726] It was an offshoot of the recommendation for the formation of a representative council by the national missionary conference held in Serampore in 1912.[727] The NMC effected a change of name later to reflect its change in perspective.

The early years of the NMC's history show how the NMC transferred its focus of interest from "mission societies" to the "Church". It has been reported in the

---

1981) 25–30; P.M. Thomas ed., "Mar Thoma Sabhayude Ecumenical Bandhangal" (Malayalam), In: *Mar Thoma sabha Directory,* (Malayalam), *op.cit.,* 139.

723   This college is affiliated to the Mahatma Gandhi University at Kottayam, India.

724   *http://www.uccollege.edu.in, visited on 5th December 2011*; "Mar Thoma Sabhayude Ecumenical Bandhangal" (Malayalam), In: P.M. Thomas ed., *Mar Thoma sabha Directory,* (Malayalam), *op.cit.,* 139; N.M. Mathew, *Mar Thoma Sabha Charithram* (Malayalam); Vol. III, *op.cit.,* 78.

725   C.V. John, *Juhanon Mar Thoma Metropolitan, Jeevithavum sandeshavum,* (Malayalam), *op.cit.,* 246.

726   Sherwood Eddy, *Pathfinders of the World Missionary Crusade,* (New York: Books for Libraries and Press, 1945) 166.

727   *Ibid.,* 55.

NMC proceedings during this period that the council should give importance to the activities of the church rather than of the mission. The NMC also supported efforts of the local leaders for the evangelisation of India.[728] This shift in importance led to the change of emphasis from "mission centric" to "church centric".[729] This was officially approved by the NMC meetings in 1919[730] and this perspective change eventually led to the transformation of the NMC into the National Christian Council (NCC) in 1923.[731] P.O. Philip, a member of the Mar Thoma Church, was the first NMC general secretary for a period of 15 years.

The Mar Thoma Church had an active role in all its proceedings. In 1979, the National Christian Council became the National Council of Churches in India (NCCI). The Metropolitans, clergy and laymen have been involved actively in different capacities, stretching from its chairmanship to a participant in its life and witness in India.[732]

The Mar Thoma Church also had a key pioneering role in the formation of the Kerala Council of Churches (KCC) in 1940 as an auxiliary wing.[733] The Mar Thoma Church has thus worked together relentlessly with other churches to strengthen the ecumenical movement in India. These efforts naturally extended to the international level, with the church being an active member of the WCC since its inception in 1948.

Engaging global ecumenism

The Mar Thoma Church has secured a berth in all institutional expressions of the modern ecumenical movement, such as the International Missionary Council (IMC), the Faith and Order commission and the Life and Work Movement, even

---

728 *Proceeding of the National Missionary Council, 1920, op.cit.,* 17.
729 *Proceeding of the National Missionary Council, 1919, op.cit.,* 16.
730 *Ibid.*
731 Kagg Baago, *A History of the National Christian Council of India, 1914–1964,* (Nagpur: NCCI, 1965), 8–20.
732 For instances the Metropolitans of the church – Alexander Mar Thoma, Philipose Mar Chrysostom Mar Thoma, and Joseph Mar Thoma – were Presidents of the NCCI. P.O Philip, Mathai Zacharia and Ipe Joseph were its general secretaries. Suresh Koshy serves as its Treasurer.
733 Members of the KCC in 1940 were viz., Malankara Mar Thoma Syrian Church, United Church of South India, Anglican Church, Basal Mission, CMS, and LMS. See, "Kerala Christian Conference" (Malayalam), In: *Malankara Sabha Tharaka,* Chingam/ Kanni (M.E 1115) (Sept/Oct, 1940), 233–239.

before the formation of the World Council of Churches (WCC) in 1948.[734] As the ecumenical spirit strengthened within the Mar Thoma Church during the 20th Century, the church leaders devoted considerable time to study ecumenism and sent its delegates to various worldwide ecumenical meetings in tandem with its own church unity efforts within the country. For instance, Abraham Mar Thoma and K.K. Kuruvilla, the then Principal of the Mar Thoma Theological Seminary, represented the Mar Thoma Church at the IMC meeting in Jerusalem in 1928, while C.P. Mathew went as a delegate to the IMC meeting at Tambaram in 1938.[735]

Leadership in WCC

The Mar Thoma Church can claim to be one of the founding members of the WCC.[736] When the WCC was being formally inaugurated at Amsterdam in 1948, the Metropolitan, Juhanon Mar Thoma, was present as one among the 147 members representing various churches in the world. In that assembly Juhanon Mar Thoma was elected to the WCC's central executive committee.[737] P. Thomas (1914–1984),[738] an ordained minister of the Mar Thoma Church and later became a bishop and suffragan Metropolitan of the church also attended the Amsterdam assembly.[739] Moreover, church member M.M. Thomas (1916–1996),[740] was the only non-western participant at the WCC's preparatory study commissions, which met at Bossey to prepare for the first WCC General Assembly in Amsterdam in 1948.[741] He was a member of the assembly study commission III on "The Church and the Disorder of Society".[742]

---

734 P.M. Thomas, ed., *Mar Thoma sabha Directory*, (Malayalam)*, op.cit.*, 140.
735 *Ibid.*, Sherwood Eddey, *Pathfinders of the World Missionary Crusade, op.cit.*, 157.
736 T.K. Thomas, "The Mar Thoma Church in the World Council of Churches", In: Mathew Daniel, ed., *Mar Thoma Sabha Saradhikal*, (Malayalam), (Tiruvalla: Mar Thoma Church Publication, 1993), 13.
737 Juhanon Mar Thoma, *Ormakalum Kurippukalum, op.cit.*, 196.
738 P. Thomas elevated as the Bishop of the Mar Thoma Church as Thomas Mar Athanasius (1914–1984) in 1953.
739 *Annual Report of the Juhanon Mar Thoma, Metropolitan, The Mar Thoma Syrian Church, Annual Report*, 1948; Juhanon Mar Thoma, *Ormakalum Kurippukalum, op.cit.*, 196.
740 M.M. Thomas served as the secretary and the Vice-President of the World Students Christian Federation during 1947–1953. He was in the Clergy Selection Committee for the selection of the writer to the priesthood in the Mar Thoma Church.
741 M.M. Thomas, *My Ecumenical Journey*, (Trivandrum: Ecumenical Publishing Centre, 1990), 20–21.
742 *Ibid.*, 21.

M.M. Thomas, the pioneer

M.M. Thomas (1916–1996) was a member of the Mar Thoma Church who played a prominent role in the life of the WCC four decades since the New Delhi Assembly in 1961. He was a pioneering ecumenical thinker and a layman. He was the moderator of the WCC's central committee during 1968–1975. He was also the chairman of the working committee of the WCC's department on "Church and Society" and also chaired the world conference on "Church and Society" in 1966. He spoke at the WCC assemblies at New Delhi and Uppsala. Thomas authored more than 50 books both in English and in his mother tongue, Malayalam. He was member of several key committees of the Mar Thoma Church, including the Sabha Council, general assembly, Episcopal nomination committee and clergy selection committee. He was appointed as the governor of Nagaland, a state in India in 1990.

M.M. Thomas' thought-world was primarily centred on the tradition of liberative-humanist faith. He was hopeful about social transformation through critical and rational engagement. For him, theology provides ideological support to the people for critical social engagement for social change. In this process, the poor and the marginalised received the key attention.

The socio-political world scenario after World War II made a favourable context for M.M. Thomas to apply his liberative-humanism concept in the agenda of the WCC and the Mar Thoma Church. There were four major concerns raised during the Amsterdam (1948) and Evanston (1954) assemblies, which forced the ecumenical movement to redefine its aims and plans of action in the aftermath of the World War II (1939–1945). This led to a rethinking of man's role in God's world.

The first major concern was reflected in the theme, "Man's Disorder and God's Design", of the first assembly in 1948. Second, the developments in Europe and Asia, especially the breakdown of the colonial empires after World War II, demanded systematic re-evaluations by the WCC of the problems and needs of the newly-formed Asian-African independent countries. The east-west division was visible in the theological and socio-political fields that made ecumenical efforts intricate.

Third, the newly emerging order after World War II forced states and churches to re-evaluate most of the faith and order, socio-ethical concerns and missionary paradigms. The fourth concern was the socio-ethical impact of the concept of "Responsible Society" in redefining the Church's role in the society. In such a context, the contribution of M.M. Thomas (1916–1996), which was in line with the ideas of J.C. Hoekendijk (1912–1975),[743] was instrumental in making a land-mark change in the ecumenical thinking of the WCC during the Evanston General Assembly of 1954.

J.C. Hoekendijk, a Dutch theologian, opened a new line of ecumenical thinking that the church should serve as the servant of the world. In his view, the church was only an instrument of God's redemptive action in the world and therefore "a church-centric missionary thinking is bound to go astray because it revolves around an illegitimate centre".[744] The gospel of the Kingdom will, therefore, be proclaimed throughout the *oikumene* (household of God). This prompted Hoekendijk to call upon the ecumenical movement to rethink the ecclesiology within the framework of the Kingdom-Gospel-Apostolate-world.[745] In this proposal, the world and the kingdom of God are co-related. The world is therefore considered as a unit and it is the scene of God's mission – *Missio Dei.*

A significant shift towards understanding mission during the second half of the 20th century was mission as *Missio Dei.* The concept of *Missio Dei* considered mission as mission of God that is derived from Trinity, the very nature of God.[746] So mission is understood in terms of the world's participation in the very nature of Trinity. Thus mission is considered as a movement from God to the world in solidarity with the incarnated and crucified Christ as well as the Holy Spirit. In the light of this understanding, mission is considered not an activity of the Church but an attribute of God.

The *Missio Dei* concept marked a departure from earlier understandings of mission in soteriological, cultural, salvation-history and ecclesiological terms and opened a new paradigm to see the mission of God in relation to Trinity, the very nature of God. It enabled the world ecumenical movement to see Missio Dei as the epicenter of the churches' and mission societies' mission in the world. This new paradigm provided ample room for the world ecumenical movement to take the world and its realities in its missionary agenda.

M.M. Thomas shared the same thought (*Missio Dei*) when he addressed the Evanston general assembly. He says:

---

743 Gerald H. Anderson, ed., *Biographical Dictionary of Christians Missions*, (Michigan: Wm. B. Erdmann Publishing Company, 1999), 297.

744 J.C. Hoekendijk, "The Church in Missionary Thinking", In: *International Review of Mission*, XLI, (1952), 332.

745 *Ibid.*

746 David J. Bosch, *Transforming Mission: Paradigm Shifts in Theology of Mission, op.cit.*, 389–393.

"If the Christian faith has a more realistic understanding of man and society, as we do believe, it must express itself in the insights Christians as citizens bring to the common pool in the common struggle of a responsible society where human freedom and social justice are real".[747]

The theological understanding of both J.C. Hoekendijk and M.M. Thomas, enabled the IMC and the WCC to ask themselves a question – should not the original meaning of the *oikoumene*, God's world, be the true focus of the ecumenical movement? This thinking enabled the WCC to shift its emphasis from the church to the whole inhabited world. This was a perspective change from the Tambaram meetings, where the IMC affirmed a "church-centric mission". These changes fuelled a shift of ecumenical emphasis from an established schema, Church and mission, to the 1960s WCC schema: God's World and Church's participation in the mission of God.

Sunand Sumithra's study on the work of M.M. Thomas has mentioned how "the necessity to express Christian faith in secular activities, the idea of participation, the inevitability of human freedom, social justice and the ideal of secular society…"[748] were accentuated in Thomas' theology as well as in the theology of the WCC. In that sense, it was through M.M. Thomas that the Mar Thoma Church could assist the WCC in formulating a new paradigm for the ecumenical thinking of the church's commitment to the world in the subsequent decades. This, in turn, influenced the Mar Thoma Church's policy to widen its ecumenical horizons, which will be dealt with in detail later.

M.M. Thomas also left behind a lasting legacy of Kingdom-centred critical theological tradition of liberation faith. This liberative tradition helped him to envision a new theological engagement for the emergence of a new humanism in India, rooted in Jesus Christ and Kingdom values. In this vision of social engagement for humanism, the liberation aspirations of those who converted from the "lower-caste" communities to the church received a key attention within the Mar Thoma Church.

This eventually helped the church to take social service and development schemes seriously in its mission praxis during the second half of the 20th Century. The major contribution of M.M. Thomas to the Mar Thoma Church was in

---

747 M.M. Thomas, "Christians in the struggle for Responsible Society in India Today", In: "Selected Addresses from Accredited Visitors' Programme", *Evanston Speaks. Reports from the Second Assembly of the World Council of Churches*, August 15–31, 1954, (Madras: CLS, 1954), 2.

748 Sundand Sumithra, *Revolution as Revelation,* (Tubingen/New Delhi, International Christian Network & The Theological Research and Communication Institute, 1984), 15.

developing a new consciousness about the need for change in the church in relation to its attitude to the converts from the "lower-caste" community.

Although the mainline members of the Mar Thoma Church were reluctant to accept M.M. Thomas' concept of liberative humanism, the church's Metropolitan and the leadership accepted it. The involvement of the Mar Thoma Church in social service and development works were the visible impacts of this theological and socio-ethical ideology of Thomas within the church during the second half of the 20th Century.

Thomas had a major role in the discussions towards a full communion agreement with the CSI and CNI. His concept of liberative humanism helped in the developement of a subaltern theology and "dalit" theology in India.

Evanston and New Delhi

The Evanston general assembly of the WCC was a milestone in the life of the Mar Thoma Church. It was at this assembly that the Mar Thoma Church's Metropolitan, Juhanon Mar Thoma, was elected as one of its presidents for a period of seven years. M.M. Thomas, his wife and three priests of the church were accredited as visitors at this assembly. Three Bishops of the church namely Juhanon Mar Thoma, Bishop Alexander Mar Theophilus later Metropolitan, Alexander Mar Thoma Metropolitan (1913–2000) and Philipose Mar Chrysostom were delegates to this assembly. The leadership of the Mar Thoma Metropolitan helped the WCC to convene its third General Assembly in the capital of India – New Delhi – in 1961, with the Metropolitan serving as its chairman.

> "We have come together in this place out of many nations because Christ who is the light of the world has shined in our hearts to give the light of the knowledge of the glory of God, and because he has set us as lights in the world and bidden us let our lights shine".[749]

Those words of Juhanon Mar Thoma, from the *New Delhi Story*, of Samuel McCrea Cavert, embody the overall mood of the third General Assembly of the WCC held from 19 November to 5 December, 1961.

It was in New Delhi that the address of M.M. Thomas brought forth the centrality of Jesus Christ in the social transformation process. He spoke of Christ being present in today's world engaged in a continuous dialogue with peoples and nations. He continued:

---

749 *The New Delhi Report: The Third Assembly of the World Council of Churches, 1961*, (London SCM Press LTD, 1962) 2.

"... in fact, the Church and the world have the same centre, Jesus Christ, it is therefore impossible to confine the work of Christ in or through the church".[750]

This eventually led M.M. Thomas' vision of "Christocentric universalism" to dominate ecumenical social action and the developmental activities of the WCC in the years after the New Delhi Assembly.

While referring to the post-colonial scenario of the Asian-African countries, Thomas pleaded for "positive responsible relations to the people's struggle for a new life".[751] The effect of these words echoed not only in the WCC's determination to "stay together" (Amsterdam) and "to grow together" (Evanston), but also to move out together into the world's struggle for social justice and international peace"[752], together with a perspective change in the ecumenical thinking – the church's participation in God's mission in the world.

An analysis of the reports of the New Delhi General Assembly shows that it was a defining moment for the future vision of the WCC – conciliar unity, unity of humankind, justice and peace, integrity of creation, and *koinonia*. The New Delhi Assembly also decided to practice unity, witness and service in "each place". The Mar Thoma Church's ecumenical participation obviously made its visible presence in the WCC through Juhanon Mar Thoma, Philipose Mar Chrysostom, M.M. Thomas, M.A. Thomas and others.

Ecumenical association for Asia

The Mar Thoma Church took an active part in the East Asia Christian Conference's (EACC) formation and development. The prominent Mar Thoma Church leaders showed practical support to the formation of a regional ecumenical association for the Asian region – Christian Conference of Asia – since its initial discussions at the IMC's meeting at Tambarm in 1936. C.P. Mathew, the Mar Thoma

---

750 T.V. Philip, *Edinburgh to Salvador. Twentieth Century Ecumenical Missiology. A Historical Study of the Ecumenical Discussions on Mission*, (New Delhi: CSS & ISPCK, 1999), 81; M.M. Thomas' vision of "Christo-centric universalism" was dominated in the ecumenical social action and the developmental activities of the WCC in the following years.

751 *The New Delhi Report: The Third Assembly of the World Council of Churches*, 1961, *op.cit.*, 27.

752 *Ibid.*, 55.

Church's delegate also supported the proposal for an ecumenical association for Asia region, which was promoted by the Tambaram meeting.[753] The Mar Thoma Church, by supporting the proposal for a regional ecumenical association, wanted to revitalise and materialize the world ecumenical efforts for missionary co-operation, and let the church's autonomous and openness values be assimilated into the Asian church's complex context, and to work jointly for the furtherance of unity and mission. It helped to further the Mar Thoma Church's ecumenical outlook and the emergence of national and international ecumenical leaders from the Mar Thoma Church.

The new ecumenical impulse and the Mar Thoma Church's inherent openness to fresh ideas were challenging its members and leaders to develop a fresh, healthy and self-reliant ecumenical spirit. Juhanon Mar Thoma, Alexander Mar Thoma, Thomas Mar Athanasius, M.M. Thomas, M.A. Thomas, T.N. Koshy an ordained minister of the Mar Thoma church and others from the Mar Thoma Church took active role in the East Asia Christian Conference's formation.

Among the 44 delegates from 21 WCC member churches and 10 Asian member national councils of the IMC, the Mar Thoma Church's bishop, Thomas Mar Athanasius represented the church and extended the church's support to the formation of the East Asia Christian Conference at Prapat in Indonesia in 1957.[754] The assembly elected a continuation committee with office-bearers. M.M. Thomas was elected as a member in the continuation committee and the working committee.[755] The Mar Thoma Church "has been part of Christian Conference of Asia from the beginning and Bishop Alexander Mar Theophilus later Metropolitan Alexander Mar Thoma (1913–2000) and M.A. Thomas an ordained minister of the Mar Thoma Church officially represented"[756] the church during the maiden meeting of the EACC, the forerunner of the Christian Conference of Asia (CCA) in Kuala Lumpur in 1959. Since then, the church has been serving it in different capacities. For instance, Joseph Mar Thoma was the president of the CCA during 2000–2005.

---

753 P.M. John, ed., *Mar Thoma Sabha Directory, op. cit.*, 140.

754 V.P. Thomas, T.P. Abraham, "Mar Thoma Sabhayile Nethruthrayathinte Savishesha Sambhavanakal – ecumenical veedhikalil" (Malayalam), In: *Episcopal Silver Jubilee Smarakopaharam*, (Tiruvalla: Mar Thoma Sabha Council, 1978), 107–137; Ninan Koshy, *A History of the Ecumenical Movement in Asia, op.cit.*, 128.

755 M.M. Thomas, *My Ecumenical Journey, op.cit.*, 209.

756 T.K. Thomas, "The Mar Thoma Church in the World Council of Churches" In: Mathew Daniel, ed., *Mar Thoma Sabha Saradhikal*, (Malayalam), (Tiruvalla: Mar Thoma Church Publication, 1993), 14.

A 'bridge church'

The Mar Thoma Church's engagement with the institutional expressions of the ecumenical movement can be seen as the expression of its self-awareness as an indigenous Indian church, as distinct from other Indian churches which have their roots in western missions and western denominations, together with its self-awareness and responsibility as participants of the ecumenical movement.[757] Although the reforms of the Mar Thoma Church was the connecting link of the church to the western CMS missionaries, the church's self-understanding about its reforms is that it "was a return to the ancient autonomy and biblical faith of the St. Thomas Christians, which it had lost as a result of foreign interferences".[758]

By asserting the distinct Indian Mar Thoma tradition, the church was trying to bring forth the importance of the unity models. However, the Mar Thoma Church's nature of openness provides its innate ability to accommodate the unity models, which were proposed by the ecumenical movement, into the life of the Mar Thoma church tradition. This has led the Mar Thoma Church to redefining of its ecclesiological position in the new ecumenical world.

Besides, the Mar Thoma Church received motivation from its positive ecumenical engagements with the MISC and CIPBC to deepen its labours towards the furtherance of ecumenism from time to time. The full communion relations with the MISC (1894) and the "occasional inter-communion" agreement with the CIBC (1936) had destroyed the logic of impracticability of the Mar Thoma Church, as a small traditional Indian church, to have full communion relations with both eastern and western churches. This is evident in the MT Metropolitan's statement that, "we enjoy friendly relation with almost all the protestant denominations in India that accepts infant baptism".[759]

---

757 This idea is evident in the Titus II Metropolitans' circular letter to all parishes of the Mar Thoma Church, and his desire to take leadership for formation of an independent united church of India. See, T.P Abraham, "Eikathinte verukal thedi" (Malayalam), In: *Conciliar Fellowship – Mar Thoma Sabhayude Veekshanam* (malayalaam), (Kottayam: St. Augustine Study Centre, 1979), 7–8; C.V. John, "Mar Thoma Sabhayum Eikya Samrambhangalum" (Malayalam), In: *Ibid.*, 43–52; Juhanon Mar Thoma, Mathews Mar Athanasius, "A Call to the Churches of Christ in India", In: *Joint Statement of Juhanon Mar Thoma and Mathews Mar Athanasius to Indian Churches*, December 21, 1952, Tiruvalla.
758 *Ibid.*
759 *Ibid.*

238

Besides, the organic union of four church traditions forming the Church of South India in 1948 motivated the Mar Thoma Church to work for the possibility of following the same example of the unity process, by engaging in ecumenical ties with both eastern and western churches.

In that process, the then Metropolitan Juhanon Mar Thoma believed that the Mar Thoma Church's strange mix of eastern liturgical autonomy and its evangelical commitments help to place the church as a "bridge church" to connect the eastern and western Protestant churches. The Mar Thoma Church's episcopal synod says:

> "We are proud that we remain a bridge church, preserving in it the best features of eastern traditional forms of worship and the Reformation principle of Luther and the Western Protestant churches".[760]

From this statement, it is evident that the Mar Thoma Church has the potential to stand as a link between the eastern and protestant churches, while keeping its autonomy and openness intact. This self-understanding of the church helped to support the "conciliar fellowship" model of unity in its praxis level and to relegate the organic model of unity.

This appeared to be the dominant model for ecumenism since the New Delhi assembly of the WCC in 1961, against the organic model of church unity. Thus the Mar Thoma Church safeguarded its distinctive Mar Thoma tradition and openness to fresh ideas, which unlocked the door for the Mar Thoma Church's way towards the "Church of Christ in India".

An appeal for unification

Manifesting the Mar Thoma Church's awareness of its autonomous church identity and openness in its Indian church unity efforts, its episcopal synod, which met on 21 December, 1952, comprising Metropolitan Juhanon Mar Thoma and Mathews Mar Athanasius, proposed a unity scheme of Indian churches. The synod's circular letter says:

> While we greatly value our autonomy and traditional forms of worship, we feel that the time has come for us to make a move towards the realisation of a Church of Christ in India. Autonomy, Biblical Faith, Eastern forms of worship, and evangelistic vision are our cherished ideals. We feel that our church must be willing to declare its readiness to become part of the Church of Christ in India.[761]

---

760   *Ibid.*
761   Juhanon Mar Thoma, Mathews Mar Athanasius, "A Call to the Churches of Christ in India", *Joint Statement of Juhanon Mar Thoma and Mathews Mar Athanasius to Indian Churches,* December 21, 1952, Tiruvalla.

This official statement of the episcopal synod, affirm the church's uncompromising attitude to preserve its autonomous Indian heritage and identity, its inherent openness to the fresh church unity efforts and its longing for the establishment of a united "Church of Christ in India". In that unity process, the Mar Thoma Church wanted its autonomous Indian church heritage to be respected and safeguarded, both in its doctrine and teachings. If a proposal for a united Church in India were to be seriously taken up for consideration, the Mar Thoma Church would be prepared to consider the ending of its separate existence for the establishment of a Church of Christ in India.[762]

The synod has made it clear that the unity would be a reality only when, "the church should have as its authority for its fundamental doctrines from the clear teachings of Bible",[763] the acceptance of historic episcopacy, the Nicene Creed and of church as the Body of Christ, and have the eastern forms of worship.[764] In such a union, the church was ready to cease its independent existence.

---

762 *Ibid.*
763 *Ibid.*
764 *Ibid.*

Chapter XIV
Quest for The 'Kingdom'

The next important stage in the ecumenical praxis of the Mar Thoma Church, simultaneously with its "conciliar" model of ecumenical engagements with the CSI and CNI, was its response to the "Kingdom of God" mission paradigm that emerged in the ecumenical movement. Ecumenical programmes also emerged after the post-World War II period, for the social, political and economic reconstruction of the world.[765] The Mar Thoma Church responded to it by adopting a "Kingdom-of-God-centred mission thought"[766] in its mission praxis during the second half of the twentieth century.

The new paradigm significantly shaped the church's self-understanding of mission and this enabled the church to confirm "that the goal of mission is to be that of witnessing the Kingdom of God, rather than implementing the agenda of the church".[767] The socio-economic context of post-Independent India appeared to the Mar Thoma Church as a fertile soil to plant its "Kingdom-of-God-centred" mission programmes by way of social services initially and later through establishing a Development Department. This was "to strive for a community of communities, where injustice and poverty no longer exists".[768] Here's an insight into the response of the Mar Thoma Church to the "kingdom-centred" ecumenical programmes – "responsible society", "just, participatory and sustainable society" and "justice, peace and the integrity of creation".

---

765   The churches' engagement in social, economic and political life of the nation has been an obvious emphasis of the WCC during the post World War II period. This led the WCC to develop three key ecumenical social action programmes namely; "Responsible Society", "Just, Participatory and Sustainable Society" and "Justice, Peace and the Integrity of Creation" to address the socio- economic and ethical concerns of nations, and developing the concept of "sustainable development".
        See, Ans van der Bent, *Commitment to God's World – A Concise Critical Survey of Ecumenical Social Thought,* (Geneva: WCC Publication, 1995), 57–77.
766   Alex Thomas, *A Historical Study of the North Kanara Mission of the Mar Thoma Church 1910–2000, op.cit.,* 142.
767   *Ibid.,* 140.
768   "Metropolitan's Letter", In: *Malankara Sabha Tharaka,* 56/4 (April, 1949), 91–92.

Implementation of such programmes in India would potentially be of considerable pedagogical and practical benefits to support my view of the Mar Thoma Church being open to fresh ideas and concepts, while being sensitive to the needs of the Indian situation at the same time. This was the natural authentic ecumenical response of an indigenous church, which respects Indian secularism and pluralism.

This chapter examines different stages of the Mar Thoma Church's "kingdom-centred" ecumenical social engagement in the Indian society. How did these actions help the church to further its wider ecumenical witness in the pluralistic Indian society? How far did the church's mission praxes help it to continue as an indigenous Indian church?[769] While we analyse these actions, what emerges is a clear picture of a church that forms an integral part of the country's national history.

It was during the period, 1948–2010, that the church's involvement in the world ecumenical movement's "kingdom-centred" initiatives gained more prominence than ever before.

---

769 The self-understanding of the Mar Thoma Church is based on its independent, autonomous and indigenous existence in India. Similarly, all St. Thomas Christian denominations in India affirm their indigenous existence. This self understanding of the Mar Thoma Christians stands in a dialogical relationship with other religious communities and Christian denominations, across the world. However, the advocates of "Hindutva movement" in India, although accept the Mar Thoma Christians' historical existence since the first century, they have not included them into the category of the indigenized religions. To them, those religions except Hinduism, Buddhism and Jainism all other religions were of foreign religions. Despite of this, most of the secular historians accept that the Mar Thoma Christians are indigenized Christians. For instance, the first Prime Minister of India – Jawaharlal Nehru – says: "You may be surprised to learn that Christianity came to India long before it went to England or Western Europe and when even in Rome it was a despised and proscribed sect. Within hundred years or so of the death of Jesus, Christian missionaries came to South India by sea. They were received courteously and permitted to preach their new faith. They converted a large number of people, and their descendants have lived here, with varying fortune, to this day."
See, Jawaharlal Nehru, *Glimpses of the World History*, Reprinted, (New Delhi: Oxford University Press, 1982), 87; A. Sreedhara Menon, *A Survey of Kerala History*, *op.cit.*, 80; Sathyanathan Clarke, "The Promise of Religious Conversion: Exploring Approaches, Exposing Myths, Expounding Modalities", In: Christine Lienemann-Perrin, Wolfgang Lienemann, ed., *Crossing Religious Borders Studies on Conversion and Religious Belonging* (Wiesbaden: Herrassowitz, 2012), 590–609.

Church and nation-building

The social context in post-independent India and the church's active response to the WCC's ecumenical programmes provided the impetus for the Mar Thoma Church's shift of mission perspective during the aforementioned period. What followed was its proactive stand in the struggle for a responsible government in Travancore, as seen earlier in this study and a shift of its mission paradigm from being "church-centred" to being "kingdom-centred".[770]

India became independent from the British in 1947 and became a fully independent and secular country on 26 November, 1950. India's economy relied heavily on agriculture before independence and remained much the same after as well. During the British period (1600–1947), most of the country's working class lived in the countryside. Under the "caste system", they were kept away from the "upper class" people under strict demarcation rules. Poverty, lack of proper health care means, lack of educational institutions, and lack of homes were widespread in the nation.

The new strategy of socio-economic change in post-Independent India, initiated by then Prime Minister Jawaharlal Nehru, provided a space for the church to participate in nation-building. The post-Independent India's socio-economic and political structures opted "for a strategy of economic development and social change, in which the state was designed to play a central role".[771] Accordingly, an Indian Constitution that envisaged an egalitarian society within a capitalist framework was adopted and a modern secular and democratic state was inaugurated.[772] Of great significance was the guarantee of religious freedom by way of a statutory provision enunciated in Article 17 of the Indian Constitution.[773] Thus, a context for a change from the collective organisation of the Indian socio-economic structure, embedded in the "caste system", to a new socio-economic order based on individual freedom and equality emerged in India.

---

770   The Mar Thoma Church's stance for the freedom of and the making of a responsible government got fruition initially on 1947, when the Travancore Kingdom decided to merge into the Indian union. Later it formed a separate state of Kerala on November 1, 1956 in the Federal Republic of India.

771   Gabriele Dietrich, Bas Wielenga, *Towards Understanding Indian Society* (Madurai: Centre for Social Analysis Tamil Nadu Theological Seminary, 1997), 141.

772   Ghanshyam Shah, "Caste, Class and the State", Seminar 367, March 1990, In: *Ibid.*, 142.

773   Article 17 of the Indian Constitution protects individual freedom; abolishes untouchability and guarantees right to equality.

Nation-building based on the country's new Constitution brought challenges to the churches, specifically to the Mar Thoma Church, with regard to its socio-political and economic witness, as the church has its bearings on India's socio, economic and cultural moorings. In this new post-independence Indian context, the ecumenical movement's "Kingdom of God-centred" mission paradigm provided a new direction to the church's mission in India. The church adopted and consolidated a mission centred on this paradigm of the ecumenical movement as the best way forward in post-independent India.

A concept takes root

The concept of the Kingdom of God is found in four Gospels and in the Pauline epistles.[774] On the basis of this, several understandings of the "Kingdom of God" can be seen in the history of Christianity. Some of such understandings are: Kingdom of God as the reign of God, Kingdom as the eschatological reign of God, and Kingdom that is identical with the *sacrum imperium*. The concept also refers to an "ideal community over which God rules and which submits to God's authority, loves the neighbour and exemplifies God's justice in a family-like egalitarian community".[775] In the Eastern Orthodox tradition, the kingdom of God and the eschatological fulfillment of creation have been associated with wilderness. Wilderness is a place of repentance, illumination and *theosis*.[776] Eastern Orthodox teaching considers *theosis* as very much the purpose of human life and is considered achievable only through a synergy (or cooperation) between human activity and God's uncreated energies (or operations).

The concept of the Kingdom of God has received a central position in India's "Dalit" theology also. The Dalit theology gives emphasis to the proclamation and witness to the reign of God by the church. In this process, the socio, political, economic and cultural dimensions of human existence need to be addressed seriously. In Dalit theology, the preferential option of the poor and declaring solidarity with the struggles of the people are part of witnessing the kingdom of God.

---

774 St. Mathew 3: 2; 4: 17; St. Mark 1: 15; Luke 13: 22–30; Romans 9: 31.
775 Eugene Teselle, "Kingdom of God, the Concept of, in the Western World", In: Daniel Patte, ed., *The Cambridge Dictionary of Christianity*, (New York: Cambridge University Press, 2010), 692.
776 Eugene Teselle, "Kingdom of God in the Eastern Orthodox Tradition: Kingodm and Wilderness", In: *Ibid.*, 492–493.

After the 1910 first World Missionary Conference held in Edinburgh, the concept of the Kingdom started getting understood in a radically different ethical and social context in the ecumenical movement.[777] It was during the period between the Stockholm Conference of the Life and Work Movement in 1925 and the Oxford Conference in 1938 that the socio-political and ethical concerns of Europe received much attention in discussions of the ecumenical movement.[778] The reality of increasing economic and political disorder during this period, and the rise of fascism and other totalitarian systems, forced the ecumenical movement to analyse the socio-political and ethical concerns of the world in the light of the "Kingdom of God" concept.

In this analysis, they reached a consensus that "every tendency to identify the Kingdom of God with a particular social structure or economic mechanism must result in moral confusion for those who maintain the system and in disillusionment for those who suffer from its limitations".[779] This made possible a critical evaluation of existing social and political order, including the Church. The socio-political and ethical analysis of the world in the context of fascism, communism and capitalism, enabled the WCC to formulate its programme called the "Responsible Society" during the post World War II context. We have already mentioned this at length earlier.[780]

The post World War II context gave rise to a favourable atmosphere globally to rethink the concept of Kingdom of God in relation to human struggles and mission. A rethinking of the Kingdom of God-world relation became necessary for addressing the socio-political and ethical concerns of the world. These analyses highlighted the unity of mankind as essential for addressing human struggles. The Willingen Conference's affirmation of mission as *Missio Dei*,[781] and the

---

777 See, D.J. Smith, "Kingdom of God" In: *Dictionary of the Ecumenical Movement, op.cit.*, 644–646; Juhanon Mar Thoma, *Christianity in India and a Brief History of the Mar Thoma Church, op.cit.*, 34–35.

778 Christine Lienemann-Perrin, "Leitvorstellungen im Ökumenischen Rat der Kirchen zur politischen Verantwortung der Kirche", In: *Die politische Verantwortung der Kirche in Südkorea und Südafrika, op.cit.*, 465–466.

779 J.H. Oldham, ed., "Report of the Conference on Church Community and State at Oxford 1937", In: *Foundations of Ecumenical Social Thought*, (Philadelphia: Fortress Press, 1966), 35.

780 See, Chapter III, 7.2. Freedom Struggle Phase: The Mar Thoma Church's Participation in the Agitations for Responsible Government in Travancore (1938–1947), 103–108.

781 The major question that the Whitby conference of the IMC in 1947 confronted was whether mission of the church means the transplanting of western church to the

subsequent understanding of the concept "Kingdom of God" as a redeemed socio-economic and political order that caters to individual and corporate freedom in the society led the WCC to formulate its programmes accordingly during the second half of the twentieth century.

The IMC understood mission as *Missio Dei, or* mission of God, as inaugurated by Jesus Christ through His incarnation, redemption and reconciliation. On the basis of this understanding, the notion of "kingdom of God" in the ecumenical movement has got a new mandate to look into the contemporary state of affairs in nations, particularly in the Third World countries, where churches are in alliance with various socio-economic and cultural exploitative structures. To dismantle those exploitative structures, churches have been called to witness the Kingdom, which envisions "an ideal society, which is characterised by equality, justice, and freedom of its members".[782]

The emerging socio-economic and human rights concerns of post-independent Asian and African countries in the global scenario since the 1960s forced the world ecumenical movement to widen the Christian concern of human rights from individual freedom to social, economical and cultural rights.[783] This was particularly evidenced in the Uppsala Assembly (1968) and Nairobi Assembly (1975) of the World Council of Churches (WCC), which saw a shift from a "western-civil-liberal view of human rights and social rights of the human community to a

---

missions fields in Asia and Africa. For J.C. Hoekendijk the church was only an instrument of God's redemptive action in the world. Therefore, "a church-centric missionary thinking is bound to go astray because it revolves around an illegitimate centre". Therefore, the gospel of the Kingdom will be proclaimed throughout the *oikumene* and he called for an attempt to rethink the ecclesiology within the framework of the Kingdom-Gospel-Apostolate-world.

See, J.C. Hoekendijk, "The Church in Missionary Thinking", In: *International Review of Mission*, XLI, (1952), 332. This concept dominated at the Willingen conference and accepted it as the new mission paradigm of the IMC. This has already dealt with details in Chapter V, 3.2.2.2. M.M. Thomas' Role in the WCC and in the Mar Thoma Church, 141–147.

782 See, D.J. Smith, "Kingdom of God", In: Nicholas Lossky ed., *Dictionary of the Ecumenical Movement, op.cit.*, 644–646.

783 The inclusion of the "Charter of Religious Liberty" in the Universal Declaration on Human Rights in 1948 ensured the right of the freedom to "change" and to "manifest" one's religion or belief in "teaching, practice, worship and observe" to the individuals. This was based on the concept of individual liberty, which was grounded in the western liberal view on human rights. See, *Article 18, United Nations Universal Declaration on Human Right (1948)*.

perception of the life interests of the third world".[784] The role of ecumenical leaders of that time, particularly M.M. Thomas, was substantial in developing the ecumenical socio-ethical thought during this period. The socio-economic and political emancipation dimension and the subsequent setting up of a new socio-economic order of the "Kingdom of God" provided a solid base to the global ecumenical movement to address the socio-ethical concerns, including the human rights concerns of the Third World, during this period. It eventually provided prominence to the Kingdom of God emphasis in the discussions of the WCC, in general, and its Commission on World Mission and Evangelism (CWME) and the sub-unit, "Church and Society", in particular.

Clearer focus on Kingdom concerns

From WCC's New Delhi Assembly (1961) through the Uppsala and *Nairobi* assemblies, this emphasis received a clarity that the church should work for the establishment of the "Kingdom-of-God" in the world. The CWME meetings from Mexico City in 1963, through Bangkok in 1972, discussed the mission paradigm elaborately, resulting in an emphasis on the concept of Christology in the Bangkok meeting. "It not only confessed Jesus and His Kingdom, but the Kingdom of Christ that begins on earth as the kingdom of the crucified, which places Christ's disciples with Him under the cross".[785] This was indeed a new awareness of the kingdom and the cross. This awareness gave emphasis on the salvation of the whole people and the whole created world.

The power of resurrection as the outcome of one's experience in the sufferings of Christ was also taken seriously during this meeting. It calls for a non-imperialistic evangelism, where the poor are considered as the central focus of the missionary paradigm. It invites the participation of churches in the struggles of the world to bring justice and to enable the marginalised to participate in the developmental processes with an aim to achieve sustainability.

---

784 See, Kim Sebastian, "Religious Conversion and Law in India: Controversy over the Freedom of Religious Act", In: Christine Lienemann- Perrin, Wolfgang Lienemann, ed., *Crossing Religious Borders Studies on Conversion and Religious Belonging, op.cit.*, 711; Jurgen Moltmann, "Christian Faith and Human Rights", In: Alan D. Falconer, ed., *Understanding Human Rights: An Interdisciplinary and Inter Faith Study* (Dublin: Irish School of Ecumenics, 1980) 182–195.

785 *Bangkok Assembly 1973, Minutes and Report of the assembly of Commissions on World Mission and Evangelism,* (Geneva: WCC Publication, 1973), 64.

This missionary outlook has enabled the WCC to focus on human struggles, justice and peace concerns more concretely in the 1980s. It was thus during this period from 1961 to 1983, that the CWME clearly moved its emphasis from Church to the Kingdom of God, and in which the church is considered as a channel to implement God's kingdom-centred mission in the world.[786]

When the "Kingdom of God" and the *Missio Dei* concepts became the centre of the ecumenical movement's emphasis, the concerns of the world, including development and the eradication of poverty received a special attention in the mission agenda.[787] These advances in the ecumenical movement led to the development of the ecumenical programme of "Just, Participatory and Sustainable Society".

The WCC's programme – "Just, Participatory and Sustainable Society" – emerged during the 1970s. This programme was WCC's response to the world in the context of the oil crises and the subsequent awareness of the concerns about national growth, which was dependant on transnational factors during the close of the 1960s.[788] These

---

786 The emphasis of the church centricism got prominence in the global ecumenical movement discussions since the IMC Conference at Tambaram in Madras in 1938. This has dealt with length in the previous chapters of this study.

787 The references on the need to work for the eradication of poverty were not a major concern of the ecumenical discussions until the WCC's General Assembly in Uppsala in 1968. The "Church and Society's" Geneva Conference in 1966 was also bypassed the need to give prime importance to the eradication of poverty in the world. However, this meeting considered the development of the Third World is essential for a new social order in the world. To implement the mandate of the Uppsala Assembly and to assist churches' participation in the development process, the WCC called a world consultation at Montreux in 1970 and in this meeting the "Commission on the Churches Participation in Development" (CCPD), was formed. Its Lima meeting in 1971 discussed elaborately the subject – "Through the Cry of the Poor". The WCC's General Assembly defined the programme for the CCPD and in the light of it, the CCPD decided to add the search for a "Just Participatory and Sustainable Society" (JPSS) to its programme. The CWME Conference in Melbourne, in 1980, focused the subject – poor – and in Section I, the subject studied under the title: "Good News to the Poor". The General Assembly of the WCC in Vancouver in 1983 has taken a step further and in its study on "Witnessing in a Divided World" took concerns of the poor seriously. This subject got further importance, when the theme "development" received a major place in the agenda of the WCC discussions.

788 Ans van der Bent, *Commitment to God's World, op.cit.*, 63–67. There was an increasing use of petroleum in the developed countries since 1960's. However, there was no production and supply regulating single agency from the Arab oil producing countries to monitor the production and supply of crude oil before 1960. It was in 1960, that the oil producing nations of the Arab world joined together and formed an organization:

developments necessitated a context to think of the need for a new programme that aims at justice through the participation of all people including the marginalised to provide sustainability for human development. This led the "Church and Society" unit of the WCC to turn with urgency to develop an ecumenical programme by addressing concerns of individual security, redistribution of material wealth and of the impact of the policy of implementing maximum consumption of resources on transnational security.[789] This resulted in the framing of the "Just, Participatory and Sustainable Society" programme that highlighted the concerted participation of Christians in the sufferings of the people. This programme was considered in the agenda of the WCC's Nairobi Assembly in 1975 and it eventually resulted in its adoption into an ecumenical programme of the 1980s.[790]

Since the 1983 Vancouver General Assembly, the WCC included deliberations on ecological concerns within its programme of "justice, peace and the integrity of creation". Ecological concerns arose out of the emerging scientific evidence on the alarming increase of greenhouse gases in the atmosphere and its consequent effect on the depletion of the ozone layer as well as the increasing danger of global warming. On the basis of these environmental concerns, the WCC's General Assembly in Canberra in 1991 gave prime importance to ecological concerns for the integrity of creation. The core concepts of these programmes were "Kingdom of God" and "God's World".[791]

'Organization of Arab Petroleum Exporting Countries', (OAPEC) "to coordinate and unify the petroleum policies of its member countries and to ensure the stabilization of oil markets in order to secure and efficient economic and regular supply of petroleum to consumers, a steady income to producers and a fair return on capital for those investing in the Petroleum industry". See, *http: //www.opec.org* visited on 22nd February 2013. Thus OPEC member countries got control of their petroleum industries and a dominant voice in the pricing of the crude oil in the world market. This organization imposed an oil embargo in 1973, on the pretext of the joint war of Syria, Jordan and Egypt with Israel in 1970. By this the OPEC imposed an embargo on selling petrol to those counties that supports Israel in the war. It badly affected US as its oil usage was rising even as domestic oil production was declining, leading to an increasing dependence on the oil importing countries. The oil embargo of the OPEC led to a fuel shortage and a sky high price hike of it throughout the decade. This made the world leaders conscious of the new world scenario that even the growth of independent nations is dependent on transnational factors. See, *www.opec.org* visited on 22nd February 2013.

789 *Ibid.*

790 Christine Lienemann-Perrin, "Leitvorstellungen im Ökumenischen Rat der Kirchen zur politischen Verantwortung der Kirche, In: *Die politische Verantwortung der Kirche in Südkorea und Südafrika, op.cit.*, 465–466.

791 *Ibid.*

These distinct shifts in mission paradigms reached the Mar Thoma Church through its leaders like Juhanon Mar Thoma (1893–1976), Alexander Mar Thoma (1913–2000) and M.M. Thomas (1916–1996),[792] who were also leaders of the global ecumenical movement in those earlier days, and later through Zacharias Mar Theophilus,[793] Joseph Mar Thoma Metropolitan,[794] Issac Mar Philoxinos[795] and Mathews George Chunakara[796].

Juhanon Mar Thoma, in his book titled, *"Christianity in India and a Brief History of the Mar Thoma Church"* "envisioned the creation of a new social order that enhances social and economic justice".[797] According to him,

> "In recent years in resurgent India, with powerful challenges like nationalism and communism, syncretism and materialism, with swift and sweeping political, economic, social and ideological changes, the task of the church has to be redefined and the techniques of Christian evangelism reoriented … There was a bold attempt by the Mar Thoma Church to lead, to create a new social dynamism for a new social order by fusing Christian values with the principles of social democracy, even at the risk of her young men being censored for dabbling in revolutionary politics or participating in subversive activities. But the task of the complete reorientation of the church – to smash the false alternatives and to create a new climate in which her concern for social and economic justice is effectively related to the Christian commitment – remains unfulfilled."[798]

---

792 M.M. Thomas was a leading ecumenist, who played a key role in shaping the WCC's ecumenical social thought during early decades of the WCC. He was the key person behind the organization and the conduct of the World Conference of the "Church and Society" at Geneva in 1966.

793 Zacharias Mar Theophulus, the Suffragan Metropolitan of the Mar Thoma Church was a member of the Central Committee and the executive committee of the WCC since 1991, a member of the executive committee member of the WCC for two consecutive terms –1991–1998, 1998–2006.

794 Joseph Mar Thoma is the current Metropolitan of the church. He served as the President of the National Council of Churches in India and the President of the Christian Conference Asia (2000–2005).

795 Issac Mar Philoxinos is a current executive committee member of the WCC since 2006.

796 Mathews George Chunakara is a member of the Mar Thoma Church. He served the Christian Conference of Asia in Hong Kong as an Executive Secretary for International Affairs (1993–2000), Asia Secretary of the World Council of Churches in Switzerland (2000–2009), and now serves as the director of the International affairs (CCIA) of WCC.

797 Alex Thomas, *A Historical Study of the North Kanara Mission of the Mar Thoma Church 1910–2000, op.cit.*, 149; See, "Metropolitan's Letter", In: *Malankara Sabha Tharaka*, 56/4 (April, 1949), 91–92.

798 Juhanon Mar Thoma, *Christianity in India and a Brief History of the Mar Thoma Church, op.cit.*, 35.

Christ, the reference point

This statement of the then Metropolitan of the Mar Thoma Church set the tone for the church in its efforts to partake in the creation of a new social order that respected justice and peace in the new independent Indian nation. The church sought to redefine its mission paradigm in such a way that Christian values were fused with the principles of social democracy. The significance of the new stance of the Metropolitan was that he was able to find in the "Kingdom-of-God-centred" ecumenical mission model a new hope for the total redemption of the Indian society.

To this end, he called upon the Indian churches to take up a concerted "work of preaching, teaching and healing and thus work for the coming of the Kingdom of God".[799] His motto was "the church must be interested where human life is interested."[800] This idea is well-reflected in the logo for the church that he framed with its motto, "Lighted to Lighten". His revolutionary step in this direction made the people of India to consider him as "the greatest revolutionary in this century".[801]

In the same way, M.M. Thomas, drawn by an outline of the critical theological tradition of liberation theology, hoped for India's social change towards a just and sustainable society through rational social engagement, in which the Kingdom-centred values – justice, peace and love – have special roles to play for the transformation of the Indian society.[802] He made it emphatic that both the Church and the world have the same centre in Jesus Christ.[803] His articulation thus stated clearly the purpose of the Church's existence in the world and the fact that its field of activity is the world.[804] Thomas says:

---

799 Juhanon Mar Thoma, Mathews Mar Athanasius, "A Call to the Churches of Christ in India," *Joint Statement of Juhanon Mar Thoma and Mathews Mar Athanasius to Indian Churches*, December 21, 1952, Tiruvalla, in *Ibid.*, 45.

800 *Dr. Juhanon Mar Thoma Jeevitavum Sandeshavum* (Malayalam), (Tiruvalla: Mar Thoma Church Publication, 1977), 285.

801 *Janayugam* a secular publication in Kerala published an article on Juhanon Mar Thoma on September 26, 1976, and in which described Juhanon Mar Thoma as "the greatest Christian revolutionary in this century". See, Janayugam, (September/1976).

802 M.M. Thomas, "Common Life in the Religiously Pluralistic India," In: *The Churches Mission and Post Modern Humanism,* edited by M.M. Thomas, (New Delhi: CSS & ISPCK, 1996), 3–4.

803 W A Visser't Hooft, ed., *The New Delhi Report, the Third Assembly of the World Council of Churches 1961* (New York: Association Press, 1962), 27.

804 M.M. Thomas, *My Ecumenical Journey* (Trivandrum: Ecumenical Publishing Centre, 1990), 126.

Christology is central to Christian theology. Every symbol, every sacrament, every doctrine in Christianity points to the simple assertion that Jesus is Christ. The Christian dialogue with the secular world and with men of other faiths is a dialogue about Christ. Christian apologetics are oriented to the assertion that God was in Christ reconciling the world to Himself.[805]

The basic point of Thomas is that Christ is the centre of all Christian rituals and therefore Jesus Christ is the most appropriate reference point for addressing all human concerns within and outside the church.[806] Thus the world and its historical realities should get prominence in the witness of the Church. This idea was communicated through the writings of Thomas that were accepted by the Mar Thoma Church leadership.[807]

---

805 M.M. Thomas, "Christological Task in India", In: *Religion and society*, (Sept/1964), 1.

806 M.M. Thomas' theology starts with man and his struggles in history and culminates in Christology. Following the stand of the 'Vatican II', and the 'World Conference on Church and Society' in 1966, M.M. Thomas also identified three revolutions in the world – scientific and technological, the revolt of the oppressed nations and classes demanding justice and the break up of the traditional integration of the church and state in the world. In these revolutions he finds the work of Christ and therefore these revolutions are a partial fulfilment of the "kingdom of God". In the light of this understanding he interpreted the "image of God" in man. It is the obligation of the man's active involvement in history "to respond to the call in freedom" to strive for a structure of ultimate meaning and sacredness. To achieve these, he advocated for the transformation of the whole social and religious systems to Christ. To him, "I think the ultimate framework of reference for Christian thought is neither God nor man in abstract, neither the metaphysics of God nor the science of man taken in isolation; but Jesus Christ, who is God-man, or rather God for man or to use Karl Barth's expression, the humanity of God". See, M.M. Thomas, *Salvation and Humanization,* (Bangalore: C.I.S.R.S, 1970), 7. Since Christ is the divine initiative to reveal himself to the World, Christ is the centre to revitalize all things within and outside of the church in the world. Jesus provided himself to the world an image of a new man on the cross, where he showed his way of life to the world. Therefore the cross is the symbol and example for every man to be imitated and it is the prototype of self giving love to be imitated by man, to generate a new humanity. For him, Christ is the Ultimate truth. Thomas' emphasis in the centrality of Christology did affirm in general affirmation of the WCC and for instance the General Assembly of Uppsala interpreted Jesus as the "New Man" by refuting the arguments of Peter Bayerhaus. Peter Bayerhaus argued that the shift from God to man would eventfully led to the replacement of theology by anthropology. See, Peter Bayerhaus, *Missions: Which Way?,* (Grand Rapids: Zondervan, 1974), 88; M.M. Thomas, *Salvation and Humanization, op.cit.,* 27; Religion and Society, (June, 1967).

807 M.M. Thomas, *My Ecumenical Journey, op.cit.,* 126. *Ibid.*

A fertile field for mission

The socio-political context of post-Independent India presented a favourable atmosphere for the Mar Thoma Church to adopt the "Kingdom of God" centred mission paradigm. The major elements in this context were the Indian Constitution's adoption of secularism[808] as a political concept in 1950, an Indian perception that Christians in the country were less patriotic[809] and a call to citizens by the first Indian Prime Minister, Jawaharlal Nehru, to partake in nation building.

The Indian Constitution's affirmation of secularism as a political concept sought to foster national integration by defeating divisive forces such as communalism and "casteism" and its by-products, regionalism and linguistic polarisation.[810]

---

808 During the third phase of the Indian National Congress (1919–1947) and during the post- independent India, the secularism emerged as a political ideology, over against the emergence of nationalism based on the interests of one or other religious communities. Therefore it stands against communalism. It has its ideological debt to "the European enlightenment, liberal democratic and Marxian social ideologies". See, M.M. Thomas, "Religious Fundamentalism and Indian Secularism – the Present Crisis" In: M.M. Thomas, *The Church's Mission and Post Modern Humanism, op.cit.*, 11.) Thus the secularism in India meant for the equal respect for all religions and cultures and the non- interference of religions or cultures in the government. India is secular as it allows its citizens both in individual and corporate level to follow any religion of their birth or adoption, but the state have no special religious affiliation. Indian secularism is safeguarded through Article 14, 15(2) and 16(2) of the Indian constitution, which provides equality all citizens before law. See, *The Constitution of the Republic of India;* M.M. Thomas, "Religious Fundamentalism and Indian Secularism – the Present Crisis", In: M.M. Thomas, *The Church's Mission and Post Modern Humanism, op.cit.*, 11–20.

809 George Thomas, *Christian Indians and Indian Nationalism, op.cit.*, 18.

810 Indian Nationalism took several forms in its history since its development during the nineteenth century. The Indian National Congress, a national political organization founded in 1885 was able to develop an idea of nationalism and a common religious identity of Hindus in India. Indian nationalism was in a sense a reassertion of Hinduism and its values. During the Indian Freedom Movement period (1857–1947), the Indian nationalism had gone to, at least three changes. First, it was during the first phase (1885–1906) of the Indian National Congress, it consolidated the liberal nationalistic forces to have had a concerted fight against the British colonialists. Secondly, during the second phase of its work (1906–1919), the nationalism gave way to militant nationalism; on the pretext of the formation of the "Muslim League" by the blessings of the British power to safeguard the interest of the Muslim minority in India in 1907. This eventually led to the two nation theory of Muhamad Ali Jinna and consequently to the division of India into India and Pakistan in 1947 at the time of

Generally in India, cultural and ideological trends affirm that different religious expressions are equally valid for some universal religious reality of God.[811] Indian culture both in ideological and cultural terms, is secular and pluralistic because it stands in continuity with the Indian constitution going back through the medieval mystic approach to the Reality of God as expressed by the *Rig Veda*: *Ekam sat vipra bahutavadanthi* (That which exists (God) is one, although sages call it by different names.) The idea of the equality of all religions and ideologies is integral to both the Indian mystic approach to the Reality and secularism. Both the concept of secularism and the mystic approach to Reality denies any ultimate reality to *nama* (name) and *rupa* (form) of religions. Moreover, the Indian secular culture affirms the multiplicity of particular expressions of that, which is deemed to be the universal Reality of God. Thus in India's cultural and ideological secularism, the freedom of religions and ideologies is respected and protected. However, the root of post-independent Indian cultural and ideological secularism hinges around the basic political ideology that developed during India's freedom struggle, especially under the patronage of Mahatma Gandhi (1869–1948) and Jawaharlal Nehru (1889–1964), to counter communalism and to attain freedom from the British colonial hegemony. It continued to be India's political ideology even after India's independence as safeguarded in Articles 14, 15 (2) 16 (2), 19 (1) and Article 25 of

---

Indian independence. Thirdly during the third phase of the Indian National Congress or the Gandhian Era (1919–1947) witnessed the emergence of Hindu communal organizations in India like Rastreeya Swayam Sevak Sangh (RSS), Hindu Mahasabha, which subscribed for a militant act to protect India from religious (Muslim) communalism and political colonialism, and to achieve this end they developed the *Hindutva Movement* later. The *Hindutva Movement* is a movement within the fundamentalist Hindu group in India, "which seeks to subjugate and homogenize the ethnic pluralities by establishing the hegemony of an imagined cultural mainstream". See, D.L. Shethi and Ashis Nandy, eds., *The Multi verse of Democracy,* (New Delhi: Sage Publications, 1996) 23. This movement is still active in India through RSS, *Bajarang Dal, Shiva Sena, Vishva Hindu Parishat,* and *Bharatiya Janatha Party.* The *Hindutva movement* strive for a Hindu country in India.

811   It should be realised at the very outset that Indian ideas of secularism is somewhat varied from that of the west; in the Indian secularism religious ethos are respected and every religion has a constitutional rights to express itself according to its faith and traditions. Therefore religious freedom is enshrined and protected in the Indian constitution. The secularism now prevalent in the west is against religious instincts and thought forms and Christianity are slowly forced out of the public squire because of anti-religious secular attitudes.

the Indian Constitution.[812] Thus Indian secularism provided a framework within which the country's different religious and ethnic communities could coexist even with atheists and supporters of Marxist and liberal ideologies. The statutory provisions sought to counter the nascent Hindu nationalism that was of a communalistic nature. It created the "social space"[813] for dialogue between different religious and ideological streams within India's national context on the meaning and goals of independent India's nationhood.

---

812 One unique feature of the Indian culture has been its "unity in diversity", which has already dealt with this study. Indian society has been a coexisting society, in which different races, religions, ideologies and languages inter-relate with each other within their set boundaries. There is also an undercurrent of religious unity and inter- religious engagements, among diverse religious faiths in India by the influence of Hindu sages. They affirm: "Truth is one and sages speak of it differently." See, *Rig Veda* 1: 164.46. This means that different religions are equally valid expressions of the universal truth. Thus both facts of unity of religions and differences of religious experiences are equally affirmed by sages. Therefore it is an undeniable fact that the *sanadhana dharma*, which affirms multi-religious and multi-cultural context and enriches Indian life and its relationships, provides a fertile soil for ecumenism and Inter-religiosity. This is the basis of the Indian cultural secularism, which was practiced during the pre-colonial period (1500 BCE – 1600 CE.). It was during the colonial period, colonialists have given some privileges to their religions. It was during the colonial period, the new ideological secularism, emerged on the pretext of the Indian majority Hindu and minority Muslim communalism. See, M.M. Thomas, "Religious Fundamentalism and Indian Secularism – the Present Crisis", In: M.M. Thomas, *The Church's Mission and Post Modern Humanism, op.cit.*, 11. However, during the post Independent India, the Constitution of the Republic of India, Article 14 safeguards the Indian secularism and guarantees equality of all citizens before Law and the equal protection of Law. Article 15 prohibits discrimination of Indian citizens on grounds of religion, race, caste, sex or place of birth. Article 16 protects the equality of opportunities to all Indian citizens in Indian Republic. Article 19(1), grants freedom of speech and expression, and Article 25, safeguards total freedom of conscience and the right to profess, practice and propagate religion.

813 "Social space" is a category in the post-modern epistemology. The post-modern epistemology demands an epistemological shift from the traditional understanding of the social space, which was considered as given and natural. For this shift of understanding the European Enlightenment provided an epistemological shift by envisaging the logic of social change on the basis of critical or rational engagement and on the notion of modern self. However, in the post-modern epistemology, "social space" is used as culturally constructed entity not a given entity. The term "social space" used here in this study is the way of a post-modern category of "social space" – a culturally constructed social space.

Thus secularism emerged as an appropriate framework to build India's future on the basis of equality, liberty and justice. In such a social space, the crucial question that the church confronted was whether it would be able to interact and enter into a dialogue with secular groups and gain insights regarding the "Kingdom of God", which longs for a social order that promotes justice, peace and freedom, on one hand, and a consensus on consciousness, values and relationships, on the other.

That would facilitate building up of a secular Indian nation, which guaranteed freedom of religions and no discrimination on the ground of religion, race or gender. In a nutshell, the task of an Indian Christian ecumenist was to make the unity of mankind possible in India's multi-religious and cultural context.

Secondly, since the colonial period, the Indian society typically, and rather unfairly, branded Christians as unpatriotic.[814] The rationale for this branding was the association of protestant missionary movements with the colonial rulers during the 19th and the 20th Centuries and their antipathy towards nationalism.[815] So the post-independent Indian society showed an antagonism towards foreign rule and the "foreign" Christian religion.

In this context, the contributions of C.F. Andrews, Sarojini Naidu, Raja Kumaru Amruth Kaur and people of that calibre in those times should never be forgotten – Indian Christians have a responsibility to keep the stories of such amazing people in their collective memory. The Mar Thoma Church, although small in size, appears to the Indian society as an indigenous traditional church. Therefore, its stance towards nationalism and nation-building carries significance and weight.[816]

---

814 George Thomas in his study on "Christian Indians and Indian Nationalism" proves that the Indian Christians were patriotic and they stood for India's freedom. See, George Thomas, *Christian Indians and Indian Nationalism, op.cit.*, 190–195. For more details see, Chapter III, 4.1. Reforms and Church Missionary Society, 45–50.

815 *Ibid.*, 195–196.

816 Although, the followers of the *Hindutva movement* reluctant to call the Mar Thoma Christians as indigenous Christians on the basis of their ideology that all religions, which are of foreign origin, are alien to India, the Mar Thoma Church's self-understanding that it is a traditional indigenous church. This has already dealt with in detail in the previous section of this study. In the light of this self-understanding, the Mar Thoma Church has been characterized to organize its indigenous talents for mission in its history during the last quarter of the nineteenth century, which we have dealt with in the previous Chapter of this study. "If India's millions are to be reached and won for Christ; it will be by India's sons." See, D.F. Bright, *The NMS, op.cit.*, 94. These words of the Mar Thoma Metropolitan, Abraham Mar Thoma reflect his affirmation of the indigenous character of the church. See, Jawaharlal Nehru, *Glimpses of World*

Jawaharlal Nehru's call to Indian citizens to work hard for nation-building in the context of the bane of communalism that was aggravated by the violence and killings in the aftermath of the India-Pakistan division. This brought a new social and political challenge to the church's participation in nation-building by keeping its missionary mandate in the light of the "Kingdom of God" concept.[817]

The three challenges detailed above created a "social space", which provided substance to the Mar Thoma Church as it changed its mission mandate from being "church-centred" to "kingdom-centred", from church's mission to God's mission and these inspired the church's participation in the nation-building process. These moves also served to defend the church's independent, autonomous and indigenous nature against the *Hindutva* trend in the country. Therefore, witnessing the "Kingdom of God" in the post-independent Indian social space was a significant concern of the church.

M.M. Thomas' Christian-socialist ideas and Juhanon Mar Thoma's attitude towards providing land and home for the homeless shaped the Kingdom-centred movement in India. Thus ecumenical programmes helped the Mar Thoma Church, to a certain extent, to realise its place in the Indian society and in Indian history.[818]

History, op.cit., 36–37. The Mar Thoma Church's revolt against the Portuguese administration in the 17th century and the "Coonan Cross Oath" (Chapter I) are forerunners of Indian liberation movement and its relevance should never be forgotten.

817 The major social and political challenges of Indian nation after independence were the national integration, creating communal harmony between Hindus and Muslims, safeguarding equal constitutional rights to the whole citizens by dismantling the "caste system", achieving social justice, Land Reforms to dismantle the age old feudal land structure and so on.

Immediately after the India – Pakistan division in 1947 by the British, hundreds of thousands of Muslims were killed in India by Hindus and more Hindus were killed in Pakistan by Muslims. Hindus from Pakistan moved to India and the Muslims from India moved to Pakistan. In this context of communal violence, Hindu-Muslim harmony and reconciliation was the primary agenda of the Indian government since the India's independence. See, Asgharali Engineer, ed., *Communal Riots in the Post Independence India*, 2nd Edition (Bombay: Sangam Books, 1997) 21–37.

818 There was a tension, which appeared in the church when it considered that the emancipation of the underprivileged millions of Indians from their social, economic and political bondages was part of its mission simultaneously with the mission of propagating the message of the Gospel in India. For the evangelical mission minded members, who uphold the "saving the souls" idea, of the church considered the new method of mission as a departure from its mission strategy and the adoption of the principle of the liberation theology of the Latin American countries in the church. However, the leadership of the church was able to bring a balance between these two in formulating

Over the last century, the church utilised the ecumenical movement's emphasis on fundamental human rights for the socio-economic emancipation of the under-privileged, which is essential for the development of a socio-economic order in India. India's "second liberation struggle" was to slay the five giants of physical poverty, namely want (basic human needs of food and shelter), disease, ignorance, squalor, and idleness. Mar Thoma Church is also conscious of the fight against the sixth poverty – poverty of aspiration.

Christ, the ever-present reality

The "Kingdom-centred" mission concept provides a basis for the church to work for the new proposed societal order, by focusing on the human life situations in India. The idea that the Mar Thoma Church got from the ecumenical movement is the ever-present reality of Jesus Christ in all socio-political and economic situations. The church also understood that Christ is unceasingly reviewing and transforming these situations.

In 1962, the CSI Synod passed a resolution, all Christian institutions, congregations and individuals to take seriously their responsibilities to the society and "the need to witness to the Kingdom of God, to set forth and establish in society both the love and righteousness of God in Christ".[819] The resolution thus underscored the need for a concerted effort by the churches and people to transform the Indian nation to a just and equitable one.

The Mar Thoma Church proactively acted on this resolution and took decisions to implement those programmes in a way that was suitable to the Indian context. For instance, the Church Council passed a resolution in 1948 aimed at providing "homes for the homeless" in India,[820] and opened up the church to address the

---

the church's mission strategies by giving equal emphasis of communicating the message of the gospel and involving in the social, economic and political emancipation activities in its mission fields. Besides, the leadership of the Mar Thoma Church accepted all programmes of the world ecumenical movement whole heartedly. But, still some members have been following a conservative attitude to those programmes as is evidenced in the case of the Metropolitan's Encyclical on 1952, which we have been dealt at length in this study. See, George Alexander, "Malankara Mar Thoma Suvishesha Prasanga Sangham, Charithra Samgraham" (Malayalam), In: George Alexander, ed., *Maramon Convention Sadabhi Valyam* (Malayalam), *op.cit.*, 160–305.

819   See, Rajah D. Paul, *Ecumenism in Action, op.cit.*, 100.
820   *Resolution 6, Mar Thoma Sabha Council Meeting held in Tiruvalla*, February 9, 1948.

social problems more intensely than before in its history. It was during this time that K.K. Kuruvilla, the then Principal of the Mar Thoma Theological Seminary, professors and students spent their weekends in the villages of Alleppey in Kerala and educated them to fight against epidemics and introduced to them a new way of tapioca farming that was common in the high-ranges of Kerala. The idea was to make people self-sufficient in their domestic food production and thereby alleviate the widespread poverty in the coastal regions.

Challenge to change mindsets

The major problem that the church leadership faced during this time was to change the ethos of the church community in a way that was congenial to the social and political involvement of its members. As we have seen already, although a group of the members of the church were ready to treat the poor and downtrodden communities in a Christian way of brotherhood, another group considered them untouchable. The task before the church was to transform the mindset of its members to respect freedom and human rights with a view to prepare for the "kingdom-centred" mission task in India. In this process, the Mar Thoma Church was able to look at the history of the "lower castes" and "outcastes" seriously and made an effort to address the caste and caste oppressions, which are unique in India through its "kingdom-centred" mission strategy.

However, the "Dalit" theologians are of the opinion that the churches, which claim the St. Thomas tradition, have not taken the history of the "dalits" (oppressed) seriously.[821] It is true that those churches including the Mar Thoma Church have not taken the history of the "dalits" as a focal point in its missionary praxis, in the same way as the "dalit theologians" do.[822] The pivotal focus of dalit theologians in analyzing the cause of social oppression in India is on India's "caste system" and "caste" oppression. But for the church, the main emphasis is the emancipation and

---

821 Sathyanathan Clarke, "The Promise of Religious Conversion: Exploring Approaches, Exposing Myths, Expounding Modalities", In: Christine Lienemann- Perrin, Wolfgang Lienemann, ed., *Crossing Religious Borders Studies on Conversion and Religious Belonging* (Wiesbaden: Herrassowitz, 2012), 590–609; Y.T. Vinayaraj, *Revisiting the Other*, (Tiruvalla: CSS, 2010), 71.

822 The "Dalit" theologians give prime focus to India's caste system and caste oppression in analyzing the cause of oppression in Indian society. The "caste" is an important category of the dalit theology in analyzing the social oppression and its symbolic representations in the society.

upliftment of the weaker sections of society from their current predicament. The history of the Mar Thoma Church reveals the assistance provided by the church towards this goal by including dalits in its mission praxis. The following analysis illustrates the strategies of the Mar Thoma Church to address the needs of poor and needy including the dalits in the society.

Two major strategies were employed by the Mar Thoma Church in its "kingdom-centred" mission praxis. These were social service schemes and social empowerment schemes that were implemented through the church's "Development Department". The church extended assistance to the society with a view to help remove poverty and provide sustenance through its social service schemes. Programmes such as "Medical Mission", "Marriage Aid Fund", "Relief Fund" and "Land and Home for Homeless" were founded towards this end. The social empowerment schemes refer to the assistance provided to the marginalised section through the church's Development Department to empower all sections of the Indian society to strive for a "community of communities, where poverty and injustice no longer exists".[823] M.A. Thomas evaluates the changes in the church during the early decades in the church:

> A remarkable thing that has happened during the last four decades is the church's growing concern for the poor, destitute, disabled, and orphans. Several institutions and organisations have sprung up all over the church to care for such neglected and marginalised people. The Mar Thomites at home and abroad support them liberally.[824]

During the 1950s the church felt that social services are essential to improve the condition of India and for this purpose, it took initiatives to start new schools, university colleges, hospitals and institutions to provide social services in order to help people come out of their marginalised social positioning. The work of the Medical Mission is worth mentioning in this context.[825] The Mar Thoma Church's

---

823 See, "Metropolitan's Letter", In: *Malankara Sabha Tharaka*, 56/4 (April, 1949), 91–92.

824 M.A. Thomas, "Mar Thoma Church's Approach to Other Religions and Mar Thoma Church's Socio-Political Involvement", In: *Mar Thoma Sabha Saradhikal*, (Malayalam), *op.cit.*, 7.

825 The Mar Thoma Church started its mission through Medial assistance to the people of India by starting a small dispensary at *Cheriyazheekal* in Kerala in 1930. By 1952, the church's Medical Mission co-ordinated the work of the different hospitals. In 1972, the Mar Thoma Medical Mission was registered as an organisation under the government of Travancore – Cochin Literary Scientific and Charitable Society Act. The Mar Thoma Church has currently three major Hospitals directly under the Church and five hospitals under the MTEA in India, besides of several village clinics. See, P.M. Thomas, ed., *Mar Thoma Sabha Directory, op. cit.*, 295–302. Ninan Varghese, "Mar Thoma Medical Mission", In: *Malankara Sabha Tharaka*, (February/2003), 21–22.

Medical Mission, founded in 1952 is dedicated to providing Indians, especially the poor, better access to health care through its hospitals.[826] Several village clinics and hospitals were started during the 1950s and the 1960s under the Mar Thoma Medical Mission. Simultaneously a question was posed as to how these mission strategies could be implemented in post-Independent Indian society more effectively, while engaging in social service activities.

The Mar Thoma Church found an answer to that question in the quintessentially Indian concept of *Ashram*. The church found this the best way to implement the "Kingdom of God-centred" mission effectively in Indian villages.[827] Says Alex Thomas, in his study on the *Kristu Mithra Ashram*, Ankola:

"During the second phase (1940–2000) a paradigm shift occurred in the Mar Thoma Church, causing it to establish a kingdom community. The *Ashram* served as a means of establishing such a community, one in which there was inter-caste and inter-faith believers. This community was intended to be a foretaste of the heavenly kingdom on earth."[828]

The Mar Thoma Church's *Ashrams* proved to be centres, where different "caste" and faith communities could co-exist and work together in villages under the rules, even when its residential membership is limited only to the members of the Mar Thoma Church.[829]

Alex Thomas further elucidates the *Ashram* "mission strategy":

Ashrams' focused on the liberation of "low caste" people. They focussed medical care for those who have no access to modern medicines. It liberated people from alcoholic addiction. It provided training in self employment programmes. Poor children were assisted in their physical, educational and spiritual growth. This *Ashram* rehabilitated the destitute and reached people with the message of the love of Christ. In other words the *Ashram* witnessed the foretaste of the Kingdom.[830]

---

826   The Mar Thoma Church's members were encouraged by the church to work through the Christian Medical Association and other governmental and private hospitals to render medical services to the poor and needy in India. The work of A.K. Tharian, George Oommen, Jacob Cherian, Sosamma, Benjamin Pulimoodu, Raju. P. George, Mammen Chandi, Roy Joseph (Singapore) and several doctors and nurses spread out all over India and all across the world rendering services to the poor and needy in India and abroad.

827   Alex Thomas, *A Historical Study of the North Kanara Mission of the Mar Thoma Church* 1910–2000, *op.cit.*, 141.

828   *Ibid.*

829   *"Sihorayile Vela"* (Work in Sihora) (Malayalam) in *Malankara Sabha Tharaka*, (February/1953), 31–32.

830   Alex Thomas, *A Historical Study of the North Kanara Mission of the Mar Thoma Church* 1910–2000, *op.cit.*, 141.

This *Ashram* mission strategy of the *Kristu Mitra Ashram* at Ankola gives us a glimpse on the mission strategy of all *Ashrams* of the Mar Thoma Church.[831] Along with evangelization, *Ashrams* were determined to equip villagers to respond to the challenges of the times.[832] We have seen earlier how the church went about implementing its new mission strategy by establishing the *Kristu Sishya Aashram*, Hoskote in Bangalore in 1947,[833] *Kristiya Bandhukula Ashram* at Satna in Madhaya Pradesh in 1952, *Christu Shanti Sangham* in Nepal in 1952, *Shanti Mandiram* in Andhra Pradesh in 1955 and *Chrisu Prema Kulam* at Bhopal in 1955.[834] Let us now turn to the *Bhoobhavanadana Prastanam* or "Land and Home for the Homeless Scheme" of the Mar Thoma Church. This was a pioneering movement, which reflects the church's positive response to the social needs of the poorest of the poor sections of the country.

Homes for the homeless

The church launched the *Bhoobhavanadana Prastanam*, when Vinoba Bhave (1895–1982), a disciple of Mahatma Gandhi, had been walking across India and requesting land from rich land owners for distributing to the landless and homeless people. With this purpose, he started the *Bhoodan* (gift of land) Movement. More than six million acres of land had been distributed this way.[835] Being influenced by the teachings of Vinoba Bhave, the then Metropolitan, Juhanon Mar Thoma, and the church leadership found that it was necessary to address this concern seriously as part of its kingdom-centred mission agenda of the church for a new social order by providing land and home to the landless and homeless. To achieve this, the church mandated *Bhoobhavanadana Prastanam* in 1968.

Since the Mar Thoma Church adopted a Kingdom-centred mission strategy, after India's independence, it felt that the first social concern that needed to be addressed

---

831 "Sihorayile Vela" (Malayalam), In: *The Malankara Sabha Tharaka*, (February/1953), 31–32.

832 *Ibid.*

833 The writer was a Local Administrative Committee member of the Hoskote Mission Centre, Nursing School and the Hospital during 2000–2004.

834 P.M. Thomas, ed., *Mar Thoma Church Directory, op.cit.*, 341–345; T.P. Abraham, *Mar Thoma Syrian Church of Malabar – A Journey Down the Centuries, op.cit.*, 575–577.

835 Sunand Sumithra, *Revolution as Revelation, op.cit.*, 37; *www.vinibavhave.org,* visited on 28th February 2013.

was the poverty and homelessness of the Indian people.[836] Juhanon Mar Thoma Metropolitan considered owning a home, the freedom to work for earning a livelihood, providing opportunities to educate and help widen the talents of children, and creating health-care awareness and opportunities were the birth right of every citizen. It thus became the duty of the church to work with the government to help people attain these.[837] He urged the church through his circulars and letters in the *Malankara Sabha Tharaka* to share their resources to meet these needs of the poor. His efforts were wholeheartedly approved and supported by the then communist chief Minister of Kerala, Achutha Menon (1913–1991), in whom the Mar Thoma Church found a sincere friend.

The Mar Thoma Church's proactive involvement in addressing the needs of the people and its openness to select beneficiaries from eligible people belonging to any religious or racial association is positively related to its response to the new "Kingdom-of-God-centred" mission paradigm, its wish to remove the ills of the economic system and also the idealism prevalent during the period. The new idealism appeared "not only in the church but also in the state and society as a whole – an urge to emerge from the yoke of colonialism and feudalism"[838] into a responsible society with "dignity and self-rule"[839]. Philipose Mar Chrysostom, the current *Valia*[840] Metropolitan of the Mar Thoma Church, says the church has been striving to achieve these. He pointed out that "it is through evangelism the church discovered man; through the reading of the Bible, it discovered Christ, and through Christ the church discovered the human, whom God created."[841] Although the Mar Thoma Church's membership did not increase much by this kind of mission praxis in the society, it did help the church to permeate Christian understanding and insights to society in depth.[842]

Church responds to society's needs

I shall now move to the church's "Land and Home for Homeless Scheme" with a view to validate the hypothesis that the church has been open to the needs of the

---

836 "Metropolitan's letter", In: *Malankara Sabha Tharaka, 56/4*, (April/1949), 91–92.
837 *Ibid.*
838 Jesudas M. Athyal and John J. Thattamannil ed., *Metropolitan Chrysostom on Mission in the Market Place, op.cit.*, 76–77.
839 *Ibid.* The first beneficiary under the *bhoobhavanadanam* scheme was a Hindu family in Kerala.
840 *Valia* Metropolitan is the Title of the Metropolitan Emiritus.
841 *Ibid.*
842 *Ibid.*

society after India's independence by adopting new ideas and programmes from the ecumenical movement and the post-independent Indian social space. This scheme started in 1968 in conjunction with the 75th birthday celebration of the then Metropolitan, who refused to reside at his newly-constructed official residence in Tiruvalla in 1967, and decided to remain at the Metropolitan's old official residence (Old Poolatheen). The Metropolitan felt that when millions of Indians were homeless, it was not morally right for him to live in a huge building. During the official inauguration of the newly-built official residence of the Metropolitan, he expressed his desire to launch a scheme of "Land and Home for the Homeless" for which he donated an amount to the church.[843]

The Mar Thoma Church took on board the Metropolitan's desire seriously. The church council met on May 8, 1968, and passed a resolution to start a *Bhoobhavanadana Prasthanam*. On August 7, 1968,[844] it also decided to collect INR 75,000 to construct 75 homes for the homeless in India and give land for 75 families irrespective of their religious affiliation to construct homes. This was done in conjunction with the Metropolitan's birthday celebrations.[845] The *Sabha* council also resolved to constitute a fund for this scheme and decided to seek voluntary contributions from church members and to utilize 10 per cent of the total collection of *Kaimuthu*[846] for this scheme. The members of the church contributed to this scheme and by 1971, it received INR 13,0863,00 besides individual land contributions towards this scheme.[847]

The *Bhoobhavanadana* "(Land and Home to the Homeless)" scheme of the church was greeted with great enthusiasm by the members of the church in Kerala, and even by the Communist-Marxist ministry of Kerala led by

---

843 Homelessness is a major concern in India. The India's Census Report of 2001 shows that 17 percent of the world homeless are living in India. See, *Permanent Shelters for Urban Homeless Populations, Tenth Report of the Commissioners of the Supreme Court of India, 2011*, In: *www.righttofoodinIndia/org/homelessness* visited on 7th December 2012.

844 *Resolutions of the Mar Thoma Sabha Council, "Bhoobhavanadana Prasthanam"* held on May 8, 1968.

845 P.M. Thomas ed., "Bhoobhavana Prasthnam, Vivaha Sahaya Fund, Durithaswasa Sahayam", In: *Mar Thoma Sabha Directory, op cit.*, 356–358; T.P. Abraham, *Malankara Mar Thoma Suriyani Sabha Noottandukaliloode, op. cit.*, 531.

846 *Kaimuthu* is a special collection from the church every year to meet the needs of the Bishops of the Church. Metropolitan's letter, In: *Malankara Sabha Tharaka*, 56/4, (April/1949), 91–92.

847 *Annual Report of the Mar Thoma Syrian Church,* May 2 and 3, 1971. See, *Malankara Sabha Tharaka* (June/ 1971), 74–75.

C. Achutha Menon.[848] It was during his ministry that the Government of Kerala launched a *Laksham Veedu Padhadhi* (Hundred Thousand Homes for Homeless) in 1972. The *Sabha* council in 1983 decided to join with the "Kerala State Housing Board" to spearhead the construction of more homes for the homeless. The "Kerala State Housing Board" decided to implement it under its auspices and with the co-operation of the Mar Thoma Church's *Boobhavanadana Prasthanam*.[849] Under this scheme the church constructed 1,000 houses for the homeless in India, spending INR 113 million including INR 20 million that the church received as grant from the government of Kerala.[850] In 1999, it was estimated that since its inception, the church alone had constructed 3,053 homes for the homeless.[851]

In 2007, the church decided to construct 1,000 homes for the homeless in conjunction with the 90th birthday of the then Metropolitan, Philipose Mar Chrysostom, and entrusted Zacharias Mar Theophilus, the Suffragan Metropolitan of the Church to take leadership of this project. The accounts of the *Navathy* (90th birthday) projects shows that as on 31 July 2008, the church received INR 162,755,378.18 and constructed 2,100 houses under this scheme.[852] Besides, this, the church constructed homes for earthquake victims in Lathur, in Madhya Pradesh, homes to people in Mexico[853] and some other places in India.

In 1971, the Mar Thoma Church initiated the "Marriage Aid Scheme" for providing financial assistance to poor parents for getting their daughters married. It also initiated a "Relief Fund" scheme to provide financial aid to people affected by natural

---

848 *Interview with Philipose Mar Chrysostom,* dated 18th July 2012.
849 *Metropolitan's Circular No. 152,* dated 6 October 1983, In: *the Mar Thoma Church,* Sabha Office Records, Tiruvalla.
850 P.M. Thomas ed., "Bhoobhavana *Prasthnam,* Vivaha Sahaya Fund, Durithaswasa Sahayam", In: *Mar Thoma Sabha Directory, op cit.,* 356–358.
851 *Ibid.*
852 *Metropolitan Navathy Memoirs,* (Tiruvalla: Mar Thoma Syrian Church, 2008), 156. The statistics showed above is besides of the schemes of the individual parishes for a "Home for Homeless". For instance the Mar Thoma Congregation in Switzerland assisted eleven families to build their houses by providing financial assistance in 2004 and one home in 2012. See, *Annual Report of the Mar Thoma Congregation Switzerland,* 2004.
853 The Mar Thoma Church encourages taking mission fields in foreign countries. The church adopted the island "Puntilla Norte" in Mexico as its mission project and decided to provide them basic infrastructures – homes, water, and education facilities and medical assistance in 2003 as the first phase of its action. 45 houses were built and handed over to the people there. See, *Mission Report of the Mar Thoma Church, Diocese of the North America –Europe Diocese, 2011.*

265

calamities, inside and outside the country. This scheme started with the church's decision to extend a helping hand to the flood and hurricane-affected Japanese in 1959. The relief fund was also utilised to help the tsunami victims in 2004. The "relief fund" scheme continues even today, and the present Metropolitan, Joseph Mar Thoma, is deeply involved in enlarging this funds and activities. The success of the *Boobhavanadana Prasthanam* and other schemes mentioned above are characterized by the church's progressive adoption of the "Kingdom of God" mission praxis and its affirmation of solidarity with the suffering people in India. The project was steered by metropolitans Juhanon Mar Thoma (1893–1976), Alexander Mar Thoma (1913–2000), Philipose Mar Chrysostom Mar Thoma and current incumbent Joseph Mar Thoma and suffragan Zacharias Mar Theophilus. We can surmise that the church's exposure to the world ecumenical movement and the post-Independent social space caused a shift in its mission praxis – from being "church-centred" to being "kingdom-centred" – and it demonstrates the openness of the church.

Sustainable society concerns

It was against the backdrop of the Mar Thoma Church's predilection for poverty alleviation and its participation in nation-building that fresh discussions on the "just, participatory and sustainable society"[854] concept based on the "kingdom of

---

854 The term "sustainable society" was first used in the working group of the WCC's "World Conference on Science and Technology for Development" organized by the sub-unit on the "Church and Society" in Bucharest in 1974. This meeting was convened in the context of the Stockholm convention on human environment by the UNO in 1972. "Sustainable community" implies "the nurturing of equitable relationship both within the human family and also between humans and ecological community as a whole in a geospecific place". See, Martin Robra, "Sustainability", In: Nicholas Lossky and et all. (eds.) *Dictionary of the Ecumenical Movement, op.cit.,* 1085. "A society will be sustainable only as long as the rate of use of non-renewable resources does not out run the increase in resources made available through technological innovations, unless the emissions of pollutants are well below of the capacity of the eco system to absorb them, and unless the need for food is at any time well below the global capacity to supply it." See, Martin Robra, "Sustainability", In: Nicholas Lossky and et al., ed., *Dictionary of the Ecumenical Movement, op.cit.,* 1084. It was the Bucharest meeting on which the idea of a "sustainable and just society" considering the imbalance between over consumption of oil in rich countries and the need for economic growth in poor countries accepted by the global ecumenical movement as a new idea, which need to be taken seriously in its discussions. The Nairobi Assembly

God" surfaced in the ecumenical movements. The term, sustainability, is defined as "development that meets the need of the present without compromising the ability of the future generations to meet their needs".[855] "The WCC's discussion on sustainability outlines three elements for an adequate definition and a responsible pattern for social formation."[856] These were one, the well-being of future generations and their right to a fulfilled life, two, the concern for justice and last, "matters concerning the present economic system".[857] On the pretext of discussions on sustainability, environmental concerns were highlighted in the WCC, particularly at its world conference on "Faith, Science and Future" at Massachusetts in USA in 1979. All these discussions eventually resulted in the WCC's adoption of the programme, "Justice, Peace and the Integrity of Creation" in its Vancouver General Assembly in 1983 which was further emphasised in its General Assemblies that followed.

The Mar Thoma Church became increasingly attentive to environmental concerns and initiated awareness-classes in the parish, the centre and the diocesan level. The church has organised conferences, encouraged tree-planting and published articles in the church's magazines since 1980s. However, it got a new momentum when the church's episcopal synod constituted the "Ecological Commission of the Mar Thoma Church"[858] in 2008 to "study on ecological awareness and to send practical recommendations to the Church council for their implementation".[859]

---

accepted this idea and included in the WCC's social thinking. During the next year the Central Committee of the WCC included it as a programme in it. The discussions on this idea reached to the Mar Thoma Church through M.M. Thomas, as he got the first hand understanding about these as the moderator of the Central Committee of the WCC since Uppsala Assembly and his leadership in the "Church and Society" wing of the WCC. See, David G. Hallmann, "Environment and Ecology", In: Nicholas Lossky and et al., (eds.) *Dictionary of the Ecumenical Movement, op.cit.,* 396–398.

855 *Brundtland Commission Report of the United Nations Organisation,* 1987.
856 M.J. Joseph, *The Eco Vision of the Earth Community,* (Bangalore: BTESSC/SATHRI, 2008), 31.
857 *Ibid.*
858 *Interview with M.J. Joseph,* dated 4th March 2013. M.J. Joseph is a retired clergy of the Mar Thoma Church. He was the Principal of the Mar Thoma Theological Seminary and the Director of the Ecumenical Christian Centre, Whitefield. He is a pioneer in studying the subject in an elaborative way in the Mar Thoma Church. He introduced study classes and worship services concerning the ecological concerns in India through the Ecumenical Christian Centre, Whitefield. He introduced curriculum for this in the Indian School of Ecumenical Theology in 1995. See, Joseph Daniel, *One Family Under Heaven: Paradigm Shifts in Ecumenism* (New Delhi: ISPCK, 2008), 31ff.
859 *Minutes of the Ecological Commission of the Mar Thoma Church,* dated 18th February 2008.

Following the recommendations of the commission, the church implemented the following steps. It started observing an environmental Sunday in the first week of June every year, when worship services and environmental awareness programmes like conferences are organised in parishes, the centre and the diocesan levels to educate people about ecological concerns. The Metropolitan's circular concerning the church's goal for the protection of God's creation is announced in all parishes and institutions of the church during the environmental Sunday service regularly. The church has encouraged parishes, as well as schools and colleges that it manages to organise meetings for planting trees on its premises on the third day of July every year in conjunction with the St. Thomas Day celebrations. Major publications of the church have set apart a section for environmental concerns to be published regularly. The church has incorporated environmental concerns in its Sunday school curriculum and has encouraged the youth to organise camps in parishes, the centre and diocesan levels to promote ecological awareness among youths for protecting God's earth.[860]

Actions of the church in this direction were well received by its members, and were also encouraged by the Government of Kerala. On 16 February, 2010, the Forest Department of the Government of Kerala distributed 100,000 new tree saplings at the Maramon Convention of the Mar Thoma Church. This was organised as a joint programme of the government and the church to address environmental concerns, particularly towards countering the problem of deforestation. The distribution of tree saplings was inaugurated by the then state Minister for Forests, Government of Kerala. M.J. Joseph is the director of this commission, and gives leadership through his eco-poems, articles and meditations.

An account the Mar Thoma Church's responses to the ecumenical programmes would not be complete without an analysis of the church's response to the concept of "Development" through social empowerment schemes. Although the idea of development was prominent after World War II, two perspective changes on development can be identified since the 1970 – the crucial role of human participation in the whole process of social, political and economic development and the importance given to "the people", who are poor and marginalised. These changes were due to the influence of liberation theology and the socio-political condition in the Third World.[861] Such an ecumenical outlook sees the development process from the point of view of the poor and the marginalised people in the society. It

---

860 *Ibid.*
861 Richard D.N. Dickinson, "Development", In: Nicholas Lossky and et al., (eds.) *Dictionary of the Ecumenical Movement, op.cit.*, 298–303.

was in this context that the church realised that although laudable and necessary are the church's charitable and developmental activities, they seldom challenge the existing social system and structures of injustice that perpetuate poverty and unequal distribution of resources.

Deconstructing social structures

This led to the realisation that social services alone would not be sufficient to expedite improvement of the economic standards of the poor citizens in India – poverty and marginalisation are interwoven with the Indian social space that was historically constructed by the "caste system". The Mar Thoma Church realised that the deconstruction of the historically-constructed social space is essential to strive for justice, peace and sustainability. It can be done by engaging indirectly in the social space and its practices with a view to replicate a new social space, with new practices and consciousness, instead of the caste-consciousness and its manifested social stratification. The church wants to deconstruct the caste structures so that justice, peace and the integrity of creation get interwoven into India's secular democratic context. To spearhead this type of kingdom-centred mission, the church decided to start the "Development Department". The following analysis is about the factors that guided the Mar Thoma Church to start the "Development Department" and about the modes adopted by the church to implement its development agenda.

In 1977, the church instituted a "Development Department", as its social service wing, to inspire church members to take up the mission to uplift the poor and marginalised in India. While emphasising its goal, Alexander Mar Thoma Metropolitan, said this was a way to, "participate in the mission for the building up of the Kingdom of God"[862] in the Indian society. The basis of the founding of the "Development Department" hinges around the WCC's mission paradigm – Kingdom of God – and its ecumenical programmes, the Indian social space generated by the "caste system" and the United Nations' Development Decade emphasis in 1961.[863]

---

862 *Circular Letter of Alexander Mar Thoma Metropolitan*, (Malayalam) *Circular No. 339*, dated 21 February 1992.

863 Besides, the first United Nations Development Decade was introduced by the UN General Assembly in 1961. The aim of this decade was to intensify its efforts to mobilize, support for measures required to accelerate progress towards self-sustained economic growth and social advancement in the developing countries. It resolved "Considering that the economic and social development of the economically less

The metropolitans of the Mar Thoma Church were instrumental in introducing the programmes of the WCC into the Church. It is their active involvement in the ecumenical movement that created a drive to start institutions in the Mar Thoma Church that gave expression to such programmes at the local level. To meet this end, initially a 'Backward Class Development Committee' was constituted in 1975 and this committee proposed the founding of a "Development Department". Having received the mandate from the sabha council and the *sabha mandalam*, the "Development Department" came into existence in 1977.[864] While emphasising its goals, Alexander Mar Thoma explains: "It is our (church's) duty to participate in the mission for the building up of the 'Kingdom of God' by standing firm on the side of God's love and justice in the society. The Development Department was started with the purpose of assisting the church to fulfil this duty."[865] By doing so, the church has opened up opportunities to the marginalised sections of the society within and outside the church.

Proactive initiatives

The Mar Thoma Church's "Development Department" thus serves as an umbrella organisation that aims at inspiring its members to uplift the Indian poor and marginalised people and help them to develop self-reliance.[866] The department focuses on two of its prime objectives: inspire church members to assist the poor and the needy within the church and bring them on par with the general socio-economic

---

developed countries is not only of primary importance to those countries but is also basic to the attainment of international peace and security and to a faster and mutually beneficial increase in the world prosperity." *1084th Plenary Meeting*, 19th December 1961, 17, In: *www.unpan.org/portals/0.../GA%20Res201710(XVI).1961.pdf*. The programmes of the UN got wide acceptance in India during these period, also indirectly prompted the church to join hands with the nations for the development. *S.www.unhistory.org/reviews/FDS_Jollly.pdf*.

864 The *sabha council* that met on August 27, 1976 resolved "to start a Development Department" under the auspices of the church. The *sabha mandalam* approved the resolution of the *sabha council* in 1977. The *sabha council*, which met on June 6, 1977, decided to terminate the functioning of the 'Backward Class Development Committee' and form the "Development Department". See, *Minutes of the Meetings of the Sabha Council* held on 27th August 1976; *The Annual Report of the Sabha Mandalam*, 1977.

865 *Ibid*. It is an independent translation of the author.

866 *Constitution of the Mar Thoma Development Department*, (Tiruvalla: Mar Thoma Church, 2010), 1–4.

status of its members; inspire members to support the poor and the marginalised sections of the society to attain the desired level of self-reliance and dignity. To achieve this goal, the church urged its members to provide socio-economic assistance to the marginalised and introduce new schemes in the realms of industry and agriculture in villages, where they reside.[867] To plan and execute programmes and schemes, the church decided to start the "Development Department" and the "Christian Agency for Rural Development" (CARD).

CARD is registered as a non-governmental organisation in 1977. It "strives for a world community of communities where poverty and injustice no longer exists"[868] and one in which "all people enjoy sustainable relations with each other based on the exercise of love and justice, participation and freedom".[869]

The primary task before the Mar Thoma Church was to help the poor and the marginalised to deconstruct their marginalised social position. The church considered it essential to create a self-consciousness of equality among the marginalised that they are capable to participate in the democratic social body of the church and society.[870] This would help them believe that they were equally capable to overcome their limitations

---

867 *Ibid.*, P.M. Thomas, ed., *Mar Thoma Sabha Directory, op.cit.*, 359–362; Joseph Mar Thoma Metropolitan, "Message from the Patron", In: the *34th Annual Report of the CARD*, 2010–2011, 4.

868 *Constitution of the Christian Agency for Rural Development, Mar Thoma Syrian Church, Tiruvalla*, 1.

869 It is a registered non-governmental organisation under the "Travancore – Cochin Literary, Scientific and Charitable Societies Registration Act XII of 1955 on 6th September 1977". See, *Constitution of the Christian Agency for Rural Development, Mar Thoma Syrian Church, Tiruvalla*, 1.; See, *34th Annual Report of the CARD*, 2010–11.

870 "Caste structure" developed a notion that there is a never-ending hierarchical human positioning in the making of man by *Brahman* (God), which we have already dealt with at length in the second chapter of this study. Those who are outside of the "caste structure" are not equated to human beings but subordinated to animals, on the ground that they are inferior in human quality and therefore they do not have the potential to reach the position of the "high caste" societies. Because of long centuries of demeaning subordination, the people in the lowest rung of society developed a sense of self-worthlessness and the inability to rise to a position at a higher level. This condition made them to think that they are inferior and their social positioning is subordinate to others in the Indian society. This made their social position in India vulnerable to marginalisation. Thus the creation of subjectivity and the emergence of the lower socio –economic and cultural positioning of the marginalised society in India was based on the Indian caste structure.

and poverty of aspirations and subjectivity[871] caused by their social positioning and subordination. The hope was that this would empower them to attain self-reliance.

The Church took upon itself the task of inspiring and educating its vast middle-class members whose social position was with the "high-caste" community to do away with its "high caste" mindset. This balancing act, together with the need to deconstruct the social position of the marginalised sections, was a Herculean task. The metropolitans, M.M. Thomas and leaders of the church took initiatives to generate public opinion that the church is the body of Christ, in which all members are equal before God. They did this by treating church members equally, while providing them pastoral and personal care, irrespective of their social position or status.

Leading by example

Here's how Metropolitan Alexander Mar Thoma reacted when he found a mother with her adolescent boy crying at the SC High School gate: He invited them to his office and enquired about the reason for her sorrow. The mother was crying because of her inability to pay the prescribed fees for his son's admission at the school. The Metropolitan promptly called the Head Master to his office and instructed him to give admission to the boy, without collecting fees from him.[872]

Despite all these efforts, the tension between those who wanted to treat the members who converted from the "lower caste" as equals and those who considered such members as "untouchables" continued for decades. This deplorable attitude was damaging the image of the church as a liberating force for the common good of every one and eventually forced the leadership of the church to make drastic constitutional changes that allowed those converts to form separate churches, as an interim measure, with all constitutional powers and responsibilities in 1980.

The Mar Thoma Church has realised that to uplift the marginalised, it would not be enough to just provide financial assistance and other services. Instead, the

---

871 Social position and subjectivity are the categories, which the post- modern epistemology uses frequently in its analysis of society and history. Subjectivity is considered by the post- modern thought that it is a human condition and the way a person led to think of him or herself. It is the self- reflexive programme through which one re-positions himself or herself in the current social discourses. See, Nick Mansfied, *Subjectivity: Theories of the Self from Freud to Haravay* (New York: New York University Press, 2000) 10.

872 It is an eye witness account of the writer, who was the Chaplain to the Alexander Mar Thoma Metropolitan during 1998–2000.

church has come to understand the imperative to form a development organisation to encourage the marginalised groups to actively participate in the decision-making process and its implementation phase. This would indirectly help them to come out of their subjection and thereby widen their spheres of influence in the society.[873] The programmes and activities of the "Development Department" and its registered charitable organisation, the CARD, could be seen in this background. Later the CARD coordinated the activities of the "Development Department".[874] To implement its activities and programmes, these organisations got financial aid from the WCC, World Vision, and Christian Agency for Social Action (CASA), and ACT Alliance.[875]

The "Development Department" and the CARD constituted its programmes in Indian villages.[876] Its foremost agenda, in a selected area, was the building up of a 'Village Development Association' (VDA)[877], constituted with democratic principles with all its members having equal rights to express their ideas on the

---

873 *Alexander Mar Thoma Metropolitan's Circular Letter to all Parishes,* Circular No. 339, dated 1ˢᵗ January 1992.

874 Three levels of the activities of the CARD can be distinguished: Management and implementation of the rural development projects, Co-ordination of the programmes of the church's "Development Department" and parishes, and dioceses, and to provide development education to project workers, lay leaders, clergy and the leaders of the weaker sections. These activities of the CARD aimed at making the developing people aware of their constitutional rights and privileges and equiping them to deconstruct their inferiority and subjectivity, and to participate in the development works in the local level.
See, A.T. Philip, *The Mar Thoma Church and the Kerala Society, op.cit.,* 60; *Christians Agency for Rural Development, Sovenir,* (Tiruvalla: 1986), 1–10.

875 *Ibid., Annual Report of the Christian Agency for Rural Development, 2010–11,* 11.

876 Major six levels of programmes of the CARD can be drawn at the beginning of its activities: 1. formation of social organizations in villages for children, youths, women and community. 2. Village improvement programmes such as financial and manpower assistance provided to the village road construction, arranging drinking water facilities. 3. Community irrigation projects. 4. Promotion of agriculture by supplying seeds. 5. Organizing credits through national banks and enabling the local people to the agricultural technologies in consultation with the government agricultural research centers. 6. Community health and sanitation programme, programme for women and children empowerment, and training for developing skills of the villagers.
See, A.T. Philip, *The Mar Thoma Church and the Kerala Society, op.cit.,* 60; *Christians Agency for Rural Development, Souvenir,* (Tiruvalla: 1986), 1–10; *Annual Report of the Christian Agency for Rural Development, 1986,* 1–5.

877 Hereafter referred as "VDA".

development of their particular village.[878] The VDA is the focal point, where community members meet for brainstorming, planning and executing their programmes by common consent.[879] The role of the CARD is the facilitation of development movements together with financial and planning assistance with expertise sought from trained staff of the church. VDAs sought to: 1) equip the marginalised sections to develop a self-consciousness of their capability to participate in the decision-making process and its implementation phase and thereby overcome their age-old subjectivity and 2) develop self-reliance and independence. In this liberation process, the Mar Thoma Church defined the rural development as "aided self-help".[880]

The message trickles down

The Development Department carries its activities at three levels: Parish, Diocese and the Church's centre levels. In 1979, the Mar Thoma Church decided to form the Development Department's local units in all parishes, with the then Metropolitan sending a circular to all parishes to implement it without fail.[881] In the circular, he exhorted church members to observe a "Development Week" in all parishes and dioceses during the first week of May and educate members of its need at the local level.[882] The village parishes constituted a "Development Department" and formed development committees under the chairmanship of the local parish priest, to chalk out and implement plans of development at the local level.[883] The development committee is authorised to take a survey of the village and make a chart for the target group, which needs assistance. The democratic participation of all people, irrespective of their religious, social or caste associations, was sought to be ensured in the local development committee.[884] In the same way, the

---

878 *Christian Agency for Rural Development, A Hand Book*, (Strictly for the Official Use of the CARD), Office of the Development Department, and CARD, Tiruvalla, 9.

879 *Ibid.*

880 *Ibid.* 3.

881 *Alexander Mar Thoma Metropolitan's Circular Letter to all Parishes*, dated 18th April 1979.

882 *Ibid.*

883 *Alexander Mar Thoma Metropolitan's Circular Letter to all Parishes*, Circular No. 339, dated 1st January 1992.

884 *Ibid.*

"Development Department" was formed at the diocesan level by taking development projects within the parameters of a particular diocese.

Among these grassroots intiatives are the "Mar Thoma Sea Coast Development Project", started in 1982 by the Adoor-Mavelikara Diocese that has aimed at uplifting the living conditions of the poor people residing in the coastal area of Trikkunnapuzaha, in Kerala. In 1979, the "South Travancore Agency for Rural Development" (STARD) was registered to serve the common masses in those areas.[885] A separate development body "Backward People Development Programmes" (BPDP) was also formed to cater to the needs of the members belonging to the marginalised sections within the church.[886]

"CARD" heads and coordinates the development work of the church at the centre level. It chalks out an organisational chart,[887] in which general administration is carried out by a general body, governing board, programme committee, director and assistant director.[888] A head office consisting of an administrative officer and office staff attended to matters related to the office. Community organisers, including project directors and staff, in consultation with people drawn from the VDA, women's association, youth clubs, children's associations, co-operative societies in local village development units, democratically chalk out plans for development and send it to the central office for approval.[889] They start implementing the project after taking approval from the centre and the programme director.

Currently CARD continues its activities through different programmes and projects in five Indian states.[890] Its major activities include different programmes for child care, food security, agricultural development and research with focus on equipping farmers through technology transfer. CARD's women's empowerment programmes deal with reproductive and child health emphasis, HIV/AIDS

885 P.M. Thomas, ed., *The Mar Thoma Sabha Directory, op. cit.*, 362.

886 P.M. Thomas, ed., *The Mar Thoma Sabha Directory, op. cit.*, 362.

887 *Christian Agency For Rural Development, A Hand Book*, (Strictly for the Official Use of the CARD), Office of the Development Department, and CARD, Tiruvalla, 1.

888 *Ibid., The Constitution of the Christian Agency for Rural Development*, (Tiruvalla: V.G.C, Press, 1979), 3–4. The general administration of the CARD is vested on the Governing Board. The Governing Board consists of the Metropolitan (chairman), the Church secretary and representatives from ancillary organisations of the church. This administrative body directs the function of the Development Department and the CARD.

889 *Ibid.*

890 "The CARD has its work in Kerala, Uttar Pradesh, Madhaya Pradesh, Chatisghhisghat, and Orrissa," See *the Annual Report of the CARD*, 2010–11.

prevention, environmental and bio-diversity protection, livelihood support, and manufacturing of value-added products of traditional craftsman.[891]

The Government of India's "Indian Council of Agricultural Research's" *Krishi Vigyan Kendras*, which is "a network in the country, aspiring to act as an interface with farmers to identify constraints and opportunities, assess innovations and adoption of location specific agricultural technologies and skills"[892] selected CARD as the Farm Science Centre for Pathanamthitta District in Kerala. This was a sign of the Indian government's recognition of the activities of CARD.

The activities and programmes of the "Development Department" and CARD helped to realise major social empowerment potentials of Indian villages. As mentioned earlier, these initiatives were offshoots of the Mar Thoma Church's effort to spread its "Kingdom of God" mission praxis to the wider Indian community. M.A. Thomas affirms that during the 1980s "things have changed and that too radically … Today the scheduled castes, whether converts or not, are uneasily accepted on equal terms. Though uncomfortable, the Syrians (Mar Thoma Christians) have yielded to social pressures".[893]

Cold response from parishes

However, the work of the Development Department at the local parish level has not received the desired result as local parishes have been showing a cold response to it. For instance, only 95 parishes started units of the development department between 1977 and 1995. The then Metropolitan did make an effort to organise branches in all parishes. He says: "It is necessary to constitute development programmes in parishes through … diocesan supervision."[894] But his efforts to organise the department in all parish levels has not been accomplished yet.

The reasons for the cold response from local parishes are economic and social. The economic reasons include the inability of local parishes to meet the needs of the wider community in which majority of them are economically, socially and

---

891 *Ibid.*
892 C.P. Robert., ed., *KVK Pathanamthitta: Retrospect,* (Kolabhagom: CARD-Krishi Vigjan Kendra, 2011), 1.
893 M.A. Thomas, "Mar Thoma Church's Approach to Other Religions and Mar Thoma Church's Socio-Political Involvement", In: *Mar Thoma Sabha Saradhikal,* (Malayalam), *op.cit.,* 5–6.
894 *Circular Letter of Alexander Mar Thoma Metropolitan,* Circular No. 428, 9 June 1995, Tiruvalla.

educationally poor. Besides this, the selection criteria of the needy and the distribution of financial assistance to them appeared to local parishes as beyond its organisational and economic potential.

The social reason has been the impracticability of bringing people of other religious communities together under the umbrella of a church's "Development Department". When people of other religions looked at it, it appeared to them as a means to attract them to the church, even though the church did not aim for it. So the majority communities around local places showed reluctance to join in it whole-heartedly. The impact of both these developmental wings of the church – CARD and the Development Department – on wider marginalised community in India deserves a separate study.

We now look at how the church has addressed the tension between those members who hang on to tradition and protected privileges, and the converts who came from the marginalised sections.

New churches for the marginalised

The decisions of the Mar Thoma Church to provide equal opportunities to the marginalised communities and ensure their participation in decision-making bodies also resulted in the springing up of so-called "new churches" for these sections of the society.[895] Although both the "Development Department" and the CARD have strived to inspire church members to support the efforts towards uplifting the marginalised and developing their self-reliance, the church has still not been able to integrate its own members belonging to the marginalised sections with those who claim to come from traditional background. This was in effect a reflection of the church's inability, to some extend, in expanding its ecumenical praxis.

The inability of those in the higher strata to integrate with those in the lower strata and vice versa stems from their subjective social positioning.

Although Metropolitan Alexander Mar Thoma (1913–2000) tried to find a way around this deep-rooted malaise by allowing men and women from the marginalised communities to participate in the decision-making and implementation process of the church, an alteration of the core attitude of church members, who belong to higher social strata, could not be achieved. The hegemonic nature of

---

895   Constitution of the Mar Thoma Church does not prohibit a member, who is converted from the marginalized section to take his/her membership in any of the church's parishes in his/her locality in conformity with the clauses for membership in the church.

the "caste system" and its approved social customs and practices denied social, symbolic and cultural capitals for the marginalised sections within the church.[896]

In fact, the church introduced several welfare measures for the marginalised that has opened new choices for the integration of both sections within the church.[897] For instance, Alexander Mar Thoma used to visit regularly all "new churches" and associate with them in their local life by spending weekends in their parishes. He himself used to pay their payment dues at the church office.

It was in this context that the Mar Thoma Church was forced to have an introspection and sought to ensure the representation of marginalised members in the church's constitutional bodies. The church found that the non-integration of its members was in fact a reflection of a larger problem deep-rooted in the Indian "caste system". This necessitated a drastic intervention in the existing social space of the church by allowing members of the marginalised section to be represented at its various constitutional bodies. The lesser number of members from the marginalised communities[898] in the local parishes, and their perceived lower social position had denied these communities any berths in the constitutional offices of the church at local, diocesan and the central levels. This was the context behind the Mar Thoma Church's effort to make separate churches comprising of the marginalised sections of its members.[899] It was only an interim measure, in one sense, to treat a long-standing malady – and this measure itself may be viewed as "separate development for separate people", or a form of apartheid that is not compatible with kingdom-centred mission.

The formation of the "new chapels" in 1971 and "new churches" for members converted from the marginalised sections by the constitutional changes in 1980 is one of the actions taken by the Mar Thoma Church to remove the ills of social positioning within the church.[900] The move aimed at deconstructing social customs and practices, subjection and social positioning into higher and lower

---

896 P.M. Thomas ed., *The Mar Thoma Sabha Directory, op.cit.*, 354.
897 *Ibid.*
898 The marginalized members of the church are mainly the converts from the "lower caste" to the Mar Thoma Church. While comparing the number of members in a local church, the number of converted members is very small.
899 A brief history of the Mar Thoma Church's members who converted from the "lower caste" background has already been dealt in this study.
900 The rationale behind the formation of the separate new churches within the Mar Thoma Church was to uplift the converted Christians to the Mar Thoma Church's existing traditional member's social and administrative level in the church. They had not received any opportunity to be part of the decision making bodies of the church,

strata by a constitutional intervention, which created separate 'new churches' for members who converted from the lower caste backgrounds. This was also meant to incorporate the marginalised into the existing administrative practices and customs within the dialogical and democratic social space in the church. The church made it clear that any baptised member can avail of its membership in any parish of the church, but it allows its members from the marginalised sections into separate parishes.

Consequently, the new parishes, or new churches, got the constitutional privilege to be represented in all the administrative organs of the church, stretching from the executive committee of local parish to the General Assembly member and sabha council at the central level. However, even when the new churches for the converted Christians did not fully integrate them into the church's mainstream life. The church's mainstream is still in favour of the conservative positioning and the traditional arrangements and "refuses to participate in radically transforming the hierarchical conventions of socio-economic life".[901] Hence the new churches are functioning as a separate entity within the Mar Thoma Church. Although it is difficult to assess the extent to which these constitutional changes may be useful for the upliftment and self-reliance of the marginalised sections within the church, it nevertheless opens a spectacular problem for both sections within the church today.

However impressive and necessary such changes have been in ensuring the participation of new converts in constitutional bodies in the church, they have seldom challenged deep-rooted social divisions and church structures. This prevents the integration of both sections of members within the church. It did eventually lead the larger society to view the church's affirmative action to improve the wellbeing of the backward and under-represented communities in a positive light, but the separate existence of "new churches" has not provided an answer to the search for dignity, equality and integration for the marginalised within the church. This critique led to an awareness within the church that separation is not a solution to this problem. On the contrary, the solution is to provide more opportunities to the marginalised to emerge as subjects of the church's total life together with the rest of its members as an integrated whole.

---

from the local parish to the centre level. Moreover it is not easy to get a berth in any one of the constitutional bodies, as they are minorities within the church.

901 Jesudas M. Atyal and John J. Thattamanil, ed., *Metropolitan Chrysostom on Mission in the Market Place, op.cit.*, 25.

Pivotal role of women

The position of women in the Mar Thoma Church historically reflected the Indian situation.[902] Like the larger Indian context, there was no concept of equality of women in the church, before the *Malankara* reforms in the nineteenth century. The role of women in the church has been confined to their participation in the worship services. However, during the period of Metropolitan Mathews Mar Athanasius (1842–1877), it was decided that women's talents could be used for the revival in the church – considered a counter-cultural act during that time. He decided to include women in the preaching and teaching ministry of the church. For instance, he invited a group of women preachers from Tamil Nadu under the leadership of Ammal to preach at the church's convention meetings during the second half of the Nineteenth Century.[903] The profound role of women in revival meetings led to the importance of women's preaching and their role to keep faith in the families of the church getting accepted within the church. Consequently, the church instructed

---

902 In the ancient *Vedic India*, women enjoyed freedom even the freedom to select her husband. During the Medieval India, women were considered as the sole property of her father, her husband and her son. This idea was perpetuated by the *Manusmrithi*, a Hindu sacred text. Thus she was forbidden to all freedom outside the family. The major reason for this shift was that the Indians wanted to protect their women from foreign attacks, especially from the Muslim invaders, who practiced polygamy. During the modern period, the Indian Constitution guaranties equality of women with men, especially equality of opportunity and equal pay for equal work. So many women are at the peak of all social, political and bureaucratic ladders. However, some women are suffering the violence afflicted on her by the family, which is based on patriarchy. Patriarchal structures perpetuate patriarchal controls, exploitation and oppression at the material and ideological levels. Since patriarchy is a part of a power relationship, it denies or restricts access to property, to education, and uses violence and social pressures to maintain its structures. It put "control over women's labour, her sexuality and her fertility" in India. See, *Pressing Against Boundaries, Report of the Faith and Order South Asian Workshop on Women and Development, 1989, op.cit.*, 13. Although, patriarchal structures are not confined to family alone, "the family is the place where males exercise domination and exploitation and often violence". See, Gabriele Dietrich, Bas Wielenga, *Towards Understanding Indian Society, op.cit.*, 38. However, the position of the Mar Thoma Christian women in the society is high in comparison with the women in general, as the former have high education through the church's schools and university colleges. The importance of women (mothers) in the Mar Thoma Christian homes, society and church are well recognized.

903 *Charithra Nikshepam 1919–1995* (Malayalam), *History of the Shree Jana Suvishesha Sevika Shgam, approved by the Jubilee Committee*, (Tiruvalla: MTSSS, 1995), 11.

that it is the duty of the mother in a family to conduct family prayer regularly every morning and evening in their homes. In 1894, Titus I, Metropolitan gave official permission to two ladies, F.S. Nicholson and Sara Mckibbin, to preach and teach in church parishes.

Titus I believed that it was only through female education that the upliftment of women can be achieved in the society. With this aim, he gave permission to start the Nicholson Girls School in 1910.[904] Metropolitan Abraham Mar Thoma took leadership to organise women in the church and formed an auxiliary organisation for women – "Mar Thoma Suvishesha Sevika Sangham" (MTSSS, the Mar Thoma Gospel Association for Women)[905] – in 1919. The MTSSS was founded with a view to facilitate the participation of women in the mission of the church, ignoring the objections of the conservative sections within the church. He appointed Kandamma and Saramma to organise its branches in each parishes, and their appointment was communicated to all parishes through a Metropolitan Circular in 1919.[906]

The activities of the MTSSS served to mobilise women in parishes, dioceses and the centre, ensure the participation of women in missionary works and to promote women's leadership in social services. The church leadership was able to mobilise women by forming MTSSS branches in each parish. In 1944, the MTSSS had about 270 branches, its number growing to 500 in 1963 and 965 in 1994. Currently, it has branches in almost all parishes and congregations in the church.[907] Simultaneously, mission centres were started under the auspices of the MTSSS in various places in India.

The emphasis on social services by the MTSSS owes its debt to the ecumenical programmes. It was during the last quarter of the 20th Century that the MTSSS started social services like employment training centres, women's hostels, tailoring schools, *curry powder* units, printing press, schools, de-addiction centres, "Salem Home" for girls and "Boys home", for children whose domestic circumstances left them with no atmosphere to have a life and sound education. MTSSS has also started a monastic order (*Ashram*) for women. The nature of the social

---

904   *Ibid.*, 13.
905   Hereafter referred as MTSSS.
906   *Metropolitan's Circular* No. 119, dated (Malayalam Era, Medam 1, 1094), 1919.
907   "Sevika Sangha samkhatanayum, Bharana Kramavum" (Malayalam), In: *Charithra Nikshepam 1919–1995*(Malayalam), *History of the Sthree Jana Suvishesha Sevika Shgam, approved by the Jubilee Committee, op.cit.,* 20.

service institutions and *Ashrams* are the same as that of the church, which have been dealt with at length earlier in this study.

The MTSSS responded robustly to the WCC's "Ecumenical Decade of Churches in Solidarity with Women" (1988–1998)[908] by organising conferences in diocesan, zonal and central levels in the church. The concern about the participation of women in the whole life of the church, including the holy orders, became an ecumenical focus since the second half of the 20th Century. In the light of these discussions, efforts were made within the Mar Thoma Church to strive for constitutional guarantees for women's full participation in the ministry.

Although the ordination of women was unacceptable to the church, it accepts that there are no theological impediments for the ordination of women. However, the tradition of the church has not permitted women to become priests.

The work of MTSSS has resulted in the church's attitude to women undergoing spectacular changes. Women used to be seated behind men during worship services. This practice has gradually changed and women now occupy almost equal status with men in the church. The church allows its women to take leadership in worship services and sermons during the service. Since 2009, the church implemented the 33 per cent reservation for women in its constitutional decision-making bodies at the parish, diocese and central levels.

However, in the mind of many members of the church, women are inferior and impure.[909] Because of this notion of impurity, women are not allowed to the 'altar' since it is *sanctum sanctorum*.[910] It nevertheless does not prevent women from expressing their opinion and even disagree with the policies of the church.

---

908 The WCC General Assembly of Vancouver in 1983 decided to give further emphasis to the needs and the contributions of women in church and society. So the central committee, which met in 1987, has decided to have a decade during which the churches would demonstrate their solidarity with women. The "Ecumenical Decade of the Churches in Solidarity with Women" (1988–1998) was launched on the Easter Sunday on 1988. "Its focus was on empowering women at all levels to participate more fully in the decisions that affect their destiny, to be partners with men in shaping the lives of their families and their societies and to be equipped for ministry in the churches in the full fellowship of the People of God." (Pauline Webb, "Women in Church and Society", In: Nicholas Lossky and et al. (eds.) *Dictionary of the Ecumenical Movement, op.cit.*, 1211;
E.V. Mathew, "Churches in the Solidarity with Women" in *Mar Thoma Sabha Saradhikal, op.cit.*, 30–35.
909 Aley T. Philip, "Mar Thoma Church and the Women", In: *Mar Thoma Sabha Saradhikal*, (Malayalam), *op.cit.*, 36–40.
910 *Ibid.*, 37.

Guided by the ecumenical movement and the social space of India since the country attained independence, the church has incorporated kingdom values and its manifestation can be seen in its activities encompassing development, social engineering and women's empowerment. These shifts were extended further in the church's practical expressions of its stand on safeguarding justice, peace and freedom in India at a critical time with these came under threat. That phase also served to underline the church's existence as an independent and indigenous Indian church.

Robust response to 'emergency'

The emergency rule is a statutory provision that is found in 'Article 352' of India's Constitution. It refers to a period of governance under the Indian President's alternate constitutional set-up, on the basis of the central cabinet's recommendations, when the nation faces internal, external or financial threat.[911] Under the emergency rule, the President can, on the advise of the country's cabinet, overrule many provisions of the constitution that guarantees the fundamental rights of citizens. Although the framers of the Indian Constitution – B.R. Ambedkar (1891–1956) and others – included this article in the Constitution, the provision was to be used

---

911 The Indian Constitution has provisions for emergency rule in three occasions. First, under article 352, the central government can exercise the absolute control during the time of emergency to preserve integrity, security and stability of the country. Second, under article 356, the President of India have the discretionary power to impose emergency on states, when he /she is satisfied that the state government can not be carried on in accordance with the Constitution of India, by the recommendations of the central cabinet. Third, under Article 360 the President of India can impose emergency when the financial condition of the country is in danger. The Indian Constitution also prevents the chances for any arbitrary use of this provision by the President of India. First, the government's decision to impose emergency can be challenged in the courts. Second, the president of India can return the central cabinet's recommendation to impose emergency rule back to the central cabinet for reconsideration, if the President finds the invocation of the emergency rule unreasonable. Third, if the government has secured the President's approval for the emergency rule, the central government must get the approval of rules by the both houses of the Indian parliament within two month, failing which the proclamation ceases to be ineffective. See, Lloyd I. Rudolph and Susanne H. Rudolph, "Redoing the Constitutional Design: From and Interventionist to a Regulatory State", In: Atul Kohli, ed., *The Success of Indian Democracy*, (New York: Cambridge University Press, 2001), 143.

only when all other constitutional provisions failed to protect national integrity and security. But, the then Prime Minister of India, Indira Gandhi (1917–1984), imposed the emergency provision to safeguard her political position on June 26, 1975.[912] The Indian government restrained freedom, under the pretext of emergency rule during 1975–1977. The Mar Thoma Church reacted to it in a robust manner, proving the hypothesis that the church is sensitive to the social and political concerns of India and that since India's independence, it always stood for a just, participatory and responsible society.

The declaration of emergency was followed by the illegal arrest and detention of political leaders, who were against the Prime Minister, and a ban on the freedom of the press. Many Indian leaders reacted against the move but a majority of them kept silent.

The Mar Thoma Church found the emergency rule as one that went against the mandate of a responsible society, as the then democratically elected Indian government and its prime minister, Indira Gandhi, choked the constitutionally guaranteed freedom of expression. For the church, responsible society is one "where freedom is the freedom of men who acknowledge responsibility to justice and public order, and where those who hold political authority or economic power are responsible for its exercise to God and the people whose welfare is affected by it".[913]

---

912 B.R. Ambedkar (1891–1956) was the chairman of the India's Constitution Drafting Committee. He hoped that the Article 356 "would never be called into operation and that (its use) would remain a dead letter".
See, *Government of India, Constituent Assembly Debates,* Vol. IX, (New Delhi: Lok Sabha Secretariat, 1949), 177.
The context for the imposition of the Emergency Rule by Indira Gandhi was complex. The social, political and economic condition of India was vulnerable after the Indo- Pakistan war in 1975. The Indian National Congress Party won the election of 1975 and Mrs. Indira Gandhi (1917–1984) became the Prime Minister of India. But she was accused of wide scale of corruption with allegations of election fraud and the misuse of the government machinery for the success of the election. The State court in response to the public interest litigation filed against her in the court accused her appropriating government funds, made a verdict, in which she was found guilty of several charges. It was followed by a widespread hue and cry for her resignation from the power. To keep her power she forced the President of India to declare emergency rule by using Article 352 of the Indian constitution on June 26, 1975. The emergency rule enabled her to rule the nation by decree, without democratic elections and complete suspension of the civil liberties.

913 "The Church and the Disorder of the Society", In: W.A. Visser't Hooft, ed., "Report of Section III", In: *the First Assembly of the WCC held in Amsterdam, August 22 – September 4, 1948,* (New York: Harper, 1949), 78.

The Mar Thoma Church, unlike several Christian churches in India that chose to remain silent, voiced its dissent of the emergency rule, and insisted on its repeal and sought to ensure the freedom of Indian citizens.[914] On August 25, 1976, Juhanon Mar Thoma, Metropolitan sent a letter to Indira Gandhi, expressing his disapproval of the emergency rule in India, his annoyance at her attempts to put leaders, who spoke against emergency behind the bar, and the ban on the freedom of press. He requested the withdrawal of emergency rule.[915] He wrote:

If you had resigned after the high court judgement, the country would have been without a government for some time. The declaration of emergency had immediate effect and brought peace and good Government everywhere. But I am sorry to say that it did not take many months for various governments to go back to the old state of inefficiency and corruption. The peace and efficiency in the educational world and the prosperity in industry and agriculture, because of non-interference of parties are lasting benefits. But a vast number of people and a growing number feel the price we have to pay is costly. With people like Morarji and others in jail and press, which has lost its freedom to write news and views, we feel a kind of depression. On behalf of thousands, I request withdrawal of emergency by gradual stages... I have one more request not to have elections and constitutional changes during the time of emergency.[916]

The Metropolitan thus saw the prolongation of emergency rule as a movement contrary to its intended meaning of establishing the security of the nation and the stability of the administration. From this perspective of solidarity with the national community that loves India's liberty, security and the freedom of the press, the Metropolitan, voiced the opinion of the Mar Thoma Church and requested Indira Gandhi (1917–1984) to repeal the emergency rule as soon as possible. Any move from the government's side aimed at subverting the intention of elections and the spirit of the Indian Constitution was considered a rebellion against the people and was entreated to be cancelled.

In addition to the letter, he penned his opinion in an article against the emergency rule and sent it to the popular Indian Bulletin *Navadarsanam* for publishing. Despite the governmental restrictions, the article was published in February 1978 and it read:

When we see the decisions of the Congress Party and the Parliament, it is evident that the emergency rule will not be repealed soon. Leaders, who are in autocratic rule, should know that the security of the nation has arrived. That realisation will not

---

914 Most of the Indian churches were silent on the emergency rule during 1975–1977.
915 *Juhanon Mar Thoma Metropolitan's Letter to Mrs. Indira Gandhi,* dated 28/5/1976.
916 *Ibid.*

happen soon. Both the judges and those who filed the litigation are the same... how long could we suffer.[917]

This article of the Metropolitan explained the stand of the church, regarding the emergency rule. It saw the emergency rule as "a setback to democracy and freedom and therefore he demanded its speedy withdrawal as well as the release of the politicians arrested in this regard".[918] Expressing such opinions in public against the emergency rule was generally done by the national political leaders, who stood against it and those who dared to face the consequences of such actions by the autocratic government. But as a patriot, who loves freedom and the concept of responsible government, the Metropolitan expressed his view, on behalf of the church, with the confidence to pay the price for the nation's freedom and with an intention to affirm the church's autonomy and independent nature.

Juhanon Mar Thoma, Metropolitan, was not able to continue voicing its opinion against the emergency rule, as he passed away on 27 September 1976. But the Mar Thoma Church continued its stand against emergency under the newly elevated Metropolitan, Alexander Mar Thoma (1913–2000). Zac Varghese concludes: "... Probably it was one of the many things that persuaded Indira Gandhi to withdraw the emergency rule, release the incarcerated politicians and trade unionists and announce general election in which she was defeated".[919]

Thus, among the reasons for the Mar Thoma Church in not identifying with the autocratic moves of the Congress party and Indira Gandhi and for assuming an independent position to fight against emergency rule are its sympathetic attitude towards the idea of a 'responsible society' and freedom. It also underlines its existence as an indigenous and autonomous Indian church that is part of India's national history. Simultaneous to the Mar Thoma Church's participation in assisting the Indian people to reach dignity and self-rule, the church never failed to spot its opportunity to express its autonomous and independent existence as an indigenous Indian Church, which is in solidarity with India's social, economic and political concerns.

---

917 "Navadarsanam", (Malayalam) (February/1978). It is an independent translation of the writer.

918 Zac Varghese and Mathew A. Kallupuram, *Glimpses of the Mar Thoma Church History, op.cit.*, 169.

919 *Ibid.*, 169.

Scholar turns bishop and ecumenist

The role of the Metropolitans in guiding the church towards witness, service and worship has been fundamental.

Born on 10th April 1913 in Kuriannoor in Kerala, India, M.G. Chandi joined the teaching staff of the CMS School, Kottayam in Kerala in 1933. After 12 years of teaching, he joined the United Theological College, Bangalore, and was ordained priest of the church in 1946. After three years of his parish ministry, he went to USA, where he secured a doctorate from the Hartford Seminary for his research on the cosmic vision in the *Bhagavat Gita*, which is a sacred text of the Hindu religion. He was consecrated bishop in 1953 and elevated to Metropolitan in 1976 and *valia* (senior) Metropolitan in 1999.[920] He was a historian, a scholar in Hinduism, a missionary bishop and an ecumenist.

Alexander was convinced that the way of the church towards progress in mission was through furthering its ecumenical engagements and addressing the needs of the poor and the marginalised. To address this issue, he realised that a vision based on the kingdom of God would provide theoretical clarity to implement his vision of mission into praxis. His passion for mission and evangelism put aside doctrinal formulations for the church with the conviction that it has already been developed in the church by his predecessors, especially Juhanon Mar Thoma. The basic difference between Juhanon and Alexander was to be seen in their different perspectives of the goal of their vocation in the church.

Juhanon Mar Thoma aimed at putting in order an ecclesiastical, doctrinal and ecumenical formulation to the existing stand of the church, in the light of the Indian context and modern ecumenical movement. Alexander's vocation was the furthering of the church's ecumenical horizon and mission work among Indian villages. In this sense, he combined the missionary spirit and enthusiasm of Abraham Mar Thoma and the ecumenical spirit of Juhanon Mar Thoma. He believed in the possibility of removing poverty and marginalisation in India. For this, he actively encouraged the church for evangelisation and micro development ventures in Indian villages. Apparently this perspective led him to spearhead the founding of the development department of the church and its registered charitable nongovernmental organisation, CARD.

---

920 Alexander Mar Thoma, *Daivakrupayude Thanalial* (Malayalam), (Tiruvalla: Mar Thoma Press, 1997); Joseph Daniel, "Alexander Mar Thoma: Malankara Mar Thoma Suriyani Sabhayude Adhyadmika Saundaryam" (Malayalam), In: *Malankara Sabha Tharaka* (April/2013), 11–13.

It was within this consciousness of evangelism-inspired vocation and the sense of kingdom- centred mission that the zeal for the church's ecumenical endeavours and mission work in Indian villages took its shape during his tenure.

Bishop with a cosmic vision

Philipose Mar Chrysostom, the twentieth Metropolitan of the church, who began his office in 1999, is convinced that the way of the church towards progress was through "critically looking at the church's history and reform heritage"[921], "to react to the hegemonic structures of the church"[922], and to fulfil the church's ecumenical task as the Catholic Church, in the context of the Mar Thoma Church's new challenges.

The unprecedented growth of the church as a global church and articulation of the church's stance in the context of starting new self-financing professional colleges in Kerala presented new challenges to the Mar Thoma Church. In the context of its growth associated with its migration to Singapore, Malaysia, Australia, Europe, South Africa, Middle-East, USA and UK he advocates a vision, which is in concurrence with his predecessors, for the total integration of the church with the land where its members migrated to.[923] He says:

> I would be very happy to see that there is no Indian church in America. The people should become the part of the land. I do not even want the Mar Thoma Church to survive. I would say that the American church should survive. The Mar Thoma, the Episcopal and other churches should all together evolve into an American Church.[924]

He believes in the possibility of the disintegration of the monolithic church structure and the local church in a migrant context as the local church in the given context. It should co-operate with the local church and traditions of the new location. Thus he shuns the continuation of the ethnic nature of the church:

---

921 Jesudas M. Athayal, "Metropolitan's Message in the 21ˢᵗ Century", In: *Darsan* (March/2007), 7–8.

922 *Ibid.*

923 Both Juhanon Mar Thoma and Alexander Mar Thoma were reluctant to start separate Mar Thoma Churches in the USA and Europe. They directed the migrant church members to join with the local church, especially in the Anglican Church. *Interview with Joseph Mar Thoma Metropolitan,* dated March, 18, 2013.

924 Jesudas M. Athyal and John J. Thattamannil, *Metropolitan Chrysostom on Mission in Market Place, op.cit.,* 125.

I am against the ethnic church. If a church remains an ethnic church, it will be really questioning the nature of the church itself. Now that the Mar Thoma Church has members from Karnataka and Tamil Nadu, we have the liturgy in Kannada, Tamil etc. I would say that that is when the Mar Thoma Church became the Church.[925]

In this process, he has advocated that the laity be brought to the centre of the church's praxis together with the clergy and bishops. He himself has set an example of this. In the WCC' Uppsala General Assembly, the Metropolitan was the official delegate of the church to the WCC's central committee. But he magnanimously stepped aside to facilitate the election of M.M. Thomas to the post. M.M. Thomas later became the moderator of the central committee.[926] This was a prophetic decision because M.M. Thomas' contribution to the liberations struggles in Africa and introducing kingdom-centred Christian socialist pattern of thinking to the WCC agenda were significant.

He has held the view that the life of the church can be renewed only through the self-criticism of its history and culture. So there is no scope for an effort to elevate the institutional image of the church to make its presence relevant in the society. He has affirmed the church's reform and oriental heritage in its history and has sought to uphold the oriental traditions. At the same time, he wants the church to be open to fresh insights from the West. He has reacted to the hierarchical structure of the church and has advocated equality of all baptised members of the church.

Mar Chrysostom's understanding of creation provides the content of his ecumenical thought. He has held that vision of God's unity encompassing the unity of the whole cosmos.[927] This has made him a cosmic person. For instance, he has often been an invited guest in major Hindu functions like the 50th year birthday celebrations of the Sri. Sri. Ravi Shankar, birthday celebrations of Amruthanandamayi, another Hindu spiritual leader, and a regular speaker in programmes organised by other religious communities in India. This has made him "one of the well known ecumenical figures in India".[928]

---

925 *Ibid.*, 119.
926 Interview with Mathews George Chunakara, Director, International Affairs, WCC, on 8 May 2013. See, M.M. Thomas, *My Ecumenical Journey, op.cit.*, 314.
927 Philipose Mar Chrysostom's address at the Chapel Service of the Gurukul Lutheran Theological College, on January 26, 2008, in Jesudas M. Athayal, "Metropolitan's Message in the 21st Century", In: *Darsan* (March/2007), 7–8; Jesudas M. Athayal was a Professor at the Gurukul Lutheran Theological College, who attended the Metropolitan's speech.
928 Konrad Raiser, "Forward", In: Jesudas M. Athayal and John J. Thattamannil ed., *Metropolitan Chrysostom on Mission in Market Place, op.cit.*, 7.

The Metropolitan's vision has enabled the church to engage with leaders of other denominations, other faiths, socio-religious and political organisations and to begin new ecumenical engagements at local levels.

A great administrator

Joseph Mar Thoma, who assumed the office of the Metropolitan in 2007, is convinced that the way of the church towards progress can be achieved through keeping its age-old traditions of ecumenical outlook and strong institutional basis. For the strong institutional basis, he has argued for the extension of the church's institutions and believed in the possibility of organising the funds for its function.

The personality of the Metropolitan has made him a great administrator. "He has combined in his personality the traditions of his illustrious forbearers, who were leaders of reforms in the church". The combination of their two traditions – the spiritual fervour and organisational leadership – has influenced his vision of the church and its mission, as well as, the ecumenical movement. As a missionary he has given emphasis to kingdom-centred mission through the church's mission centres, as he is convinced of the need to extend a helping hand of the church to the poor and needy in villages. The Metropolitan's leadership in providing relief to the earthquake victims in Lathur in Maharastra, has been appreciated by the state government authorities.

His involvement in political matters and in the peace establishment process in Sri Lanka has made him prominent in India's socio-political realms. His zeal for leading the church and the ecumenical organisations has taken shape even as he has grown in stature in India and abroad. This has made him lead the ecumenical institutions –KCC, NCCI and CCA. He has provided leadership to international aid societies ECLOF and CASA. Discussions started between the Mar Thoma Church and the Old Catholic Church for further ecumenical engagements after he assumed office as Metropolitan.

Work in progress

The Mar Thoma Church has held an independent and autonomous position within India, a position that can be appreciated in the light of the Indian secular and democratic base. This has helped the church to be part of the fabric of the national history of India. The church has stood for safeguarding the freedom of

Indian citizens and to attain justice and peace, because it has accommodated new ecumenical programmes rooted in the "Kingdom of God". On the basis of the ecumenical programmes and post-independence India's social, political and economic space, it has renounced conservative accommodation of "casteism" within the church. This has opened a road towards the integration of the traditional mainline members of the church with those from the marginalised, a work still in progress.

Chapter XV
Ecumenism in Practice – A Progress Card

The Mar Thoma Church is an indigenous autonomous and independent church and its historical disposition and existence can be traced back to the first century beginning from the St. Thomas tradition. The coming of Christianity and the founding of the church by the Apostle Thomas in India's socio-religious and cultural setting enabled it to take on an indigenous Indian church tradition, independent of the influence of the western church traditions. But it stayed rooted in the church traditions of the Orient. This helped the church to bring members from three diversified religious and ethnic communities – the *Dravidian*, the *Brahmin* and the People of the land – under its umbrella, which necessitated a dialogical relationship with brethren of other religious communities.

Historically, the church has continued this policy of dialogical interaction and engagements with other religions in India and other churches across the world. Broadly speaking, these may be regarded as constituting the Mar Thoma Church's cognitive base that has provided the context to the church within which more ecumenical engagements and its relation with other communities emerged. This achievement aided the church in becoming aware of the need for an attempt towards formulating its life principle in developing secured connectedness with India's social, religious and cultural traditions.

The success of the dialogical interaction between the Mar Thoma Church and India's socio-cultural ethos subsequently assisted the church in framing its ecumenical vision of openness and autonomy. These became the life principle of the church that guided it in its engagements with other churches and other religions. Historically, the lasting impact of the church's ecumenical outlook consists in the adoption of a separate Law of St. Thomas, the adoption of Syriac liturgy, the Persian episcopal supervision, the adoption of west Syrian liturgy, the authorization of the "mission of help" of the Church Missionary Society (CMS) by the then Metropolitan, the mutual recognition of the episcopacy, full-communion relations with the Malabar Independent Syrian Church (MISC), the Church of India, Burma and Ceylon (CIBC), the Church of India, Pakistan, Burma and Ceylon (CIPBC), the Anglican Church, the Church of South India (CSI) and the Church of North India (CNI).

Caste system – bane or boon?

But there were instances when the Mar Thoma Church failed to keep its ecumenical outlook in line with its historic praxis. One of the instances was the church's uncritical adaptation of the Indian "caste system". The Mar Thoma Church's hierarchical administrative structure for formulating and implementing the life principle of ecumenism both at the central and local level has become passive participants in the "caste system". On the other hand, the "caste system" has given the church a considerable socio-religious status that has enabled its members to be regarded on par with the traditional Indian high-caste and socio-religious classes of Brahmanical Hinduism and culture, as well as of its power and wealth. It represented a compromised compliance to the Indian socio-cultural ethos of unity in diversity and the spirit of tolerance, and to its adoption of the Indian "caste system" that made it a caste-ridden church.

But significantly, the Mar Thoma Church came to realise eventually that India's "caste system", under the hegemonic *Brahmanical* Hinduism, was contrary to its ecumenical outlook. This new insight that came about in the 19th century led the church to start mission work among the "lower caste" communities and to take them into its full membership. The incorporation of "low caste" converts to the Mar Thoma Church was not wholeheartedly welcomed by the majority of its traditional members. This eventually led to a positive discrimination of the converts from the "lower caste' communities within the church. By this time, the Mar Thoma Church had also come to realise that the bid of foreign Roman Catholic and Antiochian churches to bring it under their ecclesiastical jurisdiction was contrary to its independent tradition. These understandings created an awareness of the need to look at the bid critically and to have an introspection into its own internal life principle and historic praxis.

Harbingers of change

The above developments resulted in the "Coonan Cross Oath" in 1653 and the reforms in 1836 within the church. The Mar Thoma Church's revolt against the Portuguese administration in the 17th century, the "Coonan Cross Oath" and the reforms in the 19th century are forerunners of the Travancore socio-political emancipation movements and its relevance can never be overstated.

The reforms within the ancient church of St. Thomas, and the Mar Thoma Church's new-found existence after reforms in 1889 was partly the result of the confrontation between the church's centuries-old policy of ecumenism, openness and independence and the adoption of some of the Antiochian church's traditions. It was also partly the result of a confrontation between traditionalism and the church's openness to receive fresh ideas of reformation from the Church of England's Church Missionary Society (CMS). Those confrontations were precipitated by the ancient Mar Thoma Church's uncritical adaptations of the authority and practices of the Roman Catholic Church and the Antiochian Church, contrary to the church's inherent policy of openness and autonomy. This led the church to search for reforms within itself to maintain its centuries-old policy of ecumenism and reinstate its autonomy.

This process necessitated the Mar Thoma Church to allow its liturgy, traditions and practices to pass through the crucible of its age-old oriental liturgical base and the reform principle of *sola scriptura*. In this process, Abraham Malpan, Geevarghese Malpan, Mathews Mar Athanasius and others felt that reforms in the liturgy, ritual practices and the church's independence from the Antiochian Patriarchate were fundamental. For the implementation of these changes, the CMS missionaries' "mission of help" provided the church with ideological and bible-based theological support, and other practical help, which they had received at a crucial time. However, the church rejected the idea that the assistance of the CMS should lead to a total adoption of Anglican reform principles and a subsequent merger with the Anglican Church. The Mar Thoma Church in its traditional wisdom decided to remain an autonomous church, while keeping its liturgical base and ecumenical outlook intact. On the other hand, the adoption of reform ideas from the CMS reflects the church's inherent ability to adopt fresh ideas from the West with a view to contemporise the church. The Mar Thoma Church's new-found existence thus saw it open up to fresh ideas, while keeping its tradition. The reforms were not about founding a new church, but returning to its traditional moorings and purity.

Vision for mission

It was in this context that the Mar Thoma Church prepared itself to face the necessity of a new church structure that asserted independence and sovereignty after the loss of the verdict in the Royal Court in 1889, and the consecration of the Metropolitan Titus I by the MISC Metropolitans in 1893. The initial steps towards the assertion of autonomy were the introduction of mission work among the "lower-caste" communities and the continuation of the church's relation with the MISC by engaging in a full-Eucharistic communion relations. For the fulfilment of its mission, the church felt the need for an ancillary organisation to work among the "lower-caste" communities and to integrate them into the main stream of the church. It was a time when foreign missions were active in India, working for the country's socio-religious transformation.

The Mar Thoma Church's basic task during this time was to cherish and continue its age-old life principle of ecumenical outlook by bringing together converts from different religious and caste traditions under the church umbrella, and to create a social transformation towards the dismantling of the "caste system". To achieve this goal, the Mar Thoma Church sought to widen its vision to transcend "caste" affiliations and integrate converts from the "lower-caste" communities to its mainstream.

With evangelisation of India as the vision, the church founded the first indigenous missionary organisation, the Mar Thoma Evangelistic Association (MTEA), in India. The members of the church were inspired and were contemporised with the missionary spirit through the work of the MTEA. The missionary work of the church was independent of the work of the western mission agencies in India. The church had a wider vision of mission in India and the church's leaders had an ecumenical vision to think that the Mar Thoma Church is part of the "one, holy, catholic and apostolic" church of the creed.

Thus the church succeeded in articulating a fresh missionary understanding in the phase of the social, political and religious transformations that took place in India, in the context of western education and the revival of Indian culture during the 19th and 20th centuries.

Faith-liturgy integration

In this process the Mar Thoma Church felt the need to integrate its eastern liturgical base and its evangelical faith harmoniously and set-up a democratic administrative system to differentiate the church as an autonomous entity, independent in terms of church polity and law from the Malankara Orthodox Syrian Church, Malankara Syrian Orthodox Church (Jacobite Church), Anglican Church and the Roman Catholic Church.

The Mar Thoma Church's mission activities through the MTEA were not simply the copying of the mission strategy of the CMS mission or other foreign missions operating in India. Two mission strategies applied by the Mar Thoma Church in India are visible at this point: the incarnational model of mission and the kingdom of God model mission. The incarnational model of mission owes its debt to the CMS mission strategy and the Indian way of the *Ashram* mission paradigm. The Mar Thoma Church promoted incarnation model of mission in India, by founding its own *Ashrams* in different parts of India, so as to bring all communities, including the "lower caste", "high caste" and "out-caste" communities under the guidelines of its mission work. The kingdom-centred mission praxis was actualized through its development department and CARD.

It was on the basis of self-awareness that the Mar Thoma Church felt the need to further its mission activities in India and realised that it could be possible through missionary co-operation with the indigenous mission organisation of other Protestant churches in India. So the church joined with the first Protestant inter-denominational indigenous missionary organisation – National Missionary Society (NMS) – for its joint mission work in India. This act of the Mar Thoma Church got a significant approval from the NMS because of the church's social affiliation with the "high-caste" society and its envious social status in the princely state of Travancore.

The NMS hoped that its alliance with the Mar Thoma Church would result in a favourable condition for the converts from the "lower caste" communities to come out from their subordinate socio-religious condition and to acquire a privileged socio-religious status in India. On the other hand, the majority of the "new Christians" in India had no "high-caste" affiliations and support. This privileged position of the Mar Thoma Church helped her to develop a favourable condition for mission in India by joining hands with the NMS to work among the "lower caste" communities in India.

Thus the Mar Thoma Church continued its distinctive traditions, while opening up to partner with missionary organisations to expedite God's mission for socio-religious transformation. This was the second step to correct the church's mistake of excluding "low-caste" people and the side-lining of its missionary zeal under the guise of ethnic and "caste" solidarity.

Church in solidarity with struggles

The Mar Thoma Church expressed its solidarity with Hindu, Muslim and Christian socio-political agitations for a responsible government in the princely state of Travancore. Moreover, it felt the need to react to the decisions of a democratic government to suspend liberty of its citizens by the declaration of the emergency rule in the Republic of India in 1975.

There were mainly three reasons for this stance. First, the socio-political awareness coupled with the wider vision and the courage of the church's Metropolitans to express their views about the value of political freedom moved it to support the agitations against the autocratic moves. The leaders of the Mar Thoma Church found that the theological understanding of the church's relationship with the state vested upon her a responsibility to the society at large. This responsibility was to express solidarity with people's struggles for safeguarding political liberty from the autocratic moves of the ruling powers. Secondly, the lay-leadership of the Mar Thoma Church became involved in the Indian socio-political realm and moved the church to declare its solidarity in the struggles to safeguard liberty. The third reason behind the church's active involvement in such socio-political struggles was its self-awareness of its autonomous and indigenous existence with a prophetic mission to share its legitimate views with the government of the day about political responsibility and citizen's freedom.

Pioneering church unity

In assessing the ecumenical outlook of the Mar Thoma Church, the praxis of a notable conciliar fellowship model of ecumenism can be seen very early in the Mar Thoma Church. Even when it remained as an independent indigenous church, it opened up to other churches in receiving episcopal supervision and in engaging in full-communion, episcopal con-celebration, occasional inter-communion and inter-communion relations with the Malabar Independent Syrian Church, (MISC) Church of India, Burma and Ceylon, and Church of India, Pakistan, Burma and Ceylon. Among the Indian churches, the pioneering stance for church unity that kept individual autonomy by maintaining liturgical and doctrinal diversities, while engaging in full-communion ties and mutual administrative assistance, came from the Mar Thoma Church.

Since 1816, the attitude of both the Mar Thoma Church and the MISC was to acknowledge their common episcopacy and to show magnanimity and humility to receive episcopal supervision from the other church, whenever a need arose. From 1893 onwards, both the churches entered into full-communion relation and started the practice of consecrating the Bishop of one church by the laying-on-of-hands by the other. This practice continues even today. This happened even before concepts of inter-communion, full-communion and episcopal con-celebration surfaced in the bilateral relations between other churches in the ecumenical movement. Similarly occasional inter-communion and full communion relationship were started between the Mar Thoma Church and the CIBC, the CIPBC, and the Anglican Church even before the formation of the WCC.

In the process of ecumenical engagements with the Church of South India (CSI), the Mar Thoma Church allowed members to use their free will in receiving the Eucharist from celebrants in the CSI, who are not ordained by the laying-on-of-hands by the Bishop. When a question was raised on the integration of the SIUC ministers within the CSI through the proper laying-on-of-hands by the Bishop, the Mar Thoma Church took a pragmatic stance of accepting the ordination of the CSI ministers on the basis of the CSI constitution's guarantee of the laying-on-of-hands by the bishop as a requirement for future ordinations within the CSI. Keeping the unity of the churches, while maintaining their autonomous existence and sovereign administrative freedom, has been the central stance of the Mar Thoma Church in its ecumenical engagements. This made it an active participant in the institutional expressions of the world ecumenical movement such as the International Missionary Council, Life and Work Movement, Faith and Order Movement and the World Council of Churches. The church also took an active role in the formation of the Christian Conference of Asia, National Council of Churches in India and the Kerala Council of Churches.

The success of the dialogical interaction between the Mar Thoma Church and the ecumenical movement and its institutional expressions such as the WCC, Christian Conference of Asia (CCA), National Council of Churches in India (NCCI), and Kerala Council of Churches (KCC), subsequently helped the church in providing ecumenical leaders to these institutions in various capacities, leading from the president of the WCC to the executive committee members. Besides, the Mar Thoma Church provided ecumenical leaders such as M.M. Thomas, Juhanon Mar Thoma, M.A. Thomas, Alexander Mar Thoma, Philipose Mar Chrysostom, Joseph Mar Thoma, Zacharias Mar Theophilus, Issac Mar Philoxinos and Mathews George Chunakara to the world ecumenical movement.

Focus on 'kingdom'

The kingdom-of-God-centred theological thought propensity of M.M. Thomas and J.C. Hoekendijk enabled the ecumenical movement to ask themselves the question: Is not the original meaning of the *oikoumene*, God's world, the true focus of the ecumenical movement? This thinking enabled the WCC to shift its emphasis from church centricism to the kingdom-of-God-centered emphasis in the 1960s. Since then, the world-centered ecumenical paradigm guided the ecumenical movement in its engagement with the emerging world realities.

The study has shown that the Mar Thoma Church never expressed itself favourably on the question of the organic model of church unity, although it stayed open to church unity engagements and to the ecumenical programmes of the WCC.

Having preoccupied with its autonomous and independent identity, the church even side-lined Juhanon Metropolitan's Encyclical of 1952 "to declare its readiness to become part of the Church of Christ in India".[929]

There were mainly four reasons for this stance being taken by the church. First, the Mar Thoma Church in principle affirms the authority of the church over matters of faith and practice, and therefore whatever the Metropolitan or the bishop is doing in word, sacraments, doctrines and faith must have concurrence and continuity with the teaching of the fathers, of Ignatius of Antioch, the first 70 disciples, the apostles and St. Thomas. Even if the Metropolitan in general supported the idea of the "Church of Christ in India", the Mar Thoma Church as a whole was not in favour. The Metropolitan looked upon the organic union of the churches in India favourably because of his life-long involvement with the global ecumenical movement. It appeared to him as an appropriate model for the unity of churches in India. Besides, he considered that the merger of the churches in India would help boost concerted missionary work in India. Despite his genuine wish, the church mainstream maintained its liturgical and church traditions even after the proposed union.

Conciliar fellowship favoured

The church avoided the possible tension between the Metropolitan's views on ecumenism by sidelining his Encyclical in the subsequent ecumenical discussions with the CSI and CNI. The second reason behind this move was the basic democratic constitutional foundation of the Mar Thoma Church that safeguards the corporate function of the church in protecting its faith foundation. There should be "three-fourths majority of the laity and clergy of the General Assembly, sitting separately and simple majority in the house of bishops before it can become an act of the church".[930] Thirdly, the church never wanted to lose its independence for the sake of unity. It wanted to continue its independent existence following the spirit of tolerance and openness. Fourthly, the Mar Thoma Church wanted to continue its trend of pragmatic ecumenism by engaging in full-communion and inter-communion relations with other churches, while remaining as a self-governing and independent

---

929 Juhanon Mar Thoma, Mathews Mar Athanasius, "A Call to the Churches of Christ in India," *Joint Statement of Juhanon Mar Thoma and Mathews Mar Athanasius to Indian Churches,* December 21, 1952, Tiruvalla. For more details, see, Chapter IV, 35–36.
930 The Constitution, *The Mar Thoma Syrian Church of Malabar, op.cit.,* 6.

church. For the fulfilment of this praxis, the Mar Thoma Church found the "conciliar fellowship" model of ecumenical engagements helpful. It also found in the conciliar model potential scope for continuing its centuries-old policy of ecumenism.

The Mar Thoma Church has responded positively to various programmes of the WCC – responsible society, just, participatory and sustainable society, justice, peace and the integrity of creation – that appeared in the ecumenical movement during the second half of the twentieth century. These programmes emerged out of the ecumenical mission paradigm of the kingdom of God and the church pursued the search for a new paradigm suitable for its implementation at its micro and macro level ecumenical engagements. The WCC felt that the conciliar fellowship model was fundaments in the pursuit of such a search.

The conciliar fellowship model of ecumenism appeared to the Mar Thoma Church as a recognition and the pinnacle of its centuries-old policy of ecumenism that respects independence and inter-dependence, while allowing plurality. This model of church unity led it to search for a new conciliar model of ecumenical engagements with churches in India. The instrument was the 'Bonn Agreement' formula used for initiating bilateral talks with the Anglican Church to further the occasional inter-communion and inter-communion relations. The same method was used to achieve ecumenical relations with the CSI and CNI for full-communion relations with a common council in a conciliar way of the three churches. The success of this was visible when the Joint Council of the three churches was formed, while the three churches adopted a common name for its ecumenical activities – "Communion of Churches in India". Based on this ecumenical engagement, members of the churches have got opportunities of mutual Episcopal supervision and membership, in places where one's mother church does not exist. Thus the inter-dependence of these churches have been beneficial to its members in the context of the migration of church members to Indian cities and to Malaysia, Singapore, United Kingdom, Europe, Canada and North America.

The ecumenical programmes of the WCC indicated to the church that these would envision the emergence of a new responsible and sustainable India in the context of its post-independence scenario. For the achievement of these, the Mar Thoma Church started its kingdom-of-God-centred mission programmes such as Medical Mission, *Bhoobhavanadana Prasthanam*, and the socio-economic empowerment programmes through its development department and Christian Agency for Rural Development (CARD). These programmes infused into Indian villages provided spiritual strength, literacy, health consciousness, environment awareness and the transformation of villages as messengers of progress. Thus the church affirmed its commitments to the world and expressed its indigenous nature.

The caste scourge

This study has shown that the formation of new local churches for the converts from the "lower caste" members in the Mar Thoma Church was an instance of departure from its centuries-old ecumenical outlook. The Mar Thoma Church was successful in converting members from "lower caste" communities and making them members of the church, which was a radical step in the direction of responding positively to the negative social system of "castiesm" in India and a departure from its centuries-old policy of uncritical adaptation of the "caste system". However, the integration of the converted members with the traditional members of local parishes is still an unresolved problem within the church. Consequently, the Mar Thoma Church was forced to form constitutionally "new churches" for those who converted from the "lower caste" communities to safeguard the converted members' constitutional rights and privileges in the church.

The church is shamefully aware that its thought propensity was shaped by an age-old association with the "caste system" in India and unfortunately, it still continues at the structural level. The marginalisation of a section of its members eventually aided the church in providing a room for practicing positive discrimination. The awareness of this basic weakness has not prompted the church to crush the walls of positive discrimination within itself. That remains a weakness in its ecumenical journey thus far, but it is hoped that the awareness would eventually result in full integration into the church of members from all sections of the community.

Need for Eucharistic hospitality

The Mar Thoma Church was unsuccessful in ecumenical engagements in formulating inter-communion relations with other churches within the St. Thomas family of churches in Kerala. There were some ecumenical dialogues with the Malankara Orthodox Syrian Church, the Malankara Syrian Orthodox Church (Jacobite Church), the Syro-Malabar Rite of the Roman Catholic Church and the Chaldean Syrian Church of the East without achieving the desired results. Therefore an urgent need of the Mar Thoma Church is to make necessary steps to reach out to other churches within the St. Thomas family of churches in Kerala and its diaspora communities throughout the world to establish Eucharistic hospitality. This is indeed a major challenge too. The Mar Thoma Church's fresh ecumenical discussion with the Old Catholic Churches of the Union of Uterecht is a positive sign that testifies its continued enthusiasm for ecumenical praxis.

The Mar Thoma Church's active participation in ecumenism in the Indian social and cultural ethos, and church unity engagements with other churches were arenas where it was able to practice its ecumenical outlook of openness and autonomy. This ecumenical vision served as the dynamic life principle of the church in shaping its historic aims in relation to India's pluralistic-cultural setting, as well as its engagements with the churches across the world. Moreover, it was in this dialogical interaction with churches that the Mar Thoma Church developed a theology of its own and its connectedness with the "one, holy, catholic and apostolic Church" for maintaining church unity.

Bibliography

I. Primary Sources

A. Books

Abraham, C.E. ed. *Mar Thoma Syrian Church and the Church of North India and the Church of South India.* Tiruvalla: Mar Thoma Church, 1968.

Abraham, M.V., Abraham Philip and et al. ed. *A Study on the Malankara Mar Thoma Church Liturgy.* Manganam: TMAM Orientation Centre, 1993.

Abraham, T.P. *Malankara Mar Thoma Sabha Noottandukaliloode.* Malayalam. Tiruvalla: CSS, 2012.

Aiya, Nagam. *The Travancore State Manual.* Trivandrum: Travancore Government Press, 1906.

Alexander, George, ed. *Maramon Convention Sathabhdhi Valyam.* Malayalam. Tiruvalla: Mar Thoma Evangelistic Association, 1995.

Alexander, P.J. ed. *The Mar Thoma Church Tradition and Modernity.* Tiruvalla: The Mar Thoma Church, 2000.

Athyal, Jesudas M. and John J. Thattamannil. ed. *Metropolitan Chrysostom on Mission in the Market Place.* Tiruvalla: Christava Sahitya Samithy, 2002.

Brown, L.W. *The Indian Christians of St. Thomas.* Cambridge: Cambridge University Press, 1956.

Buchanan, Claudius. *Christian Researches in Asia; With Notes of the Translation of the Scripture.* London/Liverpool: Ward & Co, Paterson Row, Edward Howell Co, 1849.

Abraham, C.E. ed. *The Mar Thoma Syrian Church, the Church of North India, the Church of South India.* Tiruvalla: Theological Commission of the Mar Thoma Church, 1967.

Chacko, T.C. *The Concise History of the Mar Thoma Church.* Malayalam. 5th edition. Tiruvalla: Episcopal Jubilee Institute, 2001.

Chandran, J. Russell. *Joint Council of the Church of North India, The Church of South India and the Malankara Mar Thoma Syrian Church: A Brief account of the History and Meaning of its Formation.* New Delhi: ISPCK, 1984.

Charithra Nikshepam 1919–1995. Malayalam: (History of the Shree Jana Suvishesha Sevika Shgam). Tiruvalla: MTSSS, 1995.

Cherian, P. *Malabar Syrians and Church Mission Society 1816–1840.* Kottayam: Church Missionary Press, 1935.

Conciliar Fellowship – Mar Thoma Sabhayude Veekshanam. Malayalam. Kottayam: St. Augustine Study Centre, 1979.

Constitution of the Mar Thoma Development Department. Tiruvalla: Mar Thoma Church, 2010.

Constitution of the Mar Thoma Syrian Church of Malabar. English Version. Tiruvalla: Mar Thoma Press, 2002.

Daniel, K.N. *The South Indian Apostolate of St. Thomas.* Bangalore: CHAI, 1961.

Daniel, K.N. *Malankara Sabhayum Naveekaranavum.* Malayalam Version. Vol. I. Tiruvalla: 1949.

Dr. Juhanon Mar Thoma Jeevitavum Sandeshavum. Malayalaam. Tiruvalla: Mar Thoma Church Publication, 1977.

Evanston Speaks. Reports from the Second Assembly of the World Council of Churches, August 15–31, 1954. Madras: CLS, 1955.

Farquhar, J.N. *The Apostle Thomas in North India.* Manchester: University Press, 1926.

Fay, Harold E. *The Ecumenical Advance: A History of the Ecumenical Movement 1948–1968.* Geneva: WCC publication, 1978.

Fenwick, John. R.K. *The Malabar Independent Syrian Church.* Nottingham: Grove Books, 1992.

Firth, C.B. *An Introduction to Indian Church History.* Madras: CLS, 1961.

George, K.M. *Church of South India – Life in Union, 1947–1997.* New Delhi: CSS & ISPCK, 1999.

Gill, David, ed, *Gathered for Life: Official Report of VI Assembly of World Council of Churches,* 24 July – 10 August 1983, Vancouver, Canada. Geneva: World Council of Churches Publication, 1983.

Gladstone, J.W. *Keralathile Protestant Chritumathavum Bahujanaprastanagalum.* Malayalaam Version. Trivandrum: C.D – Siddi Publications, 2004.

Goodall, Norman. ed. *The New Delhi Report, the Third Assembly of the World Council of Churches 1961.* New York: Association Press, 1962.

Goodall, Norman, ed. *The Uppsala Report 1968: Official Report of the Fourth Assembly of the World Council of Churches.* Geneva: WCC Publication, 1968.

Hogg, William Richey. *Ecumenical Foundations.* New York: Harper and Brothers Publishers, 1952.

Hooft, Visser't W.A. ed. *Report of the Amsterdam Assembly of WCC.* Geneva: WCC Publication, 1948.

———. ed. *The New Delhi Report.* New York: Association Press, 1962.

———. *The Genesis and Formation of World Council of Churches.* Geneva: WCC, 1982.

Joseph, M.J. *Vishala Ecumenism.* Malayalam. Tiruvalla: Theological Literature Council, 1998.

———. ed. *Church Unity: Response of the Mar Thoma Church.* Manganam: St. Augustine Study Centre, 1981.

———. ed. *Conciliar Fellowship.* Manganam: St. Augustine study Centre, 1979.

———. *Ormakalude Theruveedhiyil.* Malayalam. Tiruvalla: CSS, 2010.

K.T. Joy. *The Mar Thoma Church: A Study of its Growth and Contribution.* Kottayam: Good Shepherd Press, 1986.

Keay, F.E. *A History of the Syrian Church in India.* Delhi: ISPCK, 1960.

Kinnamon, Michael and Brian E. Cope (ed.): *The Ecumenical Movement: An Anthology of Key Texts and Voices.* Geneva: WCC Publication, Geneva 1997.

Kinnamon, Michael ed. *Signs of the Sprit: Official Report Seventh Assembly, Canberra, Australia, 7–20 February, 1991.* Geneva: WCC Publication/Wm. Eerdmans, Grand Rapids, 1991.

Koodapuzha, Xavier. *Christianity in India.* Vadavathoor: OIRS, 1998.

Koshy, Ninan. *A History of the Ecumenical Movement in Asia.* Vol. 1, China: World Student Christian Federation, Asia and Pacific Alliance of YMCA and Christian Conference of Asia, 2004.

Kunjanpillai, Elamkulam. *Chila Kerala Charithra Prasanagal.* Malayalam. Kottayam: NBS Press, 1963.

Kuriakose, M.K. ed. History of Christianity in India Source Materials. Madras: CLS, 1982.

Kuruvilla, K.K. *A History of the Mar Thoma Church and its Doctrines.* Madras: CLS, 1951.

Lienemann-Perrin, Christine. *Die politische Verantwortung der Kirche in Südkorea und Südafrika.* München: Chr.Kaiser, 1992.

Mar Thoma Sleehaude Edavakayakunna Malankara Suriyani Sabhayude Canon, 2nd Edition. (New Delhi: Dharma Jyothi Vidhya Peedh, 2008).

Malankara Sabhayile Episcopaciyum Mar Thoma Sabhayile Stanabhisheka Shusrooshakalum. Malayalam. Tiruvalla: Mar Thoma Syrian Church, 1975.

Mar Thoma Sabha Directory. Tiruvalla: Publication Board of the Mar Thoma Syrian Church, 1999.

Mar Thoma Schoolukal. Malayalam. Tiruvalla: M.T & E.A Schools Corporate Management, 1974.

Mar Thoma Syrian Church Liturgy. 6th Edition. Tiruvalla: Mar Thoma Church Publication, 2004.

Mar Thoma, Alexander. *The Mar Thoma Church: Heritage and Mission.* Tiruvalla: National Press, 1991.

Mar Thoma, Alexander. *Daivakrupayude Thanalial.* (Malayalam). Tiruvalla: Mar Thoma Press, 1997.

Mar Thoma, Juhanon. *Christianity in India and a Brief History of the Mar Thoma Church.* Madras: K.M. Cherian, 1954.

―――. *Malankara Sabhayile Episcopaciyum Mar Thoma Sabhayile Stanabhisheka Shushrooshakalum.* Malayalam. Tiruvalla: T.A.M. Press, 1975.

―――. *Ormakalum Kurippukalum.* Malayalam. Tiruvalla: CLS, 1972.

Mathew, C.P. and M.M. Thomas. *The Indian Churches of Saint Thomas.* Delhi: ISPCK, 1967.

Mathew, C.P. and M.M. Thomas. *Indian Churches of St. Thomas.* Second Edition. New Delhi: ISPCK, 2005.

Mathew, N.M. *Malankara Mar Thoma Sabha Charithram.* Malayalam. Vols I. II. III. Tiruvalla: Mar Thoma Episcopal Jubilee Institute of Evangelism, 2003.

Mathew, N.M. *Malankara Sabaha Charithram.* Malayalam. Tiruvalla: Mar Thoma Episcopal Jubilee Institute, 2007.

McCrindle, J.W. ed. *Christian Topography of Cosmos: An Egyptian Monk,* Book III. Cambridge: Cambridge University Press, 1897.

Medlycott, A.E. *India and the Apostle Thomas: An Enquiry with a Critical Analysis of the Acta Thomae.* London: Ballantyne Press, 1905.

Menacherry, George. ed. *Indian Church History Classics. The Nazranis.* Trissur: SARAS, 1998.

Menon, Sreedhara, A. *A Survey of Kerala History.* Madras: S. Viswanathan Printers and Publishers, 1988.

Metropolitan Navathy Memoirs. Tiruvalla: Mar Thoma Syrian Church, 2008.

Milne Rae, George. *The Syrian Church in India.* Edinburgh: William Blackwood and Sons, 1896.

Mingana, Alfonso. *The Early Spread of Christianity in India.* Manchester: Bull of John Rylands Libraray, 1926.

Mundadan, A.M. *History of Christianity in India, From the Beginning up to the Middle of the Sixteenth Century.* Vol. I. Bangalore: Church History Association of India, 1989.

————. *Indian Christians Search for Identity and Struggle for Autonomy.* Bangalore: Dharamaram, 1982.

Padmanabha Menon, K.P. *History of Kerala.* Cochin: Cochin Government Press, 1924.

Panjikkaran, J.C. *The Syrian Church in Malabar.* Trichnopoly: St. Joseph's Industrial School Press, 1914.

Paton, David M., ed. *Breaking Barriers: Official Report of the Fifth Assembly of the World Council of Churches,* Nairobi, 23 November – 10 December 1975. London: SPCK and Grand Rapids, Wm B. Eerdman in collaboration with WCC, 1976.

Your Kingdom Come; Mission Perspectives, Report on the World Conference on Mission and Evangelism, Melbourne, Australia, 12–25 May 1980. Geneva: World Council of Churches, 1980.

Philip, T.V. *Edinburgh To Salvador Twentieth Century Ecumenical Missiology.* New Delhi: CSS & ISPCK, 1999.

Philip, T.V. *East of the Euphrates: Early Christianity in Asia.* New Delhi: ISPCK, 1998.

Proceedings of the Church Missionary society for 1818–1819. London: CMS College, 1819.

Church Unity Response of the Mar Thoma Church. Manganam: St. Augustine Study Centre, 1981.

Raiser, Konrad. *To Be The Church.* Geneva: WCC Publication, 1997.

————. *Ecumenism in Transition, A Paradigm Shift in the Ecumenical Movement.* Geneva: WCC Publication, 1989.

Ray, G. Milne. *The Syrian Church in India.* Edinburgh: William Blackwood and Sons, 1892.

Robert. C.P. ed. *KVK Pathanamthitta: Retrospect.* Tiruvalla: *CARD-Krishi Vigjan Kendra.* 2011.

The Joint Council of the Church of South India, the Church of North India and the Mar Thoma Syrian Church of Malabar. Mumbai: Joint Council of the CSI-C.N.I.-M.T.C, 1999.

The Lambeth Conference 1958, The Encyclical Letter from Bishops together with Resolutions and Reports. Part 2. London: SPCK, 1958.

The Malabar Mar Thoma Syrian Christian Evangelistic Association Memorandum and Articles of Association: as amended in 1106 Malayalam Era. Reprint. Tiruvalla: TAM Press, 1960.

The New Delhi Report: The Third Assembly of the World Council of Churches, 1961. London: SCM Press LTD, 1962.

Thomas, M.A. *Ormakaliloode.* Malalyalam. Tiruvalla: CLS, 1984.

————. *Orupothunamam Avasyam Illa*. Malayalam. Kottayam: Papathinkal Press, 1983.

Thomas, M.A. *Towards Wider Ecumenism*. Bangalore: Asian Trading Corporation, 1993.

Mar Thoma Sabha Saradhikal. Malayalam. Tiruvalla: Mar Thoma Church Publication, 1993.

Thomas, M.M. *My Ecumenical Journey*. Trivandrum: Ecumenical Publishing Centre, 1990.

————. *The Secular Ideologies in India and the Secular Meaning of Christ*. Madras: CLS, 1976.

————. *Towards a Theology of Contemporary Ecumenism- A Collection* of *Ecumenical gathering (1947–1975)*. Madras: CLS, 1978.

Episcopal Silver Jubilee Smarakopaharam. Malayalam Tiruvalla: Mar Thoma Sabha Council, 1978.

Tomkins, Oliver S. ed. *The Third World Conference on Faith and Order, Lund, 1952*. London: SCM, 1953.

Vadakkan Thiruvitamkur Suvishesham. Malayalam. Tiruvalla: History Publication Committee, 1950.

Varghese Zac and Mathew A. Kallumpram. *Glimpses of Mar Thoma Church History*. New Delhi: Kalpana Printing House, 2003.

Varghese, Paul. and M. Thommen. ed. *Orthodox – Mar Thoma Conversations: Some Papers and Statements from the Period 1968–70*. Kottayam: 1971.

World Council of Churches. Minutes of the Commission on Faith and Order, New Haven, 1957, Faith and Order Paper No. 25. Geneva: WCC, 1957.

Young, William G. ed. *Handbook for Source Materials for Students of Church History*. Madras: CLS, 1969.

Zaleski. *The Apostle St. Thomas in South India*. Mangalore, 1912.

B. Reports/ Minutes

Bonn Agreement. Details of Acceptance of the Bonn Agreement by Churches of the Anglican Communion. In: WEF/File 8. Lambeth Palace: Archive of the Lambeth Palace, 27th August 1971.

Mannanam Malayalam 3/MS Mill 192. Papers of W.H Mill. Oxford: Bodleian Library, 47.

Report of the Meeting of the Commission of the Anglican Communion and the Old Catholic Churches held at Bonn on Thursday, July 2, 1931. London: 1931/32.

Report of the Commissioner for scheduled castes and scheduled Tribes for the second period ending 31ˢᵗ December, 1951. Government of India, India: 1951–52.

Mar Thoma Syrian Church, General Assembly. Minutes of the Mar Thomas Syrian Church's General Assembly. Tiruvalla: 1961.

Mar Thoma Syrian Church Samudayalochana sabha. Resolution of the Mar Thoma Syrian Samudayalochana sabha, May 5, 6, 1936. Tiruvalla: 1936.

Basel Mission, India. Report of the Basel Mission in South Western India, 1912.

Central Committee of the World Council of Churches. Minutes and Reports of the Twenty fourth Meeting, Addis Ababa, January 1971. Geneva: 1971.

Christian Agency for Rural Development. Tiruvalla, India. Annual Report of the CARD. For the Years: 1980–2012.

Christians Agency for Rural Development. Sovenir. Tiruvalla: 1986.

Church of Indian Burma and Ceylon, Calcutta, India. Resolution 4, Episcopal Synod of the Church of India, Burma, and Ceylon, 1933.

Communion of Churches in India Office, Tiruvalla, India, Minutes of the Executive Committee meetings of the CSI-CNI- Mar Thoma Joint Council. For the years: 1977–2000.

Communion of Churches in India Office, Tiruvalla, India, Minutes of the Executive Committee Meetings of the Communion of Churches in India. For the years: 2000–2008.

Communion of Churches in India. Tiruvalla. Minutes of the Second Meeting of the Joint Theological Commission of the CSI-CNI.-Mar Thoma Joint Council at United Theological Collage, Bangalore, 3, 4 June, 1975. Bangalore: 1975.

Mar Thoma Syrian Church. Judgment of the Royal Court of Malabar, Seminary Case. Archives, Mar Thoma Theological Seminary Archive. Kottayam: 1889.

Kalpana of the Titus II to T.N. Koshy, the first vicar of the Malaya – Singapore, dated 1936.

Letter of Abraham Mar Thoma to Mr. K.A. Mathew, 60 Finborough Road, London, SW10, 11ᵗʰ August 1947.

Mar Koorilose, Alathur Joseph. Will to Joseph Mar Athanasius dated 1883. Malabar Independent Syrian Church. Thozhiyoor.

Mar Thoma, Juhanon and Mathews Mar Athanasius. A Call to the Churches of Christ in India. Tiruvalla dated 21ˢᵗ December 1952.

Mar Thoma Church Office, Tiruvalla, Annual Report of the Mar Thoma Church. For the years: 1945–2010.

Mar Thoma Church Office, Tiruvalla. Report of the Annual General Body of the Mar Thoma Church, on May 16, 17. Tiruvalla: 1961.

Mar Thoma Church Office, Tiruvalla. *Alexander Mar Thoma Metropolitan's Circular Letter to all Parishes, Circular No. 339*, dated 1st January 1992. Tiruvalla: 1992.

Mar Thoma Church Office. Tiruvalla. *Juhanon Mar Thoma Metropolitan's Letter to Mrs. Indira Gandhi*, dated 28/5/1976. Tiruvalla: 1976.

Mar Thoma Church Office. Tiruvalla. *Metropolitan's Circular No. 152*, dated 6 October 1983, in the Mar Thoma Church. Tiruvalla: 1983.

Mar Thoma Church Office. Tiruvalla. *Minutes of the Ecological Commission of the Mar Thoma Church*, dated 18th February 2008. Tiruvalla: 2008.

Mar Thoma Church Office. *Circular Letter of Alexander Mar Thoma Metropolitan, Circular No. 428*, 9 June 1995. Tiruvalla: 1995.

Mar Thoma Church Office. *Minutes of the Meetings of the Sabha Council* held on 27th August 1976. Tiruvalla: 1976.

Mar Thoma Church Office. Tiruvalla, India. Mar Thoma Church, *Annual Report of the Church Council of the Mar Thoma Church*. For the years: 1945–2010.

Mar Thoma Church Office. Tiruvalla, India. *O.S No. 439, of M.E 1054 (1879)*, Alapuzha civil court, Kerala, in the Mar Thoma Syrian Church Archives, Tiruvalla: 1879.

Mar Thoma Church Office. Tiruvalla, India. *Report of the Metropolitan's Committee*, July 15, 1953. Tiruvalla: 1953.

Mar Thoma Evangelistic Association, Tiruvalla, India. *23rd Annual Report of the Mar Thoma Evangelistic Association*, 1911.

Mar Thoma Evangelistic Association, Tiruvalla, India. *Annual Reports of the Mar Thoma Evangelistic Association*. 1948.

Mar Thoma Evangelistic Association, Tiruvalla, India. *Annual Report of the Mar Thoma Evangelistic Association*, 1937.

Mar Thoma Evangelistic Association, Tiruvalla, India. *Circular letter of the General Secretary of the MTEA to all parishes*. April 17, 2011.

Mar Thoma Evangelistic Association, Tiruvalla, India. *Letter of Thomas Walker to Mrs. Walker*, dated 15th February 1900. Tiruvalla: 1900.

Mar Thoma Evangelistic Association, Tiruvalla, India. *Report of the third meeting of the MTEA*, M.E. Dhanu 27, 1064, February 7, 1889. Tiruvalla: 1889.

Mar Thoma Evangelistic Association, Tiruvalla, India. *17th Annual Report of the MTEA*. M.E.1083 (1906). Tiruvalla: 1906.

Mar Thoma Syrian Church of Malabar, Tiruvalla, India. *Resolution of the Mar Thoma Syrian Samudayalochana sabha*, 1936. Tiruvalla: 1936.

Mar Thoma Syrian Church of Malabar, Circular of Mar Thoma, Juhanon. Mathews Mar Athanasius, *A Call to the Churches of Christ in India*. Tiruvalla: 1952.

Mar Thoma Syrian Church of Malabar, Tiruvalla. *Annual Report of the Juhanon Mar Thoma, Metropolitan.* Tiruvalla: 1948. Tiruvalla: 1948.

Mar Thoma Syrian Church of Malabar, Tiruvalla. Minutes of the Mar Thoma Syrian Church's General Assembly. Tirvalla: 1971. Tiruvalla: 1971.

Mar Thoma Syrian Church. *Minutes of the CSI-Mar Thoma Union Negotiations Commission,* Held at Zion Hill Aramana, Kottayam on 17th May 1974. Kottayam: 1974.

Mar Thoma Syrian Church. *Report of the Inter Church Relations Committee,* 1958. Kottayam: 1958.

Mar Thoma Syrian Church. *Minutes of the First Meeting of the Joint Theological Commission of the CSI-CNI MTC,* held at the Community Service Centre, Kilpauk, Madras on 16th January 1975. Madras: 1975.

Mar Thoma Syrian Church. *Minutes of the Second Meeting of the Joint Theological Commission of the CSI-CNI-MTC,* held at Ranson Hall of the United Theological College, Bangalore on 3rd and 4th June 1975. Bangalore: 1975.

Mar Thoma Syrian Church. Report of the Mar Thoma Theological Commission, February 27, 1973. Kottayam: 1973.

Mar Thoma Syrian Church. *Reply Letter of the CSI Moderator to the Mar Thoma Church Secretary,* dated 31/8/196. Tiruvalla: 1961.

Mar Thoma Syrian Church. *Letter of the Moderator (Reply) to the President of the Mar Thoma Theological Commission* dated 2/12/1967. Tiruvalla: 1967.

Mar Thoma Syrian Church. *Letter of the President of the Mar Thoma Theological Commission to the Moderator of the Church of South India,* dated 27/11/196. Kottayam: 1967.

Mar Thoma Syrian Church. *Minutes of the CSI – Mar Thoma Union Negotiations Commission,* Held at Zion Hill Aramana, Kottayam on 17th May 1974. Kottayam: 1974.

Mar Thoma Syrian Church. *The Report of the Joint Meetings of the Executive Committees of the C.N.I. – CSI & M.T.C* held at Charal Kunnu, *Kerala,* 11th–14th November 1999. Charal Mount: 1999.

North America- Europe Diocese of the Mar Thoma Church. Sinai Centre. *Mission Report of the Mar Thoma Church, Diocese of the North America –Europe Diocese,* 2011. New York: 2011.

Pullach Report. The Report of the Conversations 1970–72 authorized by the Lambeth Conference and the Lutheran World Federation. London: 1973.

Special Collections, Bishop College, Calcutta, India. *The People of Dohnavur to the Home Secretary, CMS,* Touring the Tinnavely Diocese, 1 Februavary 1947, Tinnavely Box, 1.

The Malabar Mar Thoma Syrian Christians Evangelistic Association: Memorandum and Articles of Association, as Amended in 1106 M.E (1931CE).

C. Periodicals and Journals

"Christian Agency for Rural Development. Tiruvalla," In: *Christian Agency for Rural Development, A Hand Book.* (Strictly for the Official Use of the CARD). Office of the Development Department, and CARD. (Tiruvalla: 1984): 1–52.

"CSI- CNI- Mar Thoma Joint Council Meeting at Nagpur." In: *Malankara Sabha Tharaka* (Aug/1978): 28–32.

"Kerala Christian Conference," (Malayalam) In: *Malankara Sabha Tharaka,* (Sept/Oct, 1940): 233–239.

"Letter of Juhanon Mar Thimotheos," In: *Malankara Sabha Tharaka*, (December, 1947): 178.

"Sihorayile Vela," (Malayalam) In: *Malankara Sabha Tharaka.* (February/1953): 31–32.

Abraham Mar Thoma, "Metropolitan's Letter." In: *Malankara Sabha Tharaka.* All issues from *1945–1975.*

Athayal, Jesudas M. "Metropolitan's Message in the 21st Century." In: *Darsan* (March, 2007): 7–8.

Circular is No. 342. In: *Malankara Sabha Tharaka.* (July/August, 1944): 4–6.

Daniel, Joseph. "Alexander Mar Thoma: Malankara Mar Thoma Suriyani Sabhayude Adhyadmika Saundaryam." (Malayalam) In: *Malankara Sabha Tharaka* (April, 2013): 11–14.

Farquhar, J.N. "The Apostle Thomas in South India." Vol. II. In: *The Bulletin of the John Ryland's Library* (January, 1927).

Goodall, Norman, "WCC and IMC relationship Issues" In: *Ecumenical Review.* IIX, (1959).

Hoekendijk, J.C. "The Church in Missionary Thinking." In: *International Review of Mission*, XLI, (1952): 332–335.

Joseph Mar Thoma, "Metropolitan's Letter." In: *Malankara Sabha Tharaka* All issues from 2000–2010.

Lienemann-Perrin, Christine: "Theological Stimuli from the Migrant Churches." In: *Ecumenical Review*, 61(2009): 381–386.

Mar Themotheos, Juhanon, "Mar Thoma Sabhayum Athinte Prathyekathayum," (Malayalam) In: *Malankara Sabha Tharaka* Vol. 4, (Febrary, 1928): 115–129.

Mar Thoma, Alexander, "Metropolitan's Letter" *Malankara Sabha Tharaka.* All issues from *1976–2000.*

Philipose Mar Chrysostom, "Metropolitan's Letter." In: *Malankara Sabha Tharaka* All issues from *2000–2008.*

Thomas, M.M. "My Pilgrimage in Mission." In: *N.C.C Review,* Vol. CIX, (October, 1989).

Thomas, M.M. "My Pilgrimage in Mission." In: *International Bulletin of Missionary Research.* 13, No. 1 (January, 1989).

Varghese, Ninan, "Mar Thoma Medical Mission," In: *Malankara Sabha Tharaka.* (February, 2003): 21–22.

Vischer, Lukas, "A Genuinely Universal Council...?," In: *The Ecumenical Review,* 22. (1970): 97–106.

D. Interviews

Interview with Chunakara, George Mathews. Director of the International Affairs, World Council of Churches, March 26, 2013.

Interview with Joseph, M.J. Director, the Ecological Commission of the Mar Thoma Church, Kottayam, March 4, 2013.

Interview with Mar Barnabas, Joseph. Episcopa, Malankara Mar Thoma Syrian Church, Zurich, May 25, 2012.

Interview with Mar Chrysostom Mar Thoma Metropolitan, Philipose. Valia Metropolitan, Malankara Mar Thoma Syrian Church, Maramon, July 18, 2012.

Interview with Mar Koorilose Metropolitan, Joseph. Malabar Independent Syrian Church. Thozhoyoor. Thozhiyoor, August 22, 2011.

Interview with Mar Thoma Metropolitan, Joseph. Sinai Mar Thoma Church, London, March 18, 2013.

Interview with Mathew T.M. Mar Thoma Syrian Church, Singapore, Former Zonal Secretary of the Mar Thoma Churches in Malaysia and Singapore, Singapore, November 12, 2011.

Interview with Mar Theophilus, Zacharias. Central Executive Committee Member of WCC 1998–2006, Chenganoor, February 18, 2012.

E. Unpublished Materials

Donald Fossett Ebright, "The National Missionary Society of India, 1905–1942: An Expression of the Movement toward Indigenization within the Indian

Christian Community" (Ph. D Dissertation. University of Chicago, Chicago, IL: 1944).

Sabu George, "A Study of the Social Involvement of the Mar Thoma Church of Malabar from 1930–1980" (Unpublished B.D. Thesis, M.T.T. Seminary, Kottayam, 1982).

J.W. Gladstone, "Protestant Christianity and People's Movement in Kerala" (Ph.D Dissertation, Department of Theology, University of Hamburg, 1983).

Thaliath Jonas, "The Synod of Diamper" (Doctoral Dissertation, OCA152. Pontifical Gregorian University, Rome: 1958).

Johnson, Arthur P.: A Study of the Theology of Evangelism in the International Missionary Council, 1921–1961. (mimeographed thesis. WCC Library, Geneva: 1969).

Daniel, Joseph, "Socio- Religous Impact of the Temple Entry Proclamation on the Christian Community in Travancore" (Unpublished B.D. Thesis, Mar Thoma Theological Seminary, Kottayam: 1998).

Kuzhinjalil, Joseph, "The Disciplinary Legislation of Synod of Diamper" (Ph.D Dissertation, Faculty of Canon Law, Oriental Institute, Rome: 1975).

"Liturgy of the Mar Thoma Episcopal Consecration, *Amalogia*" (Unpublished Handwritten Copy. Poolatheen, Tiruvalla).

Thomas, Sabu, "The Mar Thoma Church Ashram Movement: A Missiologial Evaluation With Special Reference To Christa Mitra Ashram Ankola" (Unpublished B.D. Thesis, United Theological College Bangalore, 1997).

Thomas, Alex, "A Historical Study of the North Kanara Mission of the Mar Thoma Church 1910–2000" (Unpublished D. Th Thesis, Boston University, School of Theology, 2003).

II. Secondary Sources

A. Books

A Collection of Papers Connected with the Movement of the National Church of India Madras. Madras: Cosmopolitan Press, 1893.

A Documentary History of the Faith and Order Movement: 1927–1963. St. Louis, Bethany Press, 1963.

Abraham, K.C. ed. *Christian Witness in Society.* Bangalore: Board of Theological Education –Senate of Serampore College, 1998.

Ananthamurthy, U.R. *Would the East and West Meet?* Bangalore: Ecumenical Christian Centre, 1999.

Anderson, Wilhelm. *Towards a Theology of Mission.* London: SCM Press, 1955.

Apostolic Fathers, II/2. Cambridge: Harvard University Press, 2003.

Avis, Paul. ed. *The Christian Church: An Introduction to the Major Traditions.* London: SPCK, 2002.

Azariah, V.S. *India and the Christian Movement.* Madras: The Christian Literature Society of India, 1936.

Baago, Kaggo. *A History of the National Christian Council of India, 1914–1964.* Nagpur: NCCI, 1965.

———. *Pioneers of Indigenous Christianity.* Madras: Christian Literature society, 1969.

Bangkok Assembly 1973. Minutes and Report of the assembly of Commissions on World Mission and Evangelism. Geneva: WCC Publication, 1973.

Bell, G.K.A. *Documents on Christian Unity, Third Series 1930–1948.* London: Oxford University Press, 1948.

Bent, Ans van der. *Commitment to God's World – A Concise Critical Survey of Ecumenical Social Thought.* Geneva: WCC Publication, 1995.

Bonhoeffer, Dietrich *Prisoner of God.* New York: Harper and Row, 1954.

Bosch, David J. *Transforming Missions, Paradigm Shifts in Theology of Missions.* New York: Orbis Books, 1992.

Boyd, R.H.S. *An Introduction to Indian Christian Theology.* Madras: CLS, 1969.

Briggs, John, Mercy Amba Oduyoye and Georges Tsetsis. ed. *A History of the Ecumenical Movement 1968–2000.* Vol. 3. Geneva: WCC, 2000.

Chand, Tara. *History of the Freedom Movement in India.* Vol. II. New Delhi: Publication Division: Ministry of Information and Broadcasting, 1967.

Chunakara, Mathews George, ed. *Globalization and its Impact on Human Rights.* Hong Kong: CCA & CSS, 2000.

———. *Globalization of Geo Strategic Politics and Emerging Trends in Asia.* Bangalore: Ecumenical Christian Centre, 2005.

Christine Lienemann- Perrin, Wolfgang Lienemann. ed. *Crossing Religious Borders Studies on Conversion and Religious Belonging.* Wiesbaden: Herrassowitz, 2012.

Coleman, Roger ed. *Resolutions of the Twelve Lambeth Conferences, 1867–1988.* Toronto: Anglican Book Centre, 1992.

Constitution of the Malankara Independent Syrian Church. Thozhiyoor: MISC, 1948.

Daniel, Joseph. *One Family Under Heaven: Response to Paradigm Shifts in Ecumenism.* New Delhi: ISPCK, 2008.

Daniel, Mathew. *Mar Thoma Sabha Saradhikal*. Malayalam. Tiruvalla: Mar Thoma Church Publication, 1993.

Das, Soman. *Christian Faith and Multi Form culture in India*. Bangalore: UTC, 1987.

Daughrity, Dyron B. *Bishop Stephen Neill: From Edinburgh to South India*. New York: Peter and Lang, 2008.

Davis, Noel and Martin Convoy. *World Christianity in the 20ᵗʰ Century*. London: SCM Press, 2008.

Dayton, Donald W. *The Higher Christian Life: A Bibliographical Over View*. New York: Garland Publishing, 1985.

Dietrich, Gabriele and Bas Wielenga. *Towards Understanding Indian Society*. Madurai: Centre for Social Analysis Tamil Nadu Theological Seminary, 1997.

Dietrich, Gabriele. *The Impact of New Economic Policy on Women in India and Feminist Alternatives*. Bangalore: Ecumenical Christian Centre, 1997.

Ecumenical Collaboration at the Regional, National and Local Levels. Vatican: Secretariat for Promoting Christian Unity, 1980.

Eddy, Sherwood. *Pathfinders of the World Missionary Crusade*. New York: Books for Libraries and Press, 1945.

Edith L. Blumhofer and Randall Balmer, eds., *Modern Christian Revivals*. Urbana and Chicago: University of Illinois Press, 1993.

Engineer, Asgharali. ed. *Communal Riots in the Post Independence India*. 2ⁿᵈ Edition. Bombay: Sangam Books, 1997.

Erickson, John H. *The Challenge of Our Past, Studies in Orthodox Canon Law and Church History*. New York: St. Vladimir's Seminary Press, 1991.

Faith and Order, Louvain, 1971, Study Reports and Documents, Faith and Order Paper No. 59. Geneva: World Council of Churches, 1971.

Falconer, Alan D. ed., *Understanding Human Rights: An Interdisciplinary and Inter Faith Study*. Dublin: Irish School of Ecumenics, 1980.

Fay, Harold E. ed. *A History of the Ecumenical Movement 1948–1968*. WCC, Geneva 2004.

Fenwick, John R.K. *The Forgotten Bishops*. New Jersey: Georgia's Press, 2009.

Fernando, Leonard S.J. *Christian Faith meets other Faiths- Origin's Contra Celsum and its relevance to Indian Theology*. New Delhi: ISPCK, 1998.

Frieling, Reinhard. *Amt – Laie – Pfarrer – Priester – Bishof – Papst*. Goettingen: Vandenhoeck and Ruprecht, 2002.

Gassmann, Gunther ed. *Documentary History of the Faith and Order 1963–1993, Faith and Order paper No. 159*. Geneva: WCC Publication, 1993.

George, K.K. George Zacharia and Ajith Kumar. *'Grants-in-Aid' Policies and Practices Towards Secondary Education in Kerala.* New Delhi: National Institute of Educational Planning and Administration, 2002.

Government of India, Constituent Assembly Debates. Vol. IX. New Delhi: Lok Sabha Secretariat, 1949.

Hooft, W.A. Visser't. ed., The *New Delhi Report, the Third Assembly of the World Council of Churches 1961.* New York: Association Press, 1962.

Hough, James. *The History of Christianity in India,* Vol. II. London: R.B. Seeley and W. Burnside, 1839.

Hough, James. *The History of Christianity in India From Commencement of the Christian Era* Vol. I. London/Madras: R.B. Seeley and W. Burnside, 1839.

Iyer, Krishna. *Human Rights- Their Spiritual Dimension.* Bangalore: Ecumenical Christian Centre, 1996.

Jacob, George. *Religious Life of the Ilavas of Kerala.* New Delhi: ISPCK, 1995.

Jain, L.C. *Eco Spirituality for Communal Harmony.* Bangalore: Ecumenical Christian Centre, 2003.

Johnson, E.H. *The Highest Life: A Story of Shortcomings and a Goal.* New York: A.C. Armstrong and Son, 1901.

Joseph Mar Koorilose Valiya Metropolitan Silver Jubilee Festschrift 2011. Thozhiyoor: Episcopal Silver Jubilee Festschrift, 2011.

Joseph M.J. ed. *Church unity: Response of the Mar Thoma Church.* Manganam: St. Augustine's Study Centre, 1979.

———. *The Eco Vision of the Earth Community.* Bangalore: BTESSC/SATHRI, 2008.

Joshy, Barbara R. ed., *Untouchable! Voice of the Dalit Liberation Movement.* New Delhi, 1986.

Kaeley, S.L., V.K. Bhandari and et al. *Indian History and Culture.* New Delhi, Inter University Press, 1986.

Keshishian, Aram. *Conciliar Fellowship: A Common Goal.* Geneva: World Council of Churches, 1992.

Kohli, Atul. ed. *The Success of Indian Democracy.* New York: Cambridge University Press, 2001.

Koodapuzha, Xavier. *Christianity in India.* Vadavathoor: OIRS, 1998.

Kopf, David. *British Orientalism and the Bengal Renaissance, The Dynamics of Indian Modernization 1773–1835.* Los Angles: Berkeley, 1969.

Koshy, Ninan. *Caste in the Kerala churches.* Bangalore: The Christian Institute for the Study of Religion and Society, 1968.

319

————. *A History of the Ecumenical Movement in Asia.* Vol. I. Hong Kong: WSCF, YMCA and CCA, 2004.

Kuhn, Thomas S. *The Structures of Scientific Revolution.* Chicago: University of Chicago Press, 1970.

Christian Lange, Karl Pinggera, eds. *Die altOrientalischen Kirche-Glaube und Geschichte.* New York: Cambridge University Press (WBG), 2002.

Lienemann- Perrin, Christine and Wolfgang Lienemann. ed. *Crossing Religious Borders Studies on Conversion and Religious Belonging.* Wiesbaden: Herrassowitz, 2012.

Limourus, Gennadios. ed., *Justice, Peace and Integrity of Creation –Insights from Orthodoxy.* Geneva: WCC Publication, 1990.

Livingston, James C. *Modern Christian Thought.* New York: Macmillan Publishers, 1971.

Mackenzie, G.T. *Christianity in Travancore.* Trivandrum: Travancore Government Press, 1901.

Majumdar, R.C. *An Advanced history of India.* Reprinted. London: Macmillan and Company Limited, 1953.

Mansfied, Nick. *Subjectivity: Theories of the Self from Freud to Harvey.* New York: New York University Press, 2000.

Massey, James. *Roots- Concise History of Dalits.* New Delhi: ISPCK, 2001.

Mar Thoma Sabha Saradhikal (Malayalam). Tiruvalla: Mar Thoma Syrian Church Publication, 1993.

Mathew, K.M. *Ettamathe Mothiram.* Malayalam. Kottayam: Malayala Manorama, 2008.

Mathews, Z.K. ed. *Responsible Government in a Revolutionary Age,* Church and Society. SCM, London 1966.

Meshack, Samuel. *Building God's Kingdom on Earth.* Channai: Gurukul Publication, 1999.

Moffett, S.H. *A History of Christianity in Asia,* Vol. I. San Francisco: Harper and Row, 1992.

Neill, Stephen. *Creative Tension* (Duff Lectures). Edinburgh: Edinburgh Press, 1959.

Oldham, J.H. ed. "Report of the Conference on Church Community and State at Oxford 1937." In: *Foundations of Ecumenical Social Thought.* Philadelphia: Fortress Press, 1966.

Pathil, Kuncheria. ed. *Mission in India Today.* Bangalore: Dharmaram Publications, 1988.

Paul, Babu. *Festival of life in the Global Village.* Bangalore: Ecumenical Christian Centre, 2001.

Paul, Rajaiah D. *Ecumenism in Action: A Historical Survey of the Church of South India.* Madras: CLS, 1972.

Paulos, Mar Paulos. *Encounter in Humanisation.* Tiruvalla: CSS, 2000.

Peter Moore ed. *Bishops But What Kind?.* London: SPCK, 1982.

Peter Gemeinhardt und Uwe Keuhneweg, ed. *Patristica Et Oceumenica.* Marburg: N.G. Elwert Verland, 2004.

Perumalil, H.C. and E.R. Hambye eds. *Christianity in India: A History in Ecumenical Perspective.* Alleppey: Prakashan Publications, 1972.

Philip, T.V. *Edinburgh to Salvador. Twentieth Century Ecumenical Missiology. A Historical Study of the Ecumenical Discussions on Mission.* New Delhi: CSS & ISPCK, 1999.

Podipara, Placid J. The *Thomas Christians.* Bombay: St. Paul Publication, 1970.

Premsagar, Victor. *Evangelism Dei: Mission.* Bangalore: Ecumenical Christian Centre, 2000.

Price Charles and Ian Randall. *Transforming Keswick.* U.K: OM Publishing, 2000.

Raughly, Ralph C. Jr, ed. *New Frontiers of Christianity.* New York: Association Press, 1962.

Rein, Harald. *Kirchengemeinschaft: Die Anglikanisch – Altkatholisch – Orthodoxen Beziehungen von 1870 Bis 1990 Und Ihre okumenische Relevanz.* Bern: P.Lang, 1993.

Roger E. Hedlund. Ed. *Christianity is Indian.* New Delhi: ISPCK, 2004.

Rosenkranz, Gerhard. *Die Christliche Missionsgeschichte und Theologie.* München: Christian Kaiser Verlag, 1977.

Rouse, Ruth and Stepen Charls Neill. ed. *History of the Ecumenical Movement* 1517–1948. Vol. I. 3rd edition. Geneva: WCC, 1986.

Samartha, S.J. *Between Two Cultures –Ecumenical Ministry in a Pluralistic World.* Bangalore: Asian Trading Corporation, 1997.

Samartha, S.J. *Courage for Dialogue, Ecumenical Issues in Inter-Religious Relationships.* Geneva: WCC Publication, 1979.

———. *Towards a World Community-Colombo Papers.* Geneva: WCC, 1975.

———. *One Christ Many Religions.* Bangalore: SATHRI, 1992.

Shethi, D.L. and Ashis Nandy. eds. *The Multi verse of Democracy.* New Delhi: Sage Publications, 1996.

Shenk, Wilbert R. ed. *Enlarging the Story: Perspective on Writing World Christian History.* New York: Orbis Books, 2002.

Shenoy, P.V. *Markets and Morality.* Bangalore: Ecumenical Christian Centre, 2002.

Singh, K.S. *The Schedule Castes.* New Delhi: Oxford University Press, 2002.

Sreedhara Menon, A. *A Cultural Heritage of Kerala,* 2nd. ed. Madras: V. Subramanyam, 1996.

Sreedhara Menon, A. *Kerala and Freedom Struggle.* Kottayam: D. C. Books, 1997.

Stanly, Brian. *The World Missionary Conference Edinburgh, 1910.* Cambridge: William B. Eerdmans Publishing Company, 2009.

Sumithra, Sundand. *Revolution as Revelation.* Tubingen/New Delhi, International Christian Network & The Theological Research and Communication Institute, 1984.

The First Twenty Five Years of the National Missionary Society. Bharath Khristiya Sevak Samaj, 1932.

The World Mission of the Church. Findings and recommendations of the meeting of the International Missionary Council, Tambaram, Madras Dec 12–29, 1938. London: International Missionary Council, 1938.

Thekkedath, Joseph. *History of Christianity in India,* Vol. II. Bangalore: Theological Publication of India for Church History Association of India, 1982.

Thomas, George. *Christian Indians and Indian Nationalism 1885–1950.* Frankfurt: Verlag Peter D. Lang, 1979.

Thomas, M.M. *Abraham Malpante Naveekaranam Oru Vyakyanam.* (Malayalam). Tiruvalla: TLC, 1979.

———. *Religion and Politics.* Bangalore: Ecumenical Christian Centre, 1995.

———. ed. *The Churches Mission and Post Modern Humanism.* New Delhi: CSS & ISPCK, 1996.

———. *Salvation and Humanization.* Bangalore: C.I.S.R.S, 1970.

———. *My Ecumenical Journey.* Trivandrum: Ecumenical Publishing Centre, 1990.

———. *The Church's Mission and Post Modern Humanism.* Tiruvalla: ISPCK/ CSS, 1996.

Varghese, B.G. *Human Rights, Democracy, Secular and Social Change.* Bangalore: Ecumenical Christian Centre, 1994.

Varghese, K.A. *Abraham Mar Thoma Thirumeni,* Third Edition. Tiruvalla: 1959.

Varghese, P. *Reunion Efforts of St. Thomas Christians of India (1750–1773): A Historical Critical Analysis of the Contemporary Documents.* Trissur: Marymatha Publications, 2008.

Vasanthakumar, S. ed. *Call to Ministry and Mission.* Bangalore: The Student Christian Movement of India, 1993.

Vischer, Lukas. *Conciliar Unity.* Bangalore: Faith and Order and ECC Publication, 1978.

Visible Unity and Ministry of Oversight – The Second Theological Conference held under the Meissen Agreement between the Church of England and the Evangelical Church in Germany. West Wickham: Church House Publishing, 1996.

Walls, Andrew. *The Missionary Movements in Christian History.* New York: Orbis Books, 1996.

Wolters, Hielke T. *Theology of Prophetic Participation, M.M. Thomas's Concept of Salvation and the Collective Struggle for Fuller Humanity in India.* Bangalore: ISPCK/UTC, 1996.

Weber, Max. *Religion of India: The Sociology of Hinduism and Buddhism.* New York: Oxford University Press, 1958.

Wengert, Timothy J and Charles W. Brockwell, Jr, eds. *Telling the Churches' Stories.* Michigan/Cambridge: William B. Eerdmans Publishing Company, 1995.

Williams, Collin. *New Directions in Theology Today: The Church vol. IV,* London: Lutterworth Press, 1969.

Woong, Ahn Jae. *Building a Culture of Peace in Asia Today.* Bangalore: Ecumenical Christian Centre, 2004.

World Missionary Conference 1910. *Report of Commission VIII Co-Operation and Promotion of Unity.* Edinburgh & London: Olyphant, Anderson and Ferrrier, 1910.

Yesudas, R.N. *Colonel John Munro in Travancore.* Trivandrum: Kerala Historical Society, 1977.

Zacharia, Mathai. *Beyond Ecumenism.* Tiruvalla: CSS, 2002.

B. Dictionary and Encyclopaedia

"A Syrian Catholic: A Synopsis of the History of the Syrian Church in Malabar." *The Nazranis.* Edited by George Menacherry. (Trissur: SARAS, 1998): 264–276.

Anderson, Gerald H. ed., *Biographical Dictionary of Christian Missions.* Michigan/Cambridge: Wm B. Eardmanns, 1999.

Arahraja, Wesley S. "Dialogue, Interfaith." *A Dictionary of the Ecumenical Movement.* Edited by Nicholas Lossky. Geneva: WCC Publication, 1991, 281–286.

Ayyar, Anatha Krishna, L.K. "Anthropology of the Syrian Christians." *The Nazranis.* Edited by George Menacherry. Trissur: SARAS, 1998, 485–508.

Bent, Vander Ans. "Ecumenical Conferences." *A Dictionary of the Ecumenical Movement*. Edited by Nicholas Lossky. Geneva: WCC Publication, 1991, 338–325.

Bernard. "A Brief Sketch of the History of the St. Thomas Christians." *The Nazranis*. Edited by George Menacherry. Trissur: SARAS, 1998, 293–312.

Carl-Henric Grenholm. "Responsible Society" Edited by Nicholas Lossky and others *Dictionary of the Ecumencial Movement*. Geneva: WCC Publication, 2002, 980–981.

Cathanar, George. "The Orthodoxy of the St. Thomas Christians." *The Nazranis*. Edited by George Menacherry. Trissur: SARAS, 1998, 149–186.

Cherian, P. "The Malabar Syrians and the Church Missionary Society." *The Nazranis*. Edited by George Menacherry. Trissur: SARAS, 1998, 530–536.

Costas, Orlando E. "Christian Mission in the America," Edited by James A. Scherer and Stephen B. Bevans. *New Directions in Mission and Evangelization- Theological Foundations*. Marknoll, New York: Orbis Books, 1994.

D'Cruz, D. "St. Thomas the Apostle in India." *The Nazranis*. Edited by George Menacherry. Trissur: SARAS, 1998, 334–362.

Daniel, I. "The Syrian Church of Malabar." *The Nazranis*. Edited by George Menacherry. Trissur: SARAS, 1998, 399–411.

Farquhar, J.N. "The Apostle Thomas in North India", *Indian Church History Classics, The Nazranis*. Edited by George Menacherry. Trissur: SARAS, 1998, 313–322.

Farquhar, J.N. "The Apostle Thomas in South India", *Indian Church History Classics, The Nazranis*. Edited by George Menacherry. Trissur: SARAS, 1998, 324–331.

Geddes, Michael. "A Short History of the Church of Malabar Together with the Synod of Diamper, Act III, Decree VII, Acts and Decrees of the Synod of Diamper." *The Nazranis*. Edited by George Menacherry. Trissur: SARAS, 1998, 31–112.

Hosten. "The Song of Thomas Ramban." *The Nazranis*. Edited by George Menacherry. Trissur: SARAS, 1998, 520–525.

Hough, James. "The History of Christianity on India." *The Nazranis*. Edited by George Menacherry. Trissur: SARAS, 1998, 439–445.

Job, K.E. "The Syrian Church of Malabar." *The Nazranis*. Edited by George Menacherry. Trissur: SARAS, 1998, 378–388.

Kaithanal, Philip. "Christianity in Malabar." *The Nazranis*. Edited by George Menacherry. Trissur: SARAS, 1998, 389–398.

Lanne, Emmanuel. "Conciliarity" *A Dictionary of the Ecumenical Movement.* Edited by Nicholas Lossky. Geneva: WCC Publication, 1991, 235–236.

Leeming, B. "Ecumenical Movement." *New Catholic Encyclopedia*. Vol. 5. America: McGrow Hill Book Company, 1967, 96–100.

Mackenzie, G.T. "Christianity in Travancore." *The Nazranis*. Edited by George Menacherry. Trissur: SARAS, 1998, 112–148.

Mar Thoma Church Diary. Tiruvalla: Mar Thoma Press, 2013.

Medlycott, A.E. "India and the Apostle Thomas." *The Nazranis*. Edited by George Menacherry. Trissur: SARAS, 1998, 187–264.

Medlycott, A.E. "India and the Apostle Thomas: An Enquiry with a Critical Analysis of the Acta Thomae." *Indian Church History Classics, The Nazranis*. Edited by George Menacherry. Trissur: SARAS, 1998, 188–200.

Medlycott, A.E. "St. Thomas Christians." *Catholic Encyclopedia*, Vol. XIV, New York: The Gilmary Society, 1914, 678–688.

Mingana, Alfonso. "The Early Spread of Christianity in India." *The Nazranis*. Edited by George Menacherry. Trissur: SARAS, 1998, 509–512.

Moens, I. "The Dutch in Malabar." *The Nazranis*. Edited by George Menacherry. (Trissur: SARAS, 1998): 427–438.

Daniel Patte, eds. *The Cambridge Dictionary of Christianity*. New York: Cambridge University Press, 2010.

Panikkar, K.M. "Malabar and the Dutch." *The Nazranis*. Edited by George Menacherry. Trissur: SARAS, 1998, 481–484.

Panjikaran, J.C. "The Syrian Church in Malabar." *The Nazranis*. Edited by George Menacherry. Trissur: SARAS, 1998, 277–292.

Placid. "The Syrian Church of Malabar." *The Nazranis*. Edited by George Menacherry. Trissur: SARAS, 1998, 363–367.

Samartha, Stanly J. "Abraham Mar Thoma" *Biographical Dictionary of Christian Missions.* Edited by Gerald H. Anderson. Michigan/ Cambridge: William B. Eerdmans Publishing Company, 1999, 3–4.

Stewart. "Nestorian Missionary Enterprise." *The Nazranis*. Edited by George Menacherry. Trissur: SARAS, 1998, 513–519.

Tavard, George H. "Ecumenism." *The Modern Catholic Encyclopedia*. Edited by Michael Glazier. Bangalore: Claretian Publication, 1994, 272–275.

C. Periodicals and Journals

"A Scheme for the Comprehensive History of Christianity in India." In: *Indian Church History Review*, Vol. VIII, No. 2 (1974), 89ff.

Von Arx, Urs. "Erste theologische Konsultation zwischen der Mar-Thoma-Kirche und den Altkatholischen Kirchen der Utrechter Union." Santhigiri Statement, In: *Internationale Kirchliche Zeitschrift*, 102, (Oktober–Zezember/ 2012): 315–320.

"The Constitution of the National Missionary Society of India." In: *The National Missionary Intelligencer*, Vol. X, No. 3 (March, 1916).

Baago, Kaj. "Book Review of Colonialism and Christian Missions." In: *Indian Church History Review*, (December, 1967).

————. "Indigenization and Church History", In: *Bulletin of the Church History Association of India*, Special Number (February/1976), 24–28.

Cunningham, Alexander. *Journal of the Asiatic Society in Bengal*, Vol/ xiii, (1837): 679–712.

Bosch, David J. "Ecumenicals and Evangelicals in Growing Relationships". In: *Ecumenical Review*, 40, (1988), 458–468.

Dharmaraj, A.C. "A National Consultation of Conciliar Unity." In: *NCCI Review* 1/CV111 (April, 1978).

Goodall, Norman. "WCC and IMC relationship Issues" In: *Ecumenical Review*. 1/IX, (1959).

Hambye, E.R. "Some Eastern Evidence Concerning Early and Medieval Christianity in India." In: *Indian Ecclesiastical Studies*, 9, (Sept/1970), 185–193.

Hoekendijk, J.C. "The Church in Missionary Thinking." In: *International Review of Mission*, XLI (1952): 332–333.

Koshy, Eli. "Nooramathe Vayasil Ezhuthiya Lekhanam." (Malayalam) In: *Malankara Sabha Tharaka*. (April, 2005) 13–14.

Mathew, George. "Thozhiyoor Sabhayum Mar Thoma Sabhayum." In: *Malalnkara Sabha Tharaka* (September, 1994).

Mendez, Hector. "The Grace of God: Illusion or Reality." In: *Ecumenical Review* 5/56 (July, 2004): 297.

Mundadan, Mathias. "Changing Approaches to Historiography." In: *Indian Church History Review* (June/2001), 51ff.

————. "Rewriting History: Orientations." In: *Journal of Dharama*, Vol. XXVIII, No. 2 (April/June/2003), 168.

Oommen, George. "Historiography of Indian Christianity and Challenges of Subaltern Methodology." In: *Journal of Dharama*, No. 28, 2 (April–June/2003), 21–231.

Panicker, K.N. "Alternative Historigraphies: Changing Paradigms of Power." In: *Jeevadhara*, Vol. XXXII, No. 187 (January/2002), 11ff.

Platt, Warren C. "Intercommunion between the Episcopal Church and the Polish National Catholic Church: A Survey of Its Development." In: *Internationale Kirchlicke Zeitschift 82*, (1992), 142–165.

Romanides, J. "The Ecclesiology of the St. Ignatius of Antioch." In: *The Greek Orthodox Theological Review*, VII (1961): 63–65.

Seeliger, H.R. "Apologetische Und Fundamentaltheologische Kirchengeschichtsschribung." In: *Wissenschaft Und Weisheit*, 44 (1981), 58–72.

The National Missionary Intelligencer. Vol. X, No. 2, (February, 1916).

The Statute of the Old Catholic Bishops United in the Union of Utrecht. (Beiheit zu IKZ/2001): 30.

Thomas, M.M. "Christological Task in India." In: *Religion and society* (Sept/1964): 1–3.

Varghese, V. Titus. "Convention Yogangal – Oru Thirinju Nottam." (Malayalam) In: *Mallappally Union Christian Convention, Golden Jubilee Memorial Volume*, (Mallappally, 1981): 13–20.

Webster, John C.B. "History of Christianity in India: Aims and Methods", In: *Indian Church History Review*, Vol. XIII, No. 2 (December, 1979), 87–122,

D. Electronic Sources

"Resolution of the Synod of Mavelikara of 1836, held at the St. Mary's church." In: *www.syrianchurch.org/st.gg/mavelikara_padiyola.htm*. (accessed on January, 2, 2011)

"Malankara Orthodox Syrian Church." *http://www.malankaraorthodoxchurch.in* (accessed on April, 8, 2011)

"National Missionary Society." *www.national-missionary-society-of-india/part1.com*. (accessed on March, 13, 2011)

Ralston, Helen. The Construction of Authority in the Christian Ashram Movement / La Construction de l'autorité dans le mouvement des ashrams chrétiens. In: Archives des sciences sociales des religions. N. 67/1, 1989. pp. 53–75. doi: 10.3406/assr.1989.137. In: *http://www.persee.fr/web/revues/home/prescript/article/assr_0335-5985_1989_num_67_1_1370* (accessed on April 4, 2011)

"Jnanamarga" In: *http://www.britannica.com/EBchecked/topic/304137/jnana-marga*. (accessed on April 4, 2011)

"Resolution 14, "Church Unity and Church Universal – Full Communion and Inter – Communion", Lambeth Conference, 1958." In *www.lambethcon ference.org/resolutions/1968.* (accessed on October 17, 2011)

"Thirty Nine Articles of Faith, the Church of England" In: *http://www.churchso ciety.org/issues_new/doctrine/39a/iss_doctrine_39A_intro.asp* (accessed on December 15, 2011)

"Resolution 40, Church Union – South India, Lambeth Conference Archives 1930 – Resolution." In: *www.lambethconference.org/resolutions/1930.* (acces sed on October 10, 1911)

"Resolutions from 1958, Resolution 44, Lambeth Conference Report, 1958" In: http//:*www.lambethconference.org/resolutions/1958.* (accessed on March 14, 1958)

"Resolution 47, Lambeth Conference, 1968" In: *www.lambethconference.org/re solutions/1968.* (accessed on October 17, 2011)

"United Christians College, Aluva." In: *http:/www.uccollege.edu.in.* (accessed on December 7, 2011)

Chandran, J. Russel. "A Brief History and Interpretation." In: *www.csimkd.org/ History_of_csi_html.* (accessed on June 6, 2012)

"The Church of North India." In: *www.c.n.i.synod.org.* (accessed on June 6, 2012)

"Porvoo Common Statement" In: *www.anglicancommunion.org/.../docs/.../por voo_common_statement.pdf.* (accessed on April 4, 2013)

"Ignatius of Antioch, Epistle to the Philadelphians 7:2" In: *www.earlychristian writings.com/.../ignatius-philadelphians-lightfoot.* (accessed on February 8, 2013)

"Leuenberg Agrement." In: *www.leuenberg.net.* (accessed on March 14, 2013)

Varghese Zac and Mathew Kallupuram, Metropolitan Juhanon Marthoma (1893– 1976). In: *www.lightoflife.com* (accessed on October 23, 2012)

"OPEC." In: *http://www.opec.org.* (accessed on February 22, 2013)

"Acharay Bhivave." In: *http://www.vinibavhave.org.* (accessed on February 28, 2013)

"Permanent Shelters for Urban Homeless Populations, Tenth Report of the Com missioners of the Supreme Court of India, 2011." In: *www.righttofoodi nIndia/org/homelessness.* (accessed on 7, December 2012)

STUDIEN ZUR INTERKULTURELLEN GESCHICHTE DES CHRISTENTUMS
ETUDES D'HISTOIRE INTERCULTURELLE DU CHRISTIANISME
STUDIES IN THE INTERCULTURAL HISTORY OF CHRISTIANITY

Begründet von/fondé par/founded by
Richard Friedli, Walter J. Hollenweger und / et / and Hans Jochen Margull †

Herausgegeben von/edité par/edited by

| Mariano Delgado | Jan A.B. Jongeneel | Klaus Koschorke |
| Université de Fribourg | Universiteit Utrecht | Universität München |

Frieder Ludwig
Hermannsburg

Werner Ustorf
University of Birmingham

Die Reihe "Studien zur interkulturellen Geschichte des Christentums" arbeitet im Überschneidungsgebiet von Missions- und Religionswissenschaft, Ökumenik und Interkultureller Theologie. In historischer, sozialwissenschaftlicher und theoretischer Erforschung verfolgt sie die Frage der Identität des lokalen und globalen Christentums. Sie tut dies in Anerkennung grundlegender Transformationen (z.B. Technisierung, Globalisierung, Migration, Ökologie), der Bezugnahme auf die Andersdenkenden und Andersglaubenden und im Blick auf die Zukunft der Menschheit.

The series "Studies in the Intercultural History of Christianity" operates in an area that includes the disciplines of missiology, history of religions, ecumenics and intercultural theology. Using historical, socio-cultural and theoretical approaches it addresses the question of the identity of local and global Christianity. This is done in the light of the continuing transformations (e.g. technology, globalization, migration, ecology) and the living together of people of different faiths and persuasions in the human community.

La série « Etudes de l'Histoire Interculturelle du Christianisme » étudie les points de rencontre entre missiologie, science des religions, œcuménisme et théologie interculturelle. En utilisant les approches théoriques de l'histoire et des sciences sociales, elle fournit des éléments de réponse à la question de l'identité du christianisme local et global. Pour ce faire, elle prend en considération aussi bien les transformations profondes (p. ex. technologie, globalisation, migration, écologie), que la reconnaissance de ceux qui pensent et croient d'une manière différente, le tout en relation avec l'avenir de l'humanité.

Band 48 Jochanan Hesse (ed.): "Mitten im Tod - vom Leben umfangen". Gedenkschrift für Werner Kohler. 1988.

Band 49 Elisabeth A. Kasper: Afrobrasilianische Religion. Der Mensch in der Beziehung zu Natur, Kosmoş und Gemeinschaft im Candomblé - eine tiefenpsychologische Studie. 1988.

Band 50 Charles Chikezie Agu: Secularization in Igboland. Socio-religious Change and its Challenges to the Church Among the Igbo. 1989.

Band 51 Abraham Adu Berinyuu: Pastoral Care to the Sick in Africa. An Approach to Transcultural Pastoral Theology. 1988.

Band 52 Boo-Woong Yoo: Korean Pentecostalism. Its History and Theology. 1987.

Band 53 Roger H. Hooker: Themes in Hinduism and Christianity. A Comparative Study. 1989.

Band 54 Jean-Daniel Plüss: Therapeutic and Prophetic Narratives in Worship. A Hermeneutic Study of Testimonies and Visions. Their Potential Significance for Christian Worship and Secular Society. 1988.

Band 55 John Mansford Prior: Church and Marriage in an Indonesian Village. A Study of Customary and Church Marriage among the Ata Lio of Central Flores, Indonesia, as a Paradigm of the Ecclesial Interrelationship between village and Institutional Catholicism. 1988.

Band 56 Werner Kohler: Umkehr und Umdenken. Grundzüge einer Theologie der Mission (herausgegeben von Jörg Salaquarda). 1988.

Band 57 Martin Maw: Visions of India. Fulfilment Theology, the Aryan Race Theory, and the Work of British Protestant Missionaries in Victorian India. 1990.

Band 58 Aasulv Lande: Meiji Protestantism in History and Historiography. A Comparative Study of Japanese and Western Interpretation of Early Protestantism in Japan. 1989.

Band 59 Enyi B. Udoh: Guest Christology. An interpretative view of the christological problem in Africa.1988.

Band 60 Peter Schüttke-Scherle: From Contextual to Ecumenical Theology? A Dialogue between Minjung Theology and "Theology after Auschwitz". 1989.

Band 61 Michael S. Northcott: The Church and Secularisation. Urban Industrial Mission in North East England. 1989.

Band 62 Daniel O'Connor: Gospel, Raj and Swaraj. The Missionary Years of C. F. Andrews 1904-14. 1990.

Band 63 Paul D. Matheny: Dogmatics and Ethics. The Theological Realism and Ethics of Karl Barth's Church Dogmatics. 1990.

Band 64 Warren Kinne: A People's Church? The Mindanao-Sulu Church Debacle. 1990.

Band 65 Jane Collier: The culture of economism. An exploration of barriers to faith-as-praxis. 1990.

Band 66 Michael Biehl: Der Fall Sadhu Sundar Singh. Theologie zwischen den Kulturen. 1990.

Band 67 Brian C. Castle: Hymns: The Making and Shaping of a Theology for the Whole People of God. A Comparison of the Four Last Things in Some English and Zambian Hymns in Intercultural Perspective. 1990.

Band 68 Jan A. B. Jongeneel (ed.): Experiences of the Spirit. Conference on Pentecostal and Charismatic Research in Europe at Utrecht University 1989. 1991.

Band 69 William S. Campbell: Paul's Gospel in an Intercultural Context. Jew and Gentile in the Letter to the Romans. 1991.

Band 70 Lynne Price: Interfaith Encounter and Dialogue. A Methodist Pilgrimage. 1991.

Band 71 Merrill Morse: Kosuke Koyama. A model for intercultural theology. 1991.

Band 73 Robert M. Solomon: Living in two worlds. Pastoral responses to possession in Singapore. 1994.

Band 74 James R. Krabill: The Hymnody of the Harrist Church Among the Dida of South Central Ivory Coast (1913-1949). A Historico-Religious Study. 1995.

Band 75 Jan A. B. Jongeneel a.o. (eds.): Pentecost, Mission and Ecumenism. Essays on Intercultural Theology. Festschrift in Honour of Professor Walter J. Hollenweger. 1992.

Band 76 Siga Arles: Theological Education for the Mission of the Church in India: 1947-1987. Theological Education in relation to the identification of the Task of Mission and the Development of Ministries in India: 1947-1987; with special reference to the Church of South India. 1991.

Band 77 Roswith I.H. Gerloff: A Plea for British Black Theologies. The Black Church Movement in Britain in its transatlanctic cultural and theological interaction with special reference to the Pentecostal Oneness (Apostolic) and Sabbatarian movements. 2 parts. 1992.

Band 78 Friday M. Mbon: Brotherhood of the Cross and Star. A New Religious Movement in Nigeria. 1992.

Band 79 John Samuel Pobee (ed.): Exploring Afro-christology. 1992.

Band 80 Frieder Ludwig: Kirche im kolonialen Kontext. Anglikanische Missionare und afrikanische Propheten im südöstlichen Nigeria, 1879-1918. 1992.

Band 81 Werner A. Wienecke: Die Bedeutung der Zeit in Afrika. In den traditionellen Religionen und in der missionarischen Verkündigung. 1992.

Band 82 Ukachukwu Chris Manus: Christ, the African King. New Testament Christology. 1993.

Band 83 At Ipenburg: "All Good Men". The Development of Lubwa Mission, Chinsali, Zambia, 1905-1967. 1992.

Band 84 Heinrich Schäfer: Protestantismus in Zentralamerika. Christliches Zeugnis im Spannungsfeld von US-amerikanischem Fundamentalismus, Unterdrückung und Wiederbelebung "indianischer" Kultur. 1992.

Band 85 Joseph Kufulu Mandunu: Das "Kindoki" im Licht der Sündenbocktheologie. Versuch einer christlichen Bewältigung des Hexenglaubens in Schwarz-Afrika. 1992.

Band 86 Peter Fulljames: God and Creation in intercultural perspective. Dialogue between the Theologies of Barth, Dickson, Pobee, Nyamiti and Pannenberg. 1993.

Band 87 Stephanie Lehr: "Wir leiden für den Taufschein!" Mission und Kolonialisierung am Beispiel des Landkatechumenates in Nordostzaire. 1993.

Band 88 Dhirendra Kumar Sahu: The Church of North India. A Historical and Systematic Theological Inquiry into an Ecumenical Ecclesiology. 1994.

Band 89 William W. Emilsen: Violence and Atonement. The Missionary Experiences of Mohandas Gandhi, Samuel Stokes and Verrier Elwin in India before 1935. 1994.

Band 90 Kenneth D. Gill: Toward a Contextualized Theology for the Third World. The Emergence and Development of Jesus' Name Pentecostalism in Mexico. 1994.

Band 91 Karl O. Sandnes: A New Family. Conversion and Ecclesiology in the Early Church with Cross-Cultural Comparisons. 1994.

Band 92 Jan A. B. Jongeneel: Philosophy, Science, and Theology of Mission in the 19th and 20th Centuries. A Missiological Encyclopedia. Part I: The Philosophy and Science of Mission. 1995. Second rev. ed.: 2002.

Band 93 Raymond Pfister: Soixante ans de pentecôtisme en Alsace (1930-1990). Une approche socio-historique. 1995.

Band 94 Charles R. A. Hoole: Modern Sannyasins. Protestant Missionary Contribution to Ceylon Tamil Culture. 1995.

Band 95 Amuluche Gregory Nnamani: The Paradox of a Suffering God. On the Classical, Modern-Western and Third World Struggles to harmonise the incompatible Attributes of the Trinitarian God. 1995.

Band 96 Geraldine S. Smyth: A Way of Transformation. A Theological Evaluation of the Conciliar Process of Mutual Commitment to Justice, Peace and the Integrity of Creation, World Council of Churches, 1983-1991. 1995.

Band 97 Aasulv Lande / Werner Ustorf (eds.): Mission in a Pluralist World. 1996.

Band 98 Alan Suggate: Japanese Christians and Society. With the assistance of Yamano Shigeko. 1996.

Band 99 Isolde Andrews: Deconstructing Barth. A Study of the Complementary Methods in Karl Barth and Jacques Derrida. 1996.

Band 100 Lynne Price: Faithful Uncertainty. Leslie D. Weatherhead's Methodology of Creative Evangelism. 1996.

Band 101 Jean de Dieu Mvuanda: Inculturer pour évangéliser en profondeur. Des initiations traditionnelles africaines à une initiation chrétienne engageante. 1998.

Band 102 Allison M. Howell: The Religious Itinerary of a Ghanaian People. The Kasena and the Christian Gospel. 1997.

Band 103 Lynne Price, Juan Sepúlveda & Graeme Smith (eds.): Mission Matters. 1997.

Band 104 Tharwat Kades: Die arabischen Bibelübersetzungen im 19. Jahrhundert. 1997.

Band 105 Thomas G. Dalzell: The Dramatic Encounter of Divine and Human Freedom in the Theology of Hans Urs von Balthasar. 1997.

Band 106 Jan A. B. Jongeneel: Philosophy, Science, and Theology of Mission in the 19th and 20th Centuries. A Missiological Encyclopedia. Part II: Missionary Theology. 1997.

Band 107 Werner Kohler: Unterwegs zum Verstehen der Religionen. Gesammelte Aufsätze. Herausgegeben im Auftrag der Deutschen Ostasien-Mission und der Schweizerischen Ostasien-Mission von Andreas Feldtkeller. 1998.

Band 108 Mariasusai Dhavamony: Christian Theology of Religions. A Systematic Reflection on the Christian Understanding of World Religions. 1998.

Band 109 Chinonyelu Moses Ugwu: Healing in the Nigerian Church. A Pastoral-Psychological Exploration. 1998.

Band 110 Getatchew Haile, Aasulv Lande & Samuel Rubenson (eds.): The Missionary Factor in Ethiopia: Papers from a Symposium on the Impact of European Missions on Ethiopian Society, Lund University, August 1996. 1998.

Band 111 Anthony Savari Raj: A New Hermeneutic of Reality. Raimon Panikkar's Cosmotheandric Vision. 1998.

Band 112 Jean Pierre Bwalwel: Famille et habitat. Implications éthiques de l'éclatement urbain. *Cas de la ville de Kinshasa*. 1998.

Band 113 Michael Bergunder: Die südindische Pfingstbewegung im 20. Jahrhundert. Eine historische und systematische Untersuchung. 1999.

Band 114 Alar Laats: Doctrines of the Trinity in Eastern and Western Theologies. A Study with Special Reference to K. Barth and V. Lossky. 1999.

Band 115 Afeosemime U. Adogame: Celestial Church of Christ. The Politics of Cultural Identity in a West African Prophetic – Charismatic Movement. 1999.

Band 116 Laurent W. Ramambason: Missiology: Its Subject-Matter and Method. A Study of *Mission-Doers* in Madagascar. 1999.

Band 117 Veli-Matti Kärkkäinen: Ad Ultimum Terrae. Evangelization, Proselytism and Common Witness in the Roman Catholic Pentecostal Dialogue (1990-1997). 1999.

Band 118 Julie C. Ma: When the Spirit meets the Spirits. Pentecostal Ministry among the Kankanaey Tribe in the Philippines.2000. Second rev. ed.: 2001.

Band 119 Patrick Chukwudezie Chibuko: Igbo Christian Rite of Marriage. A Proposed Rite for Study and Celebration. 1999.

Band 120 Patrick Chukwudezie Chibuko: Paschal Mystery of Christ. Foundation for Liturgical Inculturation in Africa. 1999.

Band 121 Werner Ustorf / Toshiko Murayama (eds.): Identity and Marginality. Rethinking Christianity in North East Asia. 2000.

Band 122 Ogbu U. Kalu: Power, Poverty and Prayer. The Challenges of Poverty and Pluralism in African Christianity, 1960-1996. 2000.

Band 123 Peter Cruchley-Jones: Singing the Lord's Song in a Strange Land? A Missiological Interpretation of the Ely Pastorate Churches, Cardiff. 2001.

Band 124 Paul Hedges: Preparation and Fulfilment. A History and Study of Fulfilment Theology in Modern British Thought in the Indian Context. 2001.

Band 125 Werner Ustorf: Sailing on the Next Tide. Missions, Missiology, and the Third Reich. 2000.

Band 126 Seong-Won Park: Worship in the Presbyterian Church in Korea. Its History and Implications. 2001.

Band 127 Sturla J. Stålsett: The crucified and the Crucified. A Study in the Liberation Christology of Jon Sobrino. 2003.

Band 128 Dong-Kun Kim: Jesus: From Bultman to the Third World. 2002.

Band 129 Lalsangkima Pachuau: Ethnic Identity and Christianity. A Socio-Historical and Missiological Study of Christianity in Northeast India with Special Reference to Mizoram. 2002.

Band 130 Uchenna A. Ezeh: Jesus Christ the Ancestor. An African Contextual Christology in the Light of the Major Dogmatic Christological Definitions of the Church from the Council of Nicea (325) to Chalcedon (451). 2003.

Band 131 Chun Hoi Heo: Multicultural Christology. A Korean Immigrant Perspective. 2003.

Band 132 Arun W. Jones: Christian Missions in the American Empire. Episcopalians in Northern Luzon, the Philippines, 1902-1946. 2003.

Band 133 Mary Schaller Blaufuss: Changing Goals of the American Madura Mission in India, 1830-1916. 2003.

Band 134 Young-Gwan Kim: Karl Barth's Reception in Korea. Focusing on Ecclesiology in Relation to Korean Christian Thought. 2003.

Band 135 Graeme Smith: Oxford 1937. The Universal Christian Council for Life and Work Conference. 2004.

Band 136 Uta Theilen: Gender, Race, Power and Religion. Women in the Methodist Church of Southern Africa in Post-Apartheid Society. 2005.

Band 137 Uta Blohm: Religious Traditions and Personal Stories. Women Working as Priests, Ministers and Rabbis. 2005.

Band 138 Ann Aldén: Religion in Dialogue with Late Modern Society. A Constructive Contribution to a Christian Spirituality Informed by Buddhist-Christian Encounters. 2006.

Band 139 Stephen R. Goodwin: *Fractured Land, Healing Nations.* A Contextual Analysis of the Role of Religious Faith Sodalities Towards Peace-Building in Bosnia-Herzegovina. 2006.

Band 140 Ábrahám Kovács: The History of the Free Church of Scotland's Mission to the Jews in Budapest and its Impact on the Reformed Church of Hungary. 1841–1914. 2006.

Band 141 Jørgen Skov Sørensen: Missiological Mutilations – Prospective Paralogies. Language and Power in Contemporary Mission Theory. 2007.

Band 142 José Lingna Nafafé: Colonial Encounters: Issues of Culture, Hybridity and Creolisation. Portuguese Mercantile Settlers in West Africa. 2007.

Band 143 Peter Cruchley-Jones (ed.): God at Ground Level. Reappraising Church Decline in the UK Through the Experience of Grass Roots Communities and Situations. 2008.

Band 144 Marko Kuhn: Prophetic Christianity in Western Kenya. Political, Cultural and Theological Aspects of African Independent Churches. 2008.

Band 145 Yang-Cun Jeong: Koreanische Immigrationsgemeinden in der Bundesrepublik Deutschland. Die Entstehung, Entwicklung und Zukunft der koreanischen protestantischen Immigrationsgemeinden in der Bundesrepublik Deutschland seit 1963. 2008.

Band 146 Jonas Adelin Jørgensen: Jesus Imandars and Christ Bhaktas. Two Case Studies of Interreligious Hermeneutics and Identity in Global Christianity. 2008.

Band 147 Brian K. Jennings: Leading Virtue. A Model for the Contextualisation of Christian Ethics. A Study of the Interaction and Synthesis of Methodist and Fante Moral Traditions. 2009.

Band 148 Jan A. B. Jongeneel / Peter Tze Ming Ng / Paek Chong Ku / Scott W. Sunquist / Yuko Watanabe (eds.): Christian Mission and Education in Modern China, Japan, and Korea. Historical Studies. 2009. Second ed.: 2010.

Band 149 Jan A. B. Jongeneel: Jesus Christ in World History. His Presence and Representation in Cyclical and Linear Settings. With the Assistance of Robert T. Coote. 2009.

Band 150 Richard Friedli, Jan A. B. Jongeneel, Klaus Koschorke, Theo Sundermeier, and Werner Ustorf. Intercultural Perceptions and Prospects of World Christianity. 2010.

Band 151 Benjamin Simon: From Migrants to Missionaries. Christians of African Origin in Germany. 2010.

Band 152 Pan-chiu Lai / Jason Lam (eds.): Sino-Christian Theology. A Theological Qua Cultural Movement in Contemporary China. 2010.

Band 153 Jan A. B. Jongeneel / Jiafeng Liu/ Peter Tze Ming Ng / Paek Chong Ku / Scott W. Sunquist / Yuko Watanabe (eds.): Christian Presence and Progress in North-East Asia. Historical and Comparative Studies. 2011.

Band 154 Jan A. B. Jongeneel: Utrecht University. 375 Years Mission Studies, Mission Activities, and Overseas Ministries. 2012.

Band 155 Wim H. de Boer / Peter-Ben Smit: *In necessariis unitas.*Hintergründe zu den ökumenischen Beziehungen zwischen der *Iglesia Filipina Independiente*, den Kirchen der Anglikanischen Gemeinschaft und den altkatholischen Kirchen der Utrechter Union. 2012.

Band 156 John Parratt: The Other Jesus. Christology in Asian Perspective. 2012.

Band 157 J. Kwabena Asamoah-Gyadu / Andrea Fröchtling / Andreas Kunz-Lübcke (eds.): *Babel is Everywhere!* Migrant Readings from Africa, Europe and Asia. 2013.

Band 158 Morten Sandland: Joining New Congregations – Motives, Ways and Consequences. A Comparative Study of New Congregations in a Norwegian Folk Church Context and a Thai Minority Context. 2014

Band 159 Joseph Daniel: Ecumenism in Praxis. A Historical Critique of the Malankara Mar Thoma Syrian Church. 2014

www.peterlang.com